FUNDAMENTAL RIGHTS AND LEGAL CONSEQUENCES OF CRIMINAL CONVICTION

The legal position of convicted offenders is complex, as are the social consequences that can result from a criminal conviction. After they have served their sentences, custodial or not, convicted offenders often continue to be subject to numerous restrictions, in many cases indefinitely. In short, criminal convictions can have adverse legal consequences that may affect convicted offenders in several aspects of their lives. In turn, these legal consequences can have broader social consequences. Legal consequences are often not formally part of the criminal law, but are regulated by different areas of law, such as administrative law, constitutional law, labour law, civil law and immigration law. For this reason, they are often obscured from judges as well as from defendants and their legal representatives in the courtroom. The breadth, severity, longevity and often hidden nature of these restrictions raises the question of whether offenders' fundamental rights are sufficiently protected. This book explores the nature and extent of the legal consequences of criminal convictions in Europe, Australia and the USA. It addresses the following questions: What legal consequences can a criminal conviction have? How do these consequences affect convicted offenders? And how can and should these consequences be limited by law?

Oñati International Series in Law and Society

A SERIES PUBLISHED FOR THE OÑATI INSTITUTE
FOR THE SOCIOLOGY OF LAW

Recent titles in this series

Life Imprisonment and Human Rights
Edited by Dirk van Zyl Smit and Catherine Appleton

Trust in International Police and Justice Cooperation
Edited by Saskia Hufnagel and Carole McCartney

Human Rights Encounter Legal Pluralism
Edited by Eva Brems, Giselle Corradi and Mark Goodale

Transitional Justice and the Public Sphere: Engagement, Legitimacy and Contestation
Edited by Chrisje Brants and Susanne Karstedt

Law and the Precarious Home: Socio Legal Perspectives on the Home in Insecure Times
Edited by Helen Carr, Brendan Edgeworth and Caroline Hunter

Criminologies of the Military: Militarism, National Security and Justice
Edited by Andrew Goldsmith and Ben Wadham

Law and the Precarious Home: Socio Legal Perspectives on the Home in Insecure Times
Edited by Helen Carr, Brendan Edgeworth and Caroline Hunter

Collective Bargaining and Collective Action: Labour Agency and Governance in the 21st Century?
Edited by Julia López López

For the complete list of titles in this series, see
'Oñati International Series in Law and Society' link at
www.bloomsburyprofessional.com/uk/series/
onati-international-series-in-law-and-society

Fundamental Rights and Legal Consequences of Criminal Conviction

Edited by
Sonja Meijer
Harry Annison
and
Ailbhe O'Loughlin

Oñati International Series in Law and Society

A SERIES PUBLISHED FOR THE OÑATI INSTITUTE FOR THE SOCIOLOGY OF LAW

•HART•

OXFORD • LONDON • NEW YORK • NEW DELHI • SYDNEY

HART PUBLISHING
Bloomsbury Publishing Plc
Kemp House, Chawley Park, Cumnor Hill, Oxford, OX2 9PH, UK

HART PUBLISHING, the Hart/Stag logo, BLOOMSBURY and the Diana logo are trademarks of Bloomsbury Publishing Plc

First published in Great Britain 2019

A catalogue record for this book is available from the British Library.

Library of Congress Cataloging-in-Publication data

Names: Meijer, Sonja, 1980- editor. | Annison, Harry Michael John, 1985- editor. | O'Loughlin, Ailbhe, editor. | Oñati International Institute for the Sociology of Law, sponsoring body.

Title: Fundamental rights and legal consequences of criminal conviction / edited by Sonja Meijer, Harry Annison and Ailbhe O'Loughlin.

Description: Oxford, UK ; Chicago, Illinois : Hart Publishing, 2019. | Series: Oñati international series in law and society | Includes papers presented at a workshop sponsored by the Oñati International Institute for the Sociology of Law (IISL).—ECIP acknowledgments. | Includes bibliographical references and index.

Identifiers: LCCN 2019004741 (print) | LCCN 2019006639 (ebook) | ISBN 9781509920983 (EPub) | ISBN 9781509920976 (hardback)

Subjects: LCSH: Ex-convicts—Legal status, laws, etc.—Congresses. | Judgments, Criminal—Social aspects—Congresses.

Classification: LCC K638.5 A6 (ebook) | LCC K638.5 A6 F86 2019 (print) | DDC 345/.056—dc23

LC record available at https://lccn.loc.gov/2019004741

ISBN: HB: 978-1-50992-097-6
ePDF: 978-1-50992-099-0
ePub: 978-1-50992-098-3

Typeset by Compuscript Ltd, Shannon

Acknowledgements

WE ARE GRATEFUL to the Oñati International Institute for the Sociology of Law (IISL) for accommodating a two-day workshop that enabled us to bring together a team of leading legal, socio-legal and criminological scholars from different parts of the world. At this workshop, first versions of the chapters that make up the bulk of this book were presented and discussed extensively. In Oñati, the IISL provided us with logistical and administrative support, which made our stay very pleasant. Our special thanks go to Malen Gordoa Mendizabal for making the arrangements on behalf of the IISL.

Furthermore, we would like to thank the Kooijmans Institute of the VU University Amsterdam, which allocated a fellowship to Ailbhe O'Loughlin, allowing us to work closely together on the book for two weeks at the Law Faculty.

We are grateful to Professor Dirk Van Zyl Smit, who inspired us to undertake this project. We are also thankful to Dirk Van Zyl Smit, Shadd Maruna, Fergus McNeill, Nicola Padfield and Claire Lougarre for reading a draft of the Introduction. This book, and our Introduction in particular, has benefited greatly from their thought-provoking comments.

Lastly, our thanks go to the team at Hart/Bloomsbury Publishing for copyediting and producing this book, in particular to Emily Braggins, Rosamund Jubber and Catherine Minahan. Special thanks are due to our contributing authors. Your work has given an important insight into how a criminal conviction can affect the fundamental rights of former offenders in your countries, and will no doubt inspire future collaborations and comparative work.

Sonja Meijer, Harry Annison and Ailbhe O'Loughlin
Amsterdam, Southampton and York, January 2019

Table of Contents

PART III
DANGEROUS OFFENDERS AND LEGAL CONSEQUENCES OF CRIMINAL CONVICTION

PART IV
JUVENILE OFFENDERS AND LEGAL CONSEQUENCES OF CRIMINAL CONVICTION

List of Contributors

Harry Annison
Associate Professor in Criminal Law and Criminology, School of Law, University of Southampton, England, United Kingdom

Dimitra Blitsa
Public prosecutor, LLM LSE NYU, PhD candidate Aristotle University of Thessaloniki, Greece

Nicola Carr
Associate Professor in Criminology, University of Nottingham, England, United Kingdom

Anna Coninx
Assistant Professor in Criminal and Criminal Procedural Law, University of Luzern, Switzerland

Axel Dessecker
Professor in Criminology and Criminal Law, Institute for Criminal Law and Criminal Justice Sciences, Georg August University, Göttingen, and Deputy Director, Centre for Criminology (KrimZ), Wiesbaden, Germany

Martine Herzog-Evans
Professor in Criminal Law and Criminology, University of Rheims, France

Patrick Keyzer
Head of School and Chair of Law and Public Policy, La Trobe University Law School, Melbourne, Australia

Anna Kivrakidou
Criminal defence lawyer, PhD Aristotle University of Thessaloniki, Greece

Elena Larrauri
Professor in Criminal Law and Criminology, Pompeu Fabra University, Barcelona, Spain

Krisztina Lukács
Legal advisor Constitutional Court, Hungary

Marijke Malsch
Senior researcher Netherlands Institute for the Study of Crime and Law Enforcement (NSCR), Amsterdam, the Netherlands

Christine Morgenstern
Professor in Criminal Law and Criminology, Ernst Moritz Arndt University, Greifswald, Germany

Sonja Meijer
Assistant Professor in Criminal Law, VU University Amsterdam, the Netherlands

Darren O'Donovan
Senior Lecturer in Administrative Law, Human Rights Law and International Law, La Trobe University Law School, Melbourne, Australia

Ailbhe O'Loughlin
Lecturer in Criminal Law, York Law School, University of York, England, United Kingdom

Martí Rovira
Postdoctoral Researcher in Sociology and Criminology, Department of Sociology, University of Oxford

Davíd Vig
Senior Lecturer in Criminology and Penology at the Department of Criminology, Eötvös Lorand University Budapest, Hungary

Elina van 't Zand-Kurtovic
Assistant Professor in Criminology, Leiden University, Leiden, the Netherlands

1

Introduction

SONJA MEIJER, HARRY ANNISON AND AILBHE O'LOUGHLIN

I. BACKGROUND AND AIMS

THE LEGAL POSITION of convicted offenders is complex,[1] as are the resulting social consequences (Van Zyl Smit and Snacken 2010). Convicted offenders, after they have served their sentences, custodial or not, often continue to be subject to numerous restrictions, in many cases indefinitely, due to their criminal conviction. In short, criminal convictions can have adverse legal consequences that may affect convicted offenders in several aspects of their lives. These legal consequences often are not formally part of the criminal law but are regulated by different areas of law, such as administrative law, constitutional law, labour law, civil law and immigration law. In turn, they have, and interact with, broader social consequences of conviction. For this reason, they can be obscured from judges, as well as from defendants and their legal representatives. The breadth, severity and longevity, and often hidden nature of these restrictions, raise the question of whether offenders' fundamental rights are sufficiently protected.

It is often assumed that the criminal law brings with it better procedural safeguards than, for example, civil law, but this view seems to be out-dated on the point that consequences regulated outside of criminal law can be even more far-reaching than criminal punishment itself. This is especially the case for the consequences a criminal conviction can have for immigration (Kirk and Wakefield 2018). Such consequences cause the lines between the criminal law and other areas of law to become blurred. Some scholars have expressed their concern that we might even be creating a form of second-class citizen, unable to come back from a period of punishment to lead a normal life (Thomas 2007: 189).

[1] Questions of the appropriate terminology to utilise when speaking of those who have encountered the criminal justice system are far from straightforward, especially for publications that span cultures and languages, such as this edited collection. Here, we tend to use the term 'convicted offenders', denoting individuals who have been convicted and who can either be serving their sentence or who have already served their sentence (hence terms such as 'prisoner' or 'individual under supervision' are often under-inclusive). Some chapters do focus on the consequences for people who have served their sentence, and thus in this technical sense use the term 'ex-offender'.

We can distinguish eight different domains in which offenders can experience legal consequences because of a criminal conviction: employment, education, freedom of movement, enterprise, housing, family, privacy, and immigration. Examples are the exclusion of offenders from certain jobs and/or positions (the right to work); disenfranchisement (the loss of the right to vote or the right to run for elections); the registration of fingerprints or cellular samples from ex-offenders, or registration as sex offenders (constraining the right to privacy); the refusal of a housing permit (excluding ex-offenders from living in certain areas; the right to housing); the refusal or withdrawal of professional licences, grants or contracts (the right to work and/or privacy); and measures of intensive supervision and preventive detention that restrict (ex-)offenders in their freedom of movement after they have served their (punitive) prison sentence. These consequences can be imposed automatically (by statute), by a court or by an administrative authority.

Given these adverse consequences, it is surprising that very little international comparative and empirical research has been undertaken in Europe on this subject. In the United States (US), a large body of research on the so-called 'collateral consequences of criminal convictions' exists (eg Damaska 1968a and 1968b; Demleitner 1999; Colgate Love 2001; Mauer and Chesney Lind 2003; Pinard 2006; Uggen, Manza and Thompson 2006; Uggen and Steward 2015).[2] In comparison, in Europe, only a few scholars have engaged in research on this topic (see Von Hirsch and Wasik 1997 on civil disqualifications attending conviction). Recently, European scholars have begun to point out the existence and importance of legal consequences of criminal convictions for different domains (Boone and Kurtovic 2015; Fitzgerald O'Reilly 2018).

Research in Europe has tended to focus on criminal records (Thomas 2007). Before the introduction of the European Criminal Records Information System (ECRIS) in 2012,[3] (comparative) research addressed the question of whether the European Union (EU) was in need of a European Criminal Record database (Stefanou and Xanthaki 2008; Vermeulen et al 2002). More recently, it has mainly focused on restrictions on one of the aforementioned domains, namely, convicted offenders' access to employment (see the Special Issue of the *European Journal of Probation* 2011 with contributions from France (Herzog-Evans 2011), Germany (Morgenstern 2011), England (Padfield 2011), Spain (Larrauri 2011; see also Larrauri and Jacobs 2013; Jacobs and Larrauri 2016) and the Netherlands (Boone 2011). There has also been research on Sweden (Backman 2012). Comparative research on the employment of people with criminal records in the EU has been published by Louks, Lyner and Sullivan (1998), and more recently by Buysse, Meijer and Szytniewski (2018). Less attention has

[2] We prefer to avoid the term 'collateral consequences', because, as Condry and Minson argue in the context of prisoner families, it can fail to capture the 'relational, mutual, non-linear, agentic and heterogenous properties' of the further effects of punishment on the individual and family members (quoted in Condry and Scharff Smith 2018: 12).

[3] A database that links the individual criminal records registries of EU-countries.

been given to disenfranchisement (with the exception of Tripkovic 2016), the consequences of a criminal conviction for immigration (with the exception of Blitsa, Gouldin, Jacobs and Larrauri 2016) and the right to housing (with the exception of Van Tongeren and Vols 2017). In short, this is a significant and under-researched area of law and criminology.

The aim of this book is to begin to explore the nature and extent of legal consequences of criminal convictions in Europe. What legal consequences can a criminal conviction have? How do these consequences affect convicted offenders? And how can and should these consequences be limited? 'Legal consequences' is intended here as a broad term. On the one hand, legal consequences may result directly from a criminal conviction. An example of this is that a criminal conviction may result in long periods of preventive detention, or long periods of supervision on the grounds of prevention. On the other hand, consequences may result from the exercise of legal powers. For example, the exercise of the power of national authorities to issue criminal record extracts or criminal record check certificates may result in individuals being denied employment on the grounds of a criminal conviction.

The latter consequences are also referred to in the literature as 'collateral consequences' (eg Demleitner 1999; Love, Roberts, and Klingele 2013), 'adverse (legal) consequences' (eg Damaska 1968a and 1968b) or 'civil disqualifications' (Von Hirsch and Wasik 1997). These terms are often not clearly defined, but from the description given by Von Hirsch and Wasik it follows that these disqualifications may (i) take effect automatically on conviction, (ii) be imposed by the sentencing judge, or (iii) be imposed by a regulatory agency. Although the starting point of this collection is the criminal conviction, an important finding is that some of the consequences described flow not only from a criminal conviction, but also, in some countries, from criminal record information that falls short of a conviction, such as data on charges or cautions held by the police.

It should be noted that not all of the rights as described in this book are equally protected in European countries. The European Convention on Human Rights (ECHR) protects basic (civil and political) human rights (Cliquennois and Suremain 2017). The principle of human dignity underpinning Article 3 ECHR may be drawn upon to restrict grossly disproportionate punishment (see *Vinter and others v the United Kingdom* and discussion in Annison and O'Loughlin, chapter 9 of this volume). Restrictions on liberty may be challenged under Article 5 ECHR, and preventive measures imposed after conviction may be construed as penalties in violation of Article 7 ECHR (see Annison and O'Loughlin, Dessecker, chapters 9 and 10 of this volume). Restrictions on the right to vote have been successfully challenged under Article 3 of Additional Protocol No 1 to the ECHR (see *Hirst v United Kingdom* 2005; *Scoppola v Italy* 2011). However, as Herzog-Evans shows, the protection offered by the interpretation of the European Court of Human Rights (ECtHR) is still rather minimal.

The European Social Charter (ESC) protects economic, social and cultural rights, such as the right to work (Article 15(1) ESC). The problem with this instrument, however, is that states do not have to sign up to all the provisions of this treaty. Furthermore, individuals cannot invoke the rights protected by the ESC, and the conclusions of the European Committee of Social Rights – the body monitoring the implementation of the ESC – are legally non-binding. For these reasons, the focus of the book is on human rights protected by the ECHR. While the ECHR does not contain, for instance, a right to work, some protection may be found in the Article 8 right to respect for private and family life, where the disclosure of private information such as criminal convictions is involved (see Padfield 2011). However, in some countries, such as the Netherlands, pre-employment screening does not involve direct disclosure of criminal record information to employers (see Meijer and van 't Zand-Kurtovic, chapters 5 and 14 of this volume).

Furthermore, the Charter of Fundamental Rights of the European Union contains some socio-economic rights, such as the right to engage in work (Article 15(1)) and entitlements to social security and assistance (Article 34). However, these rights apply only where Member States are implementing EU law.

This book is the result of a workshop held at the Oñati International Institute for the Sociology of Law, which brought together for the first time a number of leading legal, socio-legal and criminological scholars from different parts of the world to discuss the topic of the legal consequences of a criminal conviction. The papers that were presented at the workshop have been extensively revised and form the substantive chapters of this book. In addition, Nicola Carr and Christine Morgenstern have contributed chapters to the book, for which we are very grateful. Because of our broad approach to the term 'legal consequences', not all chapters take the same approach: some chapters deal with the wide range of legal consequences a criminal conviction can have in a certain country, while other chapters deal with a specific consequence in more detail. The normative aspects of the legal consequences of criminal conviction are dealt with by various chapters. The advantage of this approach is that authors were able to focus on the most current and relevant developments in their respective countries. The corollary of the approach, however, is that close comparisons between the different countries are difficult to make. Nevertheless, the chapters allow for the identification of broad trends, highlight a variety of significant cultural, legal and empirical similarities and differences between countries, and point the way towards principles and methods for limiting the often extensive breadth of restrictions imposed as a consequence of criminal conviction.

We have organised the papers into four parts: I. Criminological Perspectives on Legal Consequences of Criminal Conviction; II. Legal Limits on the Legal Consequences of Criminal Conviction; III. Dangerous Offenders and Legal Consequences of Criminal Conviction; and IV. Juvenile Offenders and Legal Consequences of Criminal Conviction.

In this introduction, we set out some normative debates with regard to the consequences a criminal conviction might have (section II). Furthermore, we highlight the discussions presented in the various contributions, and point out how these chapters build on previous research (section III).

II. NORMATIVE DEBATES

While there is copious scholarly work on the rationales of and justifications for state punishment, surprisingly, the principles governing legal consequences of criminal conviction have attracted little doctrinal or conceptual analysis. As the contributions to this volume demonstrate, the (more or less clearly elucidated) justifications for legal consequences of conviction often echo the purposes of sentencing, which include retributive punishment or crime prevention (whether through deterrence, incapacitation, reform or rehabilitation).

However, due to their 'hidden' nature, judges may not be aware of these consequences when passing sentence. Thus, they are often not taken into account in calculations of proportionality. Furthermore, legal consequences are often determined by administrative authorities and governed by different areas of law. Therefore, they often escape the traditional safeguards of the criminal law. In addition to these considerations, criminal convictions are often also taken as an indication of a person's status or character. Consequently, those with a criminal conviction may find their rights and opportunities restricted because they are regarded as untrustworthy or undesirable, particularly in the employment context (see Morgenstern, chapter 4 of this volume). Similarly, those who have criminal convictions may be deprived of civil and political rights, such as the right to vote, not necessarily because of what they may do in the future, but because their past offending is taken as an indication that they are not deserving of the full rights and duties of citizenship. Given their potential to negatively impact upon offenders' rights, the question of what limits should be placed on legal consequences is an important one. For this reason, the proportionality or appropriateness of legal consequences to their purpose is a theme that runs throughout this volume.

A. Prevention

Restrictions on convicted offenders' rights are often justified by national authorities as a means of preventing reoffending through incapacitation or deterrence. Malsch's chapter in this volume (chapter 3) highlights the tendency of measures of incapacitation towards net-widening and self-perpetuation, as measures of prevention or incapacitation often seem to lead to further measures.

An important contribution of this volume to the literature on the consequences of criminal conviction is that several chapters emphasise the severity of the legal consequences that can flow from criminal conviction for a serious offence. Justifications for that severity blur the line between retribution and prevention by conceiving of serious offenders as 'dangerous' individuals. In this sense, there is often an assumption that a person with a history of serious offending is more likely to reoffend seriously in the future than someone without a criminal record. As Morgenstern argues (in chapter 4 of this volume), empirical studies of reconviction rates amongst convicted offenders demonstrate that the assumption that past convictions are a reliable predictor of reoffending is often misplaced. This is particularly the case for sex offenders, who are often regarded by the public as particularly liable to reoffend but who actually have a very low rate of reconviction. Thus, in relation to dangerous offenders, the line between punishment and prevention is often blurred, and retributive justifications for lengthy periods of detention and supervision are intertwined with preventive justifications (see Annison and O'Loughlin, chapter 9 of this volume). Conversely, even minor offences can have far-reaching consequences that seem out of step with the preventive function they ostensibly seek to fulfil. In particular, chapter 8 by Blitsa and Kivrakidou on Greece highlights the sometimes arbitrary nature of restrictions that result from a criminal conviction.

Furthermore, as chapter 4 by Christine Morgenstern and chapter 5 by Sonja Meijer highlight, a previous conviction has legal consequences *within* the criminal justice system, as it is viewed as an aggravating factor in sentencing. In the German context, this is often justified by reference to the fact that the individual has reoffended despite the 'warning' effect of the previous conviction, or that reoffending is in itself evidence of a higher risk of recidivism (see Morgenstern, chapter 4).

B. Punishment

While the primary purpose of many restrictions on offenders' rights is the prevention of crime, punitive sentiments and the notion that offenders are less deserving of the rights and privileges accorded to (supposedly) law-abiding citizens are often not far below the surface. Indeed, restrictions on the right to vote are frequently conceived of as a punishment, and are defended on the grounds that offenders have broken the social contract and therefore no longer deserve to participate in civil life (see *Hirst v United Kingdom*; Herzog-Evans (chapter 11 of this volume); Lukács and Vig (chapter 6 of this volume)).

As several of the contributions to this volume demonstrate, restrictions that are primarily intended to prevent reoffending may also be experienced as punitive or stigmatising in their effects, or are applied so widely and indiscriminately that they impose hardships out of all proportion to their preventive aims (see Blitsa and Kivrakidou (chapter 8); Herzog-Evans (chapter 11); Lukács and Vig (chapter 6); Meijer (chapter 5); Annison and O'Loughlin (chapter 9); Keyzer and O'Donovan (chapter 12)). Kirkwood and McNeill (2015: 514) note that 'even under a retributivist approach to punishment, the polity has a duty to make sure that the punishment ends and that there is no punishment beyond the law ("*nulla poena sine lege*")'. Yet criminological and sociological evidence about the enduring unintended effects of punishment both for individuals and for their families, exposed by studies of desistance, suggests that this duty is commonly neglected *de facto* if not *de jure*. Some US authors have referred to collateral consequences as (invisible) punishments (Travis 2002: 16; Karlan 2004 (focusing specifically on disenfranchisement); Pinard 2010: 1215; Colgate Love 2011; Chin 2012; Thomas and Hebenton 2012: 238). Yet in Europe, the *communis opinion* of criminal law scholars seems to be that these consequences are not to be seen as punishment (Von Hirsch and Wasik 1997; Morgenstern, chapter 4 of this volume).

Some authors argue that the principle that the severity of the sentence ought to be proportionate to the seriousness of the crime requires a close connection between the conviction and the collateral consequence (Von Hirsch and Wasik 1997; and Meijer, chapter 5 of this volume). For instance, Demleitner has argued that employment restrictions should be tied to the character of the occupation, function or activity involved, and calibrated specifically to the offence (Demleitner 1999: 160). The principle of proportionality in sentencing is proposed by several contributors to this volume as a potential limit on the severity of the legal consequences of criminal conviction (Blitsa and Kivrakidou (chapter 8); Coninx (chapter 7); Meijer (chapter 5); Annison and O'Loughlin (chapter 9)).

C. Character

In the US, the absence of a criminal conviction is considered proof of good character for the purposes of naturalisation, while those with an aggravated felony conviction are automatically disqualified (Colgate Love, Roberts and Klingele 2013; Jacobs 2015; Blitsa et al 2016; Larrauri and Rovira, chapter 2 of this volume). Criminal record checks in Europe tend to be for roles in public administration, or those for which a higher standard of 'integrity' is demanded, for example private security officers, high-ranking officials in the public sector or managers in gambling companies, and people working with children[4] and vulnerable adults (Jacobs and Larrauri 2016; see Larrauri and Rovira, chapter 2 of this volume). It may also be argued that practical and legal restrictions on social and welfare rights noted by some contributors to this volume, including the right to adopt, retain custody of children, receive social security benefits or live in certain areas (see Larrauri and Rovira (chapter 2); Meijer (chapter 5)), may be linked to judgments of character or deservingness rather than the risk of recidivism. Similarly, the notion that some offenders are no longer deserving or worthy of the exercise of the rights and duties of citizenship, such as the right to vote or to serve on a jury, may say something more about how (ex-)offenders are regarded by society than about the risks they may pose.

[4] EU Directive 2011/92/EU of the European Parliament and the Council of 13 December 2011 on combating the sexual abuse and sexual exploitation of children and child pornography, and replacing Council Framework Decision 2004/68/JHA [2011] OJ L335/1.

D. Rehabilitation

Restrictions on offenders' rights are sometimes defended on the grounds that they not only protect the public, but also aid rehabilitation and eventual social reintegration. As noted by several contributors to this volume, however, the legal consequences of criminal conviction may impede the process of desistance from crime, conceived of as a personal journey towards 'long term committed compliance with the law' (McNeill 2012: 8). Such measures may therefore have the counter-productive effect of increasing the risk of reoffending in the long term. For this reason, it is important to distinguish between different forms of 'rehabilitation', and to examine their relationship with desistance and the legal consequences of a criminal conviction.

McNeill (2012: 14; see also Burke, Collett and McNeill 2018; Kirkwood and McNeill 2015) distinguishes between four, interconnected forms of rehabilitation: psychological rehabilitation, which is principally concerned with promoting positive individual-level change in the offender; legal or judicial rehabilitation ('when, how, to what extent a criminal record and the stigma it represents can ever be set aside, sealed, or surpassed'); moral rehabilitation, meaning that an offender has to pay back before he or she can trade up to a restored social position as a citizen of good character; and social rehabilitation, encompassing the informal social recognition and acceptance of the reformed offender.

Legal rehabilitation has also been referred to as a process of 'requalification': restoring to offenders their rights and duties as full citizens (McNeill 2012, citing Beccaria 1764). As such, the law views the legally rehabilitated person as deserving of membership of the community of law-abiding citizens and of the status and entitlements that accompany it (Raynor and Robertson 2009: 10). Thus, in principle, legally rehabilitated offenders should no longer be excluded from public life. However, legal or judicial rehabilitation does not necessarily track psychological, moral or social rehabilitation, and the legal consequences of a criminal conviction can continue despite the progress made by the offender towards rehabilitation in the other areas. Similarly, where the expungement of criminal records occurs automatically after a prescribed number of years (see, eg, Herzog-Evans (chapter 11) and Lukács and Vig (chapter 6)), a committed offender may be legally rehabilitated despite lacking psychological rehabilitation.

Research has shown that stable employment, particularly after the age of 26, is associated with desistance from crime (Farrall and Calverley 2006, ch 1). The same applies to having access to housing (Bahr, Davis and Ward 2013). However, a criminal record can be grounds for the denial of a social housing permit (see Meijer, chapter 5 of this volume), and there appears to be an increase in the frequency of criminal record checking for the purposes of employment in several European countries (see Larrauri and Rovira, chapter 2 of this volume). Thus, it is clear that the legal consequences of criminal conviction can pose a significant barrier to desistance and reintegration. In this sense, legal rehabilitation can be conducive to social and moral rehabilitation, as the removal of a criminal record removes many of these barriers (Maruna 2011). Furthermore, the restoration of the status of full citizen can go some way towards removing the often state-sanctioned stigmatisation and social exclusion that can result from the legal consequences of a criminal conviction. The more serious the offence, however, the longer the periods for expungement tend to be, with the result that serious offences not only carry a greater social stigma but also have legal effects for a longer period of time.

The importance of social rehabilitation has been recognised by the Council of Europe – which was founded on human rights principles – in Recommendation No R (84) 10 of the Committee of Ministers on the criminal record and rehabilitation of convicted persons (21 June 1984). After considering 'that criminal records are principally intended to provide the authorities responsible for the criminal justice system with information on the antecedents of the person on trial, in order to assist them in making a decision appropriate to that individual', the Recommendation considers 'that any other use of criminal records may jeopardise the convicted person's chances of social reintegration, and should therefore be restricted to the utmost'. The ECtHR, for its part, has recognised a form of a 'right to rehabilitation' on behalf of long-term prisoners (see Annison and O'Loughlin, chapter 9 of this volume; Meijer 2017), underpinned by human dignity and the capacity of individuals to change for the better (see *Vinter and others v the United Kingdom*). This right is limited, however, and does not extend to a right to work or other conditions conducive to social reintegration.

Social rehabilitation or social reintegration is often emphasised in relation to juvenile offenders, and children's rights standards encourage the promotion of social participation and the avoidance of stigmatisation. However, as Nicola Carr's and Elina van 't Zand-Kurtovic's contributions to this volume demonstrate (chapters 13 and 14 respectively), the consequences associated with a criminal conviction continue to impede social reintegration and desistance from crime for this group of offenders. This is the case even where young offenders have been diverted away from the criminal justice system in an attempt to reduce the negative repercussions of punishment for juveniles. Thus, the legal barriers imposed by a criminal conviction can undermine the rehabilitative aims of measures that seek to support or promote the reintegration and social rehabilitation of offenders.

III. LEGAL CONSEQUENCES OF CRIMINAL CONVICTION

A. Criminological Perspectives on Legal Consequences of Criminal Conviction

The two chapters in Part I of this book take a criminological perspective on the legal consequences of criminal conviction, drawing on examples and empirical research from Europe and the US. These contributions highlight an upward trend in the frequency and severity of collateral consequences for convicted offenders in Europe that can have negative effects not only for ex-offenders but for society as a whole.

In chapter 2, Elena Larrauri and Martí Rovira use empirical research to explore the collateral consequences of a conviction in Spain and how their scope compares to those in the US. As other contributions to this volume highlight, a European constitutional culture or culture of rights appears to offer some protection to ex-offenders. Larrauri and Rovira's study should alert readers that the 'piling on' of collateral consequences, which Uggen and Steward (2015) detect in the US, is also present in Europe, especially regarding immigrants and sexual offenders. The extent of collateral consequences in Spain is particularly striking from a comparative perspective, considering that Spain is often depicted as a relatively 'lenient' European nation (Stefanou and Xanthaki 2008; Tripkovic 2016). Consequently, the contributors call for more research on this topic from different European countries.

In chapter 3, Marijke Malsch describes forms of incapacitation that imply the taking away of opportunities to commit certain wrongs or restricting freedoms in other ways (see Malsch and Duker 2012). She argues that incapacitation is not restricted to the most invasive types of elimination of certain people, but may also refer to less comprehensive forms, such as the exclusion of offenders from certain jobs, positions or activities (like driving a car or running a particular business), as long as disabling the individual involved is the goal of the intervention or of the person issuing it. Her chapter focuses not only on the effect of the criminal law, as incapacitating interventions can also be found in both civil law and administrative law, or outside the law in a strict sense. For Malsch, disproportionate use of measures of incapacitation can increase the risk of recidivism instead of diminishing it, and disproportionate use of incapacitation can be experienced as a form of punishment by the person subject to such measures. She argues that the type of incapacitation used should bear a strong relation to the type of behaviour that is to be prevented, that it should not exceed the limits of proportionality, that decisions should be made by a court and that measures should be accompanied by interventions that aim to rehabilitate the offender.

B. Legal Limits on the Legal Consequences of Criminal Conviction

The chapters in Part II of this volume take a legal perspective on the consequences of criminal conviction and discuss their legal and normative limits. Like the previous two chapters, these contributions discuss a range of possible consequences of criminal convictions, including restrictions on employment opportunities, on the right to privacy and on political rights. In addition, Morgenstern and Meijer highlight the consequences a criminal conviction can have within the criminal justice system itself. Together, the chapters in Part II reflect the extent to which the legal consequences of criminal conviction circumvent traditional criminal law safeguards, and argue for a more robust approach to protecting fundamental rights drawing on the principle of proportionality.

Christine Morgenstern in chapter 4 explores the under-researched and under-theorised topic of 'the stain of conviction' in Germany. Taking both a criminal justice and a human rights perspective, Morgenstern argues that the state, as 'author of the conviction', must take responsibility for its consequences and counteract any that are unintended and illegitimate. In so doing, she uses penal theory and the right to privacy to point towards a more coherent theoretical approach to criminal records.

As Sonja Meijer shows in chapter 5, while criminal records in most European countries typically do not provide information on so-called 'administrative sanctions', this is currently up for debate in the Netherlands, because administrative fines can possibly become included in the Certificate of Conduct. In the Netherlands, draft legislation is in preparation that makes it possible to deny a Conduct Certificate on the basis of police intelligence. Furthermore, a permit for social housing can be refused on a screening based on police registers.

Morgenstern and Meijer not only point to the consequences that criminal convictions can subsequently have outside the criminal justice system, but also emphasise the significant consequences that can flow from a criminal conviction within the criminal justice system. For most judges, the fact an offender has a previous conviction, regardless of the nature of the offence, is enough to substantiate a risk of recidivism and to justify the imposition of pre-trial detention. Furthermore, a criminal record can be an aggravating factor in sentencing, and can even lead to sentences being automatically imposed by statute.

In chapter 6, Lukács and Vig chart the detrimental legal consequences of a conviction in Hungary, focusing particularly on restrictions on political rights. While the ECtHR has established that a blanket prohibition on the right to vote violates Article 3 of Protocol No 1 to the Convention (*Hirst v the United Kingdom* 2005), Lukács and Vig show that Hungarian courts almost always order the deprivation of political rights, as such an order is included in 95 per cent of all prison sentences. Nevertheless, under Hungarian law, as one of the aims of a prison sentence is to prevent reoffending, the law requires that the social reintegration of the convicted person should be supported not only when imposing and when executing the sentence, but also after the sentence has been served. This gives rise to a right to legal rehabilitation in Hungarian law, underpinned by human dignity. Lukács and Vig describe three methods of legal rehabilitation in Hungary, which include automatic legal rehabilitation after a certain time period, the possibility of applying to a court for rehabilitation on the grounds of 'worthiness', and the possibility of a pardon by the President of the Republic of Hungary or the Parliament as a form of clemency. Lukács and Vig argue, however, that, notwithstanding the legal rehabilitation regime, the scope and duration of detrimental consequences for convicted offenders undermine their human dignity.

In chapter 7, Anna Coninx focuses on criminal background checks in the employment context. Like many other European countries, Switzerland allows the expungement of criminal records from the 'ordinary' extract, used for employment screening purposes, once the sentence has been served or the monetary penalty has been paid and a certain waiting period has passed. This means that the record itself is deleted, by contrast to other jurisdictions, such as England and Wales, in which the conviction remains on record but the individual does not have to disclose it to employers. The idea is that after some time, an ex-offender is at no more risk of reoffending than a non-offender (see Larrauri Pijoan 2014: 58). However, serious offences are not deleted from the 'private' extract, which can be requested when the individual wishes to apply for a job involving close contact with vulnerable groups, such as children. In 2012, however, the Swiss Government took the view that 'employers, landlords, associations and other organisations of employers can ask employees, tenants or members of an association to provide a private extract' (Botschaft BBl 2012, 8857). The fact that criminal records are considered to be confidential was not even mentioned. Coninx challenges the assumption that employers have a legitimate interest in being fully informed about previous convictions. Using Rawls' general analytic method of fair decision-making, introduced in *A Theory of Justice*, she argues that although in Swiss law the access to criminal records for private employers is limited in content and time, it is still over-inclusive. According to Coninx, potential future employers should only be informed about convictions if the crime committed is related to employment and there is a considerable risk of reoffending. She also argues that it should be up to courts, and not to employers, to decide on whether an ex-offender should be disqualified from working in a specific field or from undertaking a certain activity.

In chapter 8, Dimitra Blitsa and Anna Kivrakidou seek to limit the role a person's criminal past, as depicted in his or her criminal record, plays in obtaining legitimate employment. Using Greece as a starting point, they summarise the current Greek legislation on criminal records and employment disqualifications and identify significant shortcomings. These include a lack of uniformity between the occupational barriers faced by similar professionals (eg any felony conviction is an obstacle to employment as a dentist, but not as a doctor), a lack of correspondence between the requirements of the particular job and the disqualifying crimes (eg a person who wants to work as a lifeguard must not have been convicted of defamation or tax evasion), and under-inclusive background checking (eg unlike financial crimes, crimes against life or sex offences do not constitute an obstacle to employment for doctors). They argue that employment bans must be governed by clear principles and be respectful of offenders' rights. Moving from theory to practice, they identify the key policy questions any European policymaker needs to answer when implementing employment disqualifications based on criminal records.

C. 'Dangerous' Offenders and Legal Consequences of Criminal Conviction

The contributions in Part III of this book on offenders who are categorised by the law as 'dangerous',[5] point to similarities but also to significant differences between the jurisdictions surveyed. In conjunction with the chapters relating to juveniles (in Part IV), they provide points of alignment with, but also differentiation from, measures and processes relating to more 'run of the mill' offenders (see chapter 11 by Herzog-Evans).

Harry Annison and Ailbhe O'Loughlin's (chapter 9) discussion of a prison sentence created for dangerous offenders in England and Wales points to the significant extent to which legal consequences can impact on individuals *within* the traditional confines of the criminal justice system. Their contribution focuses on the indeterminate sentence of Imprisonment for Public Protection (IPP), a measure of preventive detention that sits within a broader system of preventive justice that seeks to target individuals on the basis of the likelihood of their committing future harm (Ashworth and Zedner 2016). Those released from indeterminate prison sentences such as the IPP face onerous and highly restrictive licence conditions and the prospect of immediate recall to prison. In this sense, the legal consequences of convictions for serious offences continue to have a significant impact on the lives of offenders who have already served the punitive part of their sentences. On the strength of a detailed analysis of case law from domestic courts and the ECtHR, Annison and O'Loughlin argue that while the ECHR and English common law provide important protections to convicted offenders, the current interpretation of Article 5 ECHR fails to adequately safeguard the rights of 'dangerous' individuals serving indeterminate sentences. While Article 7 acts as an important safeguard against 'penal subversions' (Zedner 2016), Article 5 allows significant incursions into individual liberties by failing to scrutinise sentences, such as the IPP, that allow for very long periods of detention, and which hand over release decisions to administrative bodies. In light of these limitations, Annison and O'Loughlin argue that prisoners who have exceeded the punitive tariff of these sentences and are held in prison on preventive grounds should be conceived in principle as being 'beyond' their sentences. This has significant implications for how the predicament of these particular prisoners should be addressed, but also more broadly for the conceptualisation of the imprisonment of 'dangerous offenders' and such convicted offenders' journeys towards rehabilitation.

In chapter 10, Axel Dessecker describes various forms of intensive supervision in Germany: a set of individualised interventions directed at probationers

[5] The term 'dangerous offender' is here used to refer to what has been termed the modern 'monstrous' (Simon 1998), most usually serious sexual offenders, serious violent offenders and other offenders thought to pose a risk of serious physical or sexual harm.

or parolees living in the community. Empirical research shows an increasing number of offenders are subject to a form of intensive supervision in Germany, whether as an alternative to prison or upon leaving prison. Although intensive supervision can be part of the sentence imposed by the court, most cases occur in specific situations when the law orders intensive supervision as a binding legal consequence based on the assumption that the offender is dangerous. Where measures of intensive supervision are imposed post-sentence, they are classified by the German penal code as 'measures of reform and prevention' rather than punishments. Commonalities with the system in England and Wales described by Annison and O'Loughlin are readily apparent: intensive supervision is conceived of as a measure for both rehabilitation and incapacitation (with the implicit view that these goals are readily reconcilable). As in England and Wales, the system takes a hybrid approach: it is primarily crime-based (prompted by the crime committed, rather than a risk assessment), but measures are also triggered for some individuals by their categorisation (which in effects operates as a form of dangerousness trigger). The level of intervention also varies significantly, from minimal oversight to very severe intrusion into, and restrictions on, an offender's life. While intensive supervision measures are intended to be non-custodial, they often blur the distinction between custodial and non-custodial sanctions, such as in cases of compulsory residence. Dessecker concludes that, despite the potential for serious interference with offenders' rights, including their right to liberty under Article 5 ECHR, non-custodial sanctions and measures are less open to challenge on human rights grounds, as they will always appear as a less serious alternative to the imprisonment of high-risk offenders.

In chapter 11, Martine Herzog-Evans uses Anthony Bottom's (1977) concept of 'bifurcation' to compare the legal consequences of criminal conviction in France for 'run of the mill' offenders with those for 'dangerous' offenders. Her discussion of 'run of the mill' offenders surveys the right to vote, criminal records and offender supervision. She shows that, in France, two main principles explain why criminal records are not easily accessible and are easily expunged: the right to be forgotten, and the necessity of supporting the desistance process and of acknowledging achieved desistance. She shows that while very light-touch supervision for 'run of the mill' offenders means that they are subject to few restrictions, they also receive very little support. The result is that such offenders are expected to prepare their own release plan, obtain employment and housing, and engage with community agencies and the health system with little formal support.

In contrast, at the opposite end of the spectrum, dangerous offenders appear to be treated somewhat more harshly but yet tend to receive greater support. Notwithstanding superficial similarities with both the United Kingdom (UK) and Germany, Herzog-Evans shows that the French system for governing dangerous offenders differs significantly in practice from that in other jurisdictions. While common systems exist – longer periods of supervision for the dangerous, preventive detention for dangerous offenders, and a sex offender register – their use in practice is dramatically limited. 'Safety Measures', ostensibly a form of intensive supervision for dangerous offenders (coupled with the longstanding 'socio-judicial supervision') are cast by Herzog-Evans to amount, in practice, to little more than the supervision provided for 'run of the mill' offenders.

Measures of preventive detention for dangerous offenders (akin to the German system, or the Australian system discussed below) have been little used, to the point that specially-designed institutions that anticipated heavy reliance on group-work therapeutic interventions have never held more than two people at a time. A register of sex offenders exists, but the requirements it imposes on individuals are limited, and there are significant constraints on access when compared to the systems in place in the US, the UK, Switzerland and elsewhere. In short, Herzog-Evans concludes that notwithstanding such measures, dangerous offenders in France retain most of their rights, and certainly to an extent that compares positively to many other jurisdictions. Equally, however, Herzog-Evans shows that the reasons for this situation are not necessarily so positive, and offenders often lack the support needed to help them reintegrate into the community.

Contrasted with these accounts of European policy and practice (with the variations therein), Patrick Keyzer and Darren O'Donovan provide, in chapter 12, a dystopian account of current Australian practice that serves as a cautionary tale for Europe. Australia has increasingly developed a system of civil preventive detention at both State and federal level. Keyzer and O'Donovan describe how this has been coupled with the growth of data-driven policing, whereby risk increasingly underpins everyday practice. Thus on the one hand, for the dangerous offenders *du jour* (sexual and violent offenders), significant interventions exist both within and beyond imprisonment/preventive detention. On the other hand, individuals or groups who may have had few or no criminal convictions, but who nonetheless are regarded as dangerous, find themselves subject to significant criminal justice intervention. Furthermore, issues of migration are increasingly bound up in such risk-based practices: in short, the 'riskiness' (including even 'low risk' categorisation) of individuals serves as a standalone justification for deportation.

Empirical research cited by Keyzer and O'Donovan shows practitioners to have serious reservations about the risk-reduction interventions targeted at dangerous offenders. Not unlike the situation Herzog-Evans describes in France, 'high risk' individuals find themselves essentially having to develop their own 'exit strategies' from civil detention, including identifying appropriate accommodation, developing appropriate social networks and so on. The disproportionate impact on juveniles (in particular) of risk-oriented (ie data-driven) policing is becoming increasingly clear, with juveniles assailed by frequent home visits, stop and searches, and other activities with no therapeutic component. In sum, Keyzer and O'Donovan point to a 'normative drift towards rights deprivation'. This is attributed, in part, to Australia's weak constitutional law framework, which limits accountability and thus facilitates the emergence of such a trajectory.

While casting European frameworks – not least the ECHR – as particularly valuable instruments (see also Brown 2011), Keyzer and O'Donovan's chapter also presents an important cautionary tale.

D. Juvenile Offenders and Legal Consequences of Criminal Conviction

Contributors to Part IV of this book stress the importance of a criminal record regime that adequately differentiates between criminal records acquired as a juvenile and those acquired as an adult. The rationale for this is grounded in the view that the labelling and stigmatisation inherent in the mark of a criminal record impacts negatively on the rehabilitation and reintegration of juveniles.

In chapter 13, Nicola Carr likens juvenile criminal records in England and Wales to an albatross around one's neck: some childhood transgressions can never be shaken off and continue to have consequences later in life. She examines a series of legal challenges in domestic and European courts, highlighting the difficulties with the current regime and the negative impact it has had on fundamental areas of life such as education, employment, travel and family life. She describes cases in which criminal records acquired as a juvenile for minor offending have been subject to disclosure many years after the event, even where the penalty issued at the time was intended to 'divert' the child from the criminal justice system, and thus on the understanding that fewer consequences would result. These disposals may even remain on a person's criminal record *ad infinitum*, regardless of the age at which he or she acquired the record. Therefore, Carr argues that one of the main justifications for the use of diversionary disposals in England and Wales – to avoid the negative effects of contact with the criminal justice system, including the labelling of young people as offenders – is fundamentally undermined by the criminal record regime.

In legislation in England and Wales, a distinction is drawn between records of juvenile and adult offending, in that shorter time periods apply for a juvenile record to become 'spent' than for offences committed as an adult. However, as Carr argues, legal rehabilitation for juvenile offenders is still very limited, because the list of specific professions to which the legislation does not apply and the range of exceptions have expanded significantly over time. Carr considers the implications of this regime in relation to children's rights standards and highlights a paradox: greater access to the criminal records of juveniles has in many instances been justified by reference to the need to protect children.

In chapter 14, Elina van 't Zand-Kurtovic presents a critique of Dutch criminal record screening in the light of childrens' rights standards. She shows that in the Netherlands, like in England and Wales, information can be stored in the Dutch criminal record database for both adult and juvenile offenders for lengthy periods (20 years for minor offences, 30 years for more serious offences and 80 years for sexual offences). Such information is registered as soon as the police submit a case to the public prosecutor's office, so individuals who are merely suspected of an offence will acquire a criminal record without the need for a conviction. Unlike other European countries, the Netherlands does not provide for the possibility for criminal records to become spent or expunged once a juvenile reaches the age of majority. In the Netherlands, however, criminal record disclosure is highly restricted due to the weight given to the protection of privacy, and the only way for most employers to acquire information on a potential employee's criminal background is by means of an official request for a Certificate of Conduct (see also Meijer, chapter 5 of this volume). According to Dutch policy, criminal record information on juveniles can only be used for pre-employment screening purposes for two years. In cases of violent offending, this period increases to four years. While the Dutch system appears relatively lenient when compared to other systems detailed in this book, van 't Zand-Kurtovic shows, using findings from qualitative empirical research, that having acquired a criminal record as a juvenile can negatively impact young adults' entry into the Dutch labour market.

IV. REFLECTIONS

It is hoped that the analyses of different legal systems presented in this book raise a number of important issues that will stimulate further in-depth legal and criminological research on, and analysis of, the consequences of criminal convictions. Overall, it seems that during the last few decades, preventive measures have been imposed with ever greater frequency on the grounds of criminal convictions. The result of this is that the potential legal consequences of a criminal conviction are expanding in scope.

An important question that requires further research is when and how the legal consequences of criminal conviction should come to an end. A Special Issue of the *European Journal of Probation* explored in some detail the possibility for legal or judicial rehabilitation in Europe. Almost all European countries have some form of 'expunging technique', including: (i) automatic expungement; (ii) expungement by judicial decision, or (iii) expungement by an administrative decision (Thomas 2007: 94). Herzog-Evans (2011) divides automatic expunging techniques into automatic measures, granted without any requirement of the offender (ie reaching a certain age), and measures based on the absence of reconviction.

With regard to automatic expungement, the period after which a criminal record becomes expunged or spent differs between the countries described in this volume. Most countries have adopted a two-step approach to the expiry of recording periods: in the first step, criminal convictions are no longer included in the extract of the criminal record (see Blitsa and Kivrakidou (chapter 8), Morgenstern (chapter 4), Lukács and Vig (chapter 6)), nor are they relevant to the decision whether or not to provide a Conduct Certificate (Meijer (chapter 5) and Kurtovic (chapter 14)). In the second step, criminal convictions are removed from the criminal register altogether. In the latter case, much longer periods apply.

The general justification for expunging criminal records is that after some time, an ex-offender is at no more risk of reoffending than a non-offender. As noted, the expungement periods between the different countries as described in this volume differ from each other. Periods also differ between different groups of offenders, most notably with regard to convictions for sexual offences: in some countries a criminal conviction can have life-long consequences, whereas in other countries the legal consequences of sexual offences are limited in time (although the consequences tend to last longer than for other crimes). Furthermore, the systems as described in this volume distinguish between offences only according to their seriousness (as reflected in the length of the sentence imposed) and do not take into account the findings of reconviction research, including the declining risk of recidivism over time (Blumstein and Nakamura 2009; Kurlychek, Brame, and Bushway 2006, 2007; Soothill and Francis 2009). At what point is a person with a criminal record, who has remained free of further contact with the criminal justice system, at no greater risk than a counterpart of the same age? So far, very limited (criminological) research has been undertaken in Europe on this question (with the exception of Bushway, Nieuwbeerta and Blokhuis 2011 for the Netherlands) and on the implications of such research for policy. This raises the question of what criminological reconviction research can contribute to improving current systems for expunging criminal records, and thereby protect more effectively the dignity and rights of individuals.

Another question on legal rehabilitation is whether an offender should be seen as a passive recipient of legal rehabilitation (ie through the passage of time), or as an active participant in his or her own rehabilitation. Should the offender be able to influence his or her legal rehabilitation and, if so, how? Recommendation No R (84) 10 on the criminal record and rehabilitation of convicted persons is clear on this point: Member States should provide for 'an automatic rehabilitation *after a reasonably short period of time*' and should – in addition – provide 'a possibility of rehabilitation at an earlier moment *at the request of the person concerned*' (emphasis added). However, it is unclear whether all Member States provide the possibility of legal rehabilitation at the request of the ex-offender.

With regard to the question of the extent to which offenders should be able to influence the consequences of their criminal conviction, the contributions in this volume build upon previous research by describing procedures that enable ex-offenders to request legal rehabilitation from the court (see Herzog-Evans for France and Morgenstern (chapters 4 and 11 of this volume), who describes the procedure of 'elimination of the stain of conviction' in Germany). Also, this volume includes procedures in countries not described previously (see Lukács and Vig for Hungary, chapter 6 of this volume). A distinction can be made between mechanisms that allow the offender to request the sentencing judge to exempt the offender from the negative consequences of a criminal conviction at the same time as imposing a sentence (see, for instance, the 'preliminary exemption' in Hungary), and exemption methods that may be employed after the sentence has become final (see, for instance, the 'subsequent exemption' in Hungary). Usually, these exemption methods are based on merit and/or require some degree of 'worthiness'. In deciding on worthiness, various factors can be of significance: the gravity of the criminal offence; the level of culpability; whether or not the harm caused by the act in question has been repaired (damages paid); whether the offender has paid all of his or her fines; whether he or she had a record of good behaviour whilst incarcerated; and whether he or she has been of good behaviour since release (meaning that he or she has not only not been reconvicted, but also has not been on the police radar).

Another important question that follows from this is whether all ex-offenders should be eligible for legal rehabilitation: should there be a point in time for all offenders where they no longer are affected or restricted by law due to their former criminal conviction? Or is it legitimate to exclude certain offenders from being legally rehabilitated? And if so, which offenders and under what conditions?

The various contributions to this collection demonstrate that there is an urgent need for greater normative debate on the limits on legal consequences of criminal conviction. And if greater limits are desired, how this is to be achieved. As different contributions show, the ECHR offers very little protection to convicted offenders. Within the current framework of the ECHR it seems rather unlikely that the ECtHR can itself set out firmer normative limits on the legal consequences of criminal conviction. The scope of these consequences, and the differences between countries, raises the question of whether harmonisation at the EU level is perhaps needed. Another approach would be to introduce an EU directive on (legal limits on the) rights of former offenders, similar to the guidelines that are in place for victims[6] or suspects.[7]

Adding further complexity, the future relationship between the UK and the EU, and the ECHR/ECtHR, remains at time of writing (and likely for many years) an open question. This raises questions, prompted by insights provided by Keyzer and O'Donovan (in chapter 10 of this volume), about other national or supra-national mechanisms by which the concerns raised throughout this collection can satisfactorily be addressed. The far-reaching ramifications of the ratcheting-up of 'tough on crime' policy and rhetoric over recent decades in many Western nations (UK, US, Australia), and the more recent populist uprisings in parts of Europe and elsewhere (Hungary, Poland, Brazil, Philippines), make it clear that the protection of fundamental rights of convicted offenders will remain a crucial concern.

[6] Directive 2012/29/EU of the European Parliament and of the Council of 25 October 2012 establishing minimum standards on the rights, support and protection of victims of crime, and replacing Council Framework Decision 2001/220/JHA [2012] OJ L315/57.

[7] Directive 2013/48/EU of the European Parliament and of the Council of 22 October 2013 on the right of access to a lawyer in criminal proceedings and in European arrest warrant proceedings, and on the right to have a third party informed upon deprivation of liberty and to communicate with third persons and with consular authorities while deprived of liberty [2013] OJ L294/1.

REFERENCES

Ashworth, A and Zedner, L (2016) *Preventive Justice* (Oxford, Oxford University Press).

Backman, C (2012) *Criminal Records in Sweden. Regulation of Access to Criminal Records and the Use of Criminal Background Checks by Employers* (PhD Thesis. Göteborg, Department of Sociology, University of Göteborg).

Bahr, SJ, Davis, C and Ward, C (2013) 'The process of offender reintegration: perceptions of what helps prisoners reenter society' *Criminology and Criminal Justice*, 13(4), 446–49.

Beccaria, C (1764 [1963]) *On Crimes and Punishment* (trans H Pallouci) (Indianapolis, Bobbs-Merrill).

Blitsa, D, Gouldin, LP, Jacobs, J and Larrauri, E (2016) 'Criminal Records and Immigration: Comparing the United States and the European Union' *Fordham International Law Journal*, 36, 205–44.

Blumstein, A and Nakamura, K (2009) 'Redemption in the Presence of Widespread Criminal Background Checks, *Criminology*, 47, 327–59.

Boone, M (2011) 'Judicial Rehabilitation in the Netherlands: Balancing Between Safety and Privacy' *European Journal of Probation*, 3, 63–78.

Boone, M and Kurtovic, E (2015) 'Collateral Consequences and the Principle of Proportional Punishment' in F de Jong (ed), *Overarching Views of Crime and Deviancy. Rethinking the Legacy of the Utrecht School* (The Hague, Eleven International Publishing) 401–18.

Brown M (2011) 'Preventive Detention and the Control of Sex Crime: Receding visions of justice in Australian case law' *Alternative Law Journal* 36, 10–16.

Bottom, AE (1977) 'Reflections on the Renaissance of Dangerousness' *Howard Journal of Criminal Justice*, 16, 70–96.

Burke, L, Collett, S and McNeill, F (2018) *Reimagining Rehabilitation: Beyond the Individual* (London, Routledge).

Bushway, SD, Nieuwbeerta, P and Blokhuis, A (2011) 'The predictive value of criminal background checks: do age and criminal history affect time to redemption?' *American Society of Criminology*, 49, 1, 27–60.

Buysse, W, Meijer, S and Szytniewski, B (2018) *Pre-employment screening in de grensregio's van de Benelux and Germany* (The Hague, WODC).

Chin, GJ (2012) 'The New Civil Death: Rethinking Punishment in the Era of Mass Conviction' *University of Pennsylvania Law Review*, 160, 1789–1833.

Cliquennois, G and Suremain, H (eds) (2017) *Monitoring Penal Policy in Europe* (London, Routledge).

Colgate Love, M (2001) 'Deconstructing the New Infamy: A Preview of the Section's Project on Collateral Sanctions' *Criminal Justice*, 16, 30–32.

—— (2011), 'Paying Their Debt to Society: Forgiveness, Redemption, and the Uniform Collateral Consequences of Conviction Act' *Howard Law Journal*, 54(3), available at SSRN: https://ssrn.com/abstract=1802180 (last accessed 20 September 2018).

Condry, R and Scharff Smith, P (2018) 'The Sociology of Punishment and the Effects of Imprisonment on Families' in R Condry and P Scharff Smith (eds), Prisons, Punishment and the Family (Oxford, Oxford University Press).

Damaska, MR (1968a) 'Adverse Legal Consequences of Conviction and Their Removal: A Comparative Study' *The Journal of Criminal Law, Criminology, and Police Science*, 59, 347–60.

—— (1968b) 'Adverse Legal Consequences of Conviction and Their Removal: A Comparative Study (Part 2)' *The Journal of Criminal Law, Criminology, and Police Science*, 59, 542–68.

Demleitner, NV (1999) 'Preventing internal exile: the need for restrictions on collateral sentencing consequences' *Standford Law & Policy Review*, 11, 153–71.

Farrall, S and Calverley, A (2006) *Understanding Desistance from Crime: Emerging Theoretical Directions in Resettlement and Rehabilitation* (Maidenhead, Open University Press).

Fitzgerald O'Reilly, M (2018) *Uses and Consequences of a Criminal Conviction. Going on the Record of an Offender* (Basingstoke, Palgrave Macmillan).

Goffman, E (1963) *Stigma: Notes on the Management of Spoiled Identity* (London, Penguin).

Hahn, JM (1991) 'Pre-employment information services: Employers beware?' *Employee Relations Law Journal*, 17, 45–69.

Harris, PM and Keller, KS (2005) 'Ex-offenders need not apply: The criminal background check in hiring decisions' *Journal of Contemporary Criminal Justice*, 21, 6–30.

Herzog-Evans, M (2011) 'Judicial Rehabilitation in France: Helping with the Desisting Process and Acknowledging Achieved Desistance' *European Journal of Probation*, 3, 4–19.

Holzer, HJ, Raphael, S and Stoll, MA (2004) 'Will employers fire former offenders? Employer preferences, background checks, and their determinants' in M Patillo, DF Weiman and B Western (eds) *Imprisoning America: The Social Effects of Mass Incarceration* (New York, Russell Sage Foundation).

Jacobs, JB and Crepet, T (2008) 'The expanding scope, use, and availability of criminal records' *Journal of Legislation and Public Policy*, 11, 177–213.

—— and Larrauri (2016) *European Criminal Records and Ex-Offender Employment* (Oxford, Oxford University Press, Oxford Handbooks Online).

Karlan, PS (2004) 'Convictions and Doubts: Retribution, Representation, and the Debate over Felon Disenfranchisement' *Stanford Public Law and Legal Theory Working Paper Series*, available at http://papers.ssrn.com/abstract=484543 (last accessed 20 September 2018).

Kirk, DS and Wakefield, S (2018) 'Collateral Consequences of Punishment: A Critical Review and Path Forward' *Annual Review of Criminology*, 1, 171–94.

Kirkwood, S and McNeill, F (2015) 'Integration and reintegration: Comparing pathways to citizenship through asylum and criminal justice' *Criminology & Criminal Justice*, 15(5), 511–26.

Kurlychek, MC, Brame, R and Bushway, SD (2006) 'Scarlet letters and recidivism: Does an old criminal record predict future offending? *Criminology & Public Policy*, 5, 483–522.

—— (2007) ' Enduring risk: Old criminal records and prediction of future criminal involvement, *Crime and Delinquency*, 53, 64–83.

Larrauri, E (2011) 'Conviction Records in Spain: Obstacles to Reintegration of Offenders?', *European Journal of Probation*, 3, 50–62.

—— and Jacobs, JB (2013) 'A Spanish Window on European Law and Policy on Employment Discrimination Based on Criminal Record' in T Daems, S Snacken and D van Zyl Smit (eds) *European Penology?* (Oxford, Hart Publishing) 293–319.

Larrauri Pijoan, E (2014) 'Legal protections against criminal background checks in Europe', *Punishment & Society*, 16(1), 50–73.

Louks, N, Lyner, O and Sullivan, T (1998) 'The employment of people with criminal records in the European Union' *European Journal on Criminal Policy and Research*, 6, 195–210.
Malsch, M and Duker, M (eds) (2012) *Incapacitation. Trends and new perspectives* (Farnham, Ashgate).
Maruna, S (2011) 'Judicial Rehabilitation and the 'Clean Bill of Health' in Criminal Justice' *European Journal of Probation*, 3(1), 97–117.
McNeill, F (2012) 'Four forms of 'offender' rehabilitation: Towards an interdisciplinary perspective' *Legal and Criminological Psychology*, 17(1), 18–36.
Mauer, M and Chesney Lind, M (2003) *Invisible Punishment: The Collateral Consequences of Mass Imprisonment* (New York, The New Press).
Meijer, S (2017) 'Rehabilitation as a Positive Obligation' *European Journal of Crime, Criminal Law, and Criminal Justice*, 25, 145–62.
Morgenstern, C (2011) 'Judicial Rehabilitation in Germany – The Use of Criminal Records and the Removal of Recorded Convictions' *European Journal of Probation*, 3, 20–35.
Padfield, N (2011) 'Judicial rehabilitation? A view from England' *European Journal of Probation*, 3(1), 36–49.
Pinard, M (2006) 'An Integrated Perspective on the Collateral Consequences of Criminal Convictions and Reentry Issues Faced by Formerly Incarcerated Individuals' *Boston University Law Review*, 86, 623–90.
—— (2010) 'Reflections and Perspectives on Reentry and Collateral Consequences' *The Journal of Criminal Law and Criminology*, 100, 3, 1213–24.
Raynor, P and Robertson, G (eds) (2009) *Rehabilitation, Crime, and Justice* (Basingstoke, Palgrave Macmillan).
Simon, J (1998) 'Managing the Monstrous: Sex offenders and the new penology' *Psychology, Public Policy, and Law*, 4, 452–67.
Stefanou, C and Xanthaki, H (eds) (2008), *Towards a European Criminal Record* (Cambridge, Cambridge University Press).
Soothill, K and Frances, B (2009) 'When do offenders become like non-offenders?' *Howard Journal of Criminal Justice*, 48, 373–87.
Thomas, T (2007) *Criminal Records. A Database for the Criminal Justice System and Beyond* (Basingstoke, Palgrave Macmillan).
—— and Hebenton, B (2012) 'Dilemmas and consequences of prior criminal record: a criminological perspective from England and Wales' *Criminal Justice Studies: A Critical Journal of Crime, Law and Society*, DOI:10.1080/ 1478601X.2012.715583.
Travis, J (2002) 'Invisible punishment: An instrument of Social Exclusion' in M Mauer and M Chesney Lind (eds) (2003) *Invisible Punishment: The Collateral Consequences of Mass Imprisonment* (New York, The New Press) 15–36.
Tripkovic, M (2016) 'The Modern Cives Sine Suffraggio: Dimensions of Criminal Disenfranchisement in Europe' *The Howard Journal*, 55, 4–23.
Uggen, C, Manza, J and Thompson, M (2006) 'Citizenship, Democracy, and the Civic Reintegration of Criminal Offenders' *The ANNALS of the American Academy of Political and Social Science*, 605, 281–310.
—— and Steward, R (2015) 'Piling On: Collateral Consequences and Community Supervision' *Minnesota Law Review*, 99, 1871–912.
Vermeulen, G et al (2002) *Blueprint for an EU Criminal Database: Legal, Politico-Institutional & Practical Feasibility* (Antwerp, Maklu).

Van Tongeren, S and Vols, M (2017) 'The right to housing and the right to a second chance. How Dutch landlords and local authorities facilitate and frustrate the successful re-integration of ex-offenders' in M Vols and J Sidoli (eds) *People and Buildings: Comparative Housing Law* (The Hague, Eleven International Publishing) 171–90.

Von Hirsch, A and Wasik, M (1997) 'Civil Disqualifications Attending Conviction: A Suggested Conceptual Framework' *The Cambridge Law Journal*, 56, 599–626.

Van Zyl Smit, D and Snacken, S (2010) *Principles of European Prison Law and Policy* (Oxford, Oxford University Press).

Zedner, L (2016) 'Penal subversions: When is a punishment not punishment, who decides and on what grounds?' *Theoretical Criminology*, 20, 3–20.

TABLE OF CASES

European Court of Human Rights

Frodl v Austria App no 20201/04 (8 April 2010)
Hirst v the United Kingdom App no 74025/01 (6 October 2005)
Scoppola v Italy (No 3) App no 126/05 (22 May 2012)
Vinter and others v the United Kingdom App no 66069/09, 130/10, 3896/10 (9 July 2013)

Part I

Criminological Perspectives on Legal Consequences of Criminal Conviction

2

Collateral Consequences of a Conviction in Spain

ELENA LARRAURI AND MARTI ROVIRA*

I. INTRODUCTION

PREVIOUS RESEARCH IN the United States (US) has concluded that criminal convictions have adverse legal consequences beyond the limits established by the sentence imposed (Damaska 1968a, 1968b; Demleitner 1999; Colgate Love 2001; Pinard 2006; Colgate Love, Roberts and Klingele 2013). Ex-offenders have their job opportunities severely limited, their welfare and voting rights restricted, and, in the case of immigrants, have a higher chance of being deported (Uggen, Manza and Thompson 2006; Uggen and Steward 2015).

These effects have been termed 'collateral consequences' because, although they are regulated by law, they are not included in the judgments of penal courts, and therefore their impact is largely unknown to the judge, to the defendant and even to lawyers participating in the court case (Damaska 1968b; Demleitner 1999; Mauer and Chesney Lind 2003; Goulette et al 2014; Corda 2016). More specifically, collateral consequences may be defined as adverse legal effects in addition to a sentence that are: (i) typically located outside the penal code; (ii) applied by non-criminal justice institutions; and (iii) interpreted by the courts as civil regulations rather than criminal penalties (Uggen and Steward 2015: 1875).[1] This definition captures the ambivalent nature of 'collateral consequences': although they 'flow' from a criminal conviction, their effects are controlled by agencies outside the criminal justice system, and they are usually not considered during the sentencing process.

* This research has been supported by the projects *Ejecución y supervisión de la pena: Calidad de la intervención, legitimidad y reincidencia* supported by the Spanish Ministry of Economy and Competitiveness, Grant DER2015-64403-P and FEDER, EU and '*La regulación de los antecedentes penales: efecto en el acceso al mercado laboral de los jóvenes*' Supported by the Research Grants RecerCaixa (Grant RecerCaixa 2013).

[1] For a discussion of the concept, see Kirk and Wakefield 2018.

Collateral consequences can be justified as responses to public safety concerns,[2] although they have been criticised (Colgate Love 2015; Hoskins 2014; Boone and Kurtovic 2015; Roberts 2008) because they are: (i) unknown to offenders and judges during trials, and therefore might not be considered when the court decides whether to accept a guilty plea; (ii) automatic – a fact that might render the sentence disproportionate; and (iii) imposed with fewer safeguards than punishment, although their content is punitive in effect. Criminologists have also pointed out that collateral consequences are important obstacles to reintegration (Uggen, Manza and Behrens 2004; Holzer, Raphael and Stoll 2007; Western 2007; LeBel 2012; Whittle 2018; Maruna and Lageson 2018).

The literature on collateral consequences sometimes tends to overlap with the research on criminal records and sexual offender registers. In our view, the latter are both instances of collateral consequences. A criminal record is, in many ways, the first and most enduring collateral consequence, as an official label that can have effects outside the criminal justice system well after the sentence has been served. For instance, previous research has extensively shown that criminal records certificates are used by employers to discriminate[3] against former offenders (Pager 2003). The effects deriving from inclusion on a sex offender register are also a collateral consequence, particularly in the US, where the publication of an individual's name and address on a website and prohibitions on living in certain places usually extend beyond the sentence and are made mandatory by administrative regulations (Tewksbury and Lees 2006).

This chapter is directed to the following questions: Are there collateral consequences in Spain? If so, how does their scope compare to those in the US? Section II gives a broad overview of the findings of previous literature on collateral consequences in the US. Then in section III we present the results of a systematic survey of the Spanish legislation. In section IV we discuss the results, and the possibility of generalising the Spanish experience with that of other European countries.

II. RESEARCH ON COLLATERAL CONSEQUENCES IN THE US

In this section we briefly describe the previous literature on collateral consequences in the US. In order to discuss which rights are affected, we find it useful to apply the categories defined by Demleitner (1999):

(a) restricted access to employment;
(b) the denial of political rights; and
(c) the denial of social and welfare rights.

[2] For an overview, see Jacobs 2015; and Gottschalk 2015.

[3] For a discussion of how the concept of discrimination might be used in a neutral way or as a criticism, see Larrauri and Jacobs (2013: 294).

A. Restricted Access to Employment

A longstanding literature in the US highlights the problematic effects in the labour market of having a criminal record (Jacobs 2015). Every US State has laws that forbid those with a criminal record from practising certain professions. Furthermore, several federal and State laws bar convicted individuals from applying for government contracts, or from obtaining licences (see Jacobs 2015 for a comprehensive review). On the website of the Justice Centre, one can find almost 30,000 different regulations in the US that restrict access to employment (CSG Justice Centre 2016).

In addition, employers often carry out criminal background checks as part of recruitment processes (Holzer, Raphael and Stoll 2007), with one survey suggesting that 92 per cent of large companies require such checks (SHRM Society for Human Resource Management 2012).

Formally, criminal records are private information, but they are easily accessible (Jacobs and Larrauri 2012). Some information is shared online, and private companies offer the possibility, for a fee, to search court records (Bushway et al 2007; Jacobs 2015).

B. The Denial of Political Rights

One of the most frequently discussed collateral effects in the US has been limitations on political rights. In some States, prisoners and former felons are disenfranchised, and in some cases this may even lead to a life-long voting ban (Demleitner 1999; Uggen, Manza and Thompson 2006).[4] Similarly, in most States, individuals with criminal records are not allowed to hold public office (Uggen, Manza and Thompson 2006; Jacobs 2015). This contrasts with the fact that in most US States, people with criminal records may run for election (Steinacker 2003; Lippke 2009). Consequently, people with criminal records may run for election and be elected to a legislative body, but they cannot be a member of the cabinet.

Other political rights may be affected by collateral consequences. For instance, federal and State laws prohibit ex-felons from purchasing or possessing firearms, and in some States ex-felons are banned from being members of a jury (Jacobs 2015).

Focusing on immigration, in every US State, a criminal record can lead to deportation if the crime involves 'moral turpitude'. In addition, having a criminal record speeds up deportation for undocumented immigrants. Lastly, the absence of a criminal conviction is considered proof of good character for the purposes of naturalisation, and those with an aggravated felony conviction are

[4] However, more recently, Jacobs (2015) notes that there is a trend toward eliminating barriers to voting for previously convicted persons who have completed their sentence.

automatically disqualified (Colgate Love, Roberts and Klingele 2013; Jacobs 2015; Blitsa et al 2016).

C. The Denial of Social and Welfare Rights

More recently, attention to the effects of collateral consequences has extended to social and welfare issues. In certain States, criminal convictions are considered a ground for marital dissolution. Moreover, in some regions a conviction for certain offences is the basis for the termination of parental rights.[5] Furthermore, criminal records are considered in applications for adopting and fostering children (Uggen, Manza and Thompson 2006).

In addition to this, several welfare support programmes explicitly exclude people with previous convictions. For instance, federal legislation provides that some types of sex offenders or people convicted of manufacturing methamphetamines on public property are disqualified from applying for public housing (Curtis, Garlington and Schottenfeld 2013), and convicted drug offenders are ineligible for federal education loans and scholarships (Demleitner 1999; Jacobs 2015). Furthermore, claimants with a criminal record are disqualified from compensation programmes for crime victims (Jacobs 2015).

* * *

In summary, collateral consequences affect a range of rights in the US. Going beyond the punishment imposed by the sentence, the effects of a conviction pervade many different aspects of life: from professional opportunities to political and family rights and the possibility of obtaining social benefits. Collateral consequences have been seen as yet another indication of 'American exceptionalism' regarding the criminal justice system (Travis 2005; Jacobs 2015; Tonry 2016; Garland 2017). Indeed, the 'breadth, automaticity and length' of collateral consequences (Demleitner 2018: 494) has been defined as a distinguishable characteristic of the US criminal justice system, which contrasts with the situation in western European countries (Díez-Ripollés 2016). In the next section we examine how accurate this vision is.

III. RESEARCH ON COLLATERAL CONSEQUENCES IN SPAIN

Besides the early work of Damaska (1968a, 1968b) and Loucks, Lyner and Sullivan (1998),[6] there had not been much research on collateral consequences

[5] See at https://niccc.csgjusticecenter.org/.

[6] Additionally, some research was conducted on the regulation of criminal records in order to explore the possibility of creating a single Europe-wide registry of criminal records (Commission

in Europe until very recently. However, the importation of American literature has led some authors to look more closely at this domain (Larrauri and Jacobs 2013; Corda 2016). In addition, the increasing attention paid to sexual offenders and to the collateral consequences occurring after their sentences (Thomas 2007; Petrunik and Deutschmann 2008; Backman 2012; McAlinden 2012)[7] has led to an interest in investigating the situation regarding other offences. Lastly, comparative scholars have sought to understand the differences with the US (Pinard 2006; Jacobs 2015; Demleitner 2018).

In the following section we present our results from Spain, once again applying the categories defined by Demleitner (1999).

A. Restrictions on Employment

Most previous research has focused on the effects of criminal records in the labour market. The original work done by Thomas (2007) in the UK has been continued by scholars highlighting the existence of laws that restrict employment opportunities for people with criminal records in France (Herzog-Evans 2011), Germany (Morgenstern 2011), the Netherlands (Boone 2011; Buysse, Meijer and Szytniewski 2018), Spain (Larrauri 2011; Jacobs and Larrauri 2016; Rovira 2016) and Sweden (Backman 2012).[8]

As Loucks, Lyner and Sullivan (1998) explained, the majority of requests for criminal record checks in Europe are produced through 'enforced subject access'. 'Enforced access' means that the only way of finding out whether the applicant has a criminal record is to ask him or her to provide it. This is due to the fact that in the EU, criminal records are considered 'confidential', and therefore only the private individual can access his or her criminal record or give consent to access by others (Jacobs and Larrauri 2012).

Some countries allow employers to request criminal record certificates (CRCs) for all jobs, whereas regulations in other countries restrict checks to certain roles. The latter jobs tend to be those related to the public administration sector, or those for which a higher standard of 'integrity' or security is demanded, for example private security officers, high-ranking officials in the public sector or managers in gambling companies (Jacobs and Larrauri 2016).

In addition, in recent years, restrictions on sex offenders holding jobs involving close contact with children have appeared (Backman 2012; McAlinden 2012).

Staff Working Paper 2005; Stefanou and Xanthaki 2005, 2008). However, the authors look at collateral consequences in a supplemental manner only. Also, on the Internet it is not difficult to find documents ordered by UK institutions with comprehensive overviews of other national regulations regarding the possibility of requesting criminal records in the employment market (see, amongst others, KPMG 2009). However, in our view, these compilations are very descriptive and have little analytical interest.

[7] See also Dessecker (ch 10), Malsch (ch 3) and Herzog-Evans (ch 11) in this volume.

[8] See also Coninx (ch 7), Blitsa and Kivrakidou (ch 8), and Lukács and Vig (ch 6) in this volume.

In particular, Directive 2011/93/EU[9] establishes that Member States should allow employers to request information on sexual crimes for jobs involving close contact with children, and encourages the adoption of sex offender registers (Jacobs and Blitsa 2011).

By contrast to the US, we do not know in practice how many European employers actually ask for a CRC. Through research in the Central Register of Criminal Records of five jurisdictions, we can assert, however, that the frequency of criminal records certificates is not negligible. In Table 2.1 we can see the number of CRCs for each year for those countries in which this information is available. To allow for comparison, the second column shows the rate of applications for CRCs per 1,000 of the population.[10] It can be seen that in 2015 there were 4,225,379 requests for criminal records checks in the England and Wales (73 petitions per 1,000 inhabitants), 1,424,460 in Spain (31 per 1,000), 950,848 in Sweden (98 per 1,000) and 862,230 in the Netherlands (51 per 1,000). Table 2.1 also shows the substantial increase in criminal record check requests in these five countries. In most cases, this rise is related to the increasing obligations to present CRCs for jobs involving children.[11]

In addition, research has highlighted the importance of the European Union (EU) in the reconfiguration of the system for requesting criminal records for employment purposes in its Member States. Some authors have stated that the principle of free movement of workers within the EU could lead to a need to standardise collateral consequences between different countries (Loucks, Lyner and Sullivan 1998; Buysse, Meijer and Szytniewski 2018). A lack of common restrictions between countries on the access of ex-offenders to the labour market could lead to a breach of the right to enjoy equal treatment with nationals regarding access to employment. Therefore some attempts have been made in order to unify the criteria on jobs requiring criminal records at the European level.[12]

Lastly, in Spain, several laws disqualify people with criminal records from serving in a wide range of positions (Larrauri and Jacobs 2011; Larrauri and Jacobs 2013; Jacobs and Larrauri 2016). Criminal record certificates are requested for jobs in public administration. For jobs in private industry, there is no law explicitly authorising employers to ask for a CRC. Employers

[9] Directive 2011/93/EU of the European Parliament and of the Council on combating the sexual abuse and sexual exploitation of children and child pornography [2011] OJ L335/1.

[10] Formula: $\left[\left(\frac{\textit{Number of petition of criminal records certificates}}{\textit{Total population}}\right) \times 1000\right]$. The data of population comes from Eurostat (www.ec.europa.eu/eurostat) and, when not available, from the World Bank (www.data.worldbank.org).

[11] For England and Wales, see Thomas 2007; for Spain, see Rovira 2016; and for Sweden, see Backman 2012.

[12] In addition to the aforementioned Directive 2011/93/EU on sex offenders, there has also been a similar process for managerial jobs in the banking sector, as seen in the *Guidelines on the assessment of the suitability of members of the management body and key function holders* from the European Banking Authority (2012).

Table 2.1 Number of requests for criminal records certificates

	England & Wales[a]		Scotland[b]		The Netherlands[c]		Spain[d]		Sweden[e]	
Year	**N**	**‰**	**N**	**‰**	**N**	**‰**	**N**	**‰**	**N**	**‰**
1961									50,000	
1995									10,000	
1999					95,000					
2000										
2001										
2002	1,189,877	23								
2003	2,155,401	41							133,135	15
2004	2,577,459	48			135,487	8			149,860	17
2005	2,736,652	51			254,338	16			172,914	19
2006	3,182,902	59	599,107	117	279,700	17			215,719	24
2007	3,382,715	62	782,764	151	384,724	24			224,898	25
2008	3,810,614	69	881,635	169	474,751	29			275,748	30
2009	4,269,924	77	946,728	181	459,633	28			297,141	32
2010	4,219,319	76	1,039,820	198	488,631	29	1,853,870	40	363,866	39
2011	4,020,446	72	1,056,122	199	538,771	32	1,531,094	33	441,127	47
2012	4,141,451	73			563,273	34	1,665,530	36	626,651	66
2013	3,959,122	70			733,156	44	1,258,114	27	694,421	73
2014	4,049,074	71			703,860	42	1,234,195	27	768,702	80
2015	4,225,379	73			862,230	51	1,424,460	31	950,848	98
2016					968,300	57	2,894,816	62	1,050,644	107

Notes

a. Freedom of information request (UK) ref no 21567 (issued 28 February 2012) and freedom of information request (UK) ref no 1392 (issued 2015).

b. McGuinness, McNeill and Armstrong 2013.

c. van 't Zand-Kurtovic 2017.

d. Information provided to the authors by the Ministry of Justice in Spain through freedom of information requests.

e. Backman 2012 and personal communication with the author.

can request job applicants to present their own copies of their CRCs as a condition of employment.[13] However, this does not seem to be a common practice in the labour market. We carried out a survey of a random sample of individuals in Catalonia who were required to provide a CRC in person

[13] As has been mentioned, criminal records are considered confidential, and private companies are prohibited from compiling this information (Jacobs and Larrauri 2012). However, in 2015, a new law established that the names of individuals convicted of crimes against the Treasury or of smuggling will be made public, although this information is out of the reach of search engines such as Google (Rovira 2016).

during May–June 2014. Eight per cent of the CRCs were required for a job for which no law specifically required the disclosure of a CRC (Rovira 2016).

In addition, since the implementation of Directive 2011/93/EU in national legislation in 2015, a special CRC is required for all jobs involving close contact with children, particularly in the education and healthcare sectors (Rovira 2016).[14] For these positions, the candidate needs to present a CRC during the application process or, for some positions in public administration, explicitly give consent for the National Registry of Criminal Convictions to access his or her data.

B. The Denial of Political Rights

Systematic reviews of electoral systems point out that, in general, political rights can also be affected as a collateral consequence of a conviction (Uggen, Van Brakle and McLaughlin 2009; Tripkovic 2016). Regarding electoral rights, Spain allows prisoners *the right to vote* both during and after sentence. This is a probably a consequence of the recognition of all legal rights – except freedom – to prisoners, and of the principle of normalisation, according to which prisoners' lives should resemble life in the community.

The European Court of Human Rights (ECtHR) has dealt with this topic in several cases, mainly concerning the UK, and has clearly established that a blanket prohibition on the right to vote for prisoners is against Article 3 of the European Convention on Human Rights (ECHR) and that states have to take into account the nature of the offence, the length of the sentence and the individual circumstances of the offender (see, eg, *Millbank and Others v The United Kingdom*). However, the UK's ban on convicted prisoners' voting has largely remained in place.

Focusing on the possibility to *run for election*, this right is also affected by a conviction, but there seem to be greater restrictions on this right than on the right to vote (Uggen, Van Brakle and Mclaughin 2009; Tripkovic 2016). In Spain, people sentenced to emprisonment are ineligible to stand for election until the end of their sentence.[15] There are no restrictions on people sentenced to other kind of measures, nor on former prisoners.

In addition, in Spain there are restrictions on *other political rights* for people with criminal records. Ex-offenders are excluded from the possibility of obtaining a high-ranking position in government, including that of the First Minister

[14] The introduction of this law into national legislation has doubled the requests for criminal records certificates. See Table 2.1.

[15] In addition, one can be sentenced to the particular penalty of not being permitted to run for election ('*inhabilitación*') for a certain time, for instance, for crimes of rebellion, terrorism, against public administration or the State. However, this is a disqualification sentence, not properly a collateral consequence.

and other members of the cabinet.[16] Also, people with criminal records for an intentional crime are ineligible to be members of a jury,[17] or to act as attesters in a Popular Legislative Initiative.[18] In addition, criminal records are an important obstacle to obtaining a firearm permit (Palacios Blanco 2003).

Without doubt, the most dramatic collateral consequence of a conviction is the effect it has for *immigration* purposes. In this respect, 'collateral' consequences cannot be understood as secondary, since they are often more severe than the main sentence (Kirk and Wakefield 2018).

These consequences deserve particular attention, particularly for 'third-country' (ie non-European) nationals. For them, inside the 'Schengen' area, a criminal record can be a ground for denying a visa for 90 days (Blitsa et al 2016). 'Third-country' nationals with criminal records in Spain, or in countries where they lived for the last five years, are automatically excluded from obtaining an initial residence and work permit. Criminal records are also considered in the renewal of this authorisation (Long-term Residence) and in the procedures for granting nationality (Larrauri 2016). Moreover, in recent years, a criminal record has also been used as a criterion for selection for deportation in the case of irregular immigration (Fernández Bessa and Brandariz 2016).

In contrast, regarding citizens from the EU, Directive 2004/38/EC[19] establishes that criminal records cannot be the only ground for denying a residence permit, but that 'the personal conduct of the individual concerned must represent a genuine, present and sufficiently serious threat affecting one of the fundamental interests of society' (Article 27(2)).

C. The Denial of Social and Welfare Rights

Damaska (1968a, 1968b) pointed out nearly 50 years ago that in some countries, a conviction could lead to problems for pension rights, comprised a ground for divorce or could imply a problem as regards parental rights.

In our study of the current Spanish legislation, we found some collateral consequences for social and welfare rights. In particular, the consequences of a conviction are important for 'parenting rights'.[20] For instance, criminal records are considered in applications to become adoptive or foster parents. In child

[16] Law 3/2015, of 30 March, regulating the exercise of the high position of the General State Administration, Art 2.

[17] Law 5/1995, of 22 May, of the Jury, Art 9.

[18] Law 3/1984, of 26 March, of the Popular Legislative Initiative, Art 10.

[19] Directive 2004/38/EC on the right of citizens of the Union and their family members to move and reside freely within the territory of the Member States [2004] OJ L158/77.

[20] In addition, regarding divorce, previously, legislation established that a prison sentence of more than six years was a cause for 'marital separation', a legal stage prior to divorce. However, since a reform in 2003, no ground for a marital separation is needed.

custody proceedings after a couple has divorced, convictions for domestic or gender violence are also considered.[21]

Focusing on social 'welfare' rights, we found few collateral consequences, but still there were some. In particular, at the regional level (*Extremadura*), people with criminal records for drug crimes or for disorderly conduct are excluded from public housing.[22] Also, we found a mention of criminal records in a grant for participating in a training programme that excludes people with some kinds of criminal records.[23] Ex-offenders convicted of crimes related to organised crime, terrorism or the sexual abuse of children need to show remorse and pay civil liability in order to be able to obtain a pension after serving their prison sentence.[24] Therefore, having some kinds of criminal record can exclude a person from obtaining certain social welfare benefits. In addition, in Spain an individual cannot be a volunteer if he or she has certain kinds of criminal record.[25] Lastly, a person cannot get a licence to own a dangerous dog if he or she has a criminal record of certain kinds of dangerous crimes.[26]

However, collateral consequences do not seem to affect the category of welfare rights to the same extent as in the US. For instance, in 1983, a judgment of the Constitutional Court established that it is unconstitutional to restrict a person's pension rights on the basis of a criminal conviction.[27] In addition, after an intensive search we did not find any university that requests information on criminal records for entry. Some universities require CRCs for those students who wish to undertake internships in activities that involve close contact with children.[28] However, if they could not provide a 'clear' certificate, other training activities could be made available.

To sum up, in Spain there are many collateral consequences linked to a previous conviction. As in the US, in Spain a conviction can lead to serious consequences in the labour market, it can prevent the exercise of some political rights, and it can create problems for welfare rights. Indeed, the extent of collateral consequences in Spain is greater than we thought when we began this research.

[21] Law 25/2010, of 29 July, of the Civil Code of Catalonia, relative to the person and the family, Arts 222-15 and 233-11.

[22] Decree 115/2006, of 27 June, regulating the procedure of concession of public housing in the Comunidad Autónoma (region) of Extremadura, Art 7.

[23] Resolution of 20 October 2017 of the President of the Valencian Institute of Business Competitiveness (IVACE), by which the IVACE Foreign 2018 Scholarships call is opened, Art 8.

[24] Legislative Decree 8/2015, of 30 October, enacting the revised text of the General Law on Social Security, Art 274.2.

[25] Law 45/2015, of 14 October, on Volunteering, Art 8.5

[26] Royal Decree 287/2002, of 22 March, by which Law 50/1999, of 23 December, is developed on the legal regime of the possession of potentially dangerous animals, Art 3.1.

[27] Case No 114-1987, STC, 6 July 1987.

[28] University of Múrcia 2016.

To finish, we present the results of a systematic review of Spanish legislation in order to obtain a comprehensive view of current collateral consequences in this country. The results are shown in Table 2.2, following the 'domains' used by Uggen, Manza and Thompson (2006). We have followed these 'domains' because they are more detailed than the categories applied by Demleitner (1999), so they might be more helpful for examining the overall extent of collateral consequences. In addition, we have introduced four new 'domains' in order to include all collateral consequences found in our research.[29]

Based on the research of Uggen, Manza and Thompson (2006), the results in the table only refer to former inmates. However, it is important to emphasise that most collateral consequences shown in Table 2.2 are not restricted to former prisoners. In Spain, as in the US, most of these effects are not linked to a prison sentence. For instance, a person sentenced to a community sentence, a fine or probation faces the same restrictions on obtaining a job, being a member of a jury, participating in legislative popular initiatives, adopting children or obtaining social welfare benefits as former prisoners.[30]

Table 2.2 Rights and opportunities potentially affected by a felony conviction: Spain

Category	Domain	Existence of a collateral consequence (US)	Examples (US)	Existence of a collateral consequence (Spain)	Examples (Spain)
Restrictions on employment	Employment	✓	• Ban on carrying out specific occupations	✓	• Ban on carrying out specific occupations
	Serving as a public contractor*	✓[31]	• Ineligible to work as a government contractor	✓	• Ineligible to work as a government contractor
	Privacy	✓	• Registration and community notification for sex offenders	✓	• Publication of criminal records in the *National Gazette* for crimes against the Treasury or smuggling

(continued)

[29] For doing so we used the references in Jacobs 2015 and CSG Justice Centre 2016. These domains are marked with an asterisk in the table.

[30] There are some small differences for accessing some jobs. For instance, you cannot work as a prison officer or work as a civil servant in the Ministry of Justice if you have a criminal record for a prison sentence of more than three years. Also, as has been already mentioned, the right to run for elections has been restricted for offenders currently in prison (for more details, see Rovira 2016).

[31] Jacobs (2015).

Table 2.2 *(Continued)*

Category	Domain	Existence of a collateral consequence (US)	Examples (US)	Existence of a collateral consequence (Spain)	Examples (Spain)
The denial of political rights	Voting	✓	• Ban on voting	×	–
	Right to run for elections*	✓	• Ineligible to run for elections	×	– [The right is restricted only for convicted prisoners]
	Public Office	✓	• Ineligible to hold public office	✓	• Ineligible to hold public office
	Jury Service	✓	• Ineligible to serve as a member	✓	• Ineligible to serve as a member
	Firearm Ownership	✓	• Prohibition on possessing firearms	✓	• Prohibition on possessing firearms
	Immigration Status	✓	• Deportation. Denial of residence permit and nationality	✓	• Deportation. Denial of residence permit and nationality
The denial of social and welfare rights	Parental rights	✓	• Termination of parental rights; restrictions on becoming an adoptive or a foster parent	✓	• Restrictions on becoming an adoptive or a foster parent. In judgment for custody after divorce, convictions for domestic or gender violence are considered
	Marital dissolution	✓	• Allow criminal conviction as a grounds for divorce	[N/A]	– [Not applicable. No grounds for divorce are necessary in Spain]
	Public assistance	✓	• Receipt of food stamps and Temporary Assistance for Needy Families	✓	–
	Public housing	✓	• Prohibition on residing in public housing	×	• Prohibition on residing in public housing

(continued)

Table 2.2 *(Continued)*

Category	Domain	Existence of a collateral consequence (US)	Examples (US)	Existence of a collateral consequence (Spain)	Examples (Spain)
	Financial Aid	✓	• Ineligible for student grants and loans	✗	–
	Volunteer Activities*	✓[32]	• Ban on carrying out volunteer activities	✓	• Ban on carrying out volunteer activities.
	Pet Ownership*	✓[33]	• Ineligible to own/possess an animal	✓	• Ineligible for a licence to own a dangerous dog

IV. DISCUSSION

So far in this chapter we have described the Spanish context. In order to allow for future discussions, we think it is useful to compare it with the context in the US.

Collateral consequences have received wide attention in the US. This research has described collateral consequences as yet another instance of 'American Exceptionalism' (Demleitner 2018). According to our research in Spain, however, the US might not be so exceptional, as collateral consequences are also present in other countries. However, we have certainly observed differences in the degree of implementation, and therefore collateral consequences in the US may still be deemed 'extreme' for their 'breadth, automaticity and length' from a comparative perspective (Demleitner 2018: 494).

In our view, the main contrast between Spain and the US is probably due to the different conception of criminal records: 'public' in the US and confidential in Europe (Jacobs and Larrauri 2012). As a consequence, and in addition, we observe that the US differs from Spain in the following respects: more frequent use of criminal background checks for employers and the existence of a private industry carrying them out (Bushway, Stoll and Weiman 2007; Jacobs 2015; Kirk and Wakefield 2018); the extension of 'digital punishment' (Maruna and Lageson 2018); the general prevalence of disenfranchisement (removal of the right to vote) following conviction (Uggen, Manza and Thompson 2006); and broader restrictions on welfare rights on the basis of criminal records (Uggen and Steward 2015).

[32] Amongst others, see Code of Ala, para 3-1-29 (CSG Justice Centre 2016).
[33] Amongst others, see Code of Ala, para 26-1-4 (CSG Justice Centre 2016).

The extent of collateral consequences in Spain is particularly striking from a comparative perspective, considering that Spain has consistently been depicted as a relatively 'lenient' nation among European countries regarding the post-penal consequences of a conviction (Stefanou and Xanthaki 2005, 2008; Tripkovic 2016). In particular, we begin to see that the 'piling on' of collateral consequences detected by Uggen and Steward (2015) in the US is also the case in Spain, especially regarding immigrants and sexual offenders.

Collateral consequences in other European jurisdictions should be a matter of concern precisely because, by their very nature, they are mostly 'invisible', since they are commonly not contemplated by penal law but are dispersed through other regulations, and are therefore hidden from the main players in a criminal trial. It will be interesting to follow what researchers of other European countries discover as research in this topic continues. It is hoped that the different works brought together in this book will contribute towards this aim.

REFERENCES

Backman, C (2012) *Criminal Records in Sweden. Regulation of Access to Criminal Records and the Use of Criminal Background Checks by Employers* (PhD Thesis, Göteborg, Department of Sociology, University of Göteborg).

Blitsa, D, Gouldin, LP, Jacobs, J and Larrauri, E (2016) 'Criminal Records and Immigration: Comparing the United States and the European Union' *Fordham International Law Journal*, 36, 205–44.

Boone, M (2011) 'Judicial Rehabilitation in the Netherlands: Balancing Between Safety and Privacy' *European Journal of Probation*, 3, 63–78.

—— and Kurtovic, E (2015) 'Collateral Consequences and the Principle of Proportional Punishment' in F de Jong (ed), *Overarching Views of Crime and Deviancy. Rethinking the Legacy of the Utrecht School* (The Hague, Eleven International Publishing) 401–18.

Bushway, S, Briggs, S, Taxman, F, Thanner, M and Van Brakle, M (2007) 'Private Providers of Criminal History Records: Do You Get What You Pay For?' in S Bushway, MA Stoll, and DF Weiman (eds), *Barriers to Reentry? The Labor Market for Released Prisoners in Post-Industrial America* (New York, Russell Sage Foundation) 174–200.

——, Stoll, MA and Weiman, DF (2007) 'Introduction' in S Bushway, MA Stoll and DF Weiman (eds), *Barriers to Reentry? The Labor Market for Released Prisoners in Post-Industrial America* (New York, Russell Sage Foundation) 1–26.

Buysse, W, Meijer, S and Szytniewski, B (2018), *Pre-employmentscreening in de grensregio's van de Benelux en Duitsland* (The Hague, WODC).

Colgate Love, M (2001) 'Deconstructing the New Infamy: A Preview of the Section's Project on Collateral Sanctions' *Criminal Justice*, 16, 30–32.

——(2015) 'Managing Collateral Consequences in the Sentencing Process: The Revised Sentencing Articles of the Model Penal Code' *Wisconsin Law Review*, 2, 247–88.

——, Roberts, JV and Klingele, C (2013) *Collateral Consequences of Criminal Convictions: Law, Policy and Practice* (Washington, DC, Thompson Reuters Westlaw/NACDL Press).

Commission Staff Working Paper (2005) *Annex to the WHITE PAPER on exchanges of information on convictions and the effect of such convictions in the European Union*, available at https://db.eurocrim.org/db/en/doc/592.pdf (last accessed 4 January 2019).

Corda, A (2016) 'More Justice and Less Harm: Reinventing Access to Criminal History Records' *Howard Journal of Criminal Justice*, 60, 1–60.

CSG Justice Centre (2016) *The National Inventory of Collateral Consequences of Conviction*, available at https://niccc.csgjusticecenter.org/map/ (last accessed 7 June 2018).

Curtis, MA, Garlington, S and Schottenfeld, LS (2013) 'Alcohol, Drug, and Criminal History Restrictions in Public Housing' *Cityscape: A Journal of Policy Development and Research*, 15, 37–52.

Damaska, MR (1968a) 'Adverse Legal Consequences of Conviction and Their Removal: A Comparative Study' *The Journal of Criminal Law, Criminology, and Police Science*, 59, 347–60.

—— (1968b) 'Adverse Legal Consequences of Conviction and Their Removal: A Comparative Study (Part 2)' *The Journal of Criminal Law, Criminology, and Police Science*, 59, 542–68.

Demleitner, NV (1999) 'Preventing internal exile: the need for restrictions on collateral sentencing consequences' *Stanford Law & Policy Review*, 11, 153–71.

—— (2018) 'Collateral Sanctions and American Exceptionalism: A Comparative Perspective' in KR Reitz (ed), *American Exceptionalism in Crime and Punishment* (New York, Oxford University Press) 487–526.

Díez-Ripollés, JL (2016) 'Collateral Sanctions for Offenders and Ex-offenders – Contrasts between the United States of America and Nordic European Countries' *European Criminal Law Review*, 6(3), 234–307.

European Banking Authority (2012) *Guidelines on the assessment of the suitability of members of the management body and key function holders*, available at https://www.eba.europa.eu/-/guidelines-on-the-assessment-of-the-suitability-of-members-of-the-management-body-and-key-function-holders-eba-gl-2012-06- (last accessed 7 June 2018).

Fernández Bessa, C and Brandariz, JA (2016) 'Transformaciones de la penalidad migratoria en el contexto de la crisis económica: El giro gerencial del dispositivo de deportación', 4/2016 *Indret Criminología y Sistema Penal* 1–25.

Garland, D (2017) 'Penal power in America: Forms, functions and foundations' *Journal of the British Academy*, 5, 1–35.

Gottschalk, M (2015) *Caught: The Prison State and the Lockdown of American Politics* (Princeton, Princeton University Press).

Goulette, NW, Reitler, AK, Frank J, Flesher W and Travis, LF (2014) 'Criminal Justice Practitioners' Perceptions of Collateral Consequences of Criminal Conviction on Offenders' *Criminal Justice Review*, 39, 290–304.

Herzog-Evans, M (2011) 'Judicial Rehabilitation in France: Helping with the Desisting Process and Acknowledging Achieved Desistance' *European Journal of Probation*, 3, 4–19.

Holzer, HJ, Raphael, S and Stoll, MA (2007) 'The Effect of an Applicant's Criminal History on Employer Hiring Decisions and Screening Practices: Evidence from Los Angeles' in S Bushway, MA Stoll and DF Weiman (eds), *Barriers to Reentry? The Labor Market for Released Prisoners in Post-Industrial America* (New York, Russell Sage Foundation).

Hoskins, Z (2014) 'Ex-offender Restrictions' *Journal of Applied Philosophy*, 31, 33–48.
Jacobs, JB (2015) *The Eternal Criminal Record* (Cambridge, Harvard University Press).
—— and Blitsa, D (2011) 'Paedophiles, Employment Discrimination, and European Integration', *Paper 390, New York, New York University Public Law and Legal Theory Working Papers*, available at http://lsr.nellco.org/nyu_plltwp/309 (last accessed 7 June 2018).
—— and Larrauri, E (2012) 'Are Criminal Convictions a Public Matter? The USA and Spain' *Punishment & Society*, 14, 3–28.
—— and —— (2016) *European Criminal Records and Ex-Offender Employment* (Oxford, Oxford University Press, Oxford Handbooks Online).
Kirk, DS and Wakefield, S (2018) 'Collateral Consequences of Punishment: A Critical Review and Path Forward' *Annual Review of Criminology*, 1, 171–94.
KPMG (2009) *Disclosure of Criminal Records in Overseas Jurisdictions* (London, Centre for the Protection of National Infrastructure).
Larrauri, E (2011) 'Conviction Records in Spain: Obstacles to Reintegration of Offenders?' *European Journal of Probation*, 3, 50–62.
—— (2016) 'Antecedentes penales y expulsión de personas inmigrantes', 2/2016 *Indret Criminología y Sistema Penal* 1–29.
—— and Jacobs, JB (2011) 'Reinserción laboral y antecedentes penales' *Revista Electrónica de Ciencia Penal y Criminología*, 13, 1–25.
—— and Jacobs, JB (2013) 'A Spanish Window on European Law and Policy on Employment Discrimination Based on Criminal Record' in T Daems, S Snacken and D van Zyl Smit (eds), *European Penology?* (Oxford, Hart Publishing) 293–319.
LeBel, TP (2012) 'Invisible Stripes? Formerly Incarcerated Persons' Perceptions of Stigma' *Deviant Behavior*, 33, 89–107.
Lippke, RL (2009) *Rethinking Imprisonment* (Oxford, Oxford University Press).
Loucks, N, Lyner, O and Sullivan, T (1998) 'The employment of people with criminal records in the European Union' *European Journal on Criminal Policy and Research*, 6, 195–210.
Maruna, S and Lageson, SE (2018) 'Digital degradation: Stigma management in the internet age' *Punishment & Society*, 20, 113–33.
Mauer, M and Chesney Lind, M (2003) *Invisible Punishment: The Collateral Consequences of Mass Imprisonment* (New York, The New Press)
McAlinden, AM (2012) 'The governance of sexual offending across Europe: Penal policies, political economies and the institutionalization of risk' *Punishment & Society*, 14, 166–92.
McGuinness, P, McNeill, F and Armstrong, S (2013) *The use and impact of the Rehabilitation of Offenders Act (1974)* (Glasgow, The Scottish Centre for Crime and Justice Research, University of Glasgow) available at www.sccjr.ac.uk/publications/the-use-and-impact-of-the-rehabilitation-of-offenders-act-1974final-report/ (last accessed 7 June 2018).
Morgenstern, C (2011) 'Judicial Rehabilitation in Germany – The Use of Criminal Records and the Removal of Recorded Convictions', *European Journal of Probation*, 3, 20–35.
Pager, D (2003) 'The Mark of a Criminal Record' *American Journal of Sociology*, 108, 937–75.
Palacios Blanco, J (2003) 'Cuestiones sobre denegación y renovación de licencias de armas de caza: jurisprudencia aplicable' *Revista jurídica de la Comunidad de Madrid*, 17, 285–93.

Petrunik, M and Deutschmann, L (2008) 'The exclusion-inclusion spectrum in state and community response to sex offenders in Anglo-American and European jurisdictions' International journal of offender therapy and comparative criminology, 52, 499–519.

Pinard, M (2006) 'An Integrated Perspective on the Collateral Consequences of Criminal Convictions and Reentry Issues Faced by Formerly Incarcerated Individuals' *Boston University Law Review*, 86, 623–90.

Roberts, J (2008) 'The Mythical Divide Between Collateral and Direct Consequences of Criminal Convictions: Involuntary Commitment of "Sexually Violent Predators"' *University of Minnesota Law Review*, 93, 670–740.

Rovira, M (2016) *Antecedentes penales y mercado laboral* (PhD Thesis, Barcelona, Universitat Pompeu Fabra).

SHRM Society for Human Resource Management (2012) *Research Spotlight: The Use of Criminal Background Checks in Hiring Decision* (Alexandria, VA, Society for Human Resource Management).

Stefanou, C and Xanthaki, H (2005) *Financial Crime in the EU. Criminal Records as effective tools or missed opportunities* (The Hague, Kluwer Law International).

—— and Xanthaki, H (2008) *Towards a European Criminal Record* (Cambridge, Cambridge University Press).

Steinacker, A (2003) 'The Prisoner's Campaign: Felony Disenfranchisement Laws and the Right to Hold Public Office' *Brigham Young University Law Review*, 2, 801–28.

Tewksbury, R and Lees, M (2006) 'Perceptions of sex offender registration: Collateral consequences and community experiences' *Sociological Spectrum*, 26, 309–34.

Thomas, T (2007) *Criminal Records. A Database for the Criminal Justice System and Beyond* (Houndmill, Palgrave Macmillan).

Tonry, M (2016) *Sentencing Fragments: Penal Reform in America, 1975–2025* (Oxford, Oxford University Press).

Travis, J (2005) *But They All Come Back: Facing the Challenges of Prisoner Reentry* (Washington, DC, Urban Institute Press).

Tripkovic, M (2016) 'The Modern Cives Sine Suffraggio: Dimensions of Criminal Disenfranchisement in Europe' *The Howard Journal of Crime and Justice*, 55, 4–24.

Uggen, C, Van Brakle, M and Mclaughin, H (2009) 'Punishment and social exclusion: national differences in prisoner disenfranchisement' in AC Ewald and B Rottinghaus (eds), *Criminal Disenfranchisement in an International Perspective* (Cambridge, Cambridge University Press) 59–76.

——, Manza, J and Behrens, A (2004) 'Less than the Average Citizen: Stigma, Role Transition, and the Civic Reintegration of Convicted Felons' in S Maruna and R Immarigeon (eds), *After Crime and Punishment: Pathways to Offender Reintegration* (New York, Russell Sage Foundation) 258–90.

——, Manza, J and Thompson, M (2006) 'Citizenship, Democracy, and the Civic Reintegration of Criminal Offenders' *The ANNALS of the American Academy of Political and Social Science*, 605, 281–310.

—— and Steward, R (2015) 'Piling On: Collateral Consequences and Community Supervision' *Minnesota Law Review*, 99, 1871–912.

University of Múrcia (2016) Matrícula por primera vez en un título de grado (Múrcia, Universidad de Múrcia) available at www.um.es/documents/877924/3525337/MATR%C3%8DCULA+POR+PRIMERA+VEZ+EN+UN+T%C3%8DTULO+DE+GRADO.pdf/9980a8d3-7c03-4796-bee0-19eafada660b (5 February 2018) (last accessed 7 June 2018).

van 't Zand-Kurtovic, EG (2017) *Invisible bars: The impact of having a criminal record on young adults' position in the labour market* (PhD Thesis, The Hague, Eleven International Publishing).

Western, B (2007) 'The Penal System and the Labor Market' in S Bushway, MA Stoll and DF Weiman (eds), *Barriers to Reentry? The Labor Market for Released Prisoners in Post-Industrial America* (New York: Russell Sage Foundation) 335–60.

Whittle, TN (2018) 'Felony Collateral Sanctions Effects on Recidivism: A Literature Review' *Criminal Justice Policy Review*, 29, 505–24.

TABLE OF CASES

European Court of Human Rights

Millbank and Others v The United Kingdom App no 44473/14 (30 June 2016)

Spanish Constitutional Court

Case no 114-1987 (6 July 1987)

3

Incapacitation: Salutary Protection of Society or the Definitive Elimination of People?

MARIJKE MALSCH

I. INTRODUCTION

INCAPACITATION, IN THE sense used in this chapter, means rendering people harmless by removing capacities in full or in part. Incapacitation implies taking away opportunities to commit certain wrongs, or restricting freedoms in other ways (for overviews of forms of incapacitation, see Malsch and Duker 2012). Thus, incapacitation is not restricted to the most invasive types of the elimination of certain people but may also refer to less comprehensive forms, as long as disabling the individual involved is the goal of the intervention or of the person issuing it. This chapter is not restricted to criminal law; incapacitating interventions can also be found in both civil law and administrative law, or outside the law in a strict sense.

Many incapacitating interventions have a narrow scope: preventing certain future undesirable misbehaviours with the help of interventions that are more technical in nature. In their effects, however, incapacitating interventions may have consequences for the individual that are considerably wider than just being restricted in certain behaviours. Highly negative side-effects may follow from incapacitating people, and these collateral consequences deserve serious attention when imposing incapacitating measures (see Meijer, chapter 5 of this volume).

This chapter combines discussion of individual examples of incapacitation related to a criminal conviction with a macro perspective, attempting to find common characteristics between those types of incapacitation. I shall thereby identify five distinct aspects of incapacitating interventions: the actual impeding effects they have on certain behaviours; their 'mirroring' character; their naming and shaming effects; their self-reinforcing effects; and the tendency these interventions have to 'transform'. The last-mentioned aspect points to the tendency that if, for example, imprisonment is no longer possible or allowed, surveillance may serve as an alternative that has the same aim: disabling the person. Net widening seems inherent to incapacitation, and the chapter presents a number of examples of this. It ends with an evaluation of the general trend towards a greater use of incapacitation in its various forms, its advantages and its drawbacks.

II. INCAPACITATION BY LOCKING PEOPLE UP

A. The Death Penalty and Incarceration

From the standpoint of incapacitation, the death penalty is the ultimate sanction. Life ends after the penalty's execution and there is no return or redress: it is irreversible. Today, a considerable number of states worldwide still include the death penalty as an option in their criminal laws, while a slightly smaller number of countries still actually apply this penalty to perpetrators of serious crimes (Garland 2001; Garland 2011; Viano 2014).

Life imprisonment is less absolute than the death penalty; the convicted person retains his right to be alive, but certain substantial basic rights are severely limited, such as those of freedom of movement, the right to enjoy family life and the freedom of association. The freedom of expression is severely limited in prison, as is the right to privacy.

Between the 1980s and the 1990s, the lengths of prison terms imposed steadily increased, as did incarceration rates (Tonry 2004; De Waard 2017). Since 2005, a serious decrease has been observed in the number of crimes committed (De Waard 2017). All types of crime show a dramatic decline, and this trend is witnessed in all Western countries. A drop in incarceration rates accompanies this trend. Many causes have been suggested for this general drop in criminal behaviour (De Waard 2017). However, this issue of dropping crime rates has not yet been resolved and thus deserves still more scholarly attention.

Changes in the landscape of crime and incarceration rates are related to the various forms of incapacitation. Incapacitation *outside* detention may have received more attention, adding to the reduction of incarceration rates. Trends, as far as they can be identified, are not unambiguous, however, as will be illustrated. Hard statements about the causes and results of developments in this domain should thus be avoided.

B. Pre-trial and Preventive Detention

The use of various types of detention other than imprisonment imposed by a court has increased in several countries, among them the Netherlands and the UK, and some still continue to use it despite serious criticism.[1] That implies that locking up increasingly takes place *before* a court determines the defendant's guilt, as well as *after* the convict has served his penalty or mandatory treatment. These other types of detention are primarily preventive or provisional, and not punitive, in intent. *Pre-trial detention* is one of them. It is served before a court session takes place, and it is 'provisional' in the sense that no final decision has been made at that moment by a judge about the defendant's culpability (Stevens 2012; Keyzer 2013). Various recent publications have drawn attention to the extensive use of pre-trial detention and the risk of an invasion into the presumption of innocence. Having earlier convictions may increase the suspect's chance of being placed in pre-trial detention, so there seems to be a direct relation with prior offending (see Crijns et al 2016; Boone et al 2018; Meijer, chapter 5 of this volume).

A similar tendency can be perceived with respect to *preventive detention*. Several countries, among them Germany, Australia and the Netherlands, do make use of this type of detention, which is to be served *after* a prison term or mandatory treatment has terminated, by offenders who continue to pose serious risks to society (Albrecht 2012; McSherry 2012; Keyzer 2013; Van Kempen and Young 2014; see also chapters in this volume). In Germany, preventive detention was at first only applicable to habitual offenders. Over the course of time, however, offenders with less lengthy criminal records, who were expected to become dangerous in the future, also became legally subject to preventive detention. The criterion for imposing preventive detention thus has become less strict, and this development illustrates the tendency towards net widening (Albrecht 2012).

Although slightly different in form, similar types of prolonged detention are imposed in Australia and the Netherlands (McSherry et al 2009; McSherry 2012; Moerings 2012; Keyzer 2013). The Dutch type of preventive detention[2] was originally imposed primarily on addicted offenders, but, as happened earlier in Germany, its scope was widened to cover other types of offenders who commit large numbers of small crimes (Moerings 2012). The measures in the countries mentioned include a form of detention imposed on top of imprisonment on violent, sexual and/or habitual offenders, as well as on those suspected of terrorism. In some cases it can even result in a lifelong period of detention that is almost exclusively based on perceived safety risks.

As the aim of preventive detention is largely to put a person away in an institution for a period that is much longer than would be justified by the (sometimes minor) seriousness of their offending, it can be considered a form of incapacitation. According to Keyzer (2013), who identifies several types of

[1] College voor de Rechten van de Mens 2017, at mensenrechten.nl/publicaties/detail/37467.

[2] *Inrichting voor Stelselmatige Daders* (ISD), a measure permitting a period of confinement of two years for perpetrators exhibiting high rates of recidivism for relatively minor offences.

preventive detention, a limitless pursuit of security is revealed by these measures, which may end up abandoning the fundamental principle of the rule of law and human rights by locking people up for increasingly longer periods. He points to the danger that this will generate too much reliance on locking people up, rather than on research into the improvement of treatment programmes and other rehabilitative policies.

III. INCAPACITATION OUTSIDE DETENTION

A. Disqualifications

As was indicated in the introduction to this chapter, some forms of incapacitation are served outside detention. Such is the case, for example, with *disqualifications*, which present a narrowly focused form of incapacitation in a situation in which the perpetrator is not detained or has already served a prison term. Offenders who are sentenced to disqualification are, for example, forbidden to perform a certain job or activity (like driving a car), or hold a particular position or occupation (like running a particular business), with the aim of making it impossible for them to reoffend or breach certain rules in a specific domain. Disqualifications are included in criminal law, civil law, disciplinary law[3] and administrative law.

A number of centuries ago, disqualifications primarily focused on (physically) taking away the opportunity to commit crime, or removing the instruments with which crimes were committed. Before 1854, for example, the hands of men who had killed their fathers could be cut off to make it impossible for them to commit a new murder. The tongue could be removed in cases of libel, and fingers could be cut off when perjury had been committed in court, which represents a primarily symbolic, incapacitating punishment. In that era, perpetrators were regularly banished from the country or the city in which they lived and where they had committed a crime. This also represents a direct and invasive form of incapacitation (Von Hirsch and Wasik 1997; De Koster 2018).

Past and present forms of disqualification can be viewed as examples of incapacitation that mirror the crimes committed. As a consequence, disqualifications generally have a strong and focused incapacitating effect, and they have both a preventive and retributive objective. The cutting off of limbs clearly served a retributive aim, but at the same time it prevented similar future crimes, at least symbolically, by taking away the instrument with which they were committed (Malsch et al 2012). Criminal offenders have, throughout history, also routinely been removed from political life through various kinds of civil

[3] The law that regulates certain professions, such as the medical profession, the profession of attorneys.

and other disqualifications and disenfranchisements in Europe.[4] However, by the mid-twentieth century, the incidence of criminal disenfranchisement of political rights had been decreasing around the world (Tripkovic 2016).

In the present era, the preventive aspect prevails and retributive aims have become less prominent. Disqualifications in the Western world now focus more exclusively on taking away the opportunity for reoffending. Corporal punishments generally are no longer imposed in the Western world. However, the retributive element of disqualifications can still be observed in cases in which they have little or nothing to do with the crime committed, or where the seriousness of the disqualification exceeds that of the crime (Von Hirsch and Wasik 1997; Malsch et al 2012; Tripkovic 2016).

Disqualification may result in exclusion from society when someone is no longer able to carry out a particular profession. When perpetrators are obstructed from earning their living and leading a normal, law-abiding life, new crimes may follow, and this may have an adverse influence on the preventive effects intended. In this respect, disqualification may exert a similar effect to the requirement for obtaining a 'certificate of conduct' for a job. When such a certificate is refused due to a criminal history, the applicant will not be allowed to take up the position or job.

'Naming and shaming' effects may ensue when the media pay attention to the disqualification, for example, of a well-known medical doctor, a politician or a famous football player. Disqualifications thus may still have certain punitive effects, be it by means of 'naming and shaming', exclusion, or when they are not closely related to the crime committed. Yet preventive effects constitute the most common goal.

B. New and Old Orders

Other types of incapacitation outside prison exist as well, and can be found in criminal law, civil law and administrative law. The type of law used may differ between countries. In England and Wales, for example, preventive orders are often found in civil law, whereas the Netherlands more often uses criminal or administrative law.

A huge increase can be witnessed in control orders, restraining orders, protection orders, banning orders, eviction orders, anti-social behaviour

[4] See also the Special Issue of *Justitiële Verkenningen* on exile and new forms of exclusion of May 2018 (available at www.wodc.nl/onderzoeksdatabase/jv201802-verbanning-en-nieuwe-vormen-van-uitsluiting.aspx?refTitle=Gt4q_Wtp1iHzqT9VhepuHT7wURUdZzyZvCjpc-SUJSSOR-p74L5ko738BcwpmLx8pYVt6j07-sdtD2FMSnb_l3cg5pSH0DhRXrftaYUXrYbfUP3-30hYpHvRjnFXDK0HIh0&refId=MlTno9-8YeJ7xivneHxm1gKzJxaIP7gLDfP9gRXbXAoeWKWdmN0EyElrgD4RcKrNlkd-X_pBqFWMiRe7VuJ9sg2.

orders (ASBOs), etc (Zedner 2007).[5] Related and sometimes more focused orders include: football banning orders, travel restriction orders, financial reporting orders, serious crime prevention orders, extended supervision orders and violent offender orders.[6] These orders restrict freedom of movement and/or the freedom to contact another person, without actually locking up the people to which they pertain. Some of these orders have existed for a long time and their application has been widened, while many others are new. In the UK, for example, the Prevention of Terrorism Act 2005 created a control order for suspected terrorists. The order could include an 18-hour curfew, electronic tagging, a ban on the use of the garden, limitations on visitors and meetings, allowing the police to enter the house at any time to search and remove any item, and allowing the installation of monitoring equipment, the prohibition of phones and Internet access, etc.[7] Even deportation is possible under control orders. Such orders may lead to the almost total exclusion of the individual from society and can have seriously damaging effects upon the person's life (see Keyzer 2013).

Electronic monitoring can sometimes be imposed to enforce these types of orders, leading to incapacitation by other means. Those subject to electronic monitoring may feel psychologically incapacitated, as may their close family members. Orders and electronic monitoring may be experienced as punitive sanctions because of the inherent loss of freedom. Feelings of embarrassment may ensue when employers and colleagues at work, as well as family members, are aware that the person is subject to house arrest and electronic monitoring (Van der Laan 2012). This may lead to an invasion of the honour of the individual subject to these orders, which resembles the effects of disqualification. Such invasion may instil punitive effects into the individual subject to it.

There is a tendency to use administrative law and civil law (such as orders to stay away from certain shops, or from certain soccer games, issued by those shops or soccer clubs without any other authority being involved) instead of criminal law when creating new types of orders (Van der Aa et al 2012; Schuilenburg 2018; Morgenstern, chapter 4 of this volume). The use of administrative and civil law opens up the possibility to act speedily after a crime, and to avoid both the involvement of the courts and criminal law safeguards, with all the negative side-effects they may have (Malsch and Duker 2012).

[5] ASBOs and other 18 measures to counter anti-social behaviour have been replaced by six new anti-social behaviour powers in England and Wales, including the civil injunction. See at www.publicnet.co.uk/news/2015/03/25/the-end-of-the-asbo/.

[6] For the Netherlands, see Malsch and Duker 2012; Schuilenburg 2018.

[7] The Prevention of Terrorism Act 2005 was repealed in 2011 by the Terrorism Prevention and Investigation Measures Act 2011, the High Court having ruled (in 2006) that s 3 of the Act was incompatible with Art 6 ECHR.

C. Surveillance: Jobs and Companies

In the Netherlands, employers who have to decide whether to contract an individual for a certain function or position can request a 'certificate of good conduct' from a government agency, which certificate sets out all or some of the individual's convictions (Boone 2012; van 't Zand-Kurtovic 2017; other contributions to this volume). The difference from disqualification is that some applicants are made subject to such a requirement *before* they start work. For many jobs and positions, a certificate of conduct is not obligatory. Such certificates are generally requested for people working in childcare and the education of children, and for taxi drivers. For other jobs, an employer is at liberty to ask for a conduct certificate.

When an applicant is unable to provide a certificate because the government agency has refused it by reason of his or her criminal history, he or she will not obtain the position or job, leading to an exclusion from work opportunities. A criminal history, even when it is not very serious, may thus affect the offender's working life for years. This may also be the case if the misconduct has not resulted in a conviction. Consequently, people with criminal records may refrain from applying for certain jobs if they know that the employers will request a certificate, which increases the risk of further exclusion (Boone 2012; van 't Zand-Kurtovic 2017; Morgenstern, chapter 4 of this volume).

When assessing the integrity and vulnerability of large companies, government agencies such as municipalities and provinces increasingly collect data about the individuals leading them and their families. In the Netherlands, these agencies are allowed to use a variety of sources, such as registers of the Public Prosecution Service, the police, the tax authorities, commercial registers and so on. Based on the information these sources provide and by combining these various types of data, government agencies assess existing risks of organised crime, fraud, human trafficking and tax evasion (Huisman 2012). This makes it possible to permanently monitor companies and individuals perceived as being at risk of committing crime, and to make their activities impossible by refusing the licences they need for setting up and leading companies. This system of control can result in reputational harm (naming and shaming), for example when the refusal of licences and exclusions from tenders are brought out into the open and generate media attention. Exclusion through incapacitating interventions imposed on these companies and individuals may thus follow in this segment of society as well.

D. Surveillance: Individuals at Risk

Perpetrators of serious crime are put under surveillance for ever-increasing periods, even *after* having served their sentence (Albrecht 2012; Van der Laan 2012; Meijer 2013). The societal desire for safety and protection leads to several forms of control over perpetrators still supposed to be dangerous, for short or longer periods after their (conditional) release, for instance by means of alternative incapacitating interventions.

In the Netherlands, several new measures have been created that focus on monitoring or supervising an offender who either has followed mandatory treatments but still poses a risk to society, or has served the unconditional part of his sentence. In some situations the term for remaining under supervision can be extended to the rest of the ex-offender's life (Meijer 2013).

Another example is presented by the 'notification requirement' for persons convicted of a wide range of sexual offences, mandatorily imposed on the basis of the English Sexual Offences Act 2003 (Ashworth 2009; Freeman 2012; Van der Laan 2012).

These types of control have an incapacitating effect: freedoms are affected and individuals subject to such control may feel restricted psychologically (Van der Laan 2012; van 't Zand-Kurtovic 2017).

Especially with respect to sex offenders, society feels a great need to reduce the risks they pose. This is particularly the case when they have been convicted of the sexual abuse of small children. Just locking them up for long periods does not seem a sufficient measure, because the risk of a relapse when leaving prison remains substantial and the type of offence itself is highly undesirable. Therefore, some sex offenders may be subject to so-called 'chemical castration', which can be considered a direct form of incapacitation that takes away the urge to have sex. The castration of men was a more common phenomenon in earlier times, for example at the beginning of the twentieth century (Troelstra et al 2012). Chemical castration became an option in cases in which sex offenders are unable to control their urges to have sex, for example with minors. Because it is a controversial remedy, it is not used on a large scale. Chemical castration may help sex offenders to lead a 'normal' life. It does not eliminate all sexual impulses, however (Troelstra et al 2012). Various therapies, cognitive therapy among them, are provided on top of the medical treatment.

In sum, the tendency to incapacitate is partly geared towards increasing the use of various forms of detention, but it covers other measures as well, which aim to keep offenders from reoffending by making certain misbehaviours impossible, or by monitoring the individual's daily life in one way or another. The concept of incapacitation as a rationale thus influences not only people in prison, but also those who have not (yet) been convicted, as well as those who have already served their prison term.

IV. THE ASPECTS OF INCAPACITATION REVISITED

In the introduction to this chapter, I identified five aspects of incapacitating interventions: the actual impeding of certain behaviours; their 'mirroring' character; their naming and shaming effects; their self-reinforcing effects; and the inclination of these interventions to 'transform'. I revisit these five aspects below, while looking back at the various examples of incapacitation presented in the preceding sections.

A. Disabling Effects

The first and most salient aspect of incapacitation is its (physically) disabling effect. Actual undesirable behaviours are most *directly* and most *completely* impeded or made impossible by the death penalty, locking people up without a prospect of release and chemical castration (Nagin 1978; Piquero and Blumstein 2007; Troelstra et al 2012). The other interventions discussed in this chapter disable people in a more *indirect* way, are more focused on (only) one or a number of specific aspects of the individual's life while not touching others, and/or allow more opportunities for escape. Disqualifications, for example, are focused on one specific aspect of life (a job, a position, driving a car), thereby taking away the opportunity to commit a certain crime while leaving others unaffected.

B. Mirroring

The second aspect is the mirroring nature of incapacitation. 'Mirroring' the crime committed was more usual in medieval times and in the centuries directly following that period, when limbs could be cut off as a sanction.[8] In the present era, these types of physically invasive interventions and the extreme form of mirroring they present no longer exist, at least not to the same degree as in earlier ages. Some incapacitating interventions still do directly mirror the misbehaviour that gave rise to them, however. This is the case for disqualifications and for interventions aimed at forbidding activities and/or taking away the opportunity to perform certain occupations (like disqualification from driving after one has caused a fatal accident, or disqualification from a profession after a sexual crime has been committed whilst exercising that profession). This is also the case for chemical castration of offenders who have committed sexual crimes. Other incapacitating interventions, like locking people up, fines or community service, generally do not mirror the crime committed.

Von Hirsch and Wasik (1997) advocate the 'principle of sparing interventions'. Interventions should not lead to more invasions of the personal life than are necessary to reduce the risk of crime, and they should be narrowly focused and sparingly imposed. From this standpoint mirroring can be applauded,

[8] On the atimia, infamia, outlawry and attainder of former ages, see Tripkovic 2016.

because it may prevent incapacitation from having a net-widening effect. Disqualifications, which most of the time do mirror the behaviour that is to be prevented, may form an adequate and tailored reaction to crime, because they only affect those positions and behaviours that engender a risk of particular undesirable conduct. As such, mirroring, when brought about in an intelligent way, may prevent more far-reaching exclusion of the perpetrator from society.

C. Naming and Shaming

Naming and shaming constitute the third aspect of incapacitation, and they come to the fore in various forms. One of the most obvious examples of naming and shaming is when a sex offender who has served his sentence moves into a community and his criminal history becomes known in his new neighbourhood. This situation may lead to a moral panic, and the effect is accelerated when the media become involved and the Internet provides further information about the perpetrator's criminal history. But this is not the only situation in which effects of naming and shaming occur.

The effects of naming and shaming may also become manifest when an exclusion, for example from a job on basis of the refusal of a conduct certificate, or a disqualification is publicised, is covered by the media or becomes known in certain circles in society. The same may occur when an exclusion is revealed on the Internet or is included in generally accessible databases. When professionals are forbidden from exercising their occupations, or when licences are refused and this is publicised, naming and shaming effects may ensue.

In earlier times, the execution of penalties (hanging or corporal punishments) generally took place in the open air and the public could attend, which may have led to 'naming and shaming' effects on top of the direct disablement and physical harming of the individual; but that no longer happens in the Western world in the present era. Nowadays, most forms of naming and shaming take place via the media and with the aid of the Internet. As a consequence of permanent coverage by the media and the open character of the Internet, these effects will persist much longer, if not for eternity, and this may seriously harm offenders and their relatives beyond the sentence they have already served or treatment they have received.

Thus, although naming and shaming generally no longer go together with physical acts of aggression against the perpetrator, they now have a far more enduring character because the effects of naming and shaming are often lasting and damaging. For the individual or the company it affects, the – primarily psychological – damage caused by naming and shaming can be enormous. At the same time, a question may be posed about the nature of the shaming that is brought about: does the perpetrator genuinely feels guilty or ashamed, which may lead to a more honest and law-abiding attitude in the future, or does he or she only regret getting caught?

The effects of naming and shaming may lead to an even more far-reaching exclusion of the perpetrator, thereby re-enforcing the negative effects of incapacitation (Malsch and Duker 2012; van 't Zand-Kurtovic 2017). By publicising failures by professionals, potential clients are notified of certain professional misbehaviours. Potential clients then can choose whether or not to make use of the services of this professional. In this sense, publication, when carefully administered, may exert certain positive effects with regard to the protection of the public. The effects of publication and naming and shaming are therefore mixed.

D. Self-reinforcing Effects

Self-reinforcing effects seem typical of at least some incapacitating interventions. As has been argued in the Introduction, certain net-widening effects seem inherent in incapacitation. A clear example is the conduct certificate: for ever-increasing numbers and types of jobs and occupations, it has been made possible for employers to request such a certificate (Boone 2012; van 't Zand-Kurtovic 2017). This facilitation of the exclusion of increasing numbers of job applicants suggests a self-reinforcing effect.

Self-reinforcing effects have also emerged from more 'traditional' forms of incapacitation. While locking up offenders has not resulted in a reduction of recidivism, there seems to be a tendency to lock people up for ever-longer periods, without questioning the effectiveness of this approach (Liedka et al 2006; Simon 2012). With respect to interventions that aim at rehabilitation, such an approach is less likely. When a rehabilitative intervention is not successful, it is generally stopped and another, more punitive approach is chosen. Incapacitating interventions, on the other hand, even when not successful, tend to be continued and even intensified, often at the expense of more rehabilitative approaches.

The media and politicians seeking support in anticipation of elections may promote lengthier periods of incarceration because they assume that the general public are of the opinion that offenders should be punished more harshly (Roberts and Stalans 1997; Albrecht 2005; Simon 2007; Van Hattum and Meijer 2016; Van der Maden et al 2017). Self-reinforcing incapacitating trends are therefore enhanced by the punitive rhetoric employed in the political domain (see also Herzog-Evans, chapter 11 of this volume). The 'incapacitative mindset' thus may lead to a search for methods to impose restrictions on people at risk of offending for longer periods. That brings us to the final aspect of incapacitation.

E. Transformation

One type of incapacitation may be transformed into another type of incapacitation where the perpetrator is still considered to pose a risk. Transformation takes place in Germany, England and Wales, and Australia, in the guise of preventive detention, which is a form of incapacitation primarily motivated by the risks the individual poses (Albrecht 2012; McSherry 2012; Malsch and Duker 2012; Keyzer 2013). Transformation may be used to lock people up for longer periods whilst avoiding legal guarantees. Detention may also be transformed into surveillance when a continuation of incarceration is no longer legally allowed (Meijer 2013; Van Kempen and Young 2014). If that is the case, incapacitation is continued by measures of a different nature.

V. ADVANTAGES AND DRAWBACKS OF INCAPACITATION

Incapacitation has both advantages and drawbacks. Depending on the situation in which incapacitation is administered, one of these prevails.

A. Advantages

The advantages of certain incapacitating interventions that are being served outside prison have already been set out: they may be geared towards a strictly circumscribed type of behaviour, and thus steer clear of excessive social exclusion while protecting the public at the same time. The advantage over interventions of a more general nature is that incapacitation may avoid acting like scattershot: only a specific aspect of the individual's life is affected by incapacitation, and life can otherwise continue as before.

B. Escape Routes

A serious drawback of incapacitating interventions is the possibility of escape, especially when incapacitation is imposed outside detention. Apart from the death penalty and a life sentence without parole, incapacitation is never complete; routes for escape exist, and they are used. Sex offenders, for example, may (illegally) acquire testosterone or testosterone-like compounds to help them boost their sexual feelings, in spite of the chemical castration they have undergone (Troelstra et al 2012). Disqualifications may be rendered without effect when medical practitioners or therapists move to another city or country and start a new practice there. Empirical research into the enforcement of disqualifications in the Netherlands suggests that this sometimes actually happens in practice. Not all registrations are complete, or work well. Sometimes, the registers are not consulted (Malsch et al 2012).

Registration may help to prevent the use of escape routes (see also Herzog-Evans, chapter 11 of this volume). The inclusion of offenders on registers that are accessible to anyone, for example via the Internet, could assist in enforcing disqualifications and comparable interventions, and thus in protecting the public. This is possible today, for example, in the medical domain or, in some countries, as regards the directors or CEOs of large companies who have abused their positions (Braithwaite 2009). When exclusions are made public, however, risks of naming and shaming emerge. Certain advantages of incapacitation may thus result in a drawback at the same time.

C. Exclusion

Exclusion is an obvious effect of incapacitation that goes together with naming and shaming, for example when teachers or therapists are convicted of sexual crimes and this becomes known in the neighbourhoods in which they live and work (Hoskins 2014). Exclusion may lead to new crime when the individual subjected to it loses the opportunity to earn a living in a legal way, only seeks friends in criminal circles, or becomes so disappointed and distrustful that he or she sees no way out of the situation (Meijer 2013). An anomalous situation may then follow.

D. Avoidance of the Judge

Especially when an administrative or civil route is taken, there is a tendency to avoid the court when new incapacitating interventions are developed. A serious drawback then is that the guarantees of a fair trial are not included in the making of incapacitating interventions, potentially leading to a violation of the presumption of innocence. Subjects are treated as if they are guilty before their actual guilt has been established by a court after a careful investigation of the allegations. As a consequence, even innocent people would run the risk of becoming the subject of invasive incapacitating interventions, which is a highly undesirable situation (Malsch and Duker 2012).

E. Self-reinforcing Effects

The drawback with the most far-reaching consequences, however, seems to be the self-reinforcing effect of incapacitation, as illustrated in section IV.D. It may lead to ever-increasing impediments, without necessary attention being paid to more positive and hopeful measures.

Research suggests that when no rehabilitative measures are imposed during a period of incapacitation, perpetrators tend to relapse into criminal behaviour soon after release (Van der Laan 2012; Moerings 2012; Keyzer 2013). In this respect, community rehabilitation services seem to offer better prospects (Blokland and Nagin 2012). Mere incapacitation thus does not seem to offer a sufficient and enduring answer to crime; it primarily leads to exclusion. If all responses to crime and deviant harassing behaviours were aimed at disabling or disqualifying people, this would be counterproductive. It would not encourage desirable behaviours but would only prevent bad behaviour. A vicious circle can emerge when incapacitation leads to exclusions, which may lead to media attention, which may lead to naming and shaming, which then may lead to further offending and further incapacitation.

VI. CONCLUSIONS

There is a tendency in the Western world to develop incapacitating measures, by means of which (groups of) offenders are disabled from engaging in certain criminal or otherwise undesirable behaviours. This new 'wave' of incapacitation differs from incapacitation in earlier times (the Middle Ages up to the nineteenth century), in that disabling interventions are less purely physically oriented now than they were previously. Disabling interventions today are less focused on literally taking away physical abilities to perform a certain activity. The ways in which they work today are more technical and/or psychological in nature. Monitoring and surveillance have emerged as means to keep track of people and control their daily lives in a relatively less coercive way. During the twentieth century, methods of incapacitation thus seem to have become more refined and less physically invasive as a result of increasing civilisation. Yet how refined and civilised is incapacitation really, in the forms that can be witnessed in the present era? Various legal principles may be violated by the way incapacitation is administered today, such as the presumption of innocence, the finality of sentencing, the principle of proportionality and prohibitions on double punishment (see other contributions to this volume).

It is clear that several forms of incapacitation meet with general criticism from (legal) scholars (Zedner 2007; Ashworth 2009; McSherry 2012; Albrecht 2012; Simon 2012). Incapacitation would be a poor approach to large-scale societal problems if it were the dominant response. Interventions may be imposed too readily, which may lead to people being locked up or excluded for long periods too easily without due justification or due process. Disproportionate incapacitation increases the risk of recidivism instead of diminishing it, and incapacitation can become punishment when it is disproportionate.

To prevent all this from happening, the type of incapacitation used should bear a strong relation to the type of behaviour that is to be prevented. It is, moreover, necessary that incapacitation does not exceed the limits that follow from the principle of proportionality (Meijer, chapter 5 of this volume). The decision about prolonging should, as far as possible, be made by a court. Furthermore, incapacitation should generally go together with other interventions that serve different types of aims.[9] When accompanied by interventions that aim at some kind of rehabilitation of the perpetrator, such as helping him gain insight into his own behaviours and/or teaching him to lead a law-abiding life, incapacitation may have its merits.

Risks of counter-productivity should be taken seriously. The self-reinforcing effects of incapacitation need due attention, because political motivations lie at their heart. In the Western world, there is a tendency to impose interventions at an earlier stage, and to avoid decision-making by a court. Penal populism may play a role here: politicians, in anticipation of elections, seek the approval of the public by drawing attention to fears of crime and advocating swifter penalties (Roberts and Stalans 1997). The media also have a part to play in this respect, by disseminating the message that the crime rate is rising (although it is not, see De Waard 2017) and that something has to be done about it. The success of other, more inclusive routes is then neglected. This vicious circle needs serious attention and should be broken. Care should be taken that we do not become an 'incapacitation society', in which disabling people who pose a risk or a nuisance becomes a standard approach.

REFERENCES

Albrecht, HJ (2005) 'Der erweiterte Sicherheitsbegriff und seine Folge' *RAV-Infobrief*, 91, 7–19.

—— (2012) 'The incapacitation of the dangerous offender: criminal policy and legislation in the Federal Republic of Germany' in M Malsch and M Duker (eds), *Incapacitation. Trends and new perspectives* (Farnham, Ashgate) 39–62.

Ashworth, A (2009) 'Criminal law, human rights and preventative justice' in B McSherry, A Norrie and S Bronitt (eds), *Regulating deviance. The redirection of criminalization and the futures of criminal law* (Oxford and Portland, OR, Hart Publishing) 87–108.

Blokland, AAJ and Nagin, DS (2012) 'Estimating the effects of imprisonment: intended and unintended consequences of incarceration' in M Malsch and M Duker (eds), *Incapacitation. Trends and new perspectives* (Farnham, Ashgate) 221–36.

Blumstein, A, Cohen, J and Nagin, D (1978) 'Deterrence and incapacitation: estimating the effects of criminal sanctions on crime rates' (Washington, DC, National Academy of Sciences).

Boone, M (2012), 'Criminal records as an instrument of incapacitation' in M Malsch and M Duker (eds), *Incapacitation. Trends and new perspectives* (Farnham, Ashgate) 203–20.

Boone, M, Jacobs, P and Lindeman, J (2018) *DETOUR – Towards Pre-trial Detention as Ultimo Ratio – 2nd Dutch National Report on Expert Interviews* (Vienna, Institute for the Sociology of Law and Criminology).

[9] For sex offenders, for example, incapacitating responses might be accompanied by the so-called 'COSA' (Circles of Support and Accountability) approach, which aims to reintegrate sexual offenders into society (Vogelvang and Höing 2012).

Braithwaite, J (2009) 'Restorative justice for banks through negative licensing' *British Journal of Criminology*, 49, 430–50.

Crijns, JH, Leeuw, BJG and Wermink, HT (2016) *Pre-trial detention in the Netherlands: legal principles versus practical reality* (The Hague, Eleven International Publishing).

De Koster, M (2018) 'Verbanning en uitzetting in Noordwest-Europa sinds de vroegmoderne periode' *Justitiële Verkenningen*, 18, 70–85.

De Waard, J (2017) 'Criminology's dirty little secret: hoe de daling van de criminaliteit bijna geheel voorbijging aan de Nederlandse criminologie' in C Bijleveld and P van der Laan (eds), *Liber Amicorum Gerben Bruinsma* (The Hague, Boom criminologie) 333–45.

Freeman, NJ (2012) 'The public safety impact of community notification laws: rearrest of convicted sex offenders' *Crime and Delinquency*, 58(4), 539–64.

Garland, D (2001) *The Culture of Control* (Oxford, Oxford University Press).

—— (2011) 'Wat is er met de doodstraf gebeurd?' *Justitiële Verkenningen*, 37, 11–30.

Goold, BJ and Lazarus, L (2007) *Security and Human Rights* (Oxford and Portland, OR, Hart Publishing).

Hoskins, Z (2014) 'Ex-offender restrictions' *Journal of Applied Philosophy*, 31(1), 33–48.

Huisman, W (2012) 'The application of administrative law against organized crime: refusing and revoking licenses as incapacitation' in M Malsch and M Duker (eds), *Incapacitation. Trends and new perspectives* (Farnham, Ashgate) 185–202.

Keyzer, P (ed) (2013) *Preventive Detention: Asking the Fundamental Questions* (Cambridge, Intersentia).

Liedka, RV, Piehl, AM and Useem, B (2006) 'The crime-control effect of incarceration: does scale matter?' *Criminology and Public Policy*, 5(2), 245–76.

Malsch, M, Alberts, A, Keijser, J de and Nijboer, H (2012) 'Disqualification from a profession or an office: nature and actual practice' in M Malsch and M Duker (eds), *Incapacitation. Trends and new perspectives* (Farnham, Ashgate) 171–84.

—— and Duker, M (eds) (2012) *Incapacitation. Trends and new perspectives* (Farnham, Ashgate).

McSherry, B (2012) 'Post-sentence incapacitation of sex-offenders and the ethics of risk assessment' in M Malsch and M Duker (eds), *Incapacitation. Trends and new perspectives* (Farnham, Ashgate) 77–96.

——, Norrie, A and Bronitt, S (2009) *Regulating deviance. The redirection of criminalization and the futures of criminal law* (Oxford and Portland, OR, Hart Publishing).

Meijer, S (2013) 'De gedragsbeïnvloedende en vrijheidsbeperkende toezichtsmaatregel als instrument in de strijd voor de maatschappelijke (schijn)veiligheid' in M Groenhuijsen, T Kooijmans and J Ouwerkerk (eds), *Roosachtig strafrecht* (Alphen aan den Rijn, Wolters Kluwer) 385–400.

Miles, TJ and Ludwig, J (2007) 'The silence of the Lambdas: deterring incapacitation research' *Journal of Quantitative Criminology*, 23, 287–301.

Moerings, M (2012) 'The risk of the persistent offender and the Special Security Measure' in M Malsch and M Duker (eds), *Incapacitation. Trends and new perspectives* (Farnham, Ashgate) 63–76.

Nagin, D (1978) 'General deterrence: a review of the empirical evidence' in A Blumstein, J Cohen and D Nagin (eds), *Deterrence and incapacitation: estimating the effects of criminal sanctions on crime rates* (Washington, DC, National Academy of Sciences) 95–139.

Piquero, AR and Blumstein, A (2007) 'Does incapacitation reduce crime?' *Journal of Quantitative Criminology*, 23, 267–85.

Roberts, JV and Stalans, LJ (1997) *Public opinion, crime and criminal justice* (Boulder, CO, Westview).

Schuilenburg, M (2018) 'Verbanning uit het semipublieke domein. Beroepsverboden in juridisch perspectief' *Justitiële Verkenningen*, 18, 5–10.

Simon, JS (2007) 'Wake of the flood: crime, disaster, and the American risk imaginary after Katrina' *Issues in Legal Scholarship*, 4, 1–19.

Simon, J (2012) 'Total incapacitation: the penal imaginary and the rise of an extreme penal rationale in California in the 1970s' in M Malsch and M Duker (eds), *Incapacitation. Trends and new perspectives* (Farnham, Ashgate) 15–38.

Stevens, L (2012) 'Incapacitation by pre-trial detention' in M Malsch and M Duker (eds), *Incapacitation. Trends and new perspectives* (Farnham, Ashgate) 97–108.

Tonry, M (2004) *Thinking About Crime* (Oxford, Oxford University Press).

Tripkovic, M (2016) 'The modern *Cives Sine Suffraggio*: Dimensions of criminal disenfranchement in Europe' *The Howard Journal of Crime and Justice*, 55(1-2), 4–24.

Troelstra, JA, Kossen, M, Niemantsverdriet, JR and Oei, K (2012) 'Incapacitation: anti-libidinal medication in the treatment of sex-offenders' in M Malsch and M Duker (eds), *Incapacitation. Trends and new perspectives* (Farnham, Ashgate) 133–44.

Van der Laan, PH (2012) 'Part-time incapacitation: probation supervision and electronic monitoring' in M Malsch and M Duker (eds), *Incapacitation. Trends and new perspectives* (Farnham, Ashgate) 109–32.

Van der Aa, S, Lens, K, Klerx, F, Bosma, A and Bosch, M van den (2012) *Aard, omvang en handhaving van beschermingsbevelen in Nederland* (Tilburg, Intervict – Universiteit van Tilburg, The Hague, Wetenschappelijk Onderzoek en Documentatiecentrum).

Van der Maden, M, Malsch, M and De Keijser, JW (2017) 'Waarom wil de burger toch steeds dat rechters zwaarder straffen? De invloed van opleiding en informatie' *Tijdschrift voor de Rechterlijke Macht*, 5, 180–83.

Van Hattum, WF and Meijer, S (2016) 'An administrative procedure for life prisoners: the law and practice of the royal pardon in the Netherlands' in D Van Zyl Smit and C Appleton (eds), *Life Imprisonment and Human Rights* (Oxford, Hart Publishing) 141–62.

Van Kempen, PHPHMC and Young, W (2014) *Prevention of reoffending; the value of rehabilitation and the management of high risk offenders* (Cambridge, Intersentia).

van 't Zand-Kurtovic, E (2017) *Invisible bars: the impact of having a criminal record on young adults' position in the labour market* (The Hague, Eleven International Publishing).

Viano, EC (2014) 'The "other" death penalty: life in prison in the United States' in PHPHMC Van Kempen and W Young (eds), *Prevention of reoffending; the value of rehabilitation and the management of high risk offenders* (Cambridge, Intersentia) 211–32.

Vogelvang, B and Höing, M (2012) 'Combining prevention and incapacitation within a communitarian approach for released sex-offenders' in M Malsch and M Duker (eds), *Incapacitation. Trends and new perspectives* (Farnham, Ashgate) 145–70.

Von Hirsch, A and Wasik, M (1997) 'Civil disqualifications attending conviction: a suggested conceptual framework' *Cambridge Law Journal*, 56(3), 599–626.

Zedner, L (2007) 'Seeking security by eroding rights: the side-stepping of due process' in BJ Goold and L Lazarus (eds), *Security and Human Rights* (Oxford and Portland, OR, Hart Publishing) 257–76.

Part II

Legal Limits on the Legal Consequences of Criminal Conviction

4

The 'Stain of Conviction' – Penal Theory, Fundamental Rights and Criminal Records in Germany

CHRISTINE MORGENSTERN

I. INTRODUCTION

- *Case 1*: The 21-year-old A was convicted for assault and sentenced to a fine of €2,100 (70 day units at €30). Upon appeal by the public prosecutor the sentence was altered in the next instance; now the amount of the fine is €3,600 (120 day units). Between the offence and the conviction, A has qualified as a mechanic and has good a chance of finding a permanent job. He argues that the new decision significantly aggravates the sentence and impedes his future work life, because all sentences that exceed 90 day units (either fines or prison days) will appear in his certificate of conduct (*Führungszeugnis*). (OLG Nürnberg, 30 August 2006)
- *Case 2*: The 23-year-old B is suspected of domestic burglary. He broke into a house at night and goods worth €3,000 were stolen. B is unemployed and was sentenced to a suspended sentence two years previously. He is now living with his parents. The public prosecutor applies for pre-trial detention.[1]
- *Case 3*: C works as sales representative for a financial services firm. He has two previous convictions, each for several counts of fraud, dating from 1993 and 1995. He was not asked for a certificate of conduct when he was employed in 1997. In 2001, he took money from a client and promised a lucrative investment, but the money disappeared. In 2007, the client

[1] Short version of a case vignette used in a research project on pre-trial decision-making: see Hammerschick et al 2018.

claimed damages. He argued that the firm had neglected its duty to protect the client's money by not claiming a certificate of conduct from C. (BGH, 13 March 2013)

- *Case 4*: E has been working for a public enterprise as an attendant in a public bath since 2008. In 2012 his employer required a so-called 'extended certificate of conduct' from him. Since 2009 all employers whose employees have contact with children must do this. The relevant legislation was part of a reform to protect children against sex offences. The certificate disclosed a conviction for several minor drug offences and two convictions for assault; E was sentenced to a high day fine in both cases. His employer has dismissed him. E applies to the labour court. (ArbG Cottbus, 30 May 2013)

These examples of cases from Germany reveal some of the manifold problems faced by persons with convictions in law and society. They touch upon different areas of law: criminal, administrative and civil courts were involved in the relevant decision-making. This chapter explores, with the assistance of the examples, how the conviction, the sentence and their consequences continued to affect the offenders' lives for a long time. It adopts both a criminal justice and a human rights perspective, and argues that the state as author of the conviction must take responsibility for its consequences, and must counteract unintended and illegitimate consequences. It therefore is necessary to determine precisely the aim and legitimacy of the documentation of former convictions and sentences in the Federal Crime Register (*Bundeszentralregister*) and its individualised parts, the criminal record statement (*Bundeszentralregisterauszug*) and the certificate of conduct (*Führungszeugnis*). In this context, German legislation and jurisprudence come under scrutiny, including a review of their historical development. Because it can help us to understand how the role of an ex-offender as a citizen is conceptualised, not only penal theory but also the wider issue of the protection of privacy of ex-offenders will be discussed. The concluding section of the chapter analyses the findings and suggests what a more coherent theoretical approach to criminal registration could look like.

The chapter thus represents a theoretical approach to the still under-researched and under-theorised topic of previous convictions in Germany. It is based on an analysis of the relevant German legislation, jurisprudence and existing criminal justice literature (Haffke 1975; Rebmann 1983; Veh 1999; Pfeiffer 2000; Morgenstern 2011; Tolzmann 2015; Sonnen 2018). Studies focusing on the topic of previous convictions are rare in Germany, and relate either to questions of labour law (Milthaler 2006; Mölter 2012) or to data protection law (Wendel 2016). No dedicated criminological or penological studies exist. The chapter therefore is also an invitation to scholars to further investigate the consequences of criminal convictions.

II. KNOWING ABOUT CONVICTIONS – WHO CLAIMS AN INTEREST AND WHY?

A. Law Enforcement Institutions and Judiciary: Assessing the Offender

The first reason to set up comprehensive registries of convictions was to serve the judiciary – judges should be able to decide upon a case based on knowledge about the previous conduct of a person (Farcy 1990) for sentencing purposes. This seems to be self-explanatory, and usually neither scholars nor practitioners discuss it any further in literature on criminal records.[2] Indeed, the German Penal Code demands in section 46 (2) that

> [w]hen sentencing the court weighs the circumstances that speak in favour of and against the offender. Consideration shall in particular be given to ... the offender's past life, his personal and financial circumstances.[3]

The offender's prior history therefore presents one of the relevant sentencing criteria explicitly mentioned in the law. However, the law does not refer to the offender's 'prior record' or 'previous conviction' but speaks more generally of all relevant circumstances in the offender's past.

Not only in the sentencing phase but also in the pre-trial phase, previous convictions play a role in decision-making. Case example 2 on the young burglar was presented as a fictitious but realistic scenario to judges, public prosecutors and defence lawyers in a comparative research project on pre-trial decision-making (Hammerschick et al 2018).[4] Many respondents, both in the overall sample and in the German sub-group (Morgenstern 2017), assumed that because of the previous conviction, the sentence for the new offence would be an unconditional prison sentence. Neither other facts nor possible future investigations played a comparable role in this assessment. In most cases the interview partners had sought to clarify whether the previous conviction was for the same type of crime (which we left open to trigger inquiries), but some respondents simply made this assumption.

It should be noted, however, that the question of a future criminal record as a consequence of an imminent conviction is something that is important for the sentencing decision, as case 1 shows. Section 46 (1) of the German Penal Code not only demands that the sentence is based on the offender's guilt, it also demands that the consequences that the sentence will to have on the offender's future life in society must be taken into account. In the decision in case 1,

[2] Veh 1999: 111: 'essential source of insight into the offender's personality'; Schäfer et al 2017: 650 and Streng 2017 are critical about the 'undifferentiated use' of previous convictions for sentencing purposes.

[3] All translations by the author.

[4] The sample comprised almost 200 interviews from seven countries, 33 from Germany; see, for more details, Hammerschick et al 2018: 18 and 76.

the court underlined that any conviction and sentencing decision that does not consider the impact of the criminal record on the convict's future life, namely potential employment chances, is flawed.[5]

These examples of the demands of the criminal justice system are by no means exhaustive – of course previous convictions play an important role in all prognostic decisions on risk: within the sentencing procedure when a decision about the dangerousness of a person has to be made, or later, when furlough or conditional release become options, the decision-making bodies use previous convictions as an indicator for decision-making. Sections 56, 57 and 57a of the German Penal Code request that the 'former life' of the offender be taken into account when deciding upon the suspension of a prison sentence or (to a lesser degree) upon early release, and previous convictions here play a major role (Meier 2015; Dünkel 2017 with further references).

B. Public Administration: Protecting the State's Reputation

Public administration also claims an interest in knowing about previous convictions. This is relevant when the authorities have to decide upon public licences, immigration questions, medical licences or the right to carry a weapon. Knowledge about the candidate's past is deemed essential to assess his or her reliability and trustworthiness (Pfeiffer 2000; Eufinger 2017) and to reduce risks to the public.

A person's past conduct additionally is always deemed important when failures can damage the legitimacy and reputation of public authorities because that person is identified in one way or another with them. This involves some state universities requiring a certificate of conduct for students in special circumstances (VG München, 17 January 2011),[6] principally in connection with the doctoral exam. For the same reasons, special requirements apply for public authorities as employers, in particular when somebody seeks employment as a civil servant – even smaller offences may shake confidence in the applicant's personal eligibility (LArbG Berlin-Brandenburg, 31 March 2017, stating that a future teacher who had forged a metro ticket was not eligible because teachers 'must be role models who take the law seriously').

C. Private Employers and Other Private Parties: Avoiding Risks

Outside criminal courts, the most important area with regard to a person's previous conduct is employment. It is widely accepted that a future employer

[5] Similarly, OLG Frankfurt, 20 December 2017, concerning a future medical doctor, held that the fact that a sentence that will be included in the certificate of conduct normally leads to the rejection of medical approbation has to be explicitly considered.

[6] Only when there is a risk to university life and peace, as would be the case with regard to extremist offences or hate speech.

needs to know about a potential employee's prior history in order to assess his or her integrity and loyalty. This economic interest is naturally seen as legitimate when an employer is about to enter into a long-term contract. The selection procedure is described as inherently 'risky' for the potential employer – when the wrong person (unable, inefficient or dishonest) is chosen, the business risks making a loss (Milthaler 2006: 25). The employer may even feel obliged to ask for information on previous convictions, and conclude from the very fact that they are officially registered that they are significant to identifying a risk, assuming that otherwise the authorities would not keep a record of them (Tolzmann 2015: 12). This is echoed in a more recent decision by a Social Court of North Rhine-Westphalia, explaining that taking into account former convictions is necessary:

> Otherwise these … entries, that amongst others are designed to prevent potential (public and private) employers from material or other damage resulting from employing persons with convictions, evidently would not make sense. (LSG Nordrhein-Westfalen, 13 July 2015)

Although it is far from clear how much previous convictions actually tell about a person's personality, the quality of their work, their loyalty or future conduct, many scholars and legal practitioners simply assume that they do, in particular with regard to economic crimes (Veh 1999: 112; more critical Tolzmann 2015: 12). A certificate of conduct is described as an 'obvious, easy to handle and reliable instrument' to avoid any risks (OLG Naumburg, 28 March 2014). When a young man convicted for commercial fraud claimed funding for occupational re-training after his release (which normally would be available), it was rejected by the authorities:

> A conviction for commercial fraud allows for the negative assumption that he will not reliably fulfil his duties of the work contract as a car seller, because this position involves the handling of significant assets and contact with potential buyers of cars that are dependent on the integrity, honesty and respectability of their business partner. This does not need further explanation. The probability that a potential employer would employ the applicant in such a trading position tends, according to the court's opinion, towards zero. (OLG Naumburg, 28 March 2014)

Candidates for positions where the employees will have contact with children, as illustrated in case 4, are subject to further scrutiny.

Another problem is the possible liability of employers for acts of employees vis-à-vis third parties. This so far has been spelled out (only) for employers working in investment business or dealing with other financial transactions. In a leading case (as illustrated in case example 3), the court argued that a financial firm had violated its duty to the client because it had not requested its employee's criminal record and therefore did not know about his previous convictions for fraud. This type of financial firm would also violate its duties when employing somebody with such a criminal record whom they otherwise found to be a suitable candidate – which will most certainly deter most employers from taking the risk.[7] Handbooks and commentaries therefore recommend that all such employers make thorough use of all legal possibilities for background checks, with the idea that candidates with convictions should probably not be employed (Kania and Sansone 2012: 360; Stumpf 2013: 3366; Eufinger 2017: 1142).

Not having asked for a certificate of conduct in the recruitment process may additionally prevent companies from receiving compensation from their insurance companies. This was decided in various cases in which employees had stolen goods from their employers (OLG Frankfurt, 7 June 2000, in the case of a butler) or from third parties. In the case of a truck driver employed by a transport company, the employer had argued that he did not ask for a certificate because he always relied on his personal impression of candidates and wanted to give a chance to everybody. The court did not accept this and held him negligent in his duties under the insurance policy (OLG Saarbrücken, 13 July 2005).

More private parties are interested in a person's past when contracts that require a certain amount of trust between the parties are at stake, for example between landlords and tenants. Although it is legally inadmissible for a landlord to ask for a certificate of conduct (Derleder and Pellegrino 1998: 550), it seems to be regular practice, and the often desperate potential tenants obviously comply. This assumption is based on brief Internet research, with many entries reporting these kind of requests, as well as on a presentation for future landlords by a lawyer specialising in tenancy law. It is conceded that there is no legal right to require a certificate of conduct, but since 'there is no duty to rent out a house ... a certificate of conduct will regularly be requested when the landlord so requires' (Stark 2013: 3).

D. The Wider Public and Research

The public is curious, too, and crime sells. Media coverage and other reports on previous convictions react to public demand. Here, the Federal Constitutional Court and other courts have been discussing the classic conflict between two important fundamental rights – freedom of speech on one hand, and the needs and rights of the individual who wants to be left alone after serving his or her sentence on the other – in a series of decisions (eg BVerfG, 24 January 2006 and 12 March 2007; OLG Frankfurt a M, 25 May 2016). They seriously limit the media as to the possibility to publicise details of offences and offenders. For the purpose of this study, it is important to note that the courts based

[7] This issue has never been raised before a court. It would be interesting to know whether the football club Bayern Munich, which is a stock corporation, knew about this risk when they re-employed their former manager, who was convicted for tax fraud and sentenced to imprisonment for more than three years.

their arguments, inter alia, on the legislative framework of recording crimes in the Federal Register and the rules regarding the disclosure and deletion of this information.

Lastly, criminal records are of interest to criminologists and penologists. Reconviction statistics (that have existed in Germany since 2003: Jehle 2014) in particular depend on the data available in the Federal Register. Other scientific studies may also rely on the register, and scholars can apply for access (Götting 2012).

E. The 'Stain of Conviction' and the Position of the Convict: Unreliable, Not Trustworthy and Dangerous?

In concluding this section from the perspective of the person who has a record of convictions, the significant effects of registration become obvious: described as 'stigmatisation by registration' (Sonnen 2018: 514) or 'confirmation of a prejudice' (Haffke 1975: 65), the entries in the register are true labelling in the Beckerian sense (Becker 1973: 9).

German law and jurisprudence sometimes even use the term 'stain of conviction' (*Strafmakel*). Although this expression is historic and has persisted only in a special regulation, it may tell us something about the aim of registering convictions as 'penal stains' more generally. The so-called 'elimination of the stain of conviction' (*Beseitigung des Strafmakels*) can be declared for young offenders by the judge of a juvenile court (section 97, 100 Juvenile Justice Act (JJA)). It results in an earlier deletion of the entry. The juvenile has to prove a 'well-integrated', 'righteous' personality, and show 'impeccable conduct'. The wording of the law suggests that this means more than just leading a law-abiding life, but there is hardly any use of the provision in practice to clarify the prerequisites (Eisenberg 2018). For the purpose of this study, however, it is remarkable that the fact of 'being stained with a conviction' is in contrast to 'impeccable conduct', and the earlier removal of this stain depends on some sort of merit (Haffke 1975: 66).

Summing up: as long as it remains, the stain has grave consequences. A defendant in a new criminal procedure may find that it influences both the decision on pre-trial detention (see case example 2) and the sentence. In both cases, the previous conviction may directly lead to the assumption that a risk of reoffending exists – that a person is dangerous. Once a sentence is served or a person is released early under conditions, the stigma makes life outside hard: finding employment and housing become more difficult, because the fact of having convictions seems to indicate compellingly that the person is unreliable and not trustworthy.

Criminal courts and labour courts are sensitive to this effect, at least to some degree: they consider it when they pass sentence (criminal courts) and they try to restrict the duties to disclose previous convictions (labour courts) – as illustrated in cases 1 and 4, where the applicants were successful in their claims. Other courts that deal with effects rather on the periphery of the problem are less sensitive and quite clear in their view that a person with prior convictions must be seen as a risk that should and will be avoided, as case example 3 shows. As the existence of the Federal Registry Act demonstrates, the state is aware of these problems and tries to mitigate or at least regulate them by providing for various details on access to the register and its information. These will be explained in the following section.

III. CRIMINAL RECORDS IN GERMANY

A. Historical Background and Aim of the Register

Legal provisions for collecting and registering comprehensive information on the criminal background of persons date back to the late nineteenth century. Following the French example,[8] the German *Länder* adopted a Register Act in 1882, and kept registers on convictions mainly for purposes of the criminal justice system and administrative decisions on licences. Private individuals had no access to this source of information (but could request codes of conduct issued by the police). Convictions were kept in the register without time limit, and no formal removal procedures were foreseen. Although not explicitly intended, but as an aspect of deterrence that was willingly accepted, the stigmatising effect of a criminal record was recognised (Rebmann 1983: 1514). In 1919, during the early liberal and reform-oriented years of the Weimar Republic, the German Conviction Redemption Act (*Straftilgungsgesetz*) was adopted. It was motivated (as cited in Tolzmann 2015: 2) as follows:

> Who, after completion of a sentence, precisely *because* of this completion only finds closed doors; who, despite honest efforts, is over and again punished with public disregard and is hampered in his struggle for life because he once failed and has been punished, eventually loses hope and motivation to find his way into reputable civil life and will be recoiled to the path to crime.

This extract shows that the legislator connected the criminal record to the punishment itself, and reflects the very limited readiness of society to welcome back ex-offenders. It called for more tolerance within the community and introduced restrictions on access to information from the register, as well as regulations for the removal of entries.

In 1972 the Federal Central Criminal Register Act (FCCRA) came into force. The legislator argued that 'within the criminal justice system the idea of resocialisation has gained more and more impact', and that the success of

[8] The '*Casiers judiciaries*', kept in Alsace-Lorraine when it became part of the German Reich in 1871, served as a model for the German legislation (Rebmann 1983; Farcy 1990).

this concept depended not only on the way sentences were executed but 'in the same way on the legislation of criminal records'.[9] The Act thus intended 'to balance the privacy interests of the persons concerned and the public interest to protect society against persons who disregard the legal order'. The introduction of the new law prompted an interesting controversy in one of the leading journals on criminal justice. Haffke (1975), as one of the protagonists, has been cited several times already. His main argument and criticism were fundamental: before regulating the consequences of the criminal registration, the concept of the stain of conviction would need clarification, and without it the criminal registration would lack legitimacy. Not surprisingly, this criticism was rejected, with the arguments that the legislation on the register could not solve the problem of public prejudices and that precise registration was indispensable for all prognostic decisions. It was argued that 'previous convictions at least provide a precise basis', as long as they are correctly collected (Schoreit 1975: 363). This controversy has never been addressed again in German penal discourse.

In 1998, criminal legislation underwent a series of changes, mainly concentrating on a harsher approach towards sex offenders, which also affected the FCCRA. Since 2009, all employers in areas where employees have contact with children are obliged to check their employees and applicants accordingly, and request a special certificate of conduct (see case 4).

B. Access to Criminal Records

Unrestricted information is accessible mainly for the criminal justice system and certain administrative procedures (section 41 *Bundeszentralregistergesetz* (BZRG)). Requesting a so-called 'register statement' thus is possible for courts, public prosecution and prison administrations, criminal investigation departments of the police and tax authorities, and specialised administration agencies that deal with particularly sensitive areas, such as immigration, private security business, drugs and pharmaceutical products, radiation protection or flight safety.

No private individual has access to the full register. The person concerned technically remains 'master' of the information, because only he or she can apply for a certificate of conduct if needed. Two types of certificate have to be distinguished: first, the certificate of conduct for private employers; and second, the certificate of conduct for public employers and authorities that are responsible for licensing in different areas.

Following section 32 BZRG, convictions will not be included in the certificate of conduct in 12 different cases. By far the most important regulation refers to day fines and very short prison sentences: a day fine below 90 units or a prison

[9] Material by the German Parliament, BT-Drs. VI/477: 14.

sentence shorter than three months will not be included if no other entry is registered. Further restrictions on including entries in the certificate of conduct apply to juveniles; only non-suspended prison sentences of more than two years will be included. Restrictions also apply to drug addicts undergoing therapy. All other entries in the register must be included in a certificate of conduct.

As explained for case example 1, judges must take these provisions into account in the sentencing decision, and particularly must have in mind the 90-day threshold. The other great significance of these regulations lies in the fact that a person applying for a job need legally only disclose what would be included in his or her certificate (section 53 BZRG).

The certificate of conduct for personal ('private') purposes is sent only to the person making the application. It is not entirely clear in what circumstances a future employer may ask about previous convictions. In general, jurisprudence has declared such a question admissible in 'recruitment procedures for positions where the nature of work makes personal integrity indispensable'. Labour courts have clarified this in extensive case law (BAG, 20 May 1999; BAG, 20 March 2014; Tolzmann 2018: 12 and 336), which has restricted the possibilities for a future employer to ask about convictions that are only directly relevant for the particular job, for example relating to traffic offences for an application as a lorry driver, property offences for an application as a teller, and so forth. In those cases and for criminal offences that may have important implication for carrying out a particular job, a potential employee must tell the truth about his or her criminal record; if not, this is considered a breach of (pre-)contractual duties and justifies the employee's prompt dismissal. It should be noted, however, that in principle the employer may not ask to see the certificate itself, because other – in this case irrelevant – convictions could be included. This restriction was developed by the labour courts and takes into account the interpretation of Article 2 Basic Law by the German Federal Constitutional Court (FCC) (privacy). The mere existence of the certificate, however, makes it possible for the employer, who is usually in a more powerful position than the applicant, to request to see it and therefore to take note of all entries.

With regard to any workplace that has anything to do with children, the possibility to see a certificate exists officially with the so-called 'extended certificate of conduct'. Since 2010, according to section 30a BZRG and section 72a Code of Social Law, all employers in childcare, youth welfare institutions, schools, youth sports and leisure must request such an extended certificate. This includes children's football coaches, scout leaders and other volunteers in that area, making the group of persons concerned almost unmanageable. Although the prohibition on employing persons who have been convicted only relates to sexual offenders and those convicted of certain other (severe) crimes, the extended certificate of conduct makes other entries visible, and thus weakens the protection of privacy jurisprudence had developed. Again, the courts have tried to restrict the powers of and potential abuse by employers: in case 4, the labour court ruled that the fact of having convictions in itself is no reason to dismiss an employee, unless the nature of the conviction or its influence on the employee's actual working performance gives reason to do so. This was denied in case 4, and the applicant got his job back.

To avoid employers' getting to know about these kinds of legally irrelevant convictions, employers and (some) scholars often request the establishment of so-called 'employers' certificates' (Milthaler 2006, Tolzmann 2018, both referring to the Dutch example). These would be accessible by future employers, in particular to implement compliance programmes to prevent economic crimes, and would only include entries relevant to the position in question. This would give the register authority significant defining powers, but at the same time burden it with an immense additional workload. Currently no such reform is planned.

A third type of certificate of conduct for public purposes exists for presentation to a German authority. Only the person concerned can request it, but it is sent directly to the authority. Fewer restrictions apply than for private certificates, in order to enable the authorities (when they do not have unrestricted access, see above) to assess the suitability of somebody who applies for a commercial licence, or who wants to be employed by a public authority, including universities. The regulations are very wide and privilege public employers, although the interrelation between workplace requirements and possible previous convictions may be vague (very critical Tolzmann 2018: 15; more details in Morgenstern 2011).

C. Expunging the Record – the Federal Registry as Stain Remover

'Expunging techniques' (Herzog-Evans 2011) differ as between the register itself and the certificate of conduct. The legislation has created a graduated system of deadlines. The expiry of recording periods results, first, in a ban from inclusion of convictions in the certificate of conduct. In a second step, after the expiry of another period, convictions cannot longer be used and are finally removed from the register altogether (cf sections 34 and 46 FCCRA). New convictions lead to suspension of the time limits, or may lead to consideration of minor crimes too, which arguably is a huge problem as regards the social integration of multiple offenders who commit rather minor offences. Again, certain privileges apply to juveniles and drug addicts. On the other hand, stricter rules apply to those convicted of sexual offences.

Some removals of entries relate to the old age or death of persons. Other measures are based on the absence of reconviction. For ex-offenders, probably the most important regulation is section 33 FCCRA: convictions are no longer included in the certificate of conduct on the expiry of specific deadlines:

- three years after convictions for offences that were punished with a suspended sentence of less than one year;

- five years for most other convictions;
- 10 years for convictions for sexual offences resulting in a prison sentence of more than one year.

The period starts with the day of the final judgment and is extended by the length of the respective prison sentence; in the case of life sentences with parole, this extension is at least 20 years. The effect of the expiry only occurs when no reconviction has been recorded and all sentences have been fully executed. Whenever more than one conviction is recorded in the register, the latest conviction overrides and defines the expiry date.

Full redemption, with the effect that the convictions may no longer be used against a person in any criminal or other legal matter, can only be achieved after longer periods, usually three times as long as the periods mentioned above. More specifically, these periods are:

- five years for all convictions that result in a penalty of less than 90 day fine units (as long as no sentence of imprisonment exists on the register; several smaller day fines are irrelevant); of penalties of imprisonment of less than three months or, for juveniles, of less than one year (or two, if suspended);
- 10 years for convictions that result in a punishment of less than one year of imprisonment, if suspended (certain restrictions apply); in the case of juveniles, all other convictions;
- 15 years in most other cases;
- 20 years in cases of sexual offences that result in a prison sentence of more than one year.

Only a few hardship regulations exist to avoid these strict deadlines; they depend on detailed requests by the person concerned and are rarely applied (Morgenstern 2011).

IV. PENAL THEORY AND FUNDAMENTAL RIGHTS IN GERMANY

As already explained, the legislator acknowledges that convictions are an additional burden and stigma for the person affected. It is therefore necessary to ask how this finding fits into wider concepts of penal theory and, before that, how German penal theory generally is conceptualised.

Section 46 (1) of the German Penal Code determines the sentencing framework: 'The guilt of the offender is the basis for sentencing. The effects which the sentence can be expected to have on the offender's future life in society shall be taken into account.' The 'defense of the legal order' may also play a role (sections 46, 47, German Penal Code). In German doctrine, this is seen as a pragmatic way of combining two approaches that in the past had often been seen as irreconcilable – the retributive and the preventive aims (for more on combination models, Roxin 1966). The 'guilt principle' determines the imputation of criminal responsibility as such (rationale of punishment), and is rooted in the constitutional guarantee of human dignity and autonomy (Hörnle 2013). As the retributive element of the penal doctrine it serves to satisfy the demand for justice to be done, and affects the sentencing decision as far as it determines the size of the penalty (Streng 2017). In its limiting function, it prevents the deterrence and rehabilitative purposes from being applied in a way that would exceed individual guilt (BGH, 10 April 1987). The 'effects' (*Wirkungen*) of punishment mentioned in section 46 of the German Penal Code include all possible aspects of special (individual) prevention, taking into account empirical perspectives, namely the offender's personality and (criminogenic) needs (Streng 2017, with references to the many discussions on the aims of punishment (*Strafzwecke*) since the late nineteenth century, initiated by Franz von Liszt's[10] essay, 'On the Idea of Purpose in Penal Law'). Additionally, courts have sometimes considered very specific effects, such as the impact of a prison sentence on foreigners under immigration law (Schäfer et al 2017). In the execution of sentences, the only aim pursued should be special prevention, with a focus on social reintegration or resocialisation (*Resozialisierung*, Morgenstern 2015).

Crucial for the practical success of the concept of *Resozialisierung*, however, were not penal theory or penal policy but several decisions of the FCC in the 1970s. In a first step, the Court stressed that the legal citizenship of a convicted criminal remains intact, because his or her civil rights can only be restricted as far as necessary to enforce the sanction and only on a statutory basis, and declared the doctrine of limited rights in the so-called *besonderes Gewaltverhältnis* (special subordination relationship) for prisoners to be unconstitutional (BVerfG, 14 March 1972).

In 1973 the Court recognised the right to resocialisation as an integral part of constitutionally guaranteed rights. It derived it from the rights to dignity and to develop one's personality freely (Articles 1 and 2 of the German Basic Law), as well as from the duty of the state to assist groups who, for whatever reason, require social assistance (*Sozialstaatsprinzip*, Article 20). From the perspective of the constitution, this legal entitlement thus consists of both negative fundamental rights against state infringements (the right to be left alone) and positive rights to state action.

The occasion on which the Court developed this right was a post-prison situation. A TV operator planned a documentary about a spectacular crime, including publication of the name and photographs of one offender who was due to be released. In the judgment, the Court stated that

> from the point of view of the offender, this interest in resocialisation accrues from his constitutional rights in terms of Article 2 (1) in conjunction with Article 1 of the Basic Law. Viewed from the perspective of the community, the principle of the

[10] For those who are reminded of the composer of the same name, they were cousins.

> social state requires public care and assistance for those groups in the community who, because of personal weakness or fault, incapacity or social disadvantage, were adversely affected in their social development; prisoners and ex-prisoners also belong to this group. Not least, resocialisation serves the protection of the community itself: it lies in its distinct interest that the offender will not reoffend ... Not only the offender must be prepared for the return into the free human community, the community itself has to be prepared to receive him again. (BVerfGE, 5 June 1973)

While the FCC further developed how this resocialisation has to be understood and shaped as a positive right to state action and assistance only later, namely with regard to the enforcement of prison sentences (also life sentences) and prison conditions, remuneration of prison work, prison leave and so forth, it has remained the crucial decision for all cases in which an ex-offender exercises his or her right to eventually be left alone. The decisions mentioned in section II.D with regard to media coverage are all based on it.

Lastly, with regard to the disclosure of sensitive information about a person, an additional constitutional concept developed by the FCC becomes relevant, that is, 'information self-determination' (*informationelle Selbstbestimmung*). This term was coined in a German constitutional ruling relating to personal information collected during the 1983 census. The Court ruled that

> in the context of modern data processing, the protection of the individual against limitless collection, storage, use and disclosure of personal data is encompassed by the general personal rights of the German constitution. This basic right demands the capacity of the individual to determine generally the disclosure and use of this personal data. Restrictions to this informational self-determination are allowed only in case of overriding public interest. (BVerfG, 15 December 1983)

V. CRIMINOLOGICAL INSIGHTS: PREVIOUS CONDUCT, RECIDIVISM AND DESISTANCE

What remains to be discussed are criminological findings on previous convictions, both as regards their prognostic value and as regards their (negative) impact on the reintegration process for ex-offenders.

For a long time, German discussions (and prognostic instruments) on the legitimacy of considering previous convictions were more or less left without empirical findings regarding their explanatory power and validity (Haffke 1975: 78; Meier 1983: 318). Doubts in that regard existed for a long time and led to the abolition of a specific provision on recidivism that made it mandatory for judges to consider recidivism as an aggravating sentencing factor in certain cases (Meier 1983; Geiter 1988).

Meanwhile, more research exists in the field of life-course criminology, and a national reconviction study was conducted in three stages (Jehle 2014; Jehle et al 2016). Recidivism was measured over a period of three to four years for all those convicted in 1994, 2003 and 2007, and re-convictions, as registered in the Federal

Criminal Register, were recorded. The study presents reconviction data in relation to offence, sentence and previous convictions, as well as the age, gender and nationality of the offender. In such a way, for example, empirically based statements can be made on how often certain offenders commit the same offences or any other offence during the observation period, providing the necessary base rates for prognostic instruments. Additionally, the different reconviction rates relating to different sentences can be examined.

With regard to the question how far it is necessary – and therefore can be legitimate – to record previous convictions, no clear answer emerges. Nevertheless, the prognostic force of previous convictions becomes less convincing when looking at the overall picture: the majority of persons convicted, who were subject to a sentence or responses under juvenile criminal law, or – in the case of those sentenced to imprisonment – who were released from prison in the reference year 2007, did not reoffend within the three-year observation period. Only about one-third (36 per cent) were registered again. Within the following three years the reconviction rate increased to 44 per cent, and after a further three years to 48 per cent (Jehle et al 2016: 174). Most relapses happened in the first months after serving a sentence, and the longer the period without a relapse, the lower was the risk of a reconviction. Specific reconvictions for the same type of offence, in particular more serious offences, were rather the exception than the rule.

Given that prognostic and preventive purposes serve as justification for the general inclusion of *all* convictions in a criminal record, while for more than half of the persons convicted the recording of a previous conviction has no prognostic meaning, doubts as regards the principle of proportionality arise. Of course, reconviction rates for particular groups are higher – but this, for example, does not refer to sex offenders who form the target groups for even stricter recording rules; they have reconviction rates of less than 30 per cent (with only very few being repeat convictions for sex offences, this rate is between 1 and 4 per cent, depending on the specific sex offence: Jehle et al 2016: 117, 253). While the findings of the reconvictions statistics would need to be interpreted carefully in the light of different preventive purposes, the general assumption of the prognostic value of previous convictions is certainly shattered and demands further reflections on the legitimacy of the criminal records system and its use.

The second question that criminologists can try to answer is how far the practical implications of previous convictions are influencing judicial decision-making throughout the proceedings. With regard to case example 2, it has been mentioned that decision-makers in the pre-trial phase assumed that the previous conviction of a young burglar would indicate an increased sentence in the upcoming case, and it was a very strong indicator for the assumption that pre-trial detention would be ordered. The respondents supposed this either because the previous conviction indicated a risk of reoffending, or because the severity of the sentence B faced meant that there was a proper risk that he would not stand trial (ie would abscond). This study and other research from Germany

(Morgenstern 2018: 480) confirmed the enormous importance of the criminal record in pre-trial decision-making. Often, scarcely any other information about personal circumstances is taken into account, mainly because other than this information, the criminal record statement is readily available. The pre-trial decision may also have the effect of a self-fulfilling prophecy for the sentencing stage.

Third, some criminological studies are available that explored the impact of previous convictions on the future life of ex-offenders as regards the reaction of employers. Some indications emerge from a study by Wößner et al (2016) that looked at obstacles to social re-integration in the re-entry phase. It was clear that the ex-offenders regularly needed to present their certificates of conduct, regardless of legal restrictions, and for positions that should usually not come under special scrutiny, such as cleaning services in public buildings. Once they presented their certificates, they lost their jobs or were not employed (Wößner et al 2016: 26). This means that even in areas where less qualified persons do have the chance to find a job (Wirth 2006), this chance hardly exists for ex-offenders. Earlier research, however, suggested that when ex-prisoners were backed by institutional support, the readiness to employ was higher. It seems to be a promising strategy to appeal to the 'social conscience' of potential employers, for example via their umbrella organisations (Bex et al 2010). As both the legislator in the 1920s and the FCC in the 1970s have underlined, desistance from crime as the final result of resocialisation needs the community's support, or at least not public rejection.

VI. (HOW) CAN PENAL THEORY, CRIMINOLOGICAL KNOWLEDGE AND MODERN PREVENTIVE AIMS BE INTEGRATED INTO A COHERENT THEORY OF CRIMINAL RECORDS?

From a socio-legal point of view, and as supported by empirical research, the burdensome and labelling effects of criminal registration are clearly visible. From the human rights perspective – in Germany a constitutional perspective – criminal registration is a state intervention that needs justification and restriction, just like any other interference with fundamental rights. These concepts have contributed greatly to restricting access to information from the register, and have been used by the courts to limit public and media curiosity, the inquisitiveness of employers and ultimately effects detrimental to the social reintegration of ex-offenders.

However, from a criminal justice perspective, the penal concept of criminal registration itself remains unclear. Often, it is assumed that it is a 'specific consequence' of a conviction (Meier 2015: 450, similarly Schoreit 1975, Sonnen 2018). According to German penal doctrine, a conviction pronounces both the 'socio-ethical unworthiness' of the offence (*sozialethisches Unwerturteil*, see for example Meier 2015: 15) and reproach of the offender. According to this interpretation, registration is not meant to intensify these two elements (Meier 2015: 450; similarly Schoreit 1975, Veh 1999)[11] and is no more than a by-product of punishment. Therefore, seemingly, it is nothing the criminal justice system or penal theory has to worry about. Public rejection of ex-offenders is seen as inevitable evil, a societal matter that may be deplorable, but 'it has nothing to do with the register that those with previous convictions generally must expect defamation and mistrust' (Schoreit 1975: 364).

Nevertheless, registered convictions are accepted as an important sentencing factor within the judicial process. Sometimes it is argued that because of their 'warning effect' they result in aggravated guilt as regards the new offence (which was committed despite the previous warning); but usually they are taken as evidence of a higher risk of recidivism, which the new sentence has to take into account (Schäfer et al 2017; Streng 2017). As mentioned in section V, the provision on relapse as a mandatory aggravating sentencing factor was abolished from the German Penal Code. For critics, however, the abolition did not change the fundamental problem of almost automatically considering previous convictions as an aggravating sentencing factor because section 46 (2) of the German Penal Code was – and still is – interpreted in that way (Geiter 1988; Schäfer et al 2017).

Apart from this, the 'stain of conviction' has hardly been put into a theoretical penal perspective. A closer look into the literature on criminal registration reveals descriptions of legitimate aims of criminal registration that are equally elements of penal theory. In the literature it is mentioned that criminal registration has 'a certain deterring effect' (Veh 1999: 114; Rebmann 1983: 1514) or works by way of incapacitation – that is, those who are not able to present a clean certificate are 'prevented from pursuing their criminal career' in certain economic areas (critical, Tolzmann 2015: 12). The fact that some entries are not included in a certificate of conduct is partly interpreted as an incentive and even pedagogic measure to motivate a person not to commit further crimes (because then all entries would be visible in the certificate) – this is a special preventive aim as well (Haffke 1975: 67).

One of the classic German textbooks on criminal law (Jescheck and Weigend 1996), on the other hand, presents the topic of criminal records in the chapter on 'Rehabilitation'. Rehabilitation and resocialisation have different meanings in the German context (Morgenstern 2015); the first is connected to restoring the status of a person in the view of society, while the second refers mainly to the life the ex-offender leads after completing his or her sentence, in particular whether it is now law-abiding. They are, however, interconnected, since the latter may depend on the former (Morgenstern 2015; Cornel 2018). Jescheck and Weigend

[11] This is, however, the aim of the publication of a conviction, which in Germany in theory (but hardly in practice) is possible for special and rare convictions, mainly for defamation.

(1996) describe the removal of entries in the register as an element of rehabilitation (see also Morgenstern 2011), while they also identify risks to resocialisation caused by registration. They demand three necessary steps: (i) not to include minor offences in certificates of conduct for reasons of proportionality; (ii) not to include offences in certificates of conduct after a certain period if the person concerned has not reoffended; and (iii) removal of entries from the register after another period without reoffending. In the most elaborate commentary of the FCCRA we find similar remarks (Tolzmann 2015: 10), and the legislator has more or less implemented this concept.

These considerations show that criminal registration itself does serve special preventive purposes, not only because it accepts but also because it deliberately uses these effects: the idea that the criminal justice system in that way 'legalizes' or 'rubberstamps' (Haffke 1975) the 'stain of conviction' is convincing. The acknowledgement that the effects have to be mitigated by the FCCRA and jurisprudence so that they do not impede the positive preventive aim of resocialisation, in particular with regard to the use of certificates of conduct for employers, underlines this finding.

What is usually missing is the first step: how can the registration of previous convictions as such be legitimised and integrated into penal theory? The question whether 'the "stain of conviction" can be founded in social ethics at all' (Haffke 1975) still has not been sufficiently addressed. The closing lines of this chapter attempt to outline a coherent approach. While criminal registration is not a sentence or measure within the sanctions system, it remains a state-driven and inseparable effect of punishment. The main penal aim pursued – following the combination approach by Roxin (1966) – at the sentencing stage is 'just punishment', proportionate to the seriousness of the crime and the offender's guilt. How previous convictions fit into this concept is a matter of ongoing debate (Streng 2017). A previous conviction can only be relevant to the current sentencing decision on the current offence, measured by the current guilt, when it has had an impact on the latter. This can only be accepted when the new offence is associated with the previous one, for example because they are of a similar type. The level of guilt of an offender who has been sufficiently warned may be higher than that of a first-time offender. Warning effects, however, last only for a certain period, and only when the offences are by their nature comparable (Schäfer et al 2017: 650). Another way to deduce a higher level of guilt for a second (or further) offence is via the assumption that a person who repeatedly commits offences has a generally hostile attitude towards the legal order.

Both aspects must be assessed in the individual case, and the reasoning may prove to be more difficult than often assumed. For this study it is undeniable that courts need to know about previous convictions for this purpose. A reliable register therefore is necessary. It is not necessary, however, to accept almost unrestricted access for judicial authorities for periods as long as currently possible. The current system, which distinguishes between offences only according to their seriousness, does not take into account the findings of reconviction research. After a certain lapse of time the connection that could identify a higher level of guilt, as described above, is difficult to establish (Schäfer 2017; BVerfG, 16 January 1979). Longer periods of judicial access to the register for sentencing purposes therefore can hardly be legitimised with this argument. The first suggestion therefore is to allow regular access to the full register information for no longer than five years.

The second leg of justification *within* the criminal justice system is prevention. Outside the criminal justice system, *only* preventive aims justify the use of criminal records. Again, a legitimate interest in the information contained in the register is undeniable in some cases, to protect private and public employers or the public. Nevertheless, access to the register information must be seriously restricted in the light of empirical findings on recidivism and risk. In more than 50 per cent of all cases, the registered convictions cannot serve preventive purposes because they do not tell us anything – there is no reconviction, not even after nine years. Of course, in the other cases – and for special groups the base rates are much higher – they may have (restricted) prognostic value. A more differentiated system therefore is needed that could draw on the likelihood of reoffending, depending on the offenders/offences. Indeed, the *Bundesjustizamt*, as an administrative body in charge of the register, is probably not well equipped to deal with the task, which equally bears the risk of discriminating against certain groups of offenders. This would rather be the task of the sentencing judge, who knows the individual case. The second suggestion therefore is to think about a system in which the sentencing judge exerts at least some influence on whether the conviction should be included in a certificate of conduct or not (similarly, Milthaler 2006: 309; Haffke 1975: 83). Additionally, regulations for a specific employer's certificate that restrict access to information which is not necessary to prevent damage for employers because it has nothing to do with the workplace could be an option. Both strategies, however, would have to be prepared by research: studies are particularly necessary to see how far requests for certificates actually impede resocialisation of ex-offenders. This could be done, for example, by way of interviews with probationers and the probation services.

While it is true that law and jurisprudence cannot force society to accept and welcome back those who have previously committed an offence, they nevertheless must not give in to punitive moods and inadequate preventive exigencies. German law in many regards offers a reintegration-oriented approach, but legal culture still lacks coherence in translating this approach into overall practice with regard to criminal records. Further restrictions on access to the information stored in the criminal register are therefore indispensable. For the reasons given, this is the case not only for private purposes, but also as regards use by public authorities – and even for use within the criminal justice system.

REFERENCES

Becker, H (1963) *Outsiders. Studies in the sociology of deviance* (New York, NY, Free Press).

Bex, H, Grosch, B and Wirth, W (2010) 'Integrationsplanung' in HJ Kerner and E Marks (eds), *Internetdokumentation des Deutschen Präventionstages* (Hannover), available at www.praeventionstag.de/nano.cms/vortraege/id/1275 (last accessed 8 June 2018).

Cornel, H (2018) 'Zum Begriff der Resozialisierung' in H Cornel, G Kawamura-Reindl and B-R Sonnen (eds), *Handbuch der Resozialisierung*, 4th edn (Baden-Baden, Nomos) 31–62.

Derleder, P and Pellegrino, D (1998) 'Die Anbahnung des Mietverhältnisses' *Neue Zeitschrift für Mietrecht*, 1, 550–54.

Dünkel, F (2017) '§ 57 Aussetzung des Strafrestes' in U Kindhäuser, U Neumann and H-U Paeffgen (eds), *Strafgesetzbuch*, 5th edn (Munich, Beck).

Eisenberg, U (2018) *Jugendgerichtsgesetz*, 20th edn (Munich, Beck).

Eufinger, A (2017) 'Die Zuverlässigkeit des Arbeitnehmers und ihre arbeitsrechtlichen Implikationen' *Betriebsberater*, 72, 1141–46.

Farcy, J-C (1990) 'Le casier judiciaire au XIXe siècle' *Bulletin du Centre d'histoire de la France contemporaine*, 11, 5–27.

Geiter, H (1988) 'Rückfallvorschrift (§ 48) aufgehoben' *Zeitschrift für Rechtspolitik*, 20, 376–79.

Götting, B (2012) 'Das Bundeszentralregister als Instrument und Gegenstand der Forschung' in E Hilgendorf and R Rengier (eds), *Festschrift für Wolfgang Heinz zum 70. Geburtstag* (Baden-Baden, Nomos) 84–93.

Haffke, B (1975) 'Hat das Bundeszentralregister eine Konzeption? Öffentliche Strafmoral und Gesetzesplanung' *Goltdammer's Archiv für Strafrecht*, 122, 66–83.

Hammerschick et al (2018) *DETOUR – Towards Pre-trial Detention as Ultima Ratio: Comparative Report* (Vienna, IRKS), available at www.irks.at/detour/publications.html (last accessed 16 May 2018).

Herzog-Evans, M (2011) 'Judicial rehabilitation in France: Helping with the desisting process and acknowledging achieved desistance' *European Journal of Probation*, 3, 4–219.

Hörnle, T (2013) 'Moderate and non-arbitrary sentencing without guidelines: the German experience' *Law and Contemporary Problems*, 7, 189–210.

Jehle, J-M (2014) 'Approach, Structure and Outcome of the German Reconviction Study' in H-J Albrecht and J-M Jehle (eds), *National Reconviction Statistics and Studies in Europe* (Göttingen, Göttinger Universitätsverlag) 25–41.

—— et al (2016) *Legalbewährung nach strafrechtlichen Sanktionen* (Berlin, Bundesministerium der Justiz).

Jescheck, H-H and Weigend, T (1996) *Lehrbuch des Strafrechts. Allgemeiner Teil*, 5th edn (Berlin, Duncker & Humblodt).

Kania, T and Sansone, P (2012) 'Möglichkeiten und Grenzen des Pre-Employment-Screenings' *Neue Zeitschrift für Arbeitsrecht*, 29, 360–64.

Maruna, S (2011) 'Reentry as a rite of passage' *Punishment and Society*, 13, 1–27.

Meier, B-D (1983) 'Anwendung und Bedeutung der Rückfallvorschrift' *Zeitschrift für die gesamte Strafrechtswissenschaft*, 95, 317–38.
—— (2015) *Strafrechtliche Sanktionen*, 4th edn (Heidelberg, Springer).
Milthaler, A (2006) *Das Fragerecht des Arbeitsgebers nach den Vorstrafen des Bewerbers* (Frankfurt a M, Peter Lang).
Mölter, T (2012) *Überwachung und Informationsbeschaffung des Arbeitgebers* (Frankfurt a M, Kovac).
Morgenstern, C (2011) 'Judicial Rehabilitation in Germany – The Use of Criminal Records and the Removal of Recorded Convictions' *European Journal of Probation*, 3, 20–35.
—— (2015) 'Der Resozialisierungsgrundsatz – Social Reintegration as the dominant narrative for community punishment in Germany?' in G Robinson and F McNeill (eds), *Community Punishment. A European Perspective* (London, Routledge) 72–94.
—— (2017) *DETOUR – Towards Pre-trial Detention as Ultima Ratio: Second National Report on Germany* (Institut für Rechts- und Kriminalsoziologie, Vienna), available at www.irks.at/detour/publications.html (last accessed 16 May 2018).
—— (2018) *Die Untersuchungshaft* (Baden-Baden, Nomos).
Pfeiffer, J (2000) 'Die unbeschränkte Auskunft aus dem Bundeszentralregister und das Führungszeugnis' *Neue Zeitschrift für Strafrecht*, 20, 402–05.
Rebmann, K (1983) 'Einhundert Jahre Strafregisterwesen in Deutschland' *Neue Juristische Wochenschrift*, 46, 1513–17.
Roxin, C (1966) 'Sinn und Grenzen staatlicher Strafe' *Juristische Schulung*, 6, 377–82.
Schäfer, G, Sander, G and Gemmeren, G (2017) *Praxis der Strafzumessung*, 6th edn (Munich, Beck).
Schoreit, A (1975) 'Die gesetzgeberische Konzeption des Bundeszentralregistergesetzes' *Goltdammer's Archiv für Strafrecht*, 122, 362–64.
Sonnen, B-R (2018) 'Rechtsfolgen nach dem Registerrecht' in H Cornel, G Kawamura-Reindl and B-R Sonnen (eds), *Handbuch der Resozialisierung*, 4th edn (Baden-Baden, Nomos) 514–526.
Streng, F (2017) '§ 46 Grundsätze der Strafzumessung' in U Kindhäuser, U Neumann and H-U Paeffgen (eds), *Strafgesetzbuch*, 5th edn (Munich, Beck).
Stark, R (2013) *Ihre Rechte als Vermieter. Vortrag, gehalten auf der Kölner Immobilienmesse am 24. Mai 2013*, available at www.drstark.de/wp-content/uploads/…/2013-05-25-Vermieterrechte-RS1.pdf (last accessed 15 May 2018).
Stumpf, B (2013) 'Repräsentantenhaftung einer Anlageberatungsgesellschaft für von ihr eingesetzten selbstständigen Handelsvertreter' *Betriebsberater*, 68, 1039–43.
Tolzmann, G (2015) *Bundeszentralregistergesetz*, 5th edn (Stuttgart, Kohlhammer).
Veh, H-M (1999) 'Das Bundeszentralregister' *Bewährungshilfe*, 46, 111–33.
Von Liszt, F (1883) 'Der Zweckgedanke im Strafrecht' *Zeitschrift für die gesamte Strafrechtswissenschaft*, 3, 1–47.
Wendel, K (2016) *Die Vorlage einer Bundeszentralregisterauskunft vor Begründung des Arbeitsverhältnisses* (Hamburg, Kovac).
Wirth, W (2006) 'Arbeitslose Haftentlassene' *Bewährungshilfe*, 53, 137–52.
Wößner, G, Wienhausen-Knezevic, E and Gauder, K (2016) *'I was thrown in at the deep end …' Prisoner reentry: Patterns of transition from prison to community among sexual and violent offenders* (Freiburg, edition iuscrim).

TABLE OF CASES

Federal Constitutional Court

BVerfGE 33, 1 (14 March 1972, 2 BvR 41/71)
BVerfGE 35, 202 (5 June1973, 1 BvR 536/72)
BVerfGE 65, 1 (15 December 1983, 1 BvR 209, 269, 362, 420, 440, 484/83)
BVerfG, 1 BvR 1252/02 (12 March 2007)
BVerfG, 1 BvR 2602/05 (24 January 2006)
BVerfG, 2 BvL 4/77 (16 January 1979)

Supreme Court

BGH, III ZR 296/11 (13 March 2013)
BGHSt 34, 345 (10 April 1987, GSSt 1/86)

Federal Labour Court

BAG, 2 AZR 320/98 (20 May 1999)
BAG, 2 AZR 1071/12 (20 March 2014)

Higher Regional Courts

OLG Nürnberg, 2 St OLG Ss 191/06 (30 August 2006)
OLG Frankfurt a. M., 1 Ss 174/17 (20 December 2017)
LSG Nordrhein-Westfalen, L 9 AL 118/15 B ER (13 July 2015)
OLG Naumburg, 10 U 5/13 (Hs) (28 March 2014)
LSG Nordrhein-Westfalen, L 9 AL 118/15 B ER (13 July 2015)
OLG Frankfurt, 7 U 152/99 (7 June 2000)
OLG Saarbrücken, 5 U 689/04 (13 July 2005)

Regional and District Courts

ArbG Cottbus, 3 Ca 317/13 (30 May 2013)
VG München, M 3 K 08.6106 (17 January 2011)
LArbG Berlin-Brandenburg, 2 Sa122/17 (31 March 2017)
OLG Frankfurt a M, 16 U 198/15 (25 May 2016)

5

Proportionality as a Constraint on the Legal Consequences of Conviction

SONJA MEIJER

I. INTRODUCTION

IN THE NETHERLANDS, as in other countries, offenders are confronted with legal consequences as a result of a criminal conviction. This chapter focuses on state-imposed legal consequences of a criminal conviction – whether imposed by statute, by a judge at the time of sentencing or by an administrative licensing authority[1] – on offenders who have served a (custodial) sentence, completed a community sentence or paid a fine (Von Hirsch and Wasik 1997: 600). These consequences can often have a greater adverse impact on ex-offenders than the actual punishment to which they were sentenced, especially if the person was originally given a non-custodial sentence.

Very little research has been done in the Netherlands on the legal consequences of criminal convictions. This is in contrast to the expansion of the possible legal consequences a criminal conviction can have: new legislation has been introduced in recent years, and existing consequences are expanding in scope. This development is in line with that in states exercising more supervision and control over convicted offenders (Garland 2001).

This development also raises the question of what restraints are placed on the power of the state to limit the rights of convicted offenders by means of the legal consequences of a criminal conviction, especially if these consequences are regulated outside of criminal law. Within the criminal law, substantive limitations and procedural safeguards, some deriving from human rights instruments, are well developed. Those particular limitations and safeguards tend not to

[1] I do not discuss the disadvantages that convicted persons incur at the hands of private firms or individuals, nor the stigmatising effects that convicted persons may face after returning to their communities (Goffman 1963).

apply to preventive measures outside the criminal law, and yet such measures also impose significant detriments on those subject to them (see also Ashworth, Zedner and Tomlin 2013: 7).

This chapter seeks to catalogue the legal consequences of criminal convictions in the Netherlands, to assess how proportionality can serve as a limit on the power of the state to impose these consequences, and to evaluate the Dutch policy of the certificate of conduct in the light of the proportionality principle. The concept of proportionality is well developed, both normatively and legally, within criminal law. The question I would like to answer here is whether any proportionality limits apply to restrictions of convicted offenders that are regulated in administrative law. Drawing on literature on preventive justice, I would like to argue that the principle of proportionality may serve as a proper constraint on prevention outside of the criminal justice system (Steiker 2015: 194–95). The principle of proportionality may thus serve as a constraint on the power of the state outside the sphere of formal criminal regulation, and may thus serve as a constraint on the legal consequences of a criminal conviction. In the European context, the proportionality principle is also recognised as a general limit on governmental power.[2]

II. LIMITING OFFENDERS BEYOND THEIR SENTENCE IN THE NETHERLANDS

The legal consequences of a criminal conviction in the Netherlands can be classified into three categories: (i) consequences that can be imposed by a judge in a criminal procedure; (ii) consequences that can be imposed by an administrative authority in an administrative setting; and (iii) restrictions that follow automatically upon conviction (Von Hirsch and Wasik 1997: 601).

A. Consequences Imposed by a Judge in a Criminal Procedure

In the Netherlands, a risk of recidivism is one of the grounds on which pre-trial detention can be imposed. As Morgenstern has demonstrated in the German context in chapter 4 of this volume, in the Netherlands the fact that an offender has been convicted before is also a very strong indicator for the imposition of pre-trial detention. For most judges, an earlier conviction is enough to indicate a risk of recidivism, no matter what that conviction was for. Only a minority of judges are of the opinion that the suspect must have been convicted of similar offences to substantiate the risk of recidivism (Boone, Jacobs and Lindeman 2017: 81; Crijns, Leeuw and Wermink 2016: 31).

[2] Art 52, Charter of Fundamental Rights of the European Union (7 December 2000) [2000] OJ C364/01, available at www.europarl.europa.eu/charter/pdf/text_en.pdf (last accessed 9 January 2019).

Former convictions may also have consequences for the sentence that can be imposed in criminal proceedings. When imposing a sentence, a judge may take the criminal record of the offender into account. According to the 'starting points' that judges use in criminal proceedings when determining the sanction, an earlier conviction for the same type of offence can be an aggravating factor.[3] Also, since 2010, the usual maximum sentence an offence carries by statute can be increased by a third if, at the time the offender committed the crime in question, no more than five years had elapsed since he or she had been sentenced to imprisonment for a similar offence (Articles 43a–43b, Dutch Criminal Code (CC)).[4] Although research shows that judges make use of this regulation, this has not had the effect that punishments above the maximum sentence are often imposed (Struijk 2012).

Furthermore, as from January 2018, the sentencing judge can impose a measure of post-incarceration mandatory supervision (Wolf 2016; Struijk and Mevis 2016; Meijer 2013),[5] which can result in life-long supervision of offenders convicted of sexual and violent crimes after conditional release or imposition of the TBS (*terbeschikkingstelling*) measure.[6] Although the post-incarceration mandatory supervision measure constitutes a penalty, and is as such regulated by the Criminal Code, it can also be considered a consequence of conviction. This is because it can only be imposed in addition to a (suspended) prison sentence of a maximum of four years (for sexual and violent crimes) or more and/or a TBS measure. Its imposition does not imply, however, that the measure will be executed. It may only be executed if there is a risk of repetition of an offence that would legitimise the imposition of the independent supervisory safety measure, or if enforcement is needed to avoid seriously damaging behaviour towards victims and witnesses. When deciding on the execution of the measure, the court also has to decide on its duration. It may order the enforcement of the measure for two, three, four or five years. Throughout this time, the measure may be extended on an unlimited number of occasions. As a result, the supervision order may last indefinitely. Being a measure and not a sentence, according to legal theory underpinning the Criminal Code, the supervisory measure is not strictly bound by proportionality limits. It is intended to safeguard society from future harm, such as recidivism, and may therefore take as long as necessary to reduce the risk for society.

The court also has to decide on the content of the measure and may impose various conditions, whether or not combined, such as a ban on the use of drugs or alcohol, a notification requirement, a restraining order, an obligation to

[3] See at www.rechtspraak.nl/Voor-advocaten-en-juristen/Reglementen-procedures-en-formulieren/Strafrecht/Paginas/Orientatiepunten-voor-straftoemeting.aspx (last accessed 9 January 2019).

[4] *Staatsblad* 2010, 200. According to Art 43b CC, crimes that are similar are, for instance, all violent crimes ranging from common assault to manslaughter and murder.

[5] Parliamentary Papers 2014/15, 33 816, A.

[6] Art 38z CC. A TBS measure is a safety measure that can only be imposed in the case of offences that carry a sentence of four years or more, a mental disorder that was present at the time of offending and a risk for society due to this disorder (Art 37a CC).

participate in treatment (with or without clinical admission), a restriction on the right to leave the country, a ban on living in certain areas and an obligation to move (for instance, in the case of a sex offender who has been convicted of the sexual abuse of children in his or her neighbourhood). In addition, electronic monitoring may be imposed. These conditions may result in far-reaching restrictions on the liberty of convicted offenders, such as the right to freedom of movement (Article 2, Fourth Protocol to the European Convention on Human Rights (ECHR)) and the right to respect for private life (Article 8 ECHR). Furthermore, the breach of a condition may result in the deprivation of liberty with a maximum duration of six months per (extended) term (Struijk and Mevis 2016).

B. Restrictions Imposed by an Administrative Authority

Increasingly, administrative authorities can impose restrictions on ex-offenders. These restrictions are often referred to as 'collateral consequences of a criminal conviction' (Maruna 2011), 'collateral sentencing consequences' (Demleitner 1999) or 'disqualifications' (Von Hirsch and Wasik 1997). These consequences can be imposed following a criminal penalty, are regulated by administrative law, do not form part of the criminal sentence and are therefore not imposed by a judge in criminal proceedings. Unlike the restrictions mentioned in section II.A, these consequences are often not even mentioned during sentencing. Their rationale is prevention: the protection of society and the maintenance of public order. These consequences may affect convicted offenders in several aspects of their lives.

In the Netherlands, the instrument known as the 'certificate of conduct' is used for criminal background checks. A certificate is needed for the purposes of employment, study, licences, public housing permits, emigration and visas, adoption and specific memberships. In this section, I inventory the consequences that are regulated by the policy on the certificate of conduct. Other collateral consequences, which are not regulated by this policy, such as the consequences for a residence permit (Brouwer 2018) or the sharing of information on the return of offenders convicted of sexual crimes in municipalities with mayors (Boone, Van de Bunt and Siegel 2014), will be left out.

i. Employment/Study

A person convicted of a crime may be precluded from certain types of employment.[7] Unlike other countries in Europe as described in this volume,

[7] See also Art 23, Universal Declaration of Human Rights and Art 6, International Covenant on Economic, Social and Cultural Rights, which both recognise the right to work.

employers in the Netherlands do not have access to the criminal records of employees. Instead, a government agency, called COVOG (*Centraal Orgaan Verklaring Omtrent Gedrag*), can issue a certificate of conduct. This certificate, which is issued on behalf on the Minister for Justice and Security, indicates that the applicant does not have any judicial data relevant to the job in question. A certificate of conduct can also be required for traineeships, and may thus limit (mostly juvenile) ex-offenders in their choice of education (see van 't Zand-Kurtovic, chapter 14 of this volume; van 't Zand-Kurtovic 2017). Young offenders may therefore be seriously hindered on the path to creating a better future for themselves. There is no legal prohibition on hiring someone with a relevant criminal record, but for certain jobs the obligation to produce a certificate of conduct is mandatory. This is the case, for example, for childcare, education, long-term care and the taxi industry. In this way it is ensured that a person without a certificate of conduct cannot be employed in these areas (Buysse, Meijer and Szytniewski 2018).

ii. Licensing

In order to exploit business activities or a taxi company a certificate of conduct is needed. The rationale for this is that the exploitation of business activities may affect the direct environment. According to the policy of the certificate of conduct, these business activities may violate environmental regulations or regulations drawn up to maintain public order. Also, people who manage business activities are responsible for the welfare and safety of people. If these business activities involve selling products, there is the possibility of endangering people and public health in general. And by having access to the goods and funds of the company, there is also a risk of theft, embezzlement or fraud.[8]

iii. Emigration/ Visas

For emigration purposes or regarding applications for a visa (for short stays abroad) a certificate of conduct may be required. This only seems be the case if the country for which the visa is being sought requires a criminal background check. COVOG assesses whether the public order of the country in question would be threatened if the applicant were to be admitted to that country. If a person has been convicted of drug, violent and/or sexual offences, the public order of the receiving country may be endangered and a certificate of conduct can be denied.[9] So far, only three cases have been published in which the applicant

[8] See, for instance, screening profile no 50 at https://www.justis.nl/producten/vog/vog-aanvragen/naar-welke-gegevens-wordt-gekeken/screeningsprofielen.aspx (last accessed 9 January 2019).

[9] According to the screening profile 'Visa and emigration'. See at https://www.justis.nl/binaries/Screeningsprofielen%20met%20ingang%20van%201%20jan%202019_tcm34-371057.pdf (last accessed 9 January 2019).

appealed the denial of the certificate.[10] In all of these cases the Administrative Jurisdiction Division of the Council of State decided that the right to family life as protected by Article 8 ECHR was not infringed, because restrictions on this right are allowed on the basis of the protection of the rights and liberties of others, which is also the rationale of this legislation.

iv. Housing

In the Netherlands, it is standard policy that prison authorities and local authorities should work together with housing associations to provide returning ex-offenders with adequate housing and a stable environment (Association of Dutch Municipalities and Dutch Ministry of Safety & Justice 2015). Most ex-offenders depend on public housing provided by housing associations. Ex-offenders can, however, be excluded from living in certain areas. On the basis of the Inner City Problems (Special Measures) Act, the Minister of Housing, Spatial Planning and the Environment can, if so requested by the local council, designate areas in which persons seeking housing may be subjected to special requirements in order to obtain a housing permit to take up residence in public housing. This Act was introduced to address increasing social problems in particular inner-city areas of Rotterdam,[11] resulting from impoverishment caused by unemployment, poverty and social exclusion.[12] In 2017 the Act was amended and expanded in scope, so that it could also be used to limit nuisance and criminal behaviour.[13] This amendment aims to provide a legal basis for the growing practice of selective housing allocation, by providing municipalities with the power to refuse a housing permit to people with a history of anti-social or criminal behaviour.

Local authorities are entitled to demand a certificate of conduct from prospective tenants. A housing permit can be refused if the applicant cannot obtain such a certificate.[14] In addition, a housing permit can be refused on a screening based on police registers.[15] These registers contain information on allegations, records of arrest, statements of witnesses, cautions, reports of anti-social behaviour or convictions that are relevant for the assessment of whether the applicant presents a threat to the quality of life in a certain neighbourhood

[10] ABRVS 7 May 2014, ECLI:NL:RVS:2014:631, ABRVS 1 June 2016, ECLI:NL:RVS:2016:1535 and ABRVS 12 October 2011, ECLI:NL:RVS:2011:BT7437.

[11] The Act is therefore also called the 'Rotterdam Act', although nowadays it is also applicable to other cities.

[12] Explanatory Memorandum to the Inner City Problems (Special Measures) Act (Parliamentary Documents, Lower House of Parliament, 2004/05, 30091, 3).

[13] Act of 23 August 2016 for the amendment of the Inner City Problems (Special Measures) Act related to the selective housing allocation to limit nuisance and criminal behaviour, *Staatsblad* 2016, 329 ('the Urban Areas Special Measures Act') (in force since 1 January 2017).

[14] Art 5(3)(a), Inner City Problems (Special Measures) Act.

[15] Art 10a, Inner City Problems (Special Measures) Act.

due to prior nuisance and criminal behaviour. Both the applicant and all other persons who want to live at a particular address are screened by the police. During this screening, the authorities may look back for a maximum period of two years if the person is under 18 years of age, or for a maximum period of four years if the person is older than 18. Information about the applicant can be provided from the time that he or she is 14 years old. If the board comprising the mayor and local councillors has reason to suspect, on the basis of these screenings, that the housing of the prospective tenants in their area could lead to an increase in anti-social behaviour or criminal behaviour in the community, the board will, in principle, not issue the housing permit.

This measure constitutes a restriction on the right to freely choose one's residence, as protected by Article 12(1) of the International Covenant on Civil and Political Rights.[16] It also infringes the right to respect for private life, including the right to protection of personal data, providing data to third parties, as protected by Article 10 of the Dutch Constitution and Article 8 ECHR. The importance of adequate housing for a person's well-being is also recognised in Article 25(1) of the Universal Declaration of Human Rights, which holds that housing is an important aspect of the right to an adequate standard of living. Although the right to housing remains an internationally contested legal concept, many international treaties do recognise the right to adequate housing or certain elements of it.

In *Garib v the Netherlands*, the European Court of Human Rights considered the Urban Areas Special Measures Act to restrict the right to freedom of establishment, but found no violation of this human right in the fact that the applicant was denied housing because she could not meet the criterion of a minimum income. However, it remains to be seen if this will also be the case for the denial of housing because of a criminal record. If housing is denied because of a criminal past, this might constitute a problem with the right to rehabilitation.

Criminological literature shows that ex-delinquents who are homeless are likely to reoffend, whereas stable living conditions result in a significant reduction in the risk of recidivism (Metraux and Culhane 2004; Roman and Travis 2006). Research also shows that, in the Netherlands, 47.4 per cent of offenders who were homeless when they first entered detention, remained homeless after detention (Beerthuizen et al 2015: 70).[17] Furthermore, ex-prisoners more often receive a rejection in their search for rented housing (Dirkzwager et al 2015).[18]

[16] See also Art 2 of Protocol No 4 to the ECHR, and Arts 18 and 43 of the Treaty establishing the European Community.

[17] These numbers relate to the year 2012. Compared to 2011, this implies an increase (2011: 43.8 %).

[18] An important limitation of this research is that it did not include social rental housing, but only rental housing in the private sector.

Empirical research on the effects of the requirement for a certificate of conduct for a housing permit does not exist. The exact number of ex-offenders who have been excluded from housing on the basis of the Urban Areas Special Measures Act is unknown due to the lack of data. The lack of case law suggests that the housing of ex-offenders does not cause any legal problems. However, it should be noted that not all cases are published. Furthermore, this Act is aimed at ex-offenders who are already socially marginalised and not in the best position to speak out. Therefore, it might be that the ex-offenders' right to housing is restricted, and may even be violated on a larger scale (Van Tongeren and Vols 2017: 186). According to an interview the present author conducted with the Probation Service in Rotterdam, this Act has not caused any problems for the reintegration of ex-offenders, but it was also common practice for ex-offenders to by-pass this law by not registering, or by registering at another address.

v. Parental Rights

Having a criminal record may also have consequences for adoption. In the adoption process, both parents are required to produce certificates of conduct. According to policy, children are a vulnerable group, and for this reason they must be protected against possible threats, such as the danger of sexual offences. Not being issued a certificate of conduct might infringe the right to marry and found a family (Article 12 ECHR; *X v the Netherlands*).

vi. Membership

Having a criminal record may also prevent someone from becoming a member of a shooting club. This is a small category, because, unlike in, for instance, the United States, owning a gun is the exception in the Netherlands. However, it is mentioned here because, after a shooting incident in a shopping mall in Alphen aan den Rijn in 2011, the rules regarding gun licences and membership of shooting clubs have become much more strict. The certificate of conduct system is used here too. The rationale is prevention: weapons and ammunition pose a potentially serious threat to the security of society if they fall into the hands of people who are not responsible enough to deal with them. Instead of a screening with a retrospective period of four years, a retrospective period of eight years is used to decide whether past behaviour is an objection to membership.[19]

vii. Conclusions

This inventory of possible consequences that are regulated by the certificate of conduct leads to the following conclusions. First of all, in recent years the

[19] See screening profile no 85 at https://www.justis.nl/binaries/Screeningsprofielen%20met%20ingang%20van%201%20jan%202019_tcm34-371057.pdf (last accessed 9 January 2019).

consequences that can be attached to a criminal conviction have expanded in scope. The inventory illustrates that the policies have become more strict, making it easier to refuse a conduct certificate. However, some of these laws constitute a codification of an already existing practice (ie refusing a housing permit on the basis of police information). Furthermore, as has been shown, little empirical research exists on the impact of these restrictions on offenders. This is mainly due to the lack of data. Empirical data on applications for a certificate of conduct only show the number of applications; they do not make any distinction between the purposes for which certificates are requested. In recent years, both the absolute number of applications for a conduct certificate and the absolute number of refusals have expanded enormously. The number of applications rose from 134,417 in 2004 to almost a million in 2016 (see Figure 5.1).[20] Compared to the number of applications, the absolute number of refusals has remained relatively low. This number has, however, risen from 398 in 2004 to 3650 in 2016. The relative number of refusals has also remained relatively low throughout the years: from 0.30% in 2004 to 0.38% in 2016.[21] However, it is unclear whether the rise in applications is due to the fact that more employers request a certificate or whether a certificate is requested for other purposes. A further increase in the number of applications is expected now that the government further encourages the use of this instrument, for example by making the application free of charge for functions involving volunteers.[22]

Table 5.1 Number of certificates of conduct applied for 2006–16

	2006	2007	2008	2009	2010	2011	2012	2013	2014	2015	2016
Applications	279,700	384,724	474,751	459,633	488,631	523,771	563,273	733,156	703,860	862,230	968,300
Refusals	1,772	3,171	2,894	3,315	3,979	3,332	3,189	4,141	2,479	3,030	3,650
Percentage of refusals	0.63	0.82	0.60	0.72	0.81	0.618	0.568	0.56	0.35	0.35	0.4

Source: 2006–09 based on Boone 2010; 2010–16 based on annual reports of Justis/COVOG.

C. Restrictions that Follow Automatically upon Conviction

Before the introduction of the Dutch Criminal Code of 1886, punishments had automatic consequences, or 'degrading punishments' as they were called,

[20] To be exact, 968,300 applications. See the annual reports of Dienst Justis, the division of the Ministry of Justice and Security which the COVOG is a part of. See also *Parliamentary Papers II* 2015/16, 34 300 VI, no 78, p 1. The numbers concern the number of applications, which should not be confused with the number of people who have made an application. A person can apply for a certificate of conduct multiple times.

[21] See annual reports Dienst Justis.

[22] Parliamentary Papers II 2012/13, 33 400 VI, no 116 and Parliamentary Papers II 2015/16, 34 300 VI, no 2.

such as the loss of rights, banishment and forfeiture of property to the state. This so-called 'civil death' or *mort civil* historically accompanied convictions in western European countries. Individuals convicted of serious offences lost almost all political, civil and legal rights, such as the rights to enter into a contract, to marry and to sue. The ex-offender was treated as if he was already dead (Chin 2012; Ryan 1963; Damaska 1968a and 1968b). In north-western European countries, a criminal conviction was often accompanied by banishment and exile. In Amsterdam in the eighteenth century, 97 per cent of all punishments that did not lead to the death of the offender, such as corporal punishment or imprisonment, were followed by some sort of banishment (Spierenburg 1995: 53; de Koster 2018: 71).

During the parliamentary debate on the new Dutch Criminal Code in 1886, it was pointed out that these consequences would hinder the return of the offender to society and would thus promote reoffending. The legislator at the time also regarded these consequences as punishments, because they added to the overall severity of the sentence. According to the legislator, this also meant that the imposition of these additional punishments should be in the hands of the judge during criminal proceedings. By letting the judge decide on the automatic consequences, proportionality between the crime committed and the punishment was pursued. A punishment was considered to be disproportionate if it had automatic consequences. As a result, automatic consequences were abolished, and instead it became possible for the judge in the criminal procedure to impose 'additional sanctions' (Smidt 1891: 157–58). These additional sanctions still exist in the current Criminal Code, such as restrictions on the right to vote or the right to run for election,[23] and the confiscation of objects used to commit the crime and/or that present a danger to society.[24]

However, since 2011, the driving licence of someone who was previously convicted of driving under the influence loses its validity automatically by law under Article 123b of the Road Traffic Act, if at the time of committing a second offence less than five years have passed since a previous irrevocable conviction for the same offence. Since 2017, this Act is also applicable to convictions for driving under the influence of drugs.[25] Not being allowed to drive a motor vehicle for which a driving licence is required can have major consequences for the person involved and his or her private life, for example for a lorry driver who loses his job. Under Article 42a of the regulations for driving licences, a driver

[23] Art 28 CC.
[24] ibid.
[25] According to this law, a driving licence loses its validity automatically by law if the driver is convicted of driving under the influence of alcohol, drugs and/or medication, refusing a breath or blood test, and/or causing a serious traffic accident under the influence of alcohol, drugs and/or medication, or following a refusal to cooperate in a breath or blood test, as referred to in s 6 of the Road Traffic Act.

whose driving licence has become legally invalid may obtain a new licence by re-sitting a theory and practical exam, and by demonstrating his or her (medical) suitability. Because the driving licence loses its validity automatically, it prevents the possibility of an appeal. Offenders are often surprised that their driving licences have become invalid. Prevention is an important aim of this provision, but because people often are not aware of these consequences, the regulations rather miss the point (Hugen 2017).

III. PROPORTIONALITY AS A CONSTRAINT ON THE CONSEQUENCES OF CONVICTION

Assuming that proportionality may serve as a restraining principle on prevention outside the criminal law (Steiker 2015: 194–95), the question arises what limiting function this principle may have on the power of the state to limit the rights of former offenders. In criminal law, proportionality is generally associated with retribution. Consequently, punishment should be proportionate to an offender's just deserts, which is itself the product of the gravity of the offender's crime and the offender's degree of culpability for that crime (Steiker 2015: 195). Normal desert-based constraints, however, do not apply to (preventive) limitations on ex-offenders' rights (Von Hirsch and Wasik 1997: 612). This is why limitations on ex-offenders' rights may focus on risk instead of on the gravity of past criminal choices. Furthermore, a non-desert-based notion of proportionality involves the idea of suitability of means to ends. Therefore, according to Von Hirsch and Wasik, drastic interventions in people's lives ought not to be resorted to in order to achieve relatively unimportant goals. In addition, Steiker argues that instead of focusing on degrees of offence severity and offender culpability, the proportionality inquiry for preventive purposes must focus on the degree of harm sought to be averted, and on the likelihood that the harm would occur in the absence of prevention (Steiker 2015: 196).

As a result, the role of proportionality as a constraint on limiting offenders' rights after their sentence can be threefold. In this way the consequences should be proportionate to the seriousness of the harm to be averted and the probability of its occurrence in the absence of prevention. Proportionality is required between (i) the offence committed and the consequences; (ii) the consequences and the harm to be averted; and (iii) the consequences and the probability of the occurrence of the harm.

In the following subsections, I analyse how the proportionality principle serves (and should serve) as a constraint on the power of the state to restrict a person in his or her work, because this is the area covered in most of the cases. I evaluate Dutch policy and practice with regard to the certificate of conduct in the light of the principle of proportionality. I begin with an outline of the procedure concerning the issuing of this certificate.

A. The Dutch Certificate of Conduct Policy Regulations

Although in the academic literature the Dutch system of certificates of conduct has so far only been described in the context of pre-employment screening (Boone 2011; van 't Zand-Kurtovic 2017; Buysse, Meijer and Szytniewski 2018; Meijer 2015 and 2017), a certificate of conduct can be required for all kinds of purposes, as was outlined in section II.B. The procedure for the issuing of this certificate is as follows. If a person applies for a certificate of conduct, COVOG checks whether the applicant has any relevant judicial data, such as a criminal conviction, registered in the Judicial Documentation System (JDS), the criminal record register.

A retrospective period – the length of time for which the judicial data can be relevant to the assessment to issue a certificate of conduct – applies. In case of sexual offences, no limits apply to this period. In all other cases the retrospective period is limited. In those cases, in principle, a retrospective period of four years applies. However, in some instances, a different period is used. For instance, for functions that demand a high level of integrity (such as police officers) a retrospective period of 10 years applies, and for applicants who are younger than 23 years a shorter period of two years applies (unless they have been convicted of sexual offences – in which case no retrospective period applies – or of violent crimes – for which a penalty of six years or more can be imposed). If judicial data that are relevant to the request are discovered in the retrospective period, COVOG will assess all available data (even if they fall outside of the retrospective period), subject to objective and subjective criteria.

The certificate of conduct is issued if the applicant is not registered in the JDS. If the applicant does appear in this system (meaning that judicial data have been found), the question of whether a certificate of conduct can be issued is assessed using objective and subjective criteria.

The objective criterion implies an assessment 'whether the judicial data found, if repeated, given the risk for society, hinder a proper exercise of the function, task or activity for which the certificate of conduct has been requested'.[26] In other words, a relationship is required between the offence and the task, function or activity for which the certificate of conduct is requested. The risk for society is evaluated in this context, with the aid of a general screening profile and a number of specific screening profiles. The general screening profile focuses on the risk in eight areas, specified in the Policy Framework, in which the applicant may obtain power over (i) information, (ii) money, (iii) goods, (iv) services, (v) commercial relations, (vi) processes, (vii) steering organisations, and/or (viii) individuals. The certificate of conduct mentions which risk areas have been included in the risk assessment. The underlying assumption of this system is that when power is granted to a person who has not dealt honestly with a

[26] Certificate of Conduct Policy Regulations, subsection 3.2.

similar responsibility or any other relevant responsibility in the past, a risk to society may arise. In addition, specific screening profiles exist for certain professions.[27]

If the objective criterion is met (and the certificate of conduct is denied), a certificate of conduct will only be issued where the refusal of this certificate is 'obviously disproportionate': the interests of the individual in the issuance of the certificate of conduct have to be more important than the risk to society determined by the objective criterion.[28]

B. Proportionality between the Offence Committed and the Consequences

The first aspect of the proportionality principle implies that it would not be proportionate if a conviction for a minor offence were to lead to lengthy and onerous collateral consequences, if the risk considerations so indicate. An argument that supports this, according to Von Hirsch and Wasik (1997: 613) is an empirical one, namely, that the best predictor for future crimes tends to be the offender's past behaviour. They argue that if someone is convicted of a lesser crime, there is little reason to expect that he will engage in serious crimes in the future, so that onerous disqualifications are not needed.

In the Netherlands, the decision of whether or not to issue a conduct certificate is based on judicial data. According to current policy, this implies that a certificate of conduct can be denied on the basis of a criminal conviction by a court, but also on the basis of other judicial data, for instance a *strafbeschikking* (a punishment for minor offences imposed by the public prosecutor),[29] a transaction (a settlement in which the prosecutor waives prosecution if the suspect pays a fine) and a decision by the public prosecutor to dismiss the case because of prosecutorial policy.[30] Furthermore, it is not required that the conviction is irrevocable.

Despite the fact that they usually concern minor offences, these possibilities for dealing with a criminal case can result in limiting an offender's rights for

[27] For instance for politicians (01), police officers (25), lawyers, civil law notaries, bailiffs or legal advisors (55), taxi drivers (65), (family) guardians at a guardian institution, probation officers, and social workers (75), court interpreters and translators (80), for those working in health care (45), education (60) or financial services (95), in order to obtain a permit to run a business (50), more specifically a taxi business (70), or purposes other than employment, such as visas and emigration (06), being a host or foster family and adoption (40), and membership of a shooting club (85). In total there are 96 specific screening profiles. The numbers refer to the specific screening profile as mentioned in the policy. The policy can be found at https://www.justis.nl/binaries/Screeningsprofielen%20met%20ingang%20van%201%20jan%202019_tcm34-371057.pdf (last accessed 9 January 2019). Surprisingly, not all screening profiles have been published.

[28] Certificate of Conduct Policy Regulations, subsection 3.3.

[29] Art 257a Criminal Procedure Code.

[30] For instance, the Dutch policy not to prosecute minor drug offences, such as the possession of small amounts of cannabis.

substantial periods of time.[31] With regard to the retrospective period, no distinction is made between different kinds of judicial data. In principle, a retrospective period of four years is applicable whether there is conviction by a judge for a grave offence or a transaction for a minor offence. In this way, minor offences can lead to (relatively) lengthy periods during which an offender's rights may be limited.

The Netherlands differs in this regard from Germany, Belgium and Luxembourg. First of all, in those countries, extracts from the criminal register contain only *irrevocable* convictions; minor convictions, such as convictions resulting in community service orders, suspended sentences, low-level fines and even prison sentences of up to two years (Herzog-Evans (chapter 11, this volume; Morgenstern, chapter 4, this volume) are – depending on the type of extract – not mentioned (Buysse, Meijer and Szyzniewsky 2018). Therefore, these minor convictions do not play a role in the decision of employers whether to hire an employee. It is important to note that this does not necessarily mean that in the Netherlands a certificate of conduct is often refused on the basis of judicial data other than irrevocable convictions; the percentage of refusals in Table 5.1 give no indication of this. However, exact data on this point are missing: decisions of the COVOG are not published as standard. Therefore, only cases that make it to the highest administrative court provide some insight. According to these cases, a refusal on the basis of, for instance, a *strafbeschikking*[32] is quite common.

A certificate of conduct can be denied in cases where the culpability of the person concerned has not yet been determined by a criminal judge. Recently, the Secretary of Justice and Security submitted a bill that should make it possible to deny a certificate of conduct on the basis of police data for functions that require a high degree of integrity, such as functions within the prison system, the police or the public prosecution service.[33] The use of these registers is problematic, because no legal remedy exists against including this information in these registers. In addition, the Secretary of Justice and Security is currently investigating whether it is possible to deny a certificate of conduct on the basis of administratives. It is clear that the threshold to deny a certificate of conduct is lowered time and again.

With regard to this particular aspect of the proportionality principle, another aspect of the above-mentioned policy is problematic. A conviction for minor offences should not lead to lengthy and onerous collateral consequences if the risk considerations so indicate, but does that also imply that a conviction for a grave offence may lead to lengthy and onerous consequences? Should, for

[31] Paras 3.1.2 and 3.2.5 VOG-NP-RP 2013.

[32] See, eg, ABRVS 11 March 2015, ECLI:NL:RVS:2015:719. In this case, a certificate of conduct was denied for obtaining a licence to drive a taxi, because on the criminal record of the applicant there were three transactions for speeding and a dismissal for common assault because this was partly the fault of the victim.

[33] See www.internetconsultatie.nl/vogpolitiegegevens/details (last accessed 9 January 2019) and Parliamentary documents 34 300 VI, no 78.

instance, a conviction for sexual offences lead to life-long consequences? Is it proportionate that in case of sexual offences, no retrospective period applies? This also means that those convicted of these offences can never be legally rehabilitated.

C. Proportionality between the Consequences and the Harm to be Averted

Proportionality is also required between the consequences of a criminal conviction and the seriousness of the harm to be averted. It would be disproportionate if (far-reaching) consequences were to be linked to a criminal conviction in order to avoid the risk of minor offences. Furthermore, it should be noted that a risk of recidivism can never be excluded, nor the probability that someone may commit an offence in the context of his or her job.

With regard to this aspect of the proportionality principle, it can be noted that the general screening profiles tend to be over-inclusive. For example, if a person who has been convicted of theft applies for a job as a supermarket manager, an assessment has to be made whether the offence, if repeated, given the risk to society, would hinder the proper exercise of the function of supermarket manager. This assessment is made on the basis of the risk area 'money', because a supermarket manager will have access to money, which poses a risk of theft. But the assessment will also be made on the basis of the risk area of 'steering organisations', because a (supermarket) manager will have power over persons, and given this position, there is a risk of abuse of such power. In both risk areas, theft is explicitly mentioned as a risk. Most likely, a certificate of conduct will be denied in this case.

D. Proportionality between the Limitations and the Probability of the Occurrence of the Harm

Proportionality is required between the collateral consequences and the likelihood that the harm would occur in the absence of these consequences. This third aspect raises questions about how the risk of recidivism is assessed. According to Steiker (2015: 204), a robust proportionality constraint requires that the calculation of the likelihood of future harm should be an individual one, rather than a conclusive presumption based on categories defined in policy.

According to the objective criterion, it must be assessed 'whether the judicial data found, *if repeated*, given the risk for society, hinders a proper exercise of the function, task or activity for which the certificate of conduct has been requested'. The wording of this criterion implies that it is not relevant whether there is an actual risk of recidivism. As already outlined, this risk assessment is made on the basis of a general screening profile and a number of specific screening profiles. Whether or not there is an actual risk of repetition of the crime is not taken into consideration in this objective evaluation. If a risk (such as the risk of theft) is mentioned in the screening profile, the certificate of conduct will be denied. An exception can only be made on the grounds that the personal circumstances of the applicant result in a refusal of the certificate that is 'obviously disproportionate' (the subjective criterion). In other words, the risk assessment with regard to the objective criterion is not individualised but group-based. It only has to be assessed what the effects would be in the event of repetition of the crime.[34]

The risk of recidivism does seem to become more and more important in the evaluation of the objective criterion. Recently, a new Act made it possible for the probation service to provide information on the risk of recidivism to COVOG at the request of the former offender. This leaves more room to make a risk assessment on the basis of current and individual identified risks. In practice, however, this assessment is only made if requested by the applicant for the certificate of conduct or his or her lawyer.

A problem with this particular aspect of proportionality is that of low-risk/high-harm offenders (Steiker 2015: 207). In some cases a certificate of conduct is denied because the risk for society is deemed too large, even though the chance of recidivism is considered low. This is particularly the case with sexual offenders. The following case illustrates this.

In this case, a teacher was denied a certificate of conduct because he had been convicted of sexual assault.[35] This assault took place after the applicant, following the death of his mother, sought support from her best friend. The offence was therefore committed while the applicant was under great emotional stress. It was not expected that these same circumstances would occur again in situations where students under emotional stress would turn to the applicant for emotional support, because these emotional situations did not relate to him personally. Furthermore, the sexual offence was committed against an elderly woman, while the applicant's students were aged 16 to 40 years. In refusing the certificate of conduct, the Secretary of Justice and Security stated that even if the chance of recidivism is considered low, this does not mean that the risk for society is acceptable, since the impact of sexual offences is too great. According to the Administrative Jurisdiction Division of the Council of State, the denial of the certificate of conduct essentially implies that in the case of an adult who commits sexual offences, regardless of the nature of these offences, the circumstances of the case are not relevant for the assessment of the risk to society and whether the refusal of a certificate of conduct is disproportionate. Such a view is not compatible with subsection 3.3.2 of the above-mentioned policy stating that, in the case of sexual offences, whether the refusal of the certificate of conduct is disproportionate is assessed on the basis of the circumstances of the case. The mere fact that it cannot be excluded that the applicant will abuse his

[34] ABRVS 4 February 2015, ECLI:NL:RVS:2015:299.
[35] ABRVS 12 February 2014, ECLI:NL:RVS:2014:382.

position of authority does not justify the conclusion that the risk for society is not acceptable and that the refusal of the certificate of conduct is not evidently disproportionate. Therefore, the Secretary of Justice and Security wrongly did not take into account the circumstances of the case.

IV. CONCLUSION

I have argued that there are limits to the power of the state to restrict convicted offenders. One of these limits can be found the principle of proportionality. I have evaluated the Dutch policy and practice with regard to the certificate of conduct in the light of the principle of proportionality. Often, the Dutch system is mentioned as an example of how a screening system should be. It is true that this system has a lot of advantages, most important of which is the protection of privacy, because employers and others do not have direct access to (an extract from) the criminal record of the person involved. However, this system also has disadvantages, as shown in this chapter. In the Netherlands, for example, unlike in countries such as Germany, Belgium and Luxembourg, judicial data other than irrevocable convictions can be taken into account when assessing whether a certificate can be issued. Also, with regard to sexual offenders a life-long retrospective period applies, which means that these offenders can, in principle, never be legally rehabilitated. The Netherlands differs in this regard from other countries such as Germany, Belgium, Luxembourg and France, where expunging periods apply that are limited in time.

REFERENCES

Ashworth, A, Zedner, L and Tomlin, P (2013) 'Introduction' in A Ashworth, L Zedner and P Tomlin (eds), *Prevention and the Limits of the Criminal Law* (Oxford, Oxford University Press).

Association of Dutch Municipalities and Dutch Ministry of Safety & Justice (2015) *Richting aan re-integratie. Convenant re-integratie van ex-gedetineerden*, available at www.dji.nl/binaries/convenant-re-integratie-van-(ex-)-gedetineerden_tcm41-128006.pdf (last accessed 1 August 2018).

Beerthuizen, MGCJ, Beijersbergen, KA, Noordhuizen, S and Weijters, G (2015) *Vierde meting van de monitor nazorg ex-gedetineerden* (The Hague, WODC).

Boone, MM, Jacobs, P and Lindeman, J (2017), *DETOUR Towards Pre-Trial Detention As Ultima Ratio. 2nd Dutch National Report on Expert Interviews* (Utrecht, Utrecht University/Montaigne Centre).

Boone, MM, Van de Bunt, HG and Siegel, D (2014), *Gevangene van het verleden. Crisissituaties na terugkeer van zedendelinquenten in de samenleving* (Politie & Wetenschap, Apeldoorn; Universiteit Utrecht, Erasmus Universiteit Rotterdam).

Brouwer, J (2018) 'Crimmigratie en het uitzetten van strafrechtelijk veroordeelde vreemdelingen' *Justitiële verkenningen*, 44(2), 86–98.

Buysse, W, Meijer, S and Szytniewski, B (2018), *Pre-employment screening in de grensregio's van de Benelux and Germany* (The Hague, WODC).
Chin, G (2012) 'The New Civil Death: Rethinking Punishment in the Era of Mass Conviction' *University of Pennsylvania Law Review*, 160, 1790–833.
Crijns, JH, Leeuw, BJG, and Wermink, HT (2016) *Pre-trial detention in the Netherlands: legal principles versus practical reality* (The Hague, Eleven International Publishing).
Damaska, MR (1968a) 'Adverse Legal Consequences of Conviction and Their Removal: A Comparative Study' *The Journal of Criminal Law, Criminology, and Police Science*, 59, 347–60.
—— (1968b) 'Adverse Legal Consequences of Conviction and Their Removal: A Comparative Study (Part 2)' *The Journal of Criminal Law, Criminology, and Police Science*, 59, 542–68.
Demleitner, NV (1999) 'Preventing Internal Exile: The Need for Restrictions on Collateral Sentencing Consequences' *Stanford Law and Policy Review*, 11, 153–71.
Dirkzwager, A, Blokland, A, Nannes, K and Vroonland, M (2015) 'Effecten van detentie op het vinden van werk en een woning. Twee veldexperimenten' *Tijdschrift voor criminologie* 57(1), 5–30.
Garland, D (2001) *The Culture of Control* (Oxford, Oxford University Press).
Goffman (1963) *Stigma: Notes on the Management of Spoiled Identity* (London, Penguin).
Hugen, S (2017) 'De (uitbreiding) recidiveregeling ernstige verkeersdelicten' *Strafblad* 2017, 3.
Koster, M de (2018) 'Verbanning en uitzetting in Noordwest-Europa sinds de vroegmoderne periode' *Justitiële Verkenningen*, 18, 70–85.
Maruna, S (2011) 'Judicial rehabilitation and the "Clean Bill of Health" in Criminal Justice' *European Journal of Probation* 3(1), 97–117.
Meijer, S (2013) 'De gedragsbeïnvloedende en vrijheidsbeperkende maatregel' in M Groenhuijsen, T Kooijmans and J Ouwerkerk (eds), *Roosachtig strafrecht* (Deventer, Kluwer) 385–99.
—— (2015) 'De Verklaring Omtrent Gedrag: enkele kanttekeningen bij recente rechtspraak' 4(32) *Delikt & Delinkwent*, 323–34.
—— (2017) 'De invloed van de strafrechter op de bijkomende gevolgen van de straf' *Delikt & Delinkwent* 3(16), 158–69.
Metraux, S and Culhane, DP (2004) 'Homeless shelter use and reincarceration after prison release' *Journal of Criminology & Public Policy*, 3(2), 201–22.
Roman, CG and Travis, J (2006) 'Where will I sleep tomorrow? Housing, homelessness, and the returning prisoner' *Housing Policy Debate*, 17(2), 389–418.
Ryan, HRS (1963) 'Loss of Civil and Political Rights on Conviction of a Criminal Offence' *Criminal Law Quarterly*, 5, 470–96.
Smidt (1891) *Geschiedenis van het Wetboek van Strafrecht, eerste deel* (Haarlem, HD Tjeenk Willink).
Spierenburg, P (1995) 'The body and the state: early modern Europe' in N Morris and DJ Rothman (eds), *The Oxford History of the Prison* (New York, Oxford University Press) 49–77.
Steiker, CS (2015) 'Proportionality as a Limit on Preventive Justice. Promises and Pitfalls' in A Ashworth, L Zedner and P Tomlin (eds), *Prevention and the Limits of Criminal Law* (Oxford, Oxford University Press).

Struijk, S (2012) 'De toepassing van de algemene recidiveregeling in het strafrecht' *Delikt & Delinkwent*, 10(89), 966–82.
Struijk, S and Mevis, P (2016) 'Legal Constraints on the Indeterminate Control of "Dangerous" Sex Offenders in the Community: the Dutch Perspective' *Erasmus Law Review*, 2, 95–108.
Van Tongeren, S and Vols, M (2017) 'The right to housing and the right to a second chance. how Dutch landlords and local authorities facilitate and frustrate the successful re-integration of ex-offenders' in M Vols and J Sidoli (eds), *People and Buildings: Comparative Housing Law* (The Hague, Eleven International Publishing) 171–90.
Von Hirsch, A and Wasik, M (1997) 'Civil Disqualifications Attending Conviction: A Suggested Conceptual Framework' *The Cambridge Law Journal*, 56, 599–626.
van 't Zand-Kurtovic (2017) *Invisible bars. The impact of having a criminal record on young adults' position in the labour market* (The Hague, Eleven International Publishing).
Wolf, M (2016) 'Legal Control on Social Control of Sex Offenders in the Community: A European Comparative and Human Rights Perspective' *Erasmus Law Review*, 2, 39–54.

TABLE OF CASES

European Court of Human Rights

Garib v the Netherlands App no 43494/09 (6 November 2017)

European Commission of Human Rights

X v the Netherlands no 8896/80 (10 March 1981)

6

The Detrimental Legal Consequences of a Conviction in Hungary

KRISZTINA LUKÁCS AND DÁVID VIG

I. INTRODUCTION

THE FORMAL CONSEQUENCES attached to a conviction in Hungary range from the consequences attached to recidivism in criminal law to restrictions on employment or voting rights. In the present chapter we analyse those consequences that consist of criminal law restrictions, and those that fall outside of the scope of the criminal law yet are attached to a criminal conviction. All of these consequences are, however, detrimental to the legal situations of convicted offenders and, as we demonstrate, may significantly hinder social reintegration.

In Hungary the public or professional criminological or legal discussion on the consequences of a conviction is very limited. Despite some empirical research in the non-governmental civil society sector and policy-oriented research, there is a paucity of recent empirical academic research in this field. In this chapter, we outline the concepts of reintegration, rehabilitation and resettlement in the Hungarian legal and criminological discourse, and argue that detrimental legal consequences have an impact on the social rehabilitation and resettlement of convicted persons. We describe in detail the Hungarian system of legal rehabilitation, which occurs through the so-called 'exemption' – the formal point after which the detrimental legal consequences of the conviction shall disappear. We also provide an in-depth analysis of how the Constitutional Court of Hungary deals with detrimental consequences with regard to human dignity.

We further argue that it is not the criminal recording system itself that attaches any detrimental consequences to the data stored but rather sectorial laws that, for example, limit employment, and employers' practice of requesting criminal records. Furthermore, we look into how certain political rights (including the right to vote) are affected by collateral consequences. The deprivation of political rights may be less relevant for social rehabilitation and the resettlement process, yet its symbolic nature gives a clear message to convicted individuals and society on prolonged exclusion from the community.

II. REINTEGRATION, REHABILITATION, RESETTLEMENT

In Hungary, scholars and practitioners use four terms to describe the processes around an inmate's release: resettlement; rehabilitation; resocialisation; and reintegration. The differences between these terms are often not emphasised, either in the academic literature or in policy or practice, and the use of these terms is not consistent, even though they describe distinct legal, psychological and penological concepts.

From a legal point of view, in the Hungarian context, *rehabilitation* is the point at which the detrimental legal consequences attached by law to a conviction are removed by law, by a court or by an act of clemency, and the convicted person is relieved from these consequences.[1] Once this so-called legal rehabilitation happens, the person is cleared by exemption and shall be deemed to have a clean criminal record; unless otherwise provided for by law, he or she cannot be required to give an account of any conviction from which he or she has been exempted.[2] Unlike expungement, which is often used in common law legal systems, the offender does not have to file a lawsuit, as exemption happens if a certain time has passed. As opposed to pardons or clemency, the exemption is not a discretionary decision of the President or of the executive power. The time of statutory exemption differs according to the severity of the convicted person's punishment. In cases of imprisonment, the length of the sentence and the intent of the offender are also taken into account.[3] In practice, these provisions mean that if the convicted person was imprisoned for a period of between one and five years for an intentional offence, exemption happens by law after a period of five years following the last day the term of imprisonment was served.

The concept of *resocialisation* has not been fully developed in constitutional law or prison law, as no legal regulations mention it explicitly. Nevertheless, the Constitutional Court has started to develop the concept of a 'claim to resocialisation'. This is not seen as a constitutional right, however. None the less, a claim to resocialisation emerged from a 2008 decision of the Constitutional Court.[4] This decision mentioned the existence of this claim, the benefits of which are acknowledged by society. The Constitutional Court connected the claim to the right to self-determination and the right to privacy, which derive from the right

[1] Arts 98 and 99 Act C of 2012 on the Criminal Code.
[2] Art 98(2) Criminal Code.
[3] Art 100 of the Criminal Code.
[4] Decision 144/2008. (XI. 26.) AB of the Constitutional Court, ABH 2008, 1107.

to human dignity as guaranteed by the previous Constitution of Hungary.[5] This was a welcome step that built on previous decisions around the acknowledgement of the concept of resocialisation, which claimed that the restriction of rights needs to be limited to what is absolutely necessary for the protection of society.[6]

The Hungarian Criminal Enforcement Code (CEC)[7] uses the terms *reintegration and (re)settlement*. The Code demonstrates a conceptual shift from previous legislation in two respects. First, it mentions 'resettlement' as opposed to the previous term 'settlement'.[8] Resettlement is one of the purposes of the enforcement of criminal sanctions, along with retribution (the enforcement of the negative consequences outlined in the judgment). In our view, retribution remains the primary aim of the CEC, while resettlement is a secondary aim. This is because the CEC prescribes the enforcement of negative consequences as an imperative aim, whereas it merely mentions the aim of fostering resettlement and does not prescribe resettlement as an aim that is to be achieved in all circumstances.[9] Nevertheless, the CEC mentions reintegrative activities or reintegrative programmes.[10] In relation to imprisonment, these programmes aim to foster prisoners' integration into the job market, to reduce the disadvantages that resulted from their lifestyles and life circumstances prior to incarceration, as well as to develop their personalities and social competencies.[11]

The concept of rehabilitation also has a distinctive meaning in the Hungarian context. Following the crisis of the correctionalist ideology of Western welfare states at the end of the 1970s, Hungary decided to follow a rights-respecting approach to law enforcement after the regime change of 1989/90. As a result of this, a consensus emerged that mandatory treatment programmes with the ambition of rehabilitation were endangering the principle of the rule of law. During the two decades that followed, scholars such as Ruzsonyi and Miklósi worked on the concept of criminal pedagogy or criminal andragogy, which emphasised the need for educational programmes in prisons (Ruzsonyi 2014). More recently, Szabó attempted to revive and reintroduce the concept of rehabilitation (Szabó 2014). Szabó's post-correctionalist approach argues from a psychological perspective that programmes of rehabilitation should aim to achieve more than merely maintaining inmates' mental and physical well-being, as they have the potential to affect factors that contribute to desistance. From a penological perspective, Fliegauf conceptualised the differences between the three concepts of rehabilitation, resocialisation and reintegration

[5] Act XX of 1949.

[6] Decision 13/2001. (V. 14.) AB of the Constitutional Court, ABH 2001, 177, 194; and Decision 569/B/1999. AB of the Consitutional Court, ABH 2002, 1015, 1019.

[7] Act CCXL of 2013 on the Criminal Enforcement Code.

[8] Law-decree 11 of 1979.

[9] Art 83(1) Act CCXL of 2013.

[10] Arts 2, 82 and 83 Act CCXL of 2013.

[11] Art 82(5) Act CCXL of 2013.

(Vig and Fliegauf 2016). Fliegauf stated that even though the aims of the three are similar, the objectives and the methods of it are distinct: resocialisation uses educational programmes and vocational training; reintegration uses administration and probational support; and rehabilitation uses treatment programmes, and health and mental health treatment (Vig and Fliegauf 2016).

III. THE DETRIMENTAL LEGAL CONSEQUENCES OF A CONVICTION

A. The Legal Consequences of a Conviction

The detrimental legal consequences of a conviction are multifaceted and affect many aspects of life. Their impact begins at the moment of the conviction and continues while the offender serves his or her sentence. They can also continue after the sentence has been served, depending on its form and severity. These negative legal consequences may be divided into two groups. The first group includes criminal law restrictions (penal consequences), while the second group rather consists of such detrimental legal consequences as apply beyond the scope of criminal law (non-penal consequences).

As far as the first group is concerned, that is the criminal law (penal) restrictions, reoffending after a conviction may lead to a person's being classified as a recidivist, or it may be regarded as an aggravating circumstance for sentencing purposes. The respective rules are included in the Hungarian Criminal Code.[12]

A perpetrator may be classified as a recidivist only if he or she commits an intentional criminal offence after having been previously sentenced to immediate imprisonment for committing another intentional criminal offence. Primarily, it is the General Part of the Criminal Code that prescribes graver legal consequences with regard to recidivists (for example, the rules pertaining to conditional release are stricter in their case)[13].

A perpetrator qualifies as a simple repeat offender instead of a recidivist if:

(a) he or she committed the recent or the previous criminal offence negligently; or
(b) he or she was not sentenced to immediate imprisonment for committing a previous criminal offence; or
(c) he or she was sentenced to immediate imprisonment for committing an intentional criminal offence and more than three years have passed between

[12] Act C of 2012 on the Criminal Code.

[13] According to Art 38 Criminal Code, if conditional release is not excluded, the earliest possible date of a conditional release is the day after two-thirds of the sentence has been served; but in the case of a recidivist, the day after three-quarters of the sentence has been served. If the sentence imposed is not more than five years of imprisonment, the court may rule in its judgment that the convicted person may be subject to conditional release after half of the sentence has been served. This provision shall not be applied if a convicted person is a multiple recidivist. Multiple recidivists, provided that their imprisonment has to be served under a high security regime, and multiple violent recidivists shall not be subject to conditional release.

the time the prison sentence was served or had ceased to be executable and the perpetrator's committing another criminal offence. In the case of reoffending, the perpetrator's previous conviction may be considered an aggravating circumstance by the court.[14]

The detrimental legal consequences that apply beyond the scope of criminal law (the second group) are regulated in other sectoral laws. Such consequences emerge in a broad range of areas, for example in constitutional law, state administration law, labour law (eg having a clean criminal record is a precondition for being employed by public education institutions), civil law (eg only a person with a clean criminal record may act as a professional guardian) and financial law (eg if someone has not been excused from the detrimental legal consequences of a conviction, he or she shall not act as a tenderer in a public procurement procedure). Regarding their content, legal consequences may be linked to having a certain job, occupying a certain official position and losing certain existing privileges.

The criminal record of the defendant is established by the conviction; penal and non-penal restrictions alike affect the perpetrator from the moment of the conviction. Pursuant to the Criminal Code,[15] detrimental legal consequences relating to establishing criminal liability, sentencing or applying a measure shall be prescribed by an Act of Parliament.

There is a crucial question of for how long these disadvantages can have an effect on the legal relationships of the ex-offender. The Criminal Code sets out in this context that data pertaining to establishing criminal liability, the sentence imposed and the measure applied shall be included in an official public register. These data remain on the register until such time as prescribed by a separate law. According to the Criminal Code,[16] no detrimental legal consequences shall be established regarding the ex-offender after the data pertaining to his or her sentence and the measures applied against him or her have been deleted from the official public register. When the data are deleted, the individual shall be exempted from the detrimental legal consequences of the conviction. As a rule, legal restrictions apply up to the point of being granted *exemption*.

B. Exemption – Relief from the Detrimental Consequences of the Conviction

i. The Content and Rationale behind the Exemption

One of the aims of a penal sentence is to prevent another criminal offence from being committed, either by the perpetrator in question or by anyone else, in order to protect society.[17] With a view to achieving this preventive aim, the

[14] Chamber Opinion 56. BK.
[15] Art 97(1) Criminal Code.
[16] Art 97(2) Criminal Code.
[17] Art 79 Criminal Code.

social integration of the convicted person should be supported not only when imposing and when executing the sentence, but also after the sentence has been served. Accordingly, there is a need for a legal institution that makes it possible for an ex-offender, after serving his or her sentence, to reach the same legal situation he or she was in before conviction. Exemption, understood as relief from the detrimental consequences of the conviction, is considered such a legal institution in Hungary. It exempts the offender from the detrimental legal (penal and non-penal) consequences of a conviction. It is based on the presumption that after a certain amount of time the sentence imposed has fulfilled its aim and the individual is reintegrated into society. In order to allow the ex-offender to become a full member of society, the state frees the ex-offender from the burden of the legal restrictions linked to the conviction by releasing him or her from them.

Exemption is one of the legal institutions in the criminal justice system that protects the individual from the excesses of the state:

> From the point of view of constitutionality, this also means that once [rehabilitated], no general measures shall be resorted to [regarding the perpetrator] within the framework of the legal system which, without any regard to the actual criminality of the perpetrator, … amount to an additional fundamental rights restriction linked to establishing criminal liability, with an effect also beyond criminal law.[18]

Accordingly, exemption means the final realm of applying legal restrictions linked to establishing criminal liability. 'Criminal offender' status terminates with the exemption in accordance with the provisions of the Criminal Code, so – as a general consequence – the individual's status can no longer be accompanied by fundamental rights restrictions with the same content as those linked to the status of an offender.[19]

According to the case law of the Constitutional Court, the source of exemption is the fundamental right to human dignity. In the view of the Constitutional Court, it follows from the right to human dignity that the possibility of rehabilitation shall be guaranteed to convicted persons, such that they shall be provided with the possibility of leading their lives without breaking the law within the terms of a free society. This is in the interests not only of the defendant, but also of society, since the new possibilities to occupy positions and take up jobs available to those with clean criminal records, which open up through the termination of restraints applying beyond the scope of criminal law, enhance (the defendant's) chances of employment, which, in turn, decreases the cost of social care, and makes it possible for the ex-offender to avoid reoffending.[20]

[18] Decision 144/2008. (XI. 26.) AB of the Constitutional Court, ABH 2008, 1107, 1156; Decision 8/2015. (IV. 17.) AB of the Constitutional Court, Reasoning [28].

[19] Decision 144/2008. (XI. 26.) AB of the Constitutional Court, ABH 2008, 1107, 1156–1157; see also Decision 20/2013 (VII. 19.) AB of the Constitutional Court, Reasoning [35].

[20] Decision 144/2008. (XI. 26.) AB of the Constitutional Court, ABH 2008, 1107, 1132; Decision 8/2015. (IV. 17.) AB of the Constitutional Court, Reasoning [29].

ii. The Scope of Exemption

According to the Criminal Code,[21] exemption results in the ex-offender's being relieved of the detrimental legal consequences of the conviction, so he or she qualifies as a person with a clean criminal record and is no longer obliged to give an account of the conviction.

In theory, the scope of exemption is general, but in practice it only covers non-penal consequences. Namely, when someone commits another criminal offence, the perpetrator's exemption does not exclude the application of the legal consequences (eg classifying the perpetrator as a recidivist) linked by criminal law provisions to an earlier conviction (penal consequences). The reasoning behind this is that reoffending rebuts the presumption that the punishment has reached its goal, the latter being the theoretical basis for exemption.

In the case of non-penal consequences, the possibility of acquiring and exercising the rights to which citizens with clean criminal records are entitled opens up again for the person affected. Accordingly, the exempted person is granted a clean criminal record for the future. The clean criminal record is certified by an official certificate issued to the exempted person.

iii. Exemption Methods

According to the Hungarian Criminal Code, there are three different ways of granting exemption. An ex-offender may be exempted: (i) by law (an Act of Parliament, thus the Criminal Code) after a certain period of time has passed; (ii) by a court decision; or (iii) by pardon.

Exemption by law is the general method of exemption, affecting the widest range of convicted offenders, which takes effect without the act of any public authority, by the force of law, once a certain period of time has passed after the punishment has become final or has been served. The necessary length of time and how it is calculated essentially depend on the type and content of the sanction imposed.[22] The exact timing of exemption by law taking effect in the case of the various forms of punishments is established by the Criminal Code.[23]

Exemption by a court may be granted upon request, on the basis of a court decision reached in a special procedure. The rules of the respective court

[21] Art 98 Criminal Code.

[22] Accordingly, the exemption may take effect the day the judgment becomes final, the day a period of probation ends, the day the punishment has been fully served or its execution is terminated, or the day the punishment ceases to be executable, after three, five, eight or 10 years have passed after the punishment has been served in full or the punishment had ceased to be executable.

[23] Art 100 Criminal Code, for example: in the case of confinement, fine and community work, the day the judgment becomes final; in the case of a suspended imprisonment, on the last day of the probation period; in the case of imprisonment for not more than one year, imposed due to an intentional criminal offence, three years after the prison sentence has been served or has ceased to be executable; in the case of fixed-term imprisonment of more than 10 years, imposed for an intentional criminal offence, 10 years after the prison sentence has been served or has ceased to be executable.

procedure are included in the Code of Criminal Procedure. Exemption by a court is of two types: subsequent exemption and preliminary exemption.

In the case of imprisonment, the court may exempt the ex-offender at the latter's request after half of the waiting time determined by the relevant Act of Parliament has passed, provided that the ex-offender is worthy of it. This type of exemption is called 'subsequent exemption' since it may be employed after the punishment has become final, so subsequent to that. When deciding on worthiness, the court has to take into account the way of life led by the ex-offender since he or she finished serving his or her sentence, or, in the case of suspended imprisonment, since the judgment became final. The notion and the content of worthiness are not defined by the Criminal Code, and only the reasoning of the Criminal Code provides some guidance with regard to its substance. According to this guidance, when examining the perpetrator's worthiness in the case of a subsequent exemption, the following circumstances are relevant: the perpetrator's lifestyle and his or her conduct after serving the sentence; and, furthermore, the reparation of the harm caused by the act in question. In the case of suspended imprisonment, any subsequent exemption becomes void if execution of the suspended imprisonment is ordered.

The Criminal Code also provides the possibility for the court to impose a sanction in the judgment and to exempt the ex-offender at the same time. In these cases exemption is granted prior to the execution of the sentence ('preliminary exemption'). This is possible if the execution of the sentence of imprisonment is suspended by the judgment, provided that the ex-offender is worthy of it. The circumstances to be examined when deliberating on the convicted person's worthiness in the case of a preliminary exemption differ from those to be assessed in the case of a subsequent exemption, since in the case of a preliminary exemption the court has to reach a decision on the exemption at the same time as reaching a judgment. Accordingly, the following factors bear significance in particular in this regard: the gravity of the criminal offence; the level of culpability; the perpetrator's personality, lifestyle, and his or her conduct between committing the criminal offence and the conviction; reparation of the harm caused by the act in question; and the partial fault of the victim. Furthermore, any preliminary exemption also becomes void if the execution of the suspended sentence is ordered.

The Constitutional Court reviewed the constitutionality of the rules governing preliminary exemptions in Decision 8/2015. (IV. 17.) AB. There, the Constitutional Court explained that exemption by law marks the final point up to which detrimental legal consequences may apply. By comparison, both types of exemption by a court amount to an allowance, since they make exemption possible before the time required by the law for exemption has passed. Subsequent exemption by court is possible after the punishment has been served or has ceased to be executable. Based on this allowance, the ex-offender does not have to wait until the date of exemption as enshrined in the respective Act of Parliament, but instead may be exempted – if worthy of it – after half the waiting time prescribed by the corresponding Act of Parliament has passed. By contrast, preliminary exemption precludes the detrimental consequences from entering into force, thus the ex-offender is exempted the day the judgment becomes final. By law, the allowance provided by exemption by court is available to different groups of convicted offenders under different rules. The law provides for subsequent exemption exclusively for those sentenced to a fixed-term, immediate imprisonment for committing an intentional criminal offence, while preliminary exemption may be applied when the execution of the sentence imposed for either an intentional or a negligent criminal offence was suspended by the court.[24]

When reviewing the rules of preliminary exemption by courts, the Constitutional Court identified several uncertainties in practice that gave rise to constitutional problems. The exact procedural rules relating to the application of the allowance had not been established by law, neither by the Criminal Code nor by the Code of Criminal Procedure. Some procedural rules had been developed by judicial practice, but there were uncertainties around their application in practice. The only thing that followed from the text of the law in this regard was that the decision on a preliminary exemption should be reached by the court deciding on criminal liability, and that the exemption decision should be reached at the same time as reaching the judgment, so the question cannot be decided after the judgment has been delivered.[25] According to the conclusion of the Constitutional Court, it was not possible to determine on the basis of the Criminal Code's respective provisions who was entitled to initiate a decision of preliminary exemption in the interests of the defendant. Similarly, the legal rules did not contain any guidance as to when the relevant claim could be enforced. This gave rise to a particular hardship in practice, because the imposition of a suspended sentence was one of the preconditions for applying the allowance, but this would only become known to the participants in the procedure, including the defendant, once the judgment was delivered. However, the court had to rule on the preliminary exemption in the same judgment. Thus, it was not clear from what point and, in particular, until what point the claim for exemption could be raised before the court by any participant in the procedure. In addition, the detailed rules prescribing the method of submitting a related request could not be identified from the provisions reviewed by the Constitutional Court. For example, it was not clear what kind of minimal requirements the applicant should take into account when submitting or presenting his or her claim. Lastly, and in contravention of the requirement for the effective judicial protection of rights, according to the impugned rules, the judge was not obliged to include the relevant decision in the judgment, and so the ex-offender would not necessarily know whether or not the motion had actually been adjudicated upon.[26]

[24] Decision 8/2015. (IV. 17.) AB of the Constitutional Court, Reasoning [48].
[25] Decision 8/2015. (IV. 17.) AB of the Constitutional Court, Reasoning [67].
[26] Decision 8/2015. (IV. 17.) AB of the Constitutional Court, Reasoning [68].

The Constitutional Court was of the view that the uncertainties detected in the application of the rules on preliminary exemption deemed it questionable whether defendants had the possibility of being granted an allowance provided for by the Criminal Code. Due to the deficiencies of the regulations, defendants found themselves in a position in which it was dubious whether the guarantees ensuring the fairness of the relevant procedure and, in particular, the right of access to a court could prevail. At the same time, the Constitutional Court's analysis established that the provisions of the Criminal Code can be interpreted in a way that may serve as guidance for practice, and through which it may be ensured that the Criminal Code's provisions and the Fundamental Law of Hungary are in harmony. Therefore, the Constitutional Court established that when applying the rules of the Criminal Code pertaining to exemption, it is a constitutional requirement, flowing from Article XXVIII (1) of the Fundamental Law, that, when imposing a suspended sentence of imprisonment, the court shall examine the possibility of preliminary exemption by court ex officio, and shall rule on this in the judgment.[27]

The third exemption method is exemption by pardon. The President of the Republic of Hungary or the Parliament may grant exemptions to convicted persons as a form of clemency, even if this would not be possible on other grounds. Exemption by pardon takes two forms: general pardon and individual pardon. In Hungary, a general pardon may be granted by the Parliament,[28] while the right to grant individual pardons is exercised by the President.[29] The law does not prescribe any precondition with regard to exemption by pardon (such as worthiness, for example). Just as in the case of exemption by law and exemption by court, the person exempted by pardon shall be regarded as having a clear criminal record with respect to legal consequences applying beyond the scope of criminal law.

C. The Criminal Recording System and the Certificate of No Criminal Record

Criminal records have been collected and stored in a central government register since 1885. The criminal recording system and the regulations on the collection of criminal records do not attach any detrimental legal consequences to the fact that someone's data are included in the database. As discussed earlier in this chapter, some consequences are regulated in the Criminal Code, but many more of the collateral negative consequences are regulated outside the terrain of criminal legislation, most importantly in legislation regulating employment (see also section III.A) In a significant number of positions, laws prohibit

[27] Decision 8/2015. (IV. 17.) AB of the Constitutional Court, Reasoning [72]–[73].
[28] Art 1 (2) (j) Fundamental Law of Hungary.
[29] Art 9 (4) (g) Fundamental Law of Hungary.

employment of persons who have a previous criminal record. Empirical data show that in up to 36 per cent of all positions on the Hungarian job market, a clean criminal record is required, and those with no certificate of 'no criminal record' are prohibited from filling these positions (Vig 2014). In other cases, employers decide to require a clean criminal record as a precondition of the job application. This means in practice that the applicant will need to present a certificate of 'no criminal record', and this status will be known by the future employer in the cases of all applicants.

An empirical study that used content analysis of job advertisements in 2011 showed that out of the 700 job advertisements examined (available both online and offline), in 55.9 per cent of cases an application was only possible with a certificate of 'no criminal record' as required by employers. In higher-paid jobs, where more experience was required, 72.7 per cent of all employers required a certificate. In the segment of industrial production, 70 per cent required a certificate; for unskilled workers, the ratio was just above 40 per cent (Csáki and Mészáros 2012). These findings show that certificates of 'no criminal record' contribute significantly to the social marginalisation of released prisoners in practice.

Csizovszki (2013:52) used discrimination testing to understand the role the certificate of 'no criminal record' plays in social reintegration of released prisoners. Csizovszki undertook 25 phone calls and found that in his (small) sample, those with criminal records face discrimination on two levels: (i) in above 25 per cent of the applications, those with criminal records received worse offers during a phone conversation; (ii) those with criminal records received fewer calls from employers, after the first call, than the control group (applicants with clean criminal records).

Unlike other jurisdictions where employers may have direct access to the database of criminal records, in Hungary neither the individuals whose data are stored nor the employers who intend to perform criminal background checks have direct access to the database. Prior to 2009, a unified database existed, in which most affected state institutions had direct access to the datasets stored.

Following the 144/2008 decision of the Constitutional Court, the previously unified database was split into two parts in order to address right-to-privacy concerns and issues relating to informational self-determination. The Parliament adopted Act XLVII of 2009, which established three different databases: the criminal recording system; the registry of forensic biometric data; and the registry of judgments of the courts of EU Member States against Hungarian citizens.

The Act regulates these databases as separate systems. The databases are not linked to one another and are managed by different government agencies. The Prosecutor General supervises the legality of the databases.[30]

[30] Art 1 (2) Act XLVII of 2009.

The criminal recording system consists of two databases: the database of personal data and photos; and the database of criminal data.[31] The database of criminal data comprises three registries: the registry of persons with a clean criminal record who are under detrimental consequences; the registry of those who are facing a criminal procedure; and the registry of persons who are under an international travel ban.[32] These registries cannot be linked with each other, and data may only be stored until the legal conditions are fulfilled. After this period, the data must be deleted immediately.[33]

The storage of the data must fulfil one of two aims: assisting the execution of judgments of a criminal court and the certification of criminal histories or records in order to protect the interests of crime prevention, prosecution, criminal justice and national security; and assisting offenders in the exercise of their rights and protecting the rights and security of others.[34] The registry of criminal offenders contains the data of those whose criminal responsibility has been established by the judgment of the criminal court and who have not been exempted by the Criminal Code. This registry contains information from the judgment, including the type of offence, whether the offence was complete or remained at the stage of preparation or attempt, whether the offender was the perpetrator of the offence or an abettor or an accomplice, and whether the offender is a recidivist. It also contains information on the names of all courts involved in the case and the number of their decisions, the details of the criminal sanctions and the expected date of the exemption. The database also contains information from the database of the execution of punishments, including the first and last days (actual and expected) of the individual's imprisonment, the earliest possible day of his or her conditional early release, or whether the court has excluded the offender from conditional early release. This information shall be deleted at the time of exemption of the person.[35]

The 2009 Act regulates the registry of forensic biometric data, which comprises two databases: the dactyloscopic registry; and the DNA profile database.[36] The dactyloscopic registry serves identification purposes, including the identification of offenders and persons who are admitted to law enforcement facilities (including prisons and police detention centres) and those whose fingerprints did not match with fingerprints found at the crime scene and who could therefore be excluded.[37] DNA profiles are registered

[31] Art 3 (1) Act XLVII of 2009.
[32] Art 7 Act XLVII of 2009.
[33] Art 8 Act XLVII of 2009.
[34] Art 9 Act XLVII of 2009.
[35] Art 13 Act XLVII of 2009.
[36] Art 35 Act XLVII of 2009.
[37] Art 37 Act XLVII of 2009.

for the identification of offenders and of those who could be excluded from having committed an offence, and for the identification of unknown persons who have been found dead.[38]

The law prescribes different levels of access to the data stored in the above-mentioned databases. Some agencies have direct access to all data, which may be transmitted through direct electronic communications. These include the courts, investigative bodies, the police service, the prosecution service, the anti-terrorism agency, the special service for national security, the immigration authority, the President and the prison service.[39] The levels of access of these bodies differ, and none of them has universal or unlimited access to all the data. In most cases, the Act defines what type of data may be accessed and for what purpose. For instance, the police have the right to access the database in order to perform background checks when granting licences to private investigators or security guards.[40]

The Act regulates the issuing of so-called 'criminal record certificates', which are criminal record extracts through which individuals and employers, who do not have direct access to the database, may receive information on the criminal history of a named person. The certificate of criminal record is an official document issued by the agency that manages the criminal recording system, which contains information based on the records in that system. Such certificates are issued at the request of the individual applicant whose data is stored in the system. The certificate may be requested in order to establish a new legal relationship (such as a contract of employment, etc), maintain such relationships or to certify certain eligibility criteria.[41] In certain cases, government authorities may request data from the database with similar content as the certificate, for instance if legal provisions prescribe a clear criminal history as an eligibility criterion for employment at a government agency. In such cases the Act stipulates that the applicant's request or application for the position is considered to be a declaration of consent to sharing his or her criminal history data.[42]

The following facts may be certified by the criminal record certificate: the applicant fulfils the eligibility criteria as prescribed by law; the applicant has a clear criminal record; the applicant is currently not under an order of deprivation of political rights (eg under ancillary punishment); the applicant is currently not prohibited from exercising a professional activity; or which professional activities are prohibited.[43] If the facts cannot be certified based on the information

[38] Art 52 Act XLVII of 2009.
[39] Art 68 Act XLVII of 2009.
[40] Art 68 (2) (e)Act XLVII of 2009.
[41] Art 71 Act XLVII of 2009.
[42] Art 71 (2) and (2a) Act XLVII of 2009.
[43] Art 71 (3) Act XLVII of 2009.

stored in the database, the agency refuses to issue the certificate.[44] The certificate is valid for up to 90 days after the date of issue.[45]

D. Collateral Consequences versus Human Dignity: How Hungary's Constitutional Court Shaped the Regulations on Detrimental Legal Consequences of a Conviction

According to what has been said, the scope of exemption does not extend to the penal consequences. Hence, exemption does not prevent someone from being classified as a recidivist, or protect him or her from the application of the provisions pertaining to special, multiple and violent multiple recidivists. Accordingly, these legal restrictions also apply after the exemption. At the same time, exemption results in the relief of the ex-offender from the non-penal consequences of a conviction. However, this is only the general rule that allows some exceptions.

In certain cases, the non-penal consequences also prevail after the date of the exemption. These regulations embody some kind of secondary sanction, as they connect further legal consequences to the conviction. These so-called secondary legal consequences are not regulated by just one piece of law in the Hungarian system. Each restriction is found within the rules of the area of law in which the legal restriction prevails and exerts its effects. There are several types of these secondary legal consequences, and it is not possible to categorise them clearly.[46] But it is right to say that they all have their effects, mainly in the field of the labour market. Namely, they extend the waiting period to have the possibility to start working in certain jobs after the exemption date.

These secondary legal consequences may be identified by reviewing sectoral laws. The effective Hungarian laws regulate about 30 different instances where the ex-offender suffers from these secondary legal consequences.[47] The length of the waiting period is at least one year, with a maximum of 12 years. Among the jobs affected are some relating to the criminal justice system, fair trading and the economic order, to traffic safety or public order and public safety.

[44] Art 73 (1) Act XLVII of 2009.

[45] Art 74 (3) Act XLVII of 2009.

[46] Unfortunately there is no official record, nor are any statistics available concerning these consequences. It is not possible to describe the number of occasions on which these secondary legal consequences are applied.

[47] Eg Act Act LXXVIII of 2017 on Legal Practice; Act I of 2012 on the Labor Code; Act CLXII of 2011 on the Legal Status and Remuneration of Judges; Act LXXV of 2007 on the Chamber of Hungarian Auditors, the Activities of Auditors, and on the Public Oversight of Auditors; Act CXXXIII of 2005 on Security Services and the Activities of Private Investigators; Act CLV of 1997 on Consumer Protection; Act CXVI of 1996 on Atomic Energy; Act LVII of 1996 on the Prohibition of Unfair Trading Practices and Unfair Competition; Act LIII of 1994 on Judicial Enforcement.

An example of a non-penal consequence is that no one with a criminal record may be appointed as a judge in Hungary. As a secondary legal consequence, the same applies to persons with a clean criminal record, if their criminal liability for committing a criminal offence was established earlier by a court in a final judgment for a certain period after the date of exemption. The length of this period is prescribed by the relevant Act of Parliament.[48] Similarly, a person with a criminal record cannot not be elected as Chief Public Prosecutor or be appointed as a public prosecutor. As a secondary legal consequence, neither can those who have a clear criminal record but whose criminal liability was established earlier by a court in a final judgment, for a certain period after the exemption took effect. The length of the ban depends on the relevant Act of Parliament.[49]

The Constitutional Court assessed the constitutionality of such restrictions in its Decision 20/2013. (VII. 19.) AB. The assessment was based on certain provisions[50] of Act CXXXIII of 2005 on the Rules of Providing Private Security Services and the Activities of Private Investigators (the 'Private Security and Private Investigation Act'). According to the Constitutional Court, the requirement not to overstep the constitutional limits of criminal law institutions also applies where the state's penal powers beyond criminal justice are being employed. Therefore, in the context of the exemption from detrimental legal consequences,

> enforcing the right to human dignity and personal integrity includes that the state marks that final point where the scope of criminal law, understood broadly, ends. … The 'criminal offender' status terminates with the exemption as per the provisions of the Criminal Code, so – as a general consequence – it can no longer be accompanied by fundamental rights restrictions of the same content as those linked to the status of a defendant, and especially not for a period of time largely exceeding the period of exemption.[51]

Nevertheless, it may be necessary from a constitutional perspective that activities that are important, confidential or dangerous to the community should not be exercised by an ex-offender. Thus, typically, certain jobs should not be filled by former criminal offenders for a certain period of time after they have been exempted from the legal restrictions attaching to their convictions.[52]

[48] Art 4 (2) Act CLXII of 2011.

[49] Art 4 (2) Act CLXII of 2011.

[50] Art 6 (4) Private Security and Private Investigation Act: 'Persons sentenced to immediate imprisonment due to committing certain intentional criminal offences shall not carry out activities falling under this Act of Parliament for 10 years after being exempted if sentenced to less than five years of imprisonment, for 12 years after being exempted if sentenced to five or more than five years of imprisonment. Persons convicted due to committing certain intentional criminal offences shall not carry out activities falling under this Act of Parliament for eight years after being exempted if sentenced to suspended imprisonment'.

[51] Decision 144/2008. (XI. 26.) AB of the Constitutional Court, ABH 2008, 1154, 1156–1157.

[52] Decision 20/2013. (VII. 19.) AB of the Constitutional Court, Reasoning [35]–[36].

In the Decision 8/2015. (IV. 17.) AB, the Constitutional Court concluded that the regulations reviewed restricted the right to free choice of employment of former convicted persons who had been exempted by law from the detrimental legal consequences linked to their convictions for a disproportionately long period of time. According to the Constitutional Court, in the case of the restriction pertaining to the provision of private security services and private investigations, the unjustified and gravely disproportionate length of time for which the restriction applied essentially meant that the legislator applied a kind of secondary sanction against a group persons who wanted to exercise these professions and who had the requisite qualifications, solely on the basis of their past convictions. They were banned from exercising a given profession, even though the court had not imposed such a sanction on them. Restricting the fundamental right in question for such a long period of time was not justified by the particularities flowing from the nature of providing private security services and private investigations, nor by the links between these activities and the protection of property, the market economy and economic policy. Accordingly, the impugned rules were nullified by the Constitutional Court. Later on, in view of the Constitutional Court's decision, the restrictive provisions of the Private Security and Private Investigation Act relating to exemption were reformed.[53] Secondary legal restrictions continue to exist in the relevant sectoral law, but the time period of the restriction was decreased by the legislator with regard to the requirement of proportionality.

Another secondary legal consequence is the limitation on giving, granting or extending a licence to possess firearms. A constitutional issue has arisen in connection with certain provisions of Act XXIV of 2004 on Firearms and Munitions. The Hungarian Constitutional Court assessed the constitutionality of this regulation in its Decision 3102/2018. (IV. 9.) AB. According to the disputed regulation, it was not possible to give or extend a licence to possess firearms within four years of the date of an exemption, if the convicted person's criminal responsibility for one of the selected offences[54] had been established and if the prison sentence was suspended. The Constitutional Court observed that this provision attached a sanction to a criminal conviction that fell outside the scope of the system of criminal responsibility. This type of 'secondary punishment' extended the period during which the individual

[53] Art 6 (4) of the Private Security and Private Investigation Act was replaced by the following: 'Persons sentenced to immediate imprisonment due to committing certain intentional criminal offences shall not carry out activities falling under this Act of Parliament for five years after being exempted if sentenced to less than five years of imprisonment, for eight years after being exempted if sentenced to five or more than five years of imprisonment. Persons sentenced to suspended imprisonment due to committing certain intentional criminal offences shall not carry out activities falling under this Act of Parliament for three years after being exempted.'

[54] These offences are included in Art 3/A (2) (b), eg crimes against the state, human trafficking, homicide, rape, drug abuse.

could not exercise the right to choose a job or profession freely based on his or her skills. Therefore the Constitutional Court examined whether the measure chosen by the legislator was the least severe with regard to the realisation of the objective pursued.[55]

The Constitutional Court also noted that there were examples in both domestic legal history and the regulations currently in force that made a gradual transition between the detrimental consequences attached to convictions and complete exemption from them. It held that it is constitutionally justifiable for a certain range of activities that are important, confidential or which entail specific risks to the community not to be performed by former offenders, even after the exemption period. In these cases, the detrimental legal consequences that continue to exist even after the exemption are integrated into the regulations that specifically govern the given profession. However, the cautious approach taken towards these activities must be limited in scope according to the framework prescribed by the Fundamental Law of Hungary, taking into account the requirements of necessity and proportionality. Therefore, the Constitutional Court analysed whether the limitations introduced by the disputed regulation were necessary and proportionate in nature.

In connection with the necessity requirement, the Court concluded that the question of possessing firearms had to be read together with the right to life and health in practice, as well as with the need to protect public safety given the imminent danger that the possession of firearms inevitably entails. Public safety and the protection of life were considered common social interests that demanded that the possession of firearms and munitions be limited and subject to licences and specific conditions. For these reasons, the lawmaker could not be deprived of the competence to regulate and restrict the legitimate possession of firearms. Therefore, in the view of the Constitutional Court, a restriction that temporarily excluded the perpetrators of certain offences from the right to obtain licences to pursue activities that require the use of firearms could be considered reasonable – even if, due to the limitation, the individual concerned could not further exercise his or her profession.[56]

When evaluating whether the restriction on the fundamental right to freely choose a job or profession was proportionate, the Court attributed specific weight to the following aspects and circumstances. The legislator had changed the original approach embedded in the regulatory framework of 2004 by shortening the waiting period necessary to obtain the licence in 2012. The challenged restriction did not pertain to all criminal acts included in the Criminal Code. Instead it related only to certain criminal acts determined by Act XXIV of 2004. Furthermore, in 2012, the range of the criminal acts in question had

[55] Decision 3102/2018. (IV. 9.) AB of the Constitutional Court, Reasoning [58].
[56] Decision 3102/2018. (IV. 9.) AB of the Constitutional Court, Reasoning [56].

been narrowed. The Court also considered that regulations on obtaining and possessing firearms and related restrictions originated in the obligation of the state to protect fundamental rights. In the view of the Constitutional Court, ensuring the protection of human life was of overriding significance. The fulfilment of these state obligations therefore served as a basis for legal restrictions on acts and objects potentially capable of endangering life, physical integrity and health.

Based on these considerations, the Constitutional Court concluded that the disputed regulation did not entail an unnecessary or disproportionate restriction on the fundamental right to freely choose a job or profession, and thus was not unconstitutional.

E. Prisoner Disenfranchisement

According to the Fundamental Law of Hungary, if the courts have banned an offender from exercising his or her political rights, that person loses his or her right to vote.[57] The 'deprivation of political rights' is an additional, supplementary punishment,[58] which may be imposed along with imprisonment. In fact, a convicted person may be deprived of political rights if he or she is sentenced to immediate imprisonment for committing an intentional crime and he or she is deemed unworthy to participate in public affairs by the court.[59] If the convicted person is deprived of political rights, he or she loses the right to vote, may not participate in a referendum, may not hold public office, may not participate in the work of bodies of popular representation (eg the Parliament), may not be delegated to work in an international organisation, may not be promoted to any military rank, may not be granted or may not be given permission to accept decorations, may not serve as legal counsel in official proceedings, may not hold an office in a public foundation or public body, and may not serve as a senior officer of a civil society organisation.[60]

The deprivation of political rights may be ordered for a definite term, with a minimum duration of one year and a maximum duration of 10 years. The duration of the deprivation of political rights begins when the sentence becomes enforceable. Where deprivation of political rights is ordered, the period of time of imprisonment served and the period of time during which the convicted perpetrator withdraws himself from the execution of the imprisonment shall

[57] Art XXIII (6) Fundamental Law of Hungary.
[58] Art 33 (2) Criminal Code.
[59] Art 61 (1) Criminal Code.
[60] Art 61 (2) Criminal Code.

not be included in its duration. Parole is not withdrawn; the time spent on parole is included in the duration of deprivation of political rights.[61]

During imprisonment, all inmates are excluded from the passive side of the right to vote, namely, the right to be elected.[62] The regulations on the active side of the right to vote are different for prisoners who have been deprived of their political rights and those who are imprisoned but who have not been deprived of their political rights by a court.

In relation to the active right to vote, if a prisoner has been deprived of his political rights, the active right to vote is suspended during imprisonment.[63] This provision, in line with the above-mentioned provisions of the Criminal Code, means in practice that if the court decides to remove the person's political rights, the term of his or her imprisonment and the period of deprivation of political rights will accumulate, hence the actual deprivation of the right to vote will be the period of the term of the imprisonment and the term for which the deprivation of political rights had been ordered. If the court has not ordered the deprivation of political rights, the prisoner may exercise the right to vote. The prisoner shall be allowed to exercise this right at the place of confinement. Alternatively, the prison may support the exercise of the right to vote by interrupting the prison sentence for up to three days.[64]

This differentiation around the exercise of the right to vote was a result of discussions following the decision of the European Court of Human Rights in *Hirst v the United Kingdom (No 2)*.[65] Responding to this decision, the legislator changed the automatic and universal deprivation of the right to vote that pertained in Hungary prior to the present Act of CCXL of 2013. However, as the figures in Table 6.1 show, the courts almost automatically order the deprivation of political rights, and there is an alarming upward trend in the frequency of such orders. While in 2006 the share of deprivation of political rights stood at 89.53 per cent, in 2011 it was 92.37 per cent. In 2014–15, the share reached 95 per cent of all prison sentences. One may conclude that despite the individualisation of court decisions, the alarming figures and trends seen in Table 6.1 demonstrate that the deprivation of political rights is almost automatic if the offender is sentenced to an immediate prison sentence. In these cases, courts only have discretionary powers to judge whether the offender is 'deemed unworthy' to participate in public affairs. Thus, the current provisions result in almost automatic deprivation, and the practice of the judiciary is not able to hinder this.

[61] Art 62 Criminal Code.

[62] Art 121(1)(f) Act CCXL of 2013 in line with Art 2(3) Act CCIII of 2011 and Art 1(4) Act L of 2011.

[63] Art 121(2) Act CCXL of 2013.

[64] Art 131 Act CCXL of 2013.

[65] *Hirst (No 2) v the United Kingdom*, Grand Chamber judgment of 6 October 2005.

Table 6.1 Deprivation of civil rights by prison sentence

Year	Number of immediate sentences of imprisonment[66]	Number of decisions on deprivation of civil rights	Percentage of deprivation of civil rights out of all applicable sentences of imprisonment[67]
2011	10,514	9,712	92.37%
2012	9,700	9,094	93.75%
2013	9,363	8,840	94.41%
2014	10,224	9,778	95.63%
2015	9,781	9,347	95.56%
2016	9,517	9,033	94.91%

Source: The Chief Prosecution Office of Hungary, at ugyeszseg.hu/repository/mkudok245.pdf.

IV. CONCLUSION

Detrimental consequences of a conviction are widespread in Hungarian law. The Criminal Code attaches consequences to recidivism on multiple levels. Beyond the criminal law, so-called sectorial laws also pose detrimental negative consequences to the conviction. The decision of whether to impose these consequences often lies outside of the scope of the criminal law (eg employment) and the decision of the sentencing judge. Thus, the detrimental consequences attached to a conviction are almost automatic, yet are not intended by the application of criminal law. Hence they are directly linked to the punishment itself.

The present chapter has used several examples to show how collateral consequences negatively affect convicted offenders' lives and how they contribute to their social exclusion. Notwithstanding the rules of legal rehabilitation in Hungary that limit the scope of and time during which the detrimental consequences prevail, the present chapter demonstrates that these rules in their current form may undermine convicted offenders' human dignity.

REFERENCES

Csáki, A and Mészáros, M (2012) 'Fogvatartásból szabadultak munkaerő-piaci beilleszkedésének lehetőségei: diszkriminál-e az erkölcsi bizonyítvány?' in *Börtönügyi Szemle*, 31:4, 53–62.

[66] This figure contains all sentences of imprisonment, irrespective of whether the crime was committed intentionally or with negligence.

[67] Due to a lack of publicly available data, these figures are calculated with regard to all immediate sentences of imprisonment (not only those that were ordered because the offender committed an intentional crime). Hence these figures are actually higher if we deduct the sentences of imprisonment for non-intentionally committed crimes.

Csizovszki, D (2013) 'Diszkriminál-e az erkölcsi bizonyítvány?', MA Thesis (Budapest, Eötvös Lorand Tudományegyetem).
Ruzsonyi, P (2014) 'Kriminálpedagógia és az új Bv. Kódex' in F Deák and J Palló (eds), *Börtönügyi Kaleidoszkóp* (Budapest, Büntetés-végrehajtési Szervezet Tudományos Tanácsa).
Szabó, J (2014) 'Rehabilitálható-e a rehabilitáció' *Börtönügyi Szemle*, 1, 28–40.
Vig, D (2014) 'Korlátlan fájdalom? – A bebörtönzés kirekesztő hatásai a semlegesítésben és azon túl', PhD Thesis (Budapest, Eötvös Lorand Tudományegyetem).
Vig, D and Fliegauf, G (2016) 'A szabadságvesztés és az elkövetők reintegrációja' in A Borbíró, K Gönczöl, K Kerezsi and M Lévay (eds), *Kriminológia* (Budapest, Wolters Kluwer) 953–83.

TABLE OF CASES

Domestic Cases

Decision 13/2001. (V. 14.) AB of the Constitutional Court, ABH 2001, 177
Decision 569/B/1999. AB of the Constitutional Court, ABH 2002, 1015
Decision 144/2008. (XI. 26.) AB of the Constitutional Court, ABH 2008, 1107
Decision 20/2013. (VII. 19.) AB of the Constitutional Court, Reasoning [35]
Decision 8/2015. (IV. 17.) AB of the Constitutional Court, Reasoning [28]
Decision 3102/2018. (IV. 9.) AB of the Constitutional Court, Reasoning [58]
Court decision BH1986. 92
Chamber Opinion 56. BK

European Court of Human Rights

Hirst (No 2) v the United Kingdom, Grand Chamber judgment of 6 October 2005.

7

Challenging the Legitimacy and Limits of Criminal Background Checks in Switzerland

ANNA CONINX*

I. INTRODUCTION

CRIMINAL RECORDS BURDEN ex-offenders years after they have served their sentences. They work as a negative curriculum vitae (CV) and as a general character reference, and discriminate against ex-offenders in various situations, especially when applying for a job. However, keeping the criminal history of a person private might put co-workers and employers at risk of becoming a victim of crime by an ex-offender with a proven criminal background (see generally Larrauri Pijoan and Jacobs 2012: 3).

According to labour law experts, systematic criminal background checks as part of pre-employment screening have become common in Switzerland not only for positions in the security sector or in education, but also for various other positions, such as jobs in the IT industry, in the insurance industry or in the health industry (Geiser and Uttinger 2016). In any event, in the case of Switzerland it must be doubted that criminal background checks are undertaken only in 'rare and exceptional circumstances', as was asserted in relation to other European countries (see Larrauri Pijoan 2014: 50, 54).

In this chapter, I begin by sketching the main features of Swiss criminal registration law, focusing on the question of who has access for how long to what kind of data. After giving an overview of current and future law, I then engage in discussion of the legitimacy of pre-employment screening, although criminal background inquiries are also undertaken in other contexts, for example when letting a flat. Even though criminal background checks based on criminal registration are decoupled from punishment and are administrative by nature,

* Thanks to the editors and to Martino Mona for comments on an earlier draft.

the hardship they cause is comparable to that imposed by a monetary penalty or a short prison sentence, and must therefore be justified. A promising way to engage critically with the legitimacy question is to ask what kind of background checks and regulations we would be willing to accept if we found ourselves behind the veil of ignorance that John Rawls introduced in *A Theory of Justice.* I shall argue that, not knowing which position they are in, the parties behind the veil of ignorance would agree to a principle that maximises the chances for the ex-offender to re-enter the labour market without unduly burdening the security and liberty interests of the employer and the victim of crime. This is the case if the crime committed is (i) of a certain severity, (ii) job-related and (iii) there is a considerable risk of reoffending. Importantly, these criteria match the requirements of an occupational disqualification order. From that it follows that criminal background information is limited to convictions that involve such orders. This would effectively make the current 'ordinary criminal record' obsolete.

II. MAPPING THE OFFENDER REGISTRATION LAW

In June 2016, the Swiss Parliament enacted new statute that governs criminal registration and that will replace the current provisions in the Swiss Criminal Code (Articles 365–371 SCC)[1] and another statute (*VOSTRA-Verordnung*). The so-called '*Strafregistergesetz*' (StReG)[2] will most probably come in force in 2020. In principle, Switzerland follows a 'spent-model' (see generally Larrauri Pijoan 2014: 57–58), according to which a conviction is registered but expunged after the sentence has been served and a certain time has passed. According to the new law, there will be only *one* central register that contains all the information about criminal convictions. As Swiss law classifies criminal records as confidential, the register cannot be accessed by the public. Instead, there are different procedures depending on whether individuals or entities request an extract from a criminal record (a so-called *private extract*), or authorities do so (a so-called *authority extract*). With respect to the terminology, the dichotomy 'private' versus 'authority' does not mean that private extracts are only used in the private working sector or when renting a flat. On the contrary, private extracts are used within public administration, for example if someone applies for a job as a teacher in a state school. The reason why we call these extracts 'private' is that, due to the confidentiality of the data, criminal record extracts are handed out only to the person to whom the entry relates, for example to a jobseeker who is asked to provide a criminal record extract by a potential

[1] *Schweizerisches Strafgesetzbuch* of 21 December 1937.

[2] *Bundesgesetz über das Strafregister-Informationssystem VOSTRA, Strafregistergesetz* (StReG) of 17 June 2016.

employer (see Arnold Gruber 2018: Article 371(7) SCC). By contrast, 'authority extracts' can be accessed directly and without the consent of the person concerned, by specific authorities that belong to law enforcement. While it is relatively simple to substantiate why a prosecutor or a criminal judge should have access to the criminal record of a suspect in principle, it is less obvious when it comes to the private extract. In this chapter, I shall focus on the justifications for and the limits of criminal background checks undertaken by employers in the private sector, as well as by members of the public administration who do not belong to law enforcement (and who therefore do not have direct access rights, for example the principal of a state school).

A. When are Employers Allowed to Ask for a Criminal Record Extract?

It is somewhat surprising that Swiss law – except for the law on pre-employment screening for offences against minors and 'other vulnerable people' – does not clearly prescribe in what circumstances a person (typically an employer) is allowed to ask another person to provide a criminal record extract. The new criminal registry law does not address this question either. Therefore, we have to rely on general principles rather than detailed statute law.

The starting point to judge the legitimacy and the lawfulness of private criminal background checks is the confidentiality of criminal records (see Larrauri Pijoan 2014: 53, 59). In principle, an employer is allowed to ask for a criminal record extract only if there is a good reason to do so. The Swiss Civil Code names such a good reason by establishing the criterion of 'business necessity', according to which 'an employer may handle data concerning the employee only to the extent that such data concern the employee's suitability for his job or are necessary for the performance of the employment contract' (Article 328b).[3] Moreover, the Federal Act on Data Protection states that the principle of proportionality must be considered when processing personal data (Article 4(2)).[4] However, the criterion of 'business necessity' can be interpreted very widely, and the principle of proportionality does not lead to a clear-cut distinction between legitimate and illegitimate criminal background checks.

Even though one could make the argument that since criminal records are considered to be confidential, employers are *generally* not allowed to ask an applicant to provide a criminal record extract (Larrauri Pijoan 2014: 53, 59), there is plenty of room for exceptions. Moreover, in Switzerland, criminal background checks seem to be socially accepted not only in the case of pre-employment screening, but also in various other situations. In 2012, the Swiss Government took the view that 'employers, landlords, associations and other organisations

[3] Swiss Civil Code of 10 December 1907.

[4] Federal Act on Data Protection (*Bundesgesetz über den Datenschutz* (*DSG*)) of 19 June 1992.

of employers can ask employees, tenants or members of an association to provide a private extract' (Botschaft BBl 2012, 8857); the fact that criminal records are considered to be confidential was not even mentioned.

Furthermore, recently, a new law on pre-employment screening was introduced in order to better protect minors and 'other vulnerable people' (elderly people and disabled persons) from becoming victims of crime.[5] In 2014, a popular initiative was adopted that requires judges to impose a life-long restraining order on working with children or other vulnerable persons if an offender is found guilty of committing a sexual offence against children or 'other vulnerable people' (the so-called paedophile-initiative, see Botschaft BBl 2012: 8819–55). The provisions are similar to Article 10 of EU Directive 2011/92,[6] which is not applicable in Switzerland due to that country's lack of EU membership and a bilateral treaty. The launch of the paedophile-initiative gave rise to a whole new regulation on occupational disqualification that goes beyond the proposal of the initiative. Most importantly, the former *occupational* disqualification order has been extended to become a more general *activity* disqualification order (Article 67 SCC). The idea is that a convicted offender can be excluded not only from a certain profession, but also from an activity in an organised non-professional field, for example from volunteering at a children's sports club (Botschaft BBl 2012, 8849).

In order to execute activity disqualification orders, employers who offer jobs or activities in close contact with the target group are entitled to request a criminal record extract, though Parliament refrained from introducing a duty to undertake a criminal background enquiry (see Botschaft BBl 2012: 8856, Botschaft BBl 2016: 6150). If someone is applying for a position, for example, as a coach at a children's sports club, a carer at a children's day care centre, a primary school teacher, or as nursing staff in a home for elderly or disabled people, he will most probably be asked to give proof that he is not subject to an activity disqualification order with the target group by providing a criminal record certificate. The Swiss Government stressed that employers have at least a moral obligation to identify a possible recidivist (BBl Botschaft 2012: 8857), and that it might become a quality standard for schools and other educational institutions to ask their employees for criminal record extracts. However, during the political debate, organisations that offer leisure activities for children expressed concern that volunteers could be deterred by being forced to disclose full information about their criminal past (Botschaft BBl 2012: 8856). The Government addressed these concerns by introducing a new type

[5] See at www.bj.admin.ch/bj/de/home/aktuell/news/2016/ref_2016-06-030.html (last accessed 12 April 2018); see also Larrauri Pijoan (2014: 51), with further references to the development in other European countries.

[6] Directive 2011/92/EU of the European Parliament and of the Council of 13 December 2011 on combating the sexual abuse and sexual exploitation of children and child pornography, and replacing Council Framework Decision 2004/68/JHA.

of criminal record extract (the so-called *special private extracts*, Article 371a SCC; Article 42 StReG). Basically, unlike *ordinary* private extracts, *special* private extracts only give information about criminal convictions that involve activity disqualification orders relevant for jobs or activities in close contact with children or other vulnerable people. On a national level, the Swiss Federal Council refrained from *obliging* employers to ask for special extracts (BBl Botschaft 2012: 8846, 8856–57; Arnold Gruber 2018: Article 371a(12)). However, if there is an activity disqualification order, and an employer is aware of it, he is prohibited from hiring the person. In fact, as the breach of an activity prohibition order is a criminal offence (see Article 294 SCC), the employer might be found criminally liable for aiding in commission of the crime.[7] From a legal point of view, it might be wise for the employer not to ask for a special extract, even though it apparently hinders the implementation of the law on disqualification orders.

B. The Content of the Private Criminal Record Extract

Whereas law enforcement authorities, such as members of the Federal Office of Justice, criminal judges and prosecutors, have extensive rights to access a person's criminal history, the law is much more restrictive when it comes to private bodies or public administration outside law enforcement. There seems to be a consensus that ex-offenders must – at least to some extent – be protected from the negative consequences of a criminal conviction (see also Botschaft BBl 2012: 8856).

These are the most important rules concerning *ordinary* private extracts (see Articles 371 SCC; Articles 40–41 StReG):

- Private criminal record extracts contain only details about final convictions for felonies (for example murder, rape, theft, robbery) and misdemeanours (for example minor assaults or property damages) (Article 371(1) SCC; Article 40(1)(b) StReG).
- No information is given on pending criminal procedures, or if a case is dismissed or someone is acquitted (see Article 41 StReG, Botschaft BBl 2014: 5786; but see Weissenberger and Hirzel 2012: 1359).
- Information on convictions for *contraventions* (eg an act of aggression that does not cause any injury to the person or health, or sexual harassment) is only accessible if an activity disqualification order, a contact prohibition order or an exclusion order (Articles 67, 67b SCC) is imposed (Article 371(1) SCC; Article 40(1)(b)(2) StReG).

[7] Less clearly, the Swiss Government states that in the case of a recidivist, an employer must 'justify' why he hired that person, knowing that there was an existing disqualification activity order: see BBl Botschaft 2012: 8857.

- Information on suspended or partly suspended sentences[8] is only accessible until the expiry of the probationary period, as long as the defendant fulfils the condition of not committing other crimes, no stationary treatment[9] was imposed, and there are no restraining orders or expulsions[10] imposed that still apply (Article 371(3bis) SCC; Article 40(3)(b) StReG).
- No entries regarding the criminal convictions of minors are accessible in the ordinary private extract in Swiss law (see Arnold Gruber 2018: Article 371(28)). In any case, the criminal history of a minor becomes visible if he goes on to be convicted as an adult (Article 371(2) SCC; Article 40(1)(d) StReG, Botschaft BBl 2014: 5787).
- Convictions by foreign criminal courts are all registered (Article 40(1)(c) StReG).

Other rules apply for the *special* private extract. The core concept is that this type of extract discloses only information on convictions that involve an activity disqualification order, a contact prohibition order or an exclusion order with the aim of protecting minors, elderly people and disabled persons (see Botschaft 2012: 8856; Arnold Gruber 2018: Article 371a(5)). During the legislative process, the target group was extended to include patients and the health sector (see Botschaft BBl 2016: 6149; Arnold Gruber 2018: Article 371a(22)). Not only adults but also minors from the age of 10 are registered (see Article 317a(3)(c) SCC; Article 42(1)(c) StReG). The idea is that organisations or employers should only have access to information that is relevant to judge someone's qualification for a *specific* job (see Arnold Gruber 2018: Article 371a(6)). These restrictions were found necessary to keep activities with minors and other vulnerable people appealing (see Botschaft BBl 2012: 8856; Arnold Gruber 2018: Article 371a(8)). For example, while the head of a youth camp may receive information from the applicant about any restrictions he might face as regards working with children, she will not be informed about a conviction for fraud, theft or traffic violations.

The procedure is as follows. The potential employer or organisation must confirm that a person is applying for a job or an activity involving minors or other persons requiring special protection, and hand the signed confirmation to the jobseeker. The applicant must then order a special extract from the criminal

[8] A court will normally suspend the execution of a monetary penalty or a custodial sentence of no more than two years if an unsuspended sentence does not appear to be necessary in order to deter the offender from committing further felonies or misdemeanours: see Art 42 SCC.

[9] Stationary treatment (Art 59 SCC) is imposed on offenders who have been found to suffer from a serious mental disorder. It can be ordered for any felony or misdemeanour, and takes priority over the execution of the sentence. It can be prolonged indefinitely at five-year intervals, as long as the offender is considered to be at risk of reoffending.

[10] 'Expulsion' is a measure that is imposed in conjunction with a sentence. A court can – and in certain cases even must – expel foreign nationals from Switzerland for a certain length of time, or even for life in the case of recidivism, if the offender is convicted of a trigger offence such as homicide, theft, fraud, various sexual offences, etc. (see Arts 66a–66d SCC.).

record register and provide it to the employer (see Article 371a SCC). However, importantly, the Swiss Government stresses that it is up to employers or organisations also to ask for an *ordinary* private extract that contains information about all possible convictions for a certain time period (Botschaft 2012: 8856). Apparently, from the applicant's perspective, this possibility makes the limitations of the special extracts meaningless, at least as long as the entry in the ordinary private extract has not been expunged.[11] It shows that the parallelism of the ordinary extract and the special extract aims to serve primarily employers, not ex-offenders. The idea is that employers should decide how much information they want to get from jobseekers, taking into account the fact that being forced to disclose full information about their criminal past could deter volunteers. However, if a non-profit organisation wants to be fully informed about the criminal past of an applicant, according to the current law, it should not be in a worse position than other employers.

C. The Removal of Entries

In Switzerland, as in many other European countries, register entries are expunged once the sentence has been served or the monetary penalty has been paid, and once a certain waiting period has expired. The idea is that after some time, an ex-offender is at no more risk of reoffending than a non-offender (see Larrauri Pijoan 2014: 58). However, considering the fact that an offender has already endured the deserved punishment, the waiting period seems very long: as a general rule, a prison sentence is spent after two-thirds of the duration that is relevant for the authorities (see Article 371(3) SCC; Article 40(3)(a) StReG). The following examples might give an idea of how long an ex-offender has to wait after having served the sentence, until his criminal past is no longer an issue in the *ordinary* private extract:

- 20 years in the case of a custodial sentence of 10 years.[12]
- 12 years in the case of a custodial sentence of three years.[13]
- 10 years and eight months in the case of a custodial sentence of one year.[14]
- 7 years in the case of a custodial sentence of six months.[15]
- Life in the case of a life sentence.[16]

[11] See section II.C.

[12] Art 371(3) SCC in conjunction with Art 369(1)(a) SCC; Art 38(3) in conjunction with Art 40(3)(a)(1) StReG (two-thirds of 10 years' imprisonment plus a 20-year waiting period).

[13] Art 371(3) SCC in conjunction with Art 369(1)(b) SCC; Art 38(3)(a)(2) in conjunction with Art 40(3)(a) StReG (two-thirds of 3 years' imprisonment plus a 15-year waiting period).

[14] Art 371(3) SCC in conjunction with Art 369(1)(b) SCC; Art 38(3)(a)(2) in conjunction with Art 40(3)(a) StReG (two-thirds of 1 year's imprisonment plus a 15-year waiting period).

[15] Art 371(3) SCC in conjunction with Art 369(1)(c) SCC; Art 38(3)(a)(3) in conjunction with Art 40(3)(a) StReG (two-thirds of 6 months' imprisonment plus a 10-year waiting period).

[16] Art 38(3)(c) in conjunction with Art 40(3)(a) StReG.

A monetary penalty is removed after six years and eight months.[17] The same is true for convictions resulting in a suspended sentence that has not been revoked.[18] If a measure (such as stationary treatment or an activity disqualification order) is imposed in conjunction with a sentence or alone, according to current law, shorter waiting periods apply (see Article 371(4) SCC). However, these rules will change with the coming into force of the new criminal registry law (for details see Botschaft BBl 2014: 5788-89). According to the new law, the entry of an activity disqualification order will remain on the record until the last day of the prohibition, but in any case at least for seven years.[19] However, in case of a *life-long* activity disqualification order imposed to protect minors or other vulnerable people, the entry in the *ordinary* extract will be expunged after seven years and the conviction will only be visible in the *special* private extract from then on. This is an important protection for ex-offenders: for example, if an offender has been sentenced to a monetary penalty and a life-long prohibition on working with children, after seven years the entry is no longer visible in the ordinary criminal record extract; the information is only given in the special private extract. If the ex-offender applies for a job unrelated to children, etc, the employer is not able to access information about the applicant's criminal past.

If a person has several entries, *all* the entries remain until the removal period of the last entry has expired (see Botschaft BBl 2014: 5787–88). In addition, entries that have been expunged become visible again if there is a new entry (see Arnold Gruber 2018: Article 371(75)). This rule allows employers to view long chains of delinquency (see Arnold Gruber 2018: Article 371(71)). In sum, it is very difficult for recidivists to get a clean criminal record.

III. THE LEGITIMACY OF PRIVATE CRIMINAL BACKGROUND CHECKS

A. The Purpose and the Impact of the Criminal Record

With the main principles of Swiss criminal registry law in mind, I would like to turn to the more fundamental discussion about the legitimacy of criminal background checks undertaken by employers in the private sector or officials outside law enforcement. When reflecting on the legitimacy of private criminal background checks, we have to address three questions: What is the hardship of being registered as an ex-offender? How can this hardship be justified (the purpose of the registry)? How could this hardship be limited?

[17] Art 38(3)(d) in conjunction with Art 40(3)(b) StReG.
[18] Art 38(3)(d) in conjunction with Art 40(3)(b) StReG.
[19] Art 40(3)(d) StReG.

Criminal records cast a long shadow far beyond the deserved punishment. Even though in Swiss law most of register entries are eventually expunged, ex-offenders might have to share information on their criminal background with other people for many years. This is also true in cases in which someone was convicted for a minor crime and was given a one-year prison sentence; as we have seen, he has to wait for more than 10 years for the registration to be expunged. Due to negative stereotypes about ex-offenders, their chances of keeping their jobs or re-entering the job market and successfully reintegrating into society are considerably diminished. As Flake puts it, it is somehow 'cruelly ironic that perhaps the most important resource [ie employment] for turning their lives around – is also often the most elusive' (2015: 47). Larrauri Pijoan and Jacobs find the stigma of the convicted criminal 'more injurious than a community supervision, fines, or even incarceration' (2012: 4).

When it comes to the justification of the hardship of being registered as an ex-offender, it is often stated that there are legitimate safety interests in being informed about the possible criminal background of a potential business partner or employee, in order to protect property and reputation, as well as the welfare of co-workers and customers (see Arnold Gruber 2013: Article 371(10); Weissenberger and Hirzel 2012: 1362; Larrauri Pijoan and Jacobs 2012: 4). Yet it seems that there are not only straightforward safety interests at play to minimise the risk of reoffending on the job; there is also a very strong notion that a criminal conviction says something important about how trustworthy a person is in general (see Flake 2015: 68). This aspect becomes apparent when reflecting on why landlords sometimes ask tenants to provide criminal record extracts. Lastly, it is stated that law-abiding citizens also have an interest in disclosing a clean criminal record (Botschaft BBl 1998: 2169).

While today in Switzerland the legitimacy of and necessity for private criminal record extracts are hardly called into question, in the early 1990s a commission of independent legal experts suggested abolishing private criminal records due to their discriminatory character (see Bericht Expertenkommission 1993: 125–26). The commission was established to advise the Swiss Federal Council on key questions regarding revision of the Criminal Code. The experts argued that there are less intrusive means than a criminal record, such as CVs, references or personal interviews, to judge on the fitness of a person for a job. For employees working in sensitive areas (eg working with minors), the commission took the view that nobody would hire a person without a complete and comprehensive CV (see Bericht Expertenkommission 1993: 125).

This somewhat radical proposal was criticised by most of the political parties. It was argued that for safety reasons, it is necessary that employers are fully informed about possible criminal convictions, especially for jobs in the security or education sector (Botschaft BBl 1998: 2170). As a compromise, the Swiss Federal Council took the view that only information about the most serious crimes (felonies) should be accessible by privates. By contrast, misdemeanours should only be registered if an occupation disqualification order is imposed (Botschaft BBl 1998: 2169). Parliament agreed to this proposition at first. However, shortly afterwards, a cantonal initiative (*Standesinitiative*) found a majority that claimed that misdemeanours should also be part of the criminal record extract.[20] The proponents argued that if the private extract was restricted to information about felonies, serious security gaps would result (see Bericht Kommission Rechtsfragen (2006)). Since then, the legitimacy of criminal background checks undertaken by employers or officials outside law enforcement has not been criticised further in principle.

B. The Minority–Majority Problem and the Necessity for a Fairness Test

Due to the fact that the stigma of a criminal conviction – perpetuated by its entry in the criminal registration system – burdens an ex-offender far beyond his deserved punishment, we have to think about possible limitations on access to crime register information for the private sector and the public sector outside law enforcement. As a starting point, we can recall the minority–majority problem that is inherent in most democratic decisions, but which becomes even more acute if the minority is politically disenfranchised and easily marginalised, as in the case of ex-offenders (see generally Coninx 2014; Geiger 2006: 1191). Since the great majority of Swiss people will never be in the position of being an ex-offender, burdened with an entry in the criminal register, it is likely that draftsmen do not fairly consider the interest of *all* the people when making laws on criminal registration. Instead, they will most probably follow the motto, 'if you've got nothing to hide, you've got nothing to fear', which gives the impression that no genuine rights are infringed (see Loader 2007: 32). Ex-offenders' rights are likely to be seen as 'other people's rights' (Luban 2005: 243) that do not concern the rest of us. Therefore, the political debate on ex-offenders' rights is not only about striking a balance between the security interests of the public and ex-offenders' interests of liberty and privacy, but also about a minority–majority problem that typically occurs when intrusive security measures are at stake. As Jeremy Waldron (2003: 201) puts it:

> So perhaps the balance we ought to be discussing is not so much a balance between one thing we all like (liberty) and another thing we all like (security). It is more like the balance that is sometimes referred to when we say we should balance the interests of a dissident individual or minority against the interests of the community as a whole.

One could object that since ex-offenders have violated rights of other people, it is legitimate to treat them differently. Unlike, for example, racial minorities, ex-offenders could be seen as morally and legally responsible for their status.

[20] Standesinitiative 05.300 n 'Änderung von Artikel 371 StGB (Strafregister)' of 21 January 2005.

Such an argument, however, would be only partially convincing (see also Geiger 2006: 1192). It is true that offenders have forfeited certain goods or rights while serving their sentence. However, after having completed their punishment, both the principle of retribution as well as the principle of rehabilitation demand that an ex-offender should not be subject to further hardship. The fact that someone was convicted for a crime should not change the legal or moral status of that person beyond the punishment. In fact, serving the sentence should re-establish the moral and legal status of the convicted person.

Deciding to whom individual criminal history information should be made accessible entails a fundamental fairness problem. We therefore have to think about a procedure to ensure that the interests of all the people involved are considered. In order to do so, we should look for a mode of reasoning that is guided by the generalisation principle (see Gewirth 1964: 229). We may be guided by Kant's categorical imperative that states that one should only act in accordance with a maxim when one can, at the same time, will that it should become a universal law (see Kant 2008: 45 (AA IV, 421)). This formula guarantees that general rules we do not want to be applied to ourselves are not justifiable. With regard to cases of the legitimate use of criminal records among private bodies, we have to think of a situation in which we can be assured that the conflicting interests of all are recognised.

This gives rise to the question of the defining features of a situation that allows us to take a general point of view. A promising method lies in John Rawls' liberal contractarian conception of the social contract developed in *A Theory of Justice*. Rawls introduces a thought experiment by positing an idealised choice situation ('original position'), in which agents must decide upon principles of justice to govern the institutions and the basic structure in a liberal society (see Rawls 1999: 10–15; see generally Stark 2000: 314). The most important negotiating condition embodied in the original position is that the parties deliberate behind a 'veil of ignorance'. Behind the veil of ignorance, 'no one knows his place in society, his class position or social status' (Rawls 1999: 118). This arrangement allows the parties to be 'fairly situated' and 'treated equally as moral persons' (Rawls 1999: 122), because they leave aside all the particularities of their own position in society and make their decisions from a strictly impartial point of view.

Even though Rawls does not introduce his conception to specific laws, the concept has been utilised by scholars in different contexts so as to justify rights to immigrate (Mona 2007) or to ensure legitimate punishment (Dolovich 2004), legitimate killing in situations of necessity (Coninx 2012) or same-couple rights (Lister 2007). Deliberating behind the veil of ignorance forces us to evaluate the interests of all people concerned in order to define the reasons, the scope and the limits of a rule to which everyone could agree.

Another important condition of the original position is that the decision to be made is a 'choice under uncertainty' (Rawls 1999: 133). The veil of ignorance not only excludes knowledge of parties' position in society, but also knowledge of likelihoods. As a consequence, the parties have no basis for estimating probabilities and for determining the circumstances of the probable society and their position (see Rawls 1999: 134). Instead of calculating expected gains and losses, and selecting the option offering the greatest gain, we assume that each possible outcome is equally likely. In order to ensure that the interests of all are protected, the parties put themselves not only in the position in which they would like to be, but also in the position of the least advantaged person. By so doing, they decide on the options guided by the *maximin principle*: they select a rule that would (also) maximise the prospects of the worst-off person (see Rawls 1999: 132–33). The focus on the worst outcome forces the parties to evaluate their fundamental interests and to ensure that they are protected in all circumstances (see Rawls 2001: 99).

To identify the principles everyone would accept as just and fair when making information on criminal convictions accessible, the parties must put themselves alternatively in the positions in which they could find themselves once the veil is lifted. I consider here three relevant positions: the ex-offender; the employer; and the potential future victim of crime (ie crime committed by an ex-offender during his employment). Guided by the *maximin principle*, they choose a rule that maximises the protection of the security and liberty of the worst-off person.

This gives rise to the question of who occupies the worst position when it comes to criminal background screening. Having the status of an ex-offender who has to bear his conviction publicly, markedly diminishes the chances of an individual's successfully re-entering society and places restraints on his liberty and security far beyond any proportionate punishment. Apparently, it is a very vulnerable position. However, the reputation of an employer who has an ex-offender under contract who commits a crime on the job, could be considerably harmed, which in turn could lead to financial loss. Lastly, being a victim of crime robs one of the elementary goods of security and integrity (Dolovich 2004: 38). Apart from physical pain or financial loss, it might make someone fearful or traumatised. In sum, it seems that there is no clear worst-off position. Nevertheless, the veil helps to conceal the interests of the relevant social positions and to overcome the minority–majority problem. Everyone has to put himself in *all* possible positions, including the position of the ex-offender, and not just in the position of the victim of crime or the employer, to whom most people would intuitively relate.

C. Principles on Limiting Private Criminal Records

Taking the view of the employer, one might vote for a principle that allows criminal background checks without any restrictions. One could make the argument that a criminal conviction is evidence of bad character, and the employer should have the right, first, to undertake criminal background checks irrespective of the job in question and, second, if someone has a criminal background, to be able to decide whether the ex-offender is nevertheless trustworthy. However, by putting oneself in the position of the ex-offender, one quickly realises that there is a clear danger of being excluded from *all* jobs based on a general prejudice against ex-offenders. A law that permits limitless criminal background checks would be a great threat to the liberty of an ex-offender, and therefore over-inclusive. By contrast, putting oneself in the shoes of the ex-offender, one might advocate that – after serving a sentence – the information about one's criminal history should be kept confidential *in any case*. But this is under-inclusive when taking the position of the potential victim of crime. From a future victim's perspective, one could not consent to confidentiality without exception, because that would put the victim of crime at unreasonable risk of harm to his property or safety. For example, one could not agree to a rule that allows an ex-offender to apply for a position at a nursery and not disclose the fact that he has been convicted of having abused children sexually. Similarly, from the perspective of a future victim of crime, it does not seem right that a bank would not be informed about the fact that an applicant has been convicted for money laundering.

I conclude that ex-offenders should be permitted to re-enter the labour market with the fewest possible restrictions, without unduly burdening the employer's interests in security and liberty. These interests would be affected if there was a direct relationship between a previous criminal offence of a certain severity (felony or misdemeanour) and the job or activity in question, such that employing the individual would impose a considerable risk to property, or to the safety of specific individuals or the general public (similar, Flake 2015: 88).

Of course, the follow-up question is *who* is to decide on whether someone poses an unreasonable risk of committing a crime in the course of the job. Apparently, this addresses the problem of who should decide on intrusive preventive measures that go beyond the deserved sentence. My proposition is that the risk assessment should be undertaken by the authority that decides on an activity disqualification order, instead of empowering private employers to undertake criminal background checks and to decide whether the offence that was committed is relevant to the job or activity in question (see also Larrauri Pijoan 2014: 60–61).

In Switzerland, it is up to the sentencing judge to make a risk assessment and to decide on an activity disqualification order, based on detailed rules embodied in the Swiss Criminal Code. As mentioned earlier, only recently the Swiss Parliament has been busy enacting new legislation in order to determine when an ex-offender should be excluded from working or volunteering.[21] There is no need to empower private employers to undertake the same exercise during an application process. Either a judge has concluded that an offender poses

[21] See also section II.A.

an unreasonable risk to other people by carrying out a certain profession, and thus imposes an activity disqualification order, or he reasons that there is no such risk. In this case the employer should not be authorised to make his own risk assessment. Instead, by introducing the new law on activity disqualification order, Parliament has already balanced the interest of the ex-offenders in re-entering the labour market and the interests in security and liberty of the employer and the potential victim of crime. Even though the law has become harsher, especially with respect to former sexual offenders in recent years, and courts have a tendency to err on the side of safety (see generally Zedner 2012), the 'sentencing model' (Larrauri Pijoan 2014: 60–61) seems the best way to promote the reintegration of ex-offenders with non-disqualifying criminal records.

From these arguments it follows that the law on criminal records should be radically altered. Criminal record extracts that are used in an application process in the private sector and public sector outside law enforcement should only list activity disqualification orders imposed by a court. With respect to the question whether the employer is permitted to ask for an extract, the information is provided if the activity disqualification order is relevant to the job or activity in question. In fact this is not a new proposal; it corresponds to the logic and concept of the special private extract. As of now, special private extracts can only be requested by employees who apply for a job that involves regular contact with children or other vulnerable persons, and their content is restricted to convictions that involve an activity disqualification order with the target group.[22] This idea, which is based on the principle of proportionality, could be expanded to cover further risk-prone activities or jobs in the private security, transportation or finance sectors. However, the possibility to also order an *ordinary* private extract, as under the current law, must be eliminated. The key is to reveal the information about previous convictions only if it is relevant to the job or a particular activity. Such a model would make the *ordinary private criminal record* obsolete.

The argument may be summarised as follows:

- Courts, not employers, should decide whether the condition of 'job relatedness' and 'considerable risk' is met, and eventually impose an activity disqualification order.
- Criminal record extracts that are used in the private employment sector or the public sector outside law enforcement should only list convictions that involve an activity disqualification order on the basis of the model of the special private extract.
- These private extracts (on the basis of the model of the special private extract) should only be provided for specific jobs to cover further risk-prone activities, for example in education, the private security sector, transportation, or the finance sector.

[22] See also section II.A.

IV. CONCLUSION

Criminal background checks are likely to burden ex-offenders unduly many years after they have served their sentences. Even though a criminal record might cause more hardship for a person than the punishment itself, there is hardly any scholarly debate in Switzerland about how to justify this burden and hardship. On the contrary, there seems to be a consensus that employers have a legitimate interest in being fully informed about previous convictions, no matter what the conviction was for.

In this chapter, I have challenged this assumption. When it comes to the question of how to justify and to limit offender registration, we must be aware that the debate on criminal records in particular and on ex-offenders' rights in general entails a 'minority–majority problem'. Due to the fact that most of us are not in the position of ex-offenders, we tend to make unfair laws in order to maximise our own position by depriving ex-offenders of genuine rights. In order to tackle this problem, I here have utilised John Rawls' procedure for fair decision-making, which he developed in *A Theory of Justice*. I have argued that the parties behind the veil of ignorance would agree to a principle that maximises the chances of the ex-offender to re-enter the labour market without unduly burdening the security and liberty interests of the employer and the victim of crime. This is the case if the crime committed is job-related and there is a considerable risk of reoffending. I have also argued that it should be up to courts and not to employers to decide on whether an ex-offender should be disqualified from working in a specific field, or from undertaking a certain activity. In criminal law we have detailed rules on activity disqualification, and there is no need to empower employers to make their own risk assessment. Instead, criminal record extracts should only list convictions that involve an activity disqualification order based on the model of the special private extract. The information should only be provided to employers who offer jobs that involve children or other vulnerable persons, as well as risk-prone activities in the private security, transportation or the finance sectors. This would effectively make the ordinary criminal record obsolete.

REFERENCES

Arnold F and Gruber, P (2018) 'Kommentar Art 371 StGB' in MA Niggli and H Wiprächtiger (eds), *Basler Kommentar Strafrecht II, Art 1-110 StGB, JStGB*, 4th edn (Basel, Helbling & Lichtenhahn).

Coninx, A (2012) *Das Solidaritätsprinzip im Lebensnotstand: Zufall, rationale Entscheidung und Verteilungsgerechtigkeit* (Bern and Baden-Baden, Staempfli & Nomos).

Coninx, A (2014), 'Unsere Sicherheit – die Freiheit der anderen? Das Problem der selektiven Freiheitsbeschränkungen in der Sicherheitspolitik' *Zeitschrift für Schweizerisches Recht*, 133, 103–30.

Dolovich, S (2004) 'Legitimate Punishment in Liberal Democracy' *Buffalo Criminal Law Review*, 7, 307–442.

Flake, DF (2015) 'When Any Sentence is a Life Sentence: Employment Discrimination Against Ex-Offenders' *Washington University Law Review*, 93, 45–102.

Geiger, B (2006) 'The Case for Treating Ex-Offenders as a Suspect Class' *California Law Review*, 94, 1191–242.

Geiser, T and Uttinger, U (2016) 'Die Mär des Strafregisterauszugs' *Neue Zürcher Zeitung*, 5 April 2016, available at www.nzz.ch/meinung/debatte/die-maer-des-strafregisterauszugs-1.18722589 (last accessed 12 April 2018).

Gewirth, A (1964), 'The Generalization Principle' *The Philosophical Review*, 73, 229–42.

Kant, I (2008 [first published 1785]) in T Valentiner (ed), *Grundlegung zur Metaphysik der Sitten* (Stuttgart, Reclam).

Larrauri Pijoan, E (2014) 'Legal protections against criminal background checks in Europe' *Punishment & Society*, 16, 50–73.

Larrauri Pijoan, E and Jacobs, JB (2012) 'Are criminal convictions a public matter? The USA and Spain' *Punishment & Society*, 14, 3–28.

Lister, M (2007) 'A Rawlsian Argument for Extending Family-Based Immigration Benefits to Same-Sex Couples' *The University of Memphis Law Review*, 37, 745–80.

Loader, I (2007) 'The Cultural Lives of Security and Rights' in BJ Goold and L Lazarus (eds), *Security and Human Rights* (Oxford and Portland, Hart Publishing) 27–42.

Luban, D (2005) 'Eight Fallacies About Liberty and Security' in R Wilson (ed), *Human Rights in the War on Terror* (Cambridge and New York, Cambridge University Press) 242–57.

Mona, M (2007) *Das Recht auf Immigration* (Basel, Helbling & Lichtenhahn).

Rawls, J (1999) *A Theory of Justice*, revised edn (Cambridge, MA, Harvard University Press).

—— (2001) in E Kelly (ed), *Justice as Fairness – A Restatement* (Cambridge, MA, Harvard University Press).

Stark, CA (2000) 'Hypothetical Consent and Justification' *The Journal of Philosophy*, 97, 313–34.

Waldron, J (2003) 'Security and Liberty: The Image of Balance' *The Journal of Political Philosophy*, 11, 191–210.

Weissenberger, P and Hirzel, A (2012) 'Sicherheitslücken im Strafregisterrecht' *Aktuelle Juristische Praxis*, 1357–364.

Zedner, L (2012) 'Erring on the Side of Safety: Risk Assessment, Expert Knowledge, and the Criminal Court' in GR Sullivan and IH Dennis (eds), *Seeking Security: Pre-empting the commission of criminal harms* (Oxford, Hart Publishing) 219–41.

LEGISLATIVE DOCUMENTS

Bericht der Kommission für Rechtsfragen zur Standesinitiative des Kantons Tessin 'Änderung von Artikel 371 StGB (Strafregister) (2006), 22 August 2006, available at www.parlament.ch/centers/kb/Documents/2005/Kommissionsbericht_RK-S_05.300_2006-08-22.pdf (last accessed 12 April 2018).

Bericht zur Revision des Allgemeinen Teils und des Dritten Buches des Strafgesetzbuches und zu einem Bundesgesetz über die Jugendstrafrechtspflege. Erstellt auf der Grundlage der Schlussberichte der Expertenkommission (1993) (Bern, Bundesamt für Justiz, Eidgenössische Drucksachen- und Materialzentrale) 1–218.

Botschaft zur Änderung des Schweizerischen Strafgesetzbuches (Allgemeine Bestimmungen, Einführung und Anwendung des Gesetzes) und des Militärstrafgesetzes sowie zu einem Bundesgesetz über das Jugendstrafrecht (1998), 21 September 1998, BBl 1979–2417.

Botschaft zur Volksinitiative 'Pädophilie sollen nicht mehr mit Kindern arbeiten dürfen' sowie zum Bundesgesetz über das Tätigkeitsverbot und das Kontakt- und Rayonverbot (Änderung des Strafgesetzbuchs, des Militärstrafgesetzes und des Jugendstrafgesetzes) als indirekten Gegenvorschlag (2012), 10 October 2012, BBl 8819– 55.

Botschaft zum Strafregistergesetz (2014), 20 June 2014, BBl 5713–872.

Botschaft zur Änderung des Strafgesetzbuches und des Militärstrafgesetzes (Umsetzung von Art 123c BV) (2016), 3 June 2016, BBl 6115-90.

8

Relevance of a Criminal Record to Employment Opportunity: A Greek Example for Comprehensive Law Reform

DIMITRA BLITSA AND ANNA KIVRAKIDOU*

I. INTRODUCTION

ALL EUROPEAN COUNTRIES prescribe some type of criminal background check for certain public and private sector jobs and positions. However, we lack contemporary Europe-wide studies on the nature, scope and duration of criminal record-based employment disqualifications (CBED) (Damaska 1968; Louks, Lyner and Sullivan 1998; Larrauri and Jacobs 2013). The present chapter seeks to delimit the role a person's criminal past, as depicted in his criminal record, plays in obtaining legitimate employment. While we use Greece as a starting point, we believe that this research is relevant to all European countries. We start off with a synopsis of the current Greek legislation on criminal records and employment disqualifications in order to allow readers to familiarise themselves with the characteristics and shortcomings of our vetting regime and draw comparisons to their home countries.[1] Moreover, we aim to reveal the principles that should govern employment bans by focusing on offenders' rights. Moving from theory to practice, we further identify the key policy questions any European policymaker needs to answer when implementing employment disqualifications based on criminal records. Throughout the chapter, we refer to the timely findings of a working

* The authors are grateful to JB Jacobs, E Larrauri and M Rovira for their helpful comments.

[1] For comparative criminal record information, see Stefanou and Xanthaki 2008; Vermeulen et al 2002.

group (including the present authors) assembled by the Greek Ministry of Justice, tasked with rationalising employment disqualifications and promoting offenders' rehabilitation in Greece.[2]

II. CRIMINAL RECORDS AND EMPLOYMENT VETTING IN GREECE

A. Criminal Record Keeping

In Greece, a criminal record is created for every adult[3] person who has been irrevocably convicted of a misdemeanour or a felony (Article 574 of the Code of Criminal Procedure (CCP)). Criminal record registries are found at the Public Prosecutor's Offices (61 in total).[4] The registries issue two types of criminal record extracts: one intended for general use and the other for judicial use. The extracts differ with respect to the information they contain and who is entitled to access them.

Convictions appear on a 'general use' extract until the individual is 'legally' rehabilitated, that is after three or eight years for misdemeanours (depending on the sentence imposed) and 20 years for felonies, without another conviction. On certain occasions,[5] the prosecutor can reduce these time limits by half (Article 576 CCP). Legal rehabilitation is not applicable to the 'judicial use' extract. Convictions continue to appear on a 'judicial use' extract even after the afore-mentioned time limits. However, both extracts may be expunged when: (i) the record subject dies or reaches the age of 80; (ii) the conviction is annulled; (iii) the conviction is covered by an amnesty; (iv) the offence ceases being punishable; (v) the court suspended the execution of the sentence, and five years have passed without the suspension's having been revoked or cancelled; (vi) 10 years have passed since a pecuniary penalty or a low prison sentence[6] was executed and the defendant has not reoffended. Expunged records must be destroyed and cannot be used for any purpose (Article 578 CCP).

The 'general use' extract may be disclosed to the record subject and to occupational licensing authorities. The 'judicial use' extract is only available to judicial authorities, prison directors, foreign embassies and to a few occupational licensing authorities (Article 577 CCP). Otherwise, the CPP restricts disclosure to third parties.[7]

[2] Ministerial Decision 53243/27.8.15. The group was put together by Mr E Fytrakis, Secretary General for Crime Policy. The opinions expressed in this chapter are the personal views of the authors and do not necessarily represent the views of the working group, nor should they be understood to be those of the Greek Ministry of Justice.

[3] Juvenile records are not examined in this chapter.

[4] Registries keep nation-wide records of those born in their district. Records of those born abroad are kept by the Ministry of Justice.

[5] First conviction, conviction for criminal negligence or conviction for an intentional crime carrying a prison sentence up to one year or a pecuniary penalty.

[6] One month for intentional crimes and two months for criminal negligence.

[7] For further information on Greek criminal records, see Giovanoglou 2006; Gavouneli and Traianos 2008.

B. Employment Disqualifications for Convicted Individuals

Employment bans for convicted individuals are primarily regulated by the Greek state. Special administrative statutes regulate criminal background checks for certain public sector positions (eg judges, police officers and university professors). For all other public sector jobs, employment bans are regulated by the Public Servants Code.[8] In addition, convictions for specific crimes render a person ineligible for a number of private sector occupations and professions (eg lawyer, doctor, accountant, bar/gym owner, taxi driver and sailor). Each occupation is regulated by a different piece of legislation specifying which convictions constitute an obstacle to its exercise. For example, a person who wants to work in the private security industry cannot have a conviction for counterfeiting, forgery, theft, embezzlement or bribery. A person convicted of kidnapping, sexual or drug offences cannot work as a nurse. Disqualifications bar the convicted individual from applying for a particular employment. They may also result in his expulsion from office (public sector) or in the revocation of his licence (private sector). For many occupations even non-prosecution is a prerequisite.

As there is no central licensing authority, employment restrictions for private sector employment are enforced by various administrative authorities charged with occupational licensing. These authorities do not enjoy any discretion and their decisions (issuance and revocation of licences) are based on statutory provisions. In order to screen out ineligible individuals, they have access (via the competent criminal record registry) to the applicant's/professional's criminal record, and check this for convictions of disqualifying offences. Non-prosecution is proved via a certificate issued by the Public Prosecutor's Offices (Blitsa 2014a). By contrast, private sector employers do not have access to a job applicant/employee's criminal record. Nor is it legal for them to collect and process criminal record extracts (Opinions 4/2013, 101/2016 of the Hellenic Data Protection Authority).[9] Criminal background checks by private sector employers are not examined in this chapter.[10]

In parallel, where an offender's occupation requires a licence, the Greek Criminal Code (Article 67(1a) CC) allows the convicting court to render the offender ineligible to exercise his occupation for one to five years where he has committed a felony or misdemeanour that constitutes a grave violation of his professional duties and has received a prison sentence exceeding three months.[11] However, courts are disinclined to enforce Article 67(1a) CC,

[8] Law 3528/2007.

[9] However, research suggests that private employers ask job applicants to submit their general use extract (Blitsa 2014b).

[10] De jure and de facto CBED do not necessarily overlap. A state-conducted criminal background check is required in order to enter the bar. A hiring law firm may conduct an extra check. In contrast, there is no mandatory state clearance for shop assistants.

[11] Similar provisions are found in other criminal statutes (eg Art 36 of Law 4139/2013).

making the imposition of employment bans by licensing authorities the principal method of disqualification.[12] Following Directive 2011/92/EU on combating the sexual abuse and sexual exploitation of children and child pornography, the court may ban convicted child sex offenders from working closely with children for the same amount of time.[13] This ancillary sanction is mandatory for recidivist child sex offenders and is of lifelong duration (Article 67(1b)–(1c) CC).

C. Drawbacks of the Current Legal Framework

So far there has been no codification of the occupations and professions closed to convicted individuals. Hundreds of occupational laws were drafted by different legislative committees, and thus they vary considerably in scope. As occupational licensing laws are found outside the Criminal Code, criminal court judges and defence attorneys are often unaware of the effects a conviction may have on a convicted individual's employability. Academic work and case law on the subject are limited.[14] As a result, employment bans are a salient yet 'hidden' collateral consequence (Mauer and Chesney-Lind 2003; Uggen and Steward 2015).

In particular, the main drawbacks of the current occupational licensing legislation with regard to private sector employment[15] include:

(a) *lack of 'relevance' between the inherent requirements of the particular job and the disqualifying crimes.* Greek occupational laws state which crimes disqualify individuals from exercising which regulated occupation. However, more often than not, disqualifying offences lack any apparent relationship to the regulated occupation. For example, although a person who wants to work as a lifeguard may not have been convicted of homicide with intent, sexual or drug offences, other disqualifying offences include defamation and tax evasion;
(b) *lack of uniformity between the occupational bars similar professionals face.* For example, any kind of a felony conviction is an employment obstacle for dentists, but not for doctors. Such discrepancies could over-burden certain professionals. At the same time, they could prove to be under-protective of the public and even perilous for vulnerable social groups, such as minors. For example, although all personnel in a private kindergarten must go through a criminal background check, in private schools such mandatory clearance is limited to the teaching faculty;
(c) *cases of insufficient criminal background checking.* Although the list of disqualifying offences usually tends to be over-inclusive ((a) above), one

[12] German drafters of the *Strafgesetzbuch* (StGB) were divided on the ability of judges to safely rule upon technical and scientific matters related to employment disqualifications (Staikos 1953). Perhaps Greek judges share this hesitation.
[13] [2011] OJ L335/1.
[14] Administrative courts are reluctant to find occupational licensing statutes unconstitutional.
[15] The group's mandate did not cover public sector employment.

notices cases of private sector jobs where criminal background checking is under-inclusive (Aukerman 2005). For example, unlike financial crimes, crimes against life or sexual offences do not constitute an employment obstacle for doctors.[16] Moreover, there is no continuous screening of licence holders. With a few exceptions, judicial authorities are not required to inform licensing authorities of disqualifying convictions. Nor are the latter required to periodically ask for follow-up information on licence holders;[17]

(d) *inconsistency in the length of disqualifications*. Barring may last until the licence applicant's/professional's conviction no longer appears on his 'general use' extract. A 'judicial use' extract is used for the screening of some professionals.[18] This means that the ban is prolonged, or may even be of lifelong duration. Often, and without sufficient reason, Greek legislators adopt shorter or longer disqualification periods for certain jobs compared to the CPP's provisions (Blitsa 2014a; Pitsela et al 2018).

III. PRINCIPLES GOVERNING CRIMINAL BACKGROUND CHECKING FOR EMPLOYMENT PURPOSES

Criminal record-based employment vetting requires weighing up the rights of those convicted/charged with a crime and those (possibly) affected by crime, that is employers and individuals accepting (ex)offenders' professional services. In many fields of work, concerns about safety, public order, etc could arise. However, if the validity of employment disqualifications were to be based solely on the legitimate public interest at issue then any law barring (ex)offenders could be upheld (Aukerman 2005). Thus, when considering employment disqualifications, attention should be drawn to the scope and content of the following rights.

A. Right to Choose and Exercise an Occupation

Article 15(1) of the EU Charter of Fundamental Rights (Charter)[19] and Article 5(1) of the Greek Constitution guarantee one's right to pursue a freely chosen occupation.[20] However, as it is not absolute, the law may impose

[16] Law 1565/1939 prior to Law 4512/2018.

[17] See Jacobs and Blitsa 2012 for the continuous monitoring of individuals working with vulnerable groups in the UK.

[18] A judicial use extract is also used for the screening of public employees.

[19] Art 21 on non-discrimination and the relevant EU Directives do not mention discrimination based on a criminal conviction. Member States may add extra grounds of prohibited discrimination. Greek legislation does not explicitly forbid discriminatory treatment of convicted individuals in relation to employment (Blitsa 2014b).

[20] The latter as part of a person's right to freely develop his personality.

restrictions on this right (Dagtoglou 2012). According to well-established case law, in order for these restrictions to be in conformity with the Greek Constitution, they need to be (i) objectively defined; (ii) justified by an important public or social interest, which must be relevant to the nature and functions of the regulated occupation; and (iii) proportionate, that is, appropriate, necessary and not excessive in relation to the interest they are intended to protect.[21] By applying these rules to the barring of (ex)offenders, one concludes that occupational restrictions should only block those whose conviction is substantially related to the necessary qualifications and duties of the regulated employment (Blitsa 2014a).

B. Right to Personal Data Protection

Article 8 of the Charter and Article 9A of the Greek Constitution guarantee the right to protection of one's personal data.[22] Regulation 2016/679 on the protection of natural persons with regard to the processing of personal data and on the free movement of such data, applicable from May 2018, repealed the antecedent EU Directive 95/46/EC.[23] The European Convention on Human Rights (ECHR) does not include a distinct Article on the protection of personal data, but the Strasbourg Court has accepted that such data fall under the protection of Article 8 (respect for private life), as the purpose of the Council of Europe's 1981 Convention for the protection of individuals with regard to automatic processing of personal data is to secure for every individual respect for his right to privacy.[24]

According to Article 5 of Regulation 2016/679, personal data shall be: (i) collected for specified, explicit and legitimate purposes; (ii) adequate, relevant and limited to what is necessary in relation to the purposes for which they are processed; (iii) kept no longer than is necessary. Everyone has the right to obtain erasure of personal data concerning him when they are no longer necessary in relation to the purposes for which they were collected (the right to be forgotten[25]) (Article 17). According to Article 10, the processing of data relating to criminal convictions and offences shall be carried out only under the control of official authority, or when the processing is authorised by EU or national law

[21] Council of State, Plenary Judgments 3665/2005, 3314/2014.

[22] In some countries (Spain, Sweden and the Netherlands), data protection is incorporated into the Constitution but is linked to privacy or personal integrity. In others (Austria, Czech Republic and Portugal), the Constitution entails an independent article on data protection (Lachana 2017).

[23] [2016] OJ L119/1.

[24] *Rotaru v Romania* (2000).

[25] See Court of Justice of the European Union, *Google Spain SL and Google Inc v AEPD and Mario Costeja González* (2014).

providing for appropriate safeguards. The Hellenic Data Protection Authority has affirmed that the collection and processing of conviction information for employment purposes is only lawful when the data's nature is relevant to the particular occupation. It has also asserted that the CPP's provisions regarding expungement are related to the data subject's right to be forgotten (Hellenic Data Protection Authority, Opinion 4/2013).[26]

C. Right to Private Life

Article 8 ECHR provides a right to respect for one's private and family life. Similar protection is offered by Article 7 of the Charter and Article 9 of the Greek Constitution. Before the European Court of Human Rights (ECtHR), in the case of *MM v the United Kingdom* (2012), the applicant successfully challenged the Criminal Records Office of the Police Service of Northern Ireland's disclosure to employers that, some years before, she had accepted a caution for child abduction.[27] The ECtHR, having affirmed that conviction and caution data constitute 'sensitive personal data', criticised the national legislation with regard to criminal record disclosure to employers, for making no distinction based on the seriousness of the offence and the time that had elapsed since the offence was committed. The Court cautioned that 'as the conviction or caution itself recedes into the past, it becomes a part of the person's private life which must be respected'.[28] In the Court's view, the applicable legislation also lacked an assessment of the relevance of caution data to the employment sought by the offender.[29] The judgment, therefore, could be read as a call for a discretionary and proportionate criminal record disclosure scheme that would effectively balance public protection and privacy (Larrauri 2014b).

Moreover, in the case of *Sidabras and Džiautas v Lithuania* (2004), the applicants were banned from private sector occupations, due to their former KGB officer status. The ECtHR, which examined the case under Article 14 (prohibition of discrimination)[30] in conjunction with Article 8, affirmed that states have a legitimate interest in regulating employment conditions in the public and private sector. Although the Court reiterated that the Convention does not guarantee the right to have access to a particular profession, it accepted

[26] See Art 6 of the Council of Europe's 1981 Convention and Art 10 of Recommendation No R(89) 2 on the protection of personal data used for employment purposes.

[27] MM absconded with her granddaughter in order to prevent the baby's mother from taking her to Australia.

[28] *MM v the United Kingdom* (2012), para 188.

[29] In the same way, see *Schware v Board of Bar Examiners of New Mexico* (1957).

[30] Art 14 ECHR has no independent existence, but has effect in relation to the rights safeguarded by the Convention.

that a far-reaching ban on taking up private sector employment does affect 'private life', that is one's ability to develop relationships with the outside world and earn one's living. The Court noted that the Act providing for the ban on employing former KGB agents in certain public and private sector positions pursued legitimate aims, such as the protection of national security, based on their presumed lack of loyalty to the state. However, the Court stressed that an employee's loyalty to the state is not inevitably an inherent requirement for employment with private companies. In addition, the ECtHR criticised the KGB Act for not containing definitions of the prohibited private sector jobs. As a result, it was 'impossible to ascertain any reasonable link between the positions concerned and the legitimate aims sought by the ban'.[31] The judgment, therefore, asserts that state-imposed restrictions on private sector employment need to be objectively justified, precise and proportionate to the aim pursued.

D. Human Dignity

Respect for human dignity is found in Article 1 of the Charter and Article 2(1) of the Greek Constitution. Human dignity is a general 'umbrella' principle under which many fundamental rights are protected. Recent ECtHR case law obliges Member States not only to refrain from actions that may offend it, but also to take positive action in order to protect it (Mowbray 2004). Notably, before the introduction of Article 25 of the Greek Constitution, which elevated respect for the principle of proportionality, with regard to all restrictions on civil rights, to a constitutional norm, protection of human dignity served as the principle's founding ground (Dimitratos 2007). Furthermore, offenders' rights to resocialisation and rehabilitation are considered to derive from the right to human dignity (Morgenstern 2011; Archimandritou 2012; Meijer 2017). Protection of human dignity also requires the Greek state to guarantee a decent minimum living level for all individuals, and to abstain from actions that would erode it.This obligation relates, for instance, to the deprivation of a pension as a result of a criminal conviction (Fytrakis 2013),[32] but it is equally applicable to other restrictions on an offender's prospects for earning a living, such as employment disqualifications.The latter should be narrow enough so that the offender is left with reasonable opportunities to find employment and have means of subsistence.

[31] *Sidabras and Džiautas v Lithuania* (2004), para 59.

[32] In *Apostolakis v Greece* (2009), the ECtHR considered the deprivation of a public servant's pension as a result of a criminal conviction a second criminal sanction, as the deprivation was automatic, absolute and came at an age when the applicant would no longer be employable.

E. Offender Rehabilitation

It is a consistent conclusion of empirical criminology that if ex-offenders cannot obtain legitimate employment, their chances of gravitating toward crime are higher, to the detriment of mainstream society (Uggen 2000). Article 10 of the International Covenant on Civil and Political Rights requires state parties' penitentiary system to promote prisoners' social rehabilitation. The Greek state is required to care for the timely and smooth reintegration of ex-prisoners into their social, professional and family environment (Articles 81–82 of the Penitentiary Code). Additionally, the CPP's provisions regarding the limited time for which convictions appear on a 'general use' extract are intended to promote offenders' employability and rehabilitation.[33] These provisions have no value, however, when the absence of any criminal conviction, regardless of its relevance to the employment sought, constitutes an employment prerequisite. Such a request may crush all chances the convicted individual has for finding work, even as a self-employed individual, and thus for social reintegration (Hellenic Data Protection Authority, Opinion 4/2013).

F. Conclusion

In view of what has been said, it is clear not only that employment disqualifications should pursue legitimate goals, but also that the adopted measures should fit tightly with these goals (Aukerman 2005). The common denominator in any restriction imposed on the above-mentioned rights is the application of the principle of proportionality. In order not to infringe upon their right to work, personal data protection, a personal life and human dignity, and in order to promote rehabilitation, employment bans on (ex)offenders need to be: (i) restricted to offences related to the necessary abilities and skills to successfully fulfil the regulated occupation's duties and responsibilities; (ii) related to offences and sentences of a certain gravity; and (iii) conscious of lapsed time, so as to mitigate the continued effects of a past criminal punishment (Larrauri 2014a–2014b).

IV. KEY POLICY QUESTIONS AND POSSIBLE ANSWERS

Policymaking in the area of CBED needs to further blend respect for the principles mentioned with practical considerations: Which authority is best suited to enforce employment disqualifications? Which crimes are 'relevant' to the regulated occupations? And how long should employment bans last? In this section,

[33] Accompanying Report to Royal Decree 4/8 June 1938.

we suggest reforms to the Greek licensing scheme. However, it is our aspiration that our analysis is relevant to the introduction of any fair and balanced employment vetting regime.

A. Who Should Decide on the Suitability of Ex-offenders?

The first issue that needs to be decided upon is which authority will have the power to prevent convicted individuals from engaging in various employments. In recent years, Greece has witnessed a proliferation of administrative CBED statutes. At the same time, courts have been extremely reluctant to impose the ancillary sanction of Article 67(1a) CC leading to the revocation of a convicted individual's occupational licence. In any case, Article 67 CC is limited in scope, as it only covers cases of convicted individuals who already practise a certain occupation and not those who have yet to choose an occupation and apply for a licence. Arguably, the sentencing judge cannot be expected to predict and specify the defendant's future job responsibilities (Von Hirsch and Wasik 1997).

These settled limitations push towards the preservation of a parallel occupational licensing scheme. That being said, the conditions for disqualifying a convicted individual for a given profession by means of an administrative decision need to be expressly prescribed by law. The professional exclusion of offenders by legal rules that have been declared beforehand and which bind state officials (in contrast to administrative guidelines) respects the principle of legality. Representatives of professional associations should not, due to their lack of legal training and impartiality (they might be over-protective of their members and under-protective of the public), play a decisive role in the matter. However, their experience may add value to the relevant legislative process, and thus consulting them should be encouraged. Ideally, occupational licensing legislation should be enforced by a central licensing authority, as in the Netherlands (Boone 2011), responsible for all regulated employment. A central authority is likely to function better than the current system of multiple and disconnected licensing authorities. Unfortunately, due to current economic hardships, there are no plans for setting up such an authority in Greece.

B. What Makes a Conviction for a Certain Crime 'Relevant' to the Regulated Occupation?

It is true that no one can safely foresee another person's future criminal behaviour. At the same time, though, a person's criminal past might prove to be useful in order to assess his potential work performance. In order, therefore, to avoid infinitely expandable exclusions, employment disqualifications should tailor the nature of the regulated occupation to the offender's criminal past. Damaska (1968: 553) argues that convictions should be disqualifying 'only to the extent they are actually relevant to fitness for the particular occupation'. Von Hirsch and Wasik (1997: 610) suggest that we need to identify what 'makes [a particular occupation] sensitive to abuse, and what kind of potential abuse is involved'. As the occupation of banker carries with it a special risk of dishonesty, 'a fraud conviction may well suggest that risk, but a conviction for … drug abuse would not' (Von Hirsch and Wasik 1997: 610–11). Indeed, when someone commits a crime, he offends a certain interest protected by criminal law ('*Rechtsgut*' in German). For example, sexual offences offend against sexual freedom; theft offends against personal property. Positions that require the protection of a particular interest, or which place it at the professional's disposal, should not be open, at least for a period of time, to a person convicted of a crime that offends against it.

Notably, the requirement for commensurability between the disqualifying conviction and the regulated employment is present in several European countries:[34] German case law has restricted the possibilities for an employer to ask for a job applicant's past convictions when they are directly relevant to the job, relating to traffic offences for lorry drivers and property offences for tellers (Morgenstern 2011). Finnish job seekers may receive a copy of their criminal record, provided it is relevant to the job sought (Jacobs and Larrauri 2016). Moreover, the importance of 'relevance' has not escaped the attention of the ECtHR. In the case of *MM v the United Kingdom* (2012), the Court criticised the applicable disqualification legislation for lacking an assessment 'of the relevance of conviction or caution data … to the employment sought, or of the extent to which the data subject may be perceived as continuing to pose a risk such that the disclosure of the data to the employer is justified'.[35] In the case of *Thlimmenos v Greece* (2000), the applicant, a Jehovah's Witness, was barred from a chartered accountant's post because of a previous conviction for insubordination for having refused to wear a military uniform at a time of general mobilisation. Although the Court examined the applicant's complaints under Article 14 ECHR in conjunction with Article 9 (freedom of religion), it was preoccupied with the effects the applicant's crime had on his employment suitability, noting that

> states have a legitimate interest to exclude some offenders from the profession of chartered accountant … However, unlike other convictions for serious criminal offences, a conviction for refusing on religious or philosophical grounds to wear the military uniform cannot imply any dishonesty or moral turpitude likely to undermine the offender's ability to exercise this profession.[36]

[34] See Aukerman 2005 for US case law on occupational restrictions (examined under the equal protection clause), requiring a conviction substantially related to the occupation's qualifications and duties.

[35] *MM v the United Kingdom* (2012), para 204.

[36] *Thlimmenos v Greece* (2000), para 47.

What we can further deduce from the above is that employment disqualifications are mainly addressed (with the exception of positions of high public standing, eg judges) not to the offender's incapacity but to his future behaviour.[37] In other words, they primarily aim to prevent reoffending.[38] In Greece, the sanction of Article 67(1a)–(1b) CC may be imposed if the judge finds that there is a risk the convicted individual will re-abuse his occupation. If the judge is satisfied that the principal sanction is sufficient to prevent the offender from reoffending, the convicted individual will not be disqualified (Bouropoulos 1959). Notably, although court-ordered employment disqualification is classified in the Criminal Code as an ancillary sanction, it has been argued that it is a security measure[39] (ie a prophylactic measure against the individual's dangerousness) due to its inherent risk prognosis[40] (Zisiadis 1971). Whether employment disqualifications imposed by a regulatory authority as an automatic result of a criminal conviction constitute punishment,[41] as do disqualifications imposed at the sentencing stage,[42] is equally debatable (Larrauri and Jacobs 2013; Von Hirsch and Wasik 1997).[43] Regardless, however, of one's views on the nature of employment disqualifications – which cannot be pursued further here – engaging in a risk assessment makes the application of proportionality even more imperative in order to outweigh unfettered discretion. The principle of proportionality is applicable, at least in Greek theory and jurisprudence, to all fields of law, and not just criminal sanctions. Proportionality itself entails a future prognosis in order to assess the suitability of the means used to achieve a specific end, as well as careful balancing of the conflicting rights and interests (Dimitratos 2007).

That having been said, it is not always easy to separate relevant from non-relevant crimes in order to introduce needful limitations to employment disqualifications. Admittedly, there is no commonly accepted criterion that could help policymakers easily detect all crimes that present a close nexus to each regulated employment (Larrauri 2014a). Even within the borders of the

[37] CBED may also seek to preserve the status and trustworthiness of the relevant profession (Council of State, Plenary Judgment 3314/2014). These criteria, though, which stretch the notion of relevance, should be employed in a narrow range of occupations (Damaska 1968; Von Hirsch and Wasik 1997).

[38] Communication from the Commission to the Council and the European Parliament, Disqualifications arising from criminal convictions in the European Union (SEC(2006)220).

[39] See Art 70 StGB.

[40] Security measures should be proportional to the danger they are set to prevent (Mylonopoulos 2007).

[41] Criminal sanctions have three aims: (i) retribution, (ii) general deterrence, and (iii) specific deterrence (Kivrakidou 2009; Margaritis and Paraskeuopoulos 2000).

[42] Throughout the EU, conviction-based disqualifications take three forms: (i) penalty ordered by the court, (ii) additional penalty, automatically imposed as a consequence of the principal penalty, (iii) penalty ordered in administrative proceedings arising as a result of a conviction. Communication from the Commission to the Council and the European Parliament, n 38.

[43] The ECtHR's case law focuses on the nature and severity of the measure, regardless of its domestic law classification, so as to apply criminal law guarantees. See *Engel and others v the Netherlands* (1976).

same legal order, the list of regulated occupations is prone to change, and so is the list of crimes. Moreover, the practice of each occupation entails different protected interests. Inevitably, the practical application of the notion of 'relevance' demands the meticulous examination of each separate occupation. Accepting this reality, the Greek working group attempted to first codify the regulated occupations into broad categories (eg medical, educational, etc) and then match the inherent requirements of each job to the existing criminal offences, focusing on the protected interests they involve. Through this course, the group aimed to achieve correlation between offences and positions, as well as uniformity between the bars faced by similar occupations (Pitsela et al 2018). The task was a difficult one, as occupational laws not only cover clearly relevant or irrelevant crimes, but also many in between. For example, reasonable people might disagree about the effects of a battery conviction against his wife on the offender's employment as a teacher. On many occasions, the group accepted the majority vote. The group's effort to revamp Greek employment vetting scheme rules is an innovative undertaking, and it is, of course, open to further discussion and research.

Regardless, though, of one's methodology, when putting the notion of 'relevance' into practice, some further questions common to all occupations arise, which are discussed in sections i–iii following.

i. Should the Conditions of the Offence Affect its 'Relevance'?

In an effort to answer this question, the working group made a distinction between 'general' and 'on duty' relevance. Generally relevant are those crimes that constitute an obstacle to employment regardless of whether they were committed during the perpetrator's personal or professional life. In contrast, 'on duty' relevant crimes are those that constitute an obstacle only when the perpetrator committed them at work or by taking advantage of his profession. For example, negligent manslaughter should be an 'on duty' relevant crime for doctors: if a doctor caused the death of another through negligent or reckless driving, this should not lead to the revocation of his licence; if, however, he caused the death of a patient as a result of medical malpractice, he could lose his licence. In contrast, sexual offences against minors should be a 'generally' relevant crime for child-centered positions. If a person is convicted of a sexual offence against a minor, he should be prevented from working as a teacher, no matter when or where he committed the crime.This division between 'generally' and 'on duty' relevant crimes does not exist in Greek occupational licensing laws.[44] However, its proposed introduction, by the working group, mirrors other Greek criminal provisions (Pitsela et al 2018).[45]

[44] But see Art 52 Law 1026/1980.

[45] For example, Art 262 CC provides for an aggravating factor leading to a higher penalty in the case of a public servant who commits a felony or misdemeanour while on duty or by taking advantage of his status.

ii. Should the Penalty Imposed by the Court Impact on the 'Relevance' of the Offence?

In the case of *MM v the United Kingdom* (2012), the ECtHR stressed the importance the seriousness of the offence has for assessing whether the convicted job seeker continues to pose a risk. Moreover, in the field of criminal law, the principle of proportionality requires a sanction that fits the seriousness of the offence. In line with this principle, Article 79 CC requires the sentencing judge to evaluate the seriousness of the offence committed, as well as the offender's personality. On top of that, Article 67(1a) CC takes into account the gravity of the sentence imposed, by requiring a minimum sentence of three months' imprisonment, regardless of the penalty prescribed by law for the offence. The Article further requires a grave violation of professional duties in order to correlate the gravity of the act and of the principal sanction, on the one hand, and the ancillary sanction, on the other (Pavlou 1991).

Given, therefore, that the seriousness of the penalty reflects the seriousness of the criminal act, occupational licensing legislation should also factor in the criminal penalty imposed. In particular, the working group favoured excluding from the disqualification process convictions for which the perpetrator received a minor sentence (Pitsela et al 2018). In our view, a low-level sentence reflecting minor criminal behaviour, for a crime that would otherwise be disqualifying for the regulated employment, should not have a bearing on the offender's employment suitability.

iii. Should a Final Decision be a Prerequisite for the Offender's Disqualification?

Occupational licensing legislation is uncertain as to the level of procedural maturity required for the imposition of employment disqualifications. Sometimes an irrevocable criminal decision is required; in other cases a decision subject to an appeal will do. Nevertheless, in several cases, pending charges suffice for the imposition of a disqualification. By contrast, court-ordered employment disqualifications are enforced when the criminal conviction becomes irrevocable (Article 67(2)-65 CC). Serious issues arise here, such as respect for the presumption of innocence (Article 6(2) ECHR) (Blitsa 2014a). Regardless of one's views on whether an employment disqualification ordered in administrative proceedings amounts to a criminal penalty, one cannot but concede that (i) its imposition is dependent upon a previous/parallel criminal procedure, the outcome of which has a decisive bearing on it, and (ii) the consequences of the disqualification for the defendant may be greater than those of the sanction imposed by the criminal court. Barring an individual from the exercise of an occupation because of a crime germane to his qualifications and functions, before his natural judge has a chance to decide on his guilt, therefore collides with the defendant's defence rights.

Admittedly, with regard to the use of information on sexual offences, special provisions are found in several European countries, for example expungement is prolonged, disclosure to employers is mandatory or it involves pre-conviction information (Boone 2011; Herzog-Evans 2011; Morgenstern 2011). When dealing with child sexual abuse, should pending charges be enough to bar the accused from working with children? Cinematography helps paint a picture here: in Vinterberg's film, *The Hunt*, a kindergarten teacher's life in a Danish village is seriously disrupted as one of his students falsely accuses him of sexual assault. On the other hand, one cannot forget the case of 'the Soham murders'. In 2002, Ian Huntley, a school caretaker, murdered two 10-year-old girls. The police had not informed the school that, from 1995 to 1999, Huntley was the subject of nine separate allegations of sexual offences, including unlawful underage sex, rape and indecent assault of a minor, which never led to charges. This notorious case put pressure on the British Government to ratchet up criminal background checking (Jacobs and Blitsa 2012).[46]

How can one balance these realities? It is true that criminal trials may take a long time before offering the assurance of a criminal conviction. At the same time, children are a special group of vulnerable people. The Greek Constitution explicitly requires childhood to be protected by the state (Article 21). As a result, even before a final verdict is reached, prevention of (further) victimisation is necessary. In view of the above, and in order to have a safe indication of the person's unsuitability, as a rule, only irrevocable convicting decisions should constitute an obstacle to employment. Only in exceptional occasions, when a more significant (compared to the rights of the accused) interest is at stake, such as the protection of minors or national security,[47] should revocable decisions or even pending charges disqualify the individual from his chosen occupation (Blitsa 2014a; Pitsela et al 2018). Even then, a final acquittal by the competent criminal court should lead to the lifting of the disqualification imposed.

C. How Long Should Offenders be Barred from Certain Occupations? Should they be Able to Challenge their Disqualification?

In Greece, the ancillary sanction of Article 67(1) CC cannot exceed five years, except in the case of recidivist child sex offenders, when it is of lifelong duration.

[46] Notably, Huntley's girlfriend was employed at the girls' school (Larrauri 2014b).

[47] See ECtHR, *Leander v Sweden* (1987), where the applicant was lawfully barred from a security-sensitive position on account of police information. In *DMT and DKI v Bulgaria* (2012), two police officers were suspended from office due to criminal charges against them. The Court accepted that the suspension served a legitimate aim, but found a violation of Art 8 ECHR because the suspension, during which the applicants could not work in the public or private sector, was prolonged. Compare to *Karov v Bulgaria* (2006).

In addition, individual character examination is required in order to assess the length of the principal sentence and of the court-ordered disqualification (Article 79 CC). In contrast, the duration of CBED ordered by licensing authorities varies considerably. While it is usually matched to the time for which the conviction appears on the individual's 'general use' or 'judicial use' extract, occupational laws may prescribe shorter or longer disqualification periods for certain positions, making the duration of employment disqualifications difficult to foresee and the relevant legislative choices hard to comprehend.

Regardless of the disqualification procedure, the licence applicant's/professional's criminal record serves as a proxy for the prognosis of future harm, and consequently for the length of his professional exclusion. Should this risk prediction be individual or group-based? Notably, the age of the record and what the person has done in the meantime are equally important to the record's content in assessing the risk of reoffending (Aukerman 2005). Bushway, Nieuwbeerta and Blokland (2011) argue that the offender's age and number of criminal convictions affect his probability of reoffending, and should thus be considered in the context of record expungement. Admittedly, however, it is not feasible to apply purely subjective criteria for the disqualification of ex-offenders, by adopting a case-by-case approach. Especially when disqualifications are ordered by regulatory bodies rather than judges, clear, objective and predetermined rules are necessary for the imposition of restrictions on offenders' rights. At the same time, a fixed period of time for expungement eligibility or for the lifting of an employment ban may be over-inclusive in the case of offenders who have quickly grown out of crime. The Council of Europe's Recommendation No R(84) 10 on the criminal record and rehabilitation of convicted persons calls on Member States to provide for an automatic legal rehabilitation after a reasonably short period of time and, if appropriate, for a possibility of earlier legal rehabilitation at the request of the person concerned.

In light of the above, we support the modification of the current Greek occupational licensing legislation so as to include unified,[48] yet fair and balanced, time limitations to employment disqualifications, which take into account the seriousness of the committed crime, the execution of the sentence and the absence of recidivism. Nonetheless, recognising that 'one-size-fits-all' policies unnecessarily disadvantage certain offenders, and in order to reward rehabilitation, we favour an exceptional and additional possibility to the automatic (ie after a certain period of time has elapsed) 'legal' rehabilitation procedure, which allows for individual rehabilitation assessments (Pitsela et al 2018).[49] In particular, the convicted individual should be able to apply to a judicial authority to shorten the disqualification period, provided he proves that he has

[48] With few exceptions, eg employment that involves regular and close contact with children.

[49] See Herzog-Evans 2011 for French discretionary rehabilitation procedures. See also Art 70a StGB.

been rehabilitated and that the reduction of time is necessary for him to find employment.[50] This option should not be limited to petty crimes or sentences and should be subject to review. The gravity of an ex-offender's offences should not deprive him of a chance to honestly prove that he is capable of irreproachable life choices.

V. EPILOGUE

The present chapter does not claim to have covered all matters relating to CBED. Employment barring of (ex)offenders is a multifaceted issue, which touches upon several fields of law: constitutional, criminal, labour and administrative (Larrauri and Jacobs 2013). What is more, employment vetting of (ex)offenders is a difficult task that must strike the right balance between conflicting public and individual rights and interests. Such a composite subject cannot be exhausted within the limits of a single chapter in a book. It is hoped, though, that our research has revealed the importance of the guarantees of the rule of law for the adoption of employment disqualifications based on prior criminal activity.

The principle of proportionality advises against over-broad exclusion policies. Limitations on employment disqualifications based on the relevance, seriousness, time and circumstances of the disqualifying crime, and restrictions on the ban's duration, should respect offenders' rights and promote rehabilitation and, ultimately, social cohesion. Employment barring should not be viewed as a block but rather as a penetrable net, which would constrain clearly unsuitable individuals but allow those whose prior criminal behaviour is unrelated to the content of their chosen professional activity, or whose link to their criminal past is ruptured, to re-establish themselves professionally in society. Only then may equilibrium between security and liberty, exclusion and restoration be achieved. It is our hope that the present chapter will spark further national or European research, and motivate criminal justice policymakers to regulate employment disqualifications more clearly, fairly and efficiently.

REFERENCES

Archimandritou, M (2012) *Η Φυλάκιση ως Τρόπος Κράτησης και ως Μορφή Έκτισης της Ποινής* (Σάκκουλας Αθήνα - Θεσσαλονίκη).

Aukerman MJ (2005) 'The Somewhat Suspect Class: Towards a Constitutional Framework for Evaluating Occupational Restrictions Affecting People with Criminal Records' *Journal of Law in Society*, 7(1), 1–65.

[50] Similar opportunities should be offered to rehabilitated drug-addicted offenders (Pitsela et al 2018).

Blitsa, D (2014a) 'Η Διάκριση στον Τομέα της Εργασίας λόγω Προηγούμενης Ποινικής Καταδίκης (Μέρος Α)' *Ποινική Δικαιοσύνη*, 7, 626–32.

—— (2014b) 'Η Διάκριση στον Τομέα της Εργασίας λόγω Προηγούμενης Ποινικής Καταδίκης (Μέρος Β)' *Ποινική Δικαιοσύνη*, 8, 739–52.

Boone, M (2011) 'Judicial Rehabilitation in the Netherlands. Balancing between Safety and Privacy' *European Journal of Probation*, 3(1), 63–78.

Bouropoulos, A (1959) Ερμηνεία Ποινικού Δικαίου-Γενικό Μέρος Ι (Αφοί Π. Σάκκουλα).

Bushway, S, Nieuwbeerta, P and Blokland, A (2011) 'The Predictive Value of Criminal Background Checks: Do Age and Criminal History Affect Time to Redemption?' *American Society of Criminology*, 49(1), 27–60.

Dagtoglou, P (2012) *Συνταγματικό Δίκαιο–Ατομικά Δικαιώματα* (Σάκκουλας Αθήνα-Θεσσαλονίκη).

Damaska, M (1968) 'Adverse Legal Consequences of Conviction and Their Removal: A Comparative Study (Part 2)' *The Journal of Criminal Law, Criminology and Police Science*, 59(4), 542–68.

Dimitratos, N (2007) 'Αρχή της Αναλογικότητας και Επιβολή Ποινικών Κυρώσεων στην Ελληνική Έννομη Τάξη' *Νομικό Βήμα*, 55, 45–52.

Fytrakis, E (2013) 'Η Στέρηση της Σύνταξης ως Ποινή' *Νομικό Βήμα*, 66, 2766–88.

Gavouneli, M and Traianos, P (2008) 'The European Criminal Record in Greece' in C Stefanou and H Xanthaki (eds), *Towards a European Criminal Record* (Cambridge, Cambridge University Press).

Giovanoglou, S (2006) *Θεσμικά Προβλήματα της Κοινωνικής Επανένταξης των Αποφυλακιζομένων* (Σάκκουλας Αθήνα-Θεσσαλονίκη).

Hellenic Data Protection Authority, Opinions 4/2013 and 101/2016.

Herzog-Evans, M (2011) 'Judicial Rehabilitation in France: Helping with the Desisting Process and Acknowledging Achieved Distance' *European Journal of Probation*, 3(1), 4–19.

Jacobs, JB and Larrauri, E (2016) 'European Criminal Records and Ex-Offender Employment' in *Oxford Handbooks Online* (Oxford, Oxford University Press).

Jacobs, JB and Blitsa, D (2012) 'US, EU & UK Employment Vetting as Strategy for Preventing Convicted Sex Offenders from Gaining Access to Children' *European Journal of Crime, Criminal Law and Criminal Justice*, 20(3), 265–96.

Kivrakidou, A (2009) *Η Αρχή της Αναλογικότητας κατά την Επιμέτρηση της Ποινής* (Διπλωματική Εργασία, Αριστοτέλειο Πανεπιστήμιο Θεσσαλονίκης).

Lachana, KC (2017) *Η κατά το Ελληνικό Δίκαιο Ποινική Προστασία των Προσωπικών Δεδομένων στο Πλαίσιο της Αστυνομικής και Δικαστικής Συνεργασίας σε Ποινικές Υποθέσεις: Προκλήσεις και Προοπτικές* (Διατριβή επί Διδακτορία, Αριστοτέλειο Πανεπιστήμιο Θεσσαλονίκης)

Larrauri, E (2014a) 'Legal Protections against Criminal Background Checks in Europe' *Punishment and Society*, 16(1), 50–73.

—— (2014b) 'Criminal Record Disclosure and the Right to Privacy' *Criminal Law Review*, 10, 723–37.

Larrauri, E and Jacobs, JB (2013) 'A Spanish Window on European Law and Policy on Employment Discrimination Based on Criminal Record' in T Daems, D Van Zyl Smit and S Snacken (eds), *European Penology?* (Oxford, Hart Publishing).

Louks, N, Lyner, O and Sullivan, T (1998) 'The Employment of People with Criminal Records in the European Union' *European Journal on Criminal Policy and Research*, 6(2), 195–210.

Margaritis, L and Paraskeuopoulos, N (2000) *Ποινολογία* (Σάκκουλας Αθήνα-Θεσσαλονίκη).
Mauer, M and Chesney-Lind, M (eds) (2003) *Invisible Punishment: The Collateral Consequences of Mass Imprisonment* (New York, The New Press).
Meijer, S (2017) 'Rehabilitation as a Positive Obligation' *European Journal of Crime, Criminal Law and Criminal Justice*, 25(2) 145–62.
Morgenstern, C (2011) 'Judicial Rehabilitation in Germany – The Use of Criminal Records and the Removal of Recorded Convictions' *European Journal of Probation*, 3(1), 20–35.
Mowbray, A (2004) *The Development of Positive Obligations under the European Convention of Human Rights by the European Court of Human Rights* (Oxford, Hart Publishing).
Mylonopoulos, C (2007) *Ποινικό Δίκαιο-Γενικό Μέρος I* (Π.Ν. Σάκκουλας).
Pitsela et al (2018), 'Έκθεση για τον Εξορθολογισμό των Κωλυμάτων Επαγγελματικής Επανένταξης Αποφυλακισθέντων και εν γένει Ποινικώς Διωχθέντων Προσώπων' σε Φυτράκης Ε. (επ), *Αόρατες ποινές. Ευρωπαϊκή διάσταση-Ελληνική προοπτική* (Υπουργείο Δικαιοσύνης, Διαφάνειας και Ανθρωπίνων Δικαιωμάτων, Αθήνα: Εθνικό Τυπογραφείο).
Pavlou, S (1991) 'Οι Αρχές της Αναλογίας κατά την Επιβολή Παρεπόμενων Ποινών: Ένα Εγγυητικό "Επιμετρητικό" Πρόχωμα' *Υπεράσπιση*, 731–41.
Staikos, A (1953) *Επίτομος Ερμηνεία Ελληνικού Ποινικού Κώδικος, τόμος I* (Μ. Φραγκούλης).
Stefanou, C and Xanthaki H (eds) (2008) *Towards a European Criminal Record* (Cambridge, Cambridge University Press).
Uggen, C (2000) 'Work as a Turning Point in the Life Course of Criminals: A Duration Model of Age, Employment, and Recidivism' *American Sociological Review*, 67, 529–46.
Uggen, C and Steward, R (2015) 'Piling On: Collateral Consequences and Community Supervision' *Minnesota Law Review*, 99(5), 1871–912.
Vermeulen, G et al (2002) *Blueprint for an EU Criminal Database: Legal, Politico-Institutional & Practical Feasibility* (Antwerp, Maklu).
Von Hirsch, A and Wasik, M (1997) 'Disqualifications Attending Conviction: A Suggested Conceptual Framework' *Cambridge Law Journal*, 56(3), 599–626.
Zisiadis, I (1971) *Ποινικόν Δίκαιον-Γενικό Μέρος, τόμος Α* (Αφοί Π.Σάκκουλα).

TABLE OF CASES

Domestic Cases

Greek Council of State, Plenary Judgments 3665/2005 and 3314/2014.

US Cases

United States Supreme Court, *Schware v Board of Bar Examiners of New Mexico* 353 US 232 (1957).

Court of Justice of the European Union

Case C-131/12 *Google Spain SL and Google Inc v AEPD and Mario Costeja González* ECLI:EU:C:2014:317

European Court of Human Rights

Apostolakis v Greece App no 39574/07 (22 October 2009)
DMT and DKI v Bulgaria App no 29476/06 (24 July 2012)
Engel and others v the Netherlands App nos 5100/71, 5101/71, 5102/71, 5354/72, 5370/72 (8 June 1976)
Karov v Bulgaria App no 45964/99 (16 November 2006)
Leander v Sweden App no 9248/81 (21 March 1987)
MM v the United Kingdom App no 24029/07 (13 November 2012)
Rotaru v Romania App no 28341/95 (4 May 2000)
Sidabras and Džiautas v Lithuania App nos 55480/00 and 59330/00 (27 July 2004)
Thlimmenos v Greece App no 34369/97 (6 April 2000)

Part III

Dangerous Offenders and Legal Consequences of Criminal Conviction

9

Fundamental Rights and Indeterminate Sentencing in England and Wales: The Value and Limits of a Right to Rehabilitation

HARRY ANNISON AND AILBHE O'LOUGHLIN*

I. INTRODUCTION

THIS CHAPTER EXAMINES a far-reaching and controversial sentencing measure targeted at 'dangerous offenders' in England and Wales: the indeterminate sentence of imprisonment for public protection (IPP), introduced by the Criminal Justice Act (CJA) 2003. In the context of this edited collection, this chapter has two primary aims: first, to point to the extent to which legal consequences can impact on individuals *within* the traditional confines of the criminal justice system. Second, to point to the distance travelled by the European Court of Human Rights (ECtHR) (and the domestic English courts) in beginning to recognise a right to rehabilitation, but also the important limits – in terms of both practical barriers and conceptual restrictions – that have been placed on this. In doing so, this chapter examines specific issues facing thousands of individuals in England and Wales who have been branded 'dangerous', while also pointing to conceptual considerations that resonate more deeply – both across 'types' of offenders and across national boundaries.

The last two decades have seen a 'preventive turn' in Anglo-American criminal law (Carvalho 2017) and the more general rise of 'preventive justice' as a

* Thanks to Sonja Meijer, Lucia Zedner and attendees at the Oñati workshop for comments on earlier drafts.

dominant orientation of the criminal justice system (Ashworth and Zedner 2014). Associated with growing concern to predict and minimise risks to the security of citizens, Anglo-American nations have seen an increasing desire to identify, segregate and, by means that have varied over time, 'eliminate' threatening, dangerous 'others' from society (Pratt 1997; Rutherford 2006). As the contributions by Dessecker and Keyzer and O'Donovan to this edited collection demonstrate, such trends have also emerged and continue to have important effects elsewhere in Europe, and in Australia.

One of the most restrictive measures taken against the 'dangerous' is preventive detention. Such measures have raised major concerns regarding the extent to which they circumvent traditional criminal law safeguards, undermine rights enshrined in the European Convention of Human Rights (ECHR) and other international treaties, and impose punishment beyond what is proportionate to the crime committed (McSherry et al 2009; Brown 2011; Ashworth and Zedner 2014).

Similarly to a life sentence, the IPP sentence is composed of a determinate period of detention for the purposes of punishment (the 'tariff'), followed by an indeterminate period of detention for the purposes of public protection, during which the prisoner may apply to the Parole Board for release. For its proponents in the British Government, the IPP was an effort at ensuring that those who were highly likely to commit further serious offences were detained in prison long enough to receive appropriate rehabilitative interventions (Annison 2015: chapter 3). For its critics, it was an example of 'tough' political posturing on crime and an effort to warehouse troubled individuals (Prison Reform Trust 2007: 6).

The implementation of the IPP had dramatic effects on the prison and probation system of England and Wales, which have in turn had detrimental impacts on the lives of individuals caught up by 'one of the least carefully planned and implemented pieces of legislation in the history of British sentencing' (Jacobson and Hough 2010). Due to a failure to provide adequate resources for the rehabilitative programmes IPP prisoners were required to complete to prove their suitability for release, many were, and some continue to be, detained well beyond their tariff. While no further IPP sentences may be imposed following the abolition of the IPP by the Legal Aid, Sentencing and Punishment of Offenders (LASPO) Act 2012, increasing numbers of individuals released from prison are being recalled due to breaches of their IPP licences.

The problems faced by IPP prisoners speak more generally to barriers to reintegration faced by offenders in England and Wales, as well as to normative questions about what the criminal justice system is seeking to accomplish, and the sometimes unintended or unforeseen consequences of the means through which it pursues its aims. Specifically, in this chapter, we focus on a succession of legal challenges to the IPP in domestic courts and before the ECtHR. While judgments of the ECtHR recognising a 'right to rehabilitation' (van Zyl Smit et al 2014) for prisoners serving indeterminate sentences appear at first to be progressive, we argue that, ultimately, the Court fails fundamentally to challenge the problematic logic of the IPP sentence. We suggest that, in order to begin to address the problems facing IPP prisoners, the post-tariff period of the IPP sentence must be distinct in practice (and experience) from the *punitive* pre-tariff period. But beyond this, we argue that insights from developments in the desistance literature must be drawn upon to avoid a problematically narrow notion of 'rehabilitation' that focuses solely on reductions in the risk of recidivism.

To do this, we first briefly set out the history of the IPP sentence and the problems it created, before discussing legal challenges and relevant legal judgments from the UK courts and the ECtHR. Then we consider the successive waves of legal challenges brought against the IPP sentence in the UK courts and the ECtHR, and critique the extent to which the courts have been willing to take an activist approach to upholding the rights of individuals subject to the IPP sentence. We then explore the importance and implications of the pre-/post-tariff distinction, and suggest that the post-tariff *preventive* element of the IPP should be distinct in terms of practice from the pre-tariff *punitive* element of the sentence. Lastly, we draw on insights from the desistance from crime literature to argue for a more nuanced and holistic conception of rehabilitation. In so doing, our specific discussion of issues relating to the indeterminate imprisonment of 'dangerous offenders' in England and Wales speaks to more general considerations regarding the potential for coercive preventive measures imposed after conviction to undermine the longer-term goal of desistance from crime.

II. THE CREATION OF THE IPP SENTENCE AND ITS EFFECTS

An IPP sentence is structured similarly to a standard life sentence.[1] When such sentences were imposed, the trial judge set a minimum term equivalent to the determinate sentence that would otherwise have been imposed for the offence (the 'tariff') – the punitive element. After expiry of the tariff, the offender would be released on licence *only* if the Parole Board was satisfied that he no longer posed a risk to the public – the preventive element.

Offenders were brought within the scope of the IPP sentence if they had previously committed one of 153 'specified offences' set out in schedule 15 to the CJA 2003, which was also 'serious' (carrying a maximum sentence of at least 10 years' imprisonment). Under section 225(1)(b) of the 2003 Act, if the judge was then 'of the opinion that there is a significant risk to members of

[1] For detailed discussion of life imprisonment and issues therein, see van Zyl Smit and Appleton 2016.

the public of serious harm occasioned by the commission by [the offender] of further specified offences', an IPP sentence had to be imposed. The court was not compelled to commission or consult any specific expert reports (Sentencing Guidelines Council 2008).[2]

The first opportunity for a parole hearing comes, in theory, at the end of the tariff period. In practice, IPP prisoners must rely on the smooth working of the penal system to afford them the opportunity to engage in appropriate rehabilitative courses addressing risk factors for offending and to move to lower-security category prisons at appropriate intervals. Furthermore, the Probation Service, Prison Service and Parole Board must be in a position to enable a swift and meaningful parole hearing. If released, the individual remains under licence supervision for life, although an application can be made for this to be cancelled 10 years following release. Unless the licence is cancelled, a released prisoner can be recalled to prison at any time. Recall may be due to new criminal charges, or to a breach of licence conditions that does not constitute a criminal offence (Padfield 2016).

At a practical level, the IPP sentence had serious negative effects soon after its introduction. Within a year of its creation, approximately 150 IPP sentences were being imposed per month (Prison Reform Trust 2007), with over 3,000 IPP prisoners incarcerated by October 2007 (Prison Reform Trust 2007).[3] There was originally no minimum tariff period. While the average tariff period for a life-sentenced prisoner was then approximately 13 years,[4] the tariff period of an IPP prisoner could be measured in months, if not weeks.[5] In the first year, the average tariff length of an IPP sentence was two years and six months (Home Office 2006: 139). This influx of 'life'-sentenced prisoners with short tariffs was the logical result of a governmental effort to exert greater powers of control over offenders thought to be dangerous. For the key politicians involved, it was an opportunity to overcome the unwillingness of what they perceived to be an unduly liberal judiciary to sufficiently protect the public (Annison 2014a, 2014b).

In 2008, Home Office estimates suggested that the IPP population would reach 25,000 by 2012, an extraordinary figure if reforms were not forthcoming (Annison 2015: 113). It increasingly became clear that the Prison Service did not have the resources required to help indeterminate prisoners to move towards release, and the Parole Board did not have the resources to ensure timely hearings. Furthermore, there were concerns that the sentence was damaging the mental health of IPP prisoners; that it was unfair and unjust; and, given all of this, that is was simply unsustainable (Annison 2015: chapter 4).

[2] An amendment to the sentence in 2008 reintroduced discretion for the trial judge (Criminal Justice and Immigration Act 2008).

[3] Further, only 13 had been released on licence (Prison Reform Trust 2007).

[4] In 2002 the average tariff given to those sentenced to a mandatory life sentence was 13.2 years, while by 2009 this had increased to 17.5 years (Prison Reform Trust 2012: 21).

[5] The shortest reported tariff for an IPP prisoner sentenced under the 2003 Act was 28 days (HM Chief Inspectors of Prisons and Probation 2008: 2).

Relatively minor, but important, amendments to the legislation were made in 2008, to introduce greater judicial discretion and to limit the IPP sentence to those whose offence was 'worth' at least four years' imprisonment (see Annison 2015: chapter 6). This led to the overall average tariff increasing to three years and five months (HM Chief Inspector of Prisons 2016b: 23). Efforts were also made to improve the management of IPP prisoners and to increase resources to hasten their progression through the custodial estate (HM Chief Inspectors of Prisons and Probation 2008: 17).

Problems nonetheless continued. Having lost legitimacy amongst much of the criminal justice community, the sentence was abolished by LASPO 2012 (Annison 2015: chapter 7). However, the 2008 amendments and 2012 abolition did not have retrospective effect. Therefore there remained, and still remains, a large body of prisoners 'left behind', who continue to serve this indeterminate sentence, whether in prison or on licence in the community.

In total, 8,711 IPP sentences were imposed by the courts prior to 2012 (HM Chief Inspector of Prisons 2016b: 10). While sections of the IPP population may have a similar risk profile or offending history to those serving life sentences, many of those caught up in the system (designed originally for prisoners with lengthy tariffs) would otherwise have been released after one to two years. While the Parole Board has made some progress in processing IPP prisoners, approximately 2,700 of the prisoners sentenced to IPP are currently in prison.[6] Over 89 per cent of these prisoners are beyond their tariff expiry date – the date at which they would have been released had they received a determinate sentence.

Recall of IPP prisoners to prison is a growing problem. Latest records show the population of such prisoners has reached almost 1,000. The Prisons Inspectorate has described the rate of recall as 'concerning' (HM Chief Inspector of Prisons 2016b: 25). As noted, recalls can – and often do – occur for technical breaches of conditions that do not, in themselves, constitute a new criminal offence. Recalled IPP prisoners must then against demonstrate their safety for release to the Parole Board. They therefore tend to find themselves tangled up once again in the problems they faced when initially seeking to progress towards release from the prison system. Thus, the effects of the IPP sentence do not end once an individual is released from prison.

The criticisms levelled at the IPP sentence prior to its abolition remain, and indeed have become more urgent. A recent thematic report by the Chief Inspector of Prisons (HM Chief Inspector of Prisons 2016b) has pointed to the on-going challenges faced by IPP prisoners. These include the under-resourcing of the systems intended to help prisoners to progress towards release; the flawed assumptions underpinning their sentences; the stigma attaching to the 'dangerous' label; and the difficulties of proving a reduction in risk to the Parole Board through participation in offending behaviour programmes. Research conducted by one of the authors has also pointed to the 'iatrogenic' effects of

[6] Unless otherwise stated, statistics are taken from Ministry of Justice (2018).

indeterminate detention (Annison 2018)[7] and demonstrated the harms experienced by families of IPP prisoners (Annison and Condry 2019).

In a particularly acute form, IPP prisoners are faced with a confluence of the general problems and pressures that currently beset the penal system of England and Wales. Two-thirds of prisons are overcrowded, and safety in prisons is declining rapidly. Serious assaults in prison have more than doubled in the last three years, rates of self-harm are at the highest levels ever recorded, and self-inflicted deaths are rising to near record levels (HM Chief Inspector of Prisons 2016a; Prison Reform Trust 2016). Between 2010 and 2015, the budget for prisons and probation was reduced by a quarter. Sustained staff cuts have seen the number of operational frontline staff also fall by a quarter: 6,500 fewer staff without a reduction in prisoner numbers (indeed a small increase over the same period). While some limited improvements in numbers are now being achieved, the ongoing departures of long-serving prison officers (at a rate of nearly 10 per cent per year) means that the service is becoming increasingly inexperienced.

III. THE EXTENT AND LIMITS OF LEGAL CHALLENGES TO INDETERMINATE SENTENCING

In this section, we consider the successive waves of legal challenges brought against the IPP sentence in the British House of Lords (as the final court of appeal was then known) and, later, the UK Supreme Court and ECtHR. The most developed and significant line of cases relates to the problems faced by post-tariff prisoners. We see that a recurring trope is a focus on the Government's failure to adequately resource an overstretched prison system. More principled concerns with the inherently problematic nature of the IPP sentence itself emerge unevenly from the judgments, with varying, and ultimately limited, substantive effects.

The first case concerning the IPP to reach the House of Lords was that of *James, Lee and Wells*,[8] an appeal taken by a group of IPP prisoners following initial applications for judicial review. The case was argued both on the grounds of the 'irrationality', or '*Wednesbury* unreasonableness',[9] of the Secretary of State's failure to properly resource the system for IPP prisoners, and on the basis of Article 5(1) and (4) ECHR.[10] The appellants sought to argue that the systemic issues they faced (set out in section II) meant that their ongoing detention was unlawful.

[7] This term refers to the harmful and counter-productive effects of the indeterminate sentence, and the prisoners' experiences of their efforts to move towards release, within a system that was ostensibly justified by its ability to better 'heal', to rehabilitate, that individual.

[8] The judgment was delivered shortly before the UK Supreme Court was established, replacing the House of Lords as the UK's highest court.

[9] *Associated Provincial Picture Houses Ltd v Wednesbury Corp* (1947).

[10] Art 5 concerns the deprivation of liberty and the conditions under which detention is, and is not, considered lawful.

In its judgment, the House of Lords agreed with the earlier judgment of the High Court in *Wells*[11] and of the Court of Appeal in *Walker and Wells*[12] holding that the Secretary of State had 'failed deplorably' in his public law duty to provide adequate resources to allow the 'Dangerous Offender' provisions of the CJA 2005 to function as Parliament had intended.[13] This failure had by this time been accepted by the Secretary of State.[14] However, the Law Lords shared the view of the Court of Appeal in *Walker and Wells*[15] that it was impossible to regard post-tariff IPP prisoners as 'unlawfully detained' given that, under section 28 of the Crime (Sentences) Act 1997, IPP prisoners could only be released once the Parole Board was satisfied that detention was no longer necessary for the protection of the public.

Further, the House of Lords considered that it was compelled by law to adopt a restrictive interpretation of the obligations of the Secretary of State, the Prison Service and the Parole Board towards IPP prisoners.[16] Most notably, their Lordships recognised that section 142(1) of the CJA 2003 – which sets out the various purposes of sentencing, including rehabilitation – was expressly disapplied from the 'Dangerous Offender' provisions by section 142(2)(c) of the 2003 Act.[17] This was interpreted as a clear statement from government that 'the first and obvious purpose of these provisions is the protection of the public from the risks posed by dangerous offenders'.[18] The reform and rehabilitation of offenders was a secondary consideration, at best.

Accepting that the failure to resource the IPP system adequately had caused substantial delays and other problems for many prisoners, Lord Hope nonetheless resisted any notion that there had been 'a breakdown of [an] extreme kind' that might break the causal link with the original public protection objective of the sentencing court.[19] The House of Lords did, however, hold out the possibility that, for reasons of 'common humanity', a 'prolonged failure' to enable a prisoner to demonstrate that he was safe for release might result in a breach of Article 5(1) ECHR.[20]

The House held that Article 5(4) was concerned with procedure rather than substance, and that it was up to the Parole Board to decide what, and how much, information was needed to decide on a prisoner's suitability for release. Therefore, notwithstanding the argument that for many IPP prisoners Parole

[11] It was heard with an appeal from the subsequent High Court case of *R (James) v Secretary of State for Justice* (2007).

[12] *R (Wells) v Parole Board; R (Walker) v Secretary of State for the Home Department* (2008).

[13] *James, Lee and Wells* (2009), [3] (Lord Hope).

[14] ibid [28] (Lord Brown).

[15] *R (Wells) v Parole Board; R (Walker) v Secretary of State for the Home Department* (2008).

[16] ibid [5]–[6], [21] (Lord Hope); [36]–[37], [51], [61]–[62] (Lord Brown); [123], [126] (Lord Judge).

[17] ibid [48] (Lord Brown).

[18] ibid [100] (Lord Judge).

[19] ibid [15] (Lord Hope).

[20] ibid [128] (Lord Judge).

Board hearings constituted an empty exercise, Article 5(4) was not breached. The result, therefore, was a finding that the Secretary of State had acted unlawfully, but only on the common law ground of 'irrationality': the Article 5(1) and (4) claims were not upheld.

The ECtHR had the chance to decide on the matter itself in the subsequent case of *James, Wells and Lee v the United Kingdom*. On 18 September 2012, the Court held that the continued post-tariff detention of three applicants (all IPP prisoners) in the absence of access to rehabilitative programmes was arbitrary and therefore breached Article 5(1) ECHR.[21] Contradicting the House of Lords in *James, Lee and Wells*, the ECtHR held that rehabilitation *was* one of the purposes of the applicants' detention. The Court inferred this from the general principle that 'a real opportunity for rehabilitation is a necessary element of any part of the detention which is to be justified solely by reference to public protection'.[22] Accordingly, following tariff expiry, 'the need for access to rehabilitative treatment … became all the more pressing'.[23]

The ECtHR made clear that while it was agreed by all parties that the continued detention of the prisoners was lawful given the relevant UK legislation,[24]

> compliance with national law is not [necessarily] sufficient in order for a deprivation of liberty to be considered 'lawful'. Article 5(1) also requires that any deprivation of liberty should be in keeping with the purpose of protecting the individual from arbitrariness.[25]

The Court further noted:

> In the context of Article 5 § 1 (a), a concern may arise in the case of persons who, having served the punishment element of their sentences, are in detention solely because of the risk they pose to the public *if there are no special measures, instruments or institutions in place*, other than those available to ordinary long-term prisoners, *aimed at reducing the danger they present and at limiting the duration of their detention to what is strictly necessary* in order to prevent them from committing further offences.[26]

The Court concluded that until steps were taken to progress the applicants through the prison system by providing them with access to rehabilitative courses, their detention would be arbitrary under Article 5(1).

Notably, the ECtHR rejected the British Government's argument that a finding of a breach of Article 5(1) would inevitably lead to the release of truly dangerous individuals. It stated, rather, that while such a situation would be

[21] *James, Wells and Lee v the United Kingdom* (2012). The judgment became final on 12 February 2013, when a request for referral to the Grand Chamber was rejected.

[22] *James, Wells and Lee*, [209].

[23] ibid [220].

[24] ibid [200].

[25] ibid [191].

[26] ibid [194] (emphasis added).

'regrettable', it was far from clear that, but for the initial statutory presumption of dangerousness, the claimants would have been sentenced to IPP.[27]

The ECtHR was troubled by the mandatory nature of the original provisions in the CJA 2003, noting that 'the applicants were assumed to constitute a risk and there was little scope to counter that assumption' and that 'risk having been established, the sentencing judge had no power to impose any sentence but an indeterminate sentence of imprisonment'.[28] Notwithstanding these concerns, the Court did not rule that the IPP sentence was unlawful in itself: instead, the failure to resource the system adequately was crucial to the judgment.

The 'special measures' principle cited in *James, Wells and Lee* (quoted above) can be understood as akin to a proportionality constraint: rehabilitative interventions are required to reduce the period of detention to the shortest period necessary to protect the public. This principle was derived from the Strasbourg Court's jurisprudence in the earlier case of *M v Germany*,[29] which concerned an applicant who challenged his post-sentence preventive detention, or *Sicherungsverwahrung*, on the grounds of both Article 5.1(a) and Article 7.

It is notable, however, that although the ECtHR expressed concern at the lack of special measures for prisoners detained for preventive purposes, it made no reference in *James, Wells and Lee* to the concern in *M v Germany* there was 'no substantial difference between the execution of a prison sentence and that of a preventive detention order'.[30] As the IPP sentence is composed of a punitive tariff followed by a preventive period that, as the Court noted, 'is to be justified solely by reference to public protection', it could be argued that the Court should have examined in more detail the material conditions of detention. We take up this point in section IV.

An opportunity for the UK Supreme Court to respond to the ECtHR judgment came in *Kaiyam*,[31] a case brought by four applicants[32] asserting that failures by the Parole Board and the Prison Service to enable their reasonable progression towards release breached their Article 5(1) ECHR rights and the Secretary of State's public law duty recognised in *James, Lee and Wells*.

Notwithstanding what van Zyl Smit and others (van Zyl Smit et al 2014) had earlier rightly cast as the British upper courts' significant resistance to recognising a general 'right to rehabilitation' for prisoners serving indeterminate sentences, the Supreme Court followed the ECtHR in accepting that the purpose of the IPP and life sentences *does* include rehabilitation.[33] Nevertheless, the Supreme Court expressed deep concern over the implications of the ECtHR's

[27] ibid [217]. Indeed, had the 2008 amendments been in force at the time they were sentenced, it would have been impossible to sentence two of the three claimants to IPP.

[28] ibid [204].

[29] *M v Germany* (2010).

[30] ibid [110].

[31] *Kaiyam* (2014).

[32] Three had been sentenced to IPP; the fourth had been given an automatic life sentence under LASPO 2012.

[33] *Kaiyam* [35]–[36] (Lord Mance and Lord Hughes).

ruling, holding that the Strasbourg Court had relied on 'an over-expanded and inappropriate reading of the word "unlawful" in article 5(1)(a)'.[34]

In line with previous case law, including the preceding High Court and Court of Appeal judgments in *Wells* and *Walker and Wells*, the Supreme Court observed a 'real difficulty about accepting a proposition that Convention rights require a life or IPP prisoners' release before the Parole Board is satisfied that his detention is no longer required for the protection of the public.[35] This was, in part, because this would mean that section 28(6)(b) of the Crime (Sentences) Act 1997 (governing the release of indeterminate-sentenced prisoners) was in conflict with Convention rights, but further because it would lead, in the Court's view, to

> the possibility … that detention could, at least post-tariff, fluctuate between the lawful and unlawful, depending on whether a prisoner serving a sentence of IPP was being offered appropriate opportunity to progress in his or her sentence.[36]

The alternative course charted by the Supreme Court was rather to conclude that the duty to afford rehabilitative interventions and support prisoners' efforts to progress towards release 'is analogous, at an earlier stage, to the duty involved under Article 5(4)'. Consequently:

> A duty to facilitate release can and should therefore be implied as an ancillary duty – a duty not affecting the lawfulness of detention, but sounding in damages if breached.[37]

Applying this to the principle to the facts, the Supreme Court held that the failings of the Ministry of Justice and its penal systems did not render the claimants' detention arbitrary under Article 5(1) ECHR. Rather, it asserted that the prisoner's detention 'remains the direct causal consequence of his indefinite sentence until his risk is judged by the independent Parole Board to be such as to permit his release on licence'.[38] The appropriate award was ruled, therefore, to be damages for legitimate frustration and anxiety, not release.

The judgment observed that the findings of a breach as regards two of the prisoners were 'a further regrettable consequence of the manner in which the seriously flawed system of imprisonment for public protection came to be introduced without sufficient funding to cope with it'.[39] Notwithstanding the injustices arguably suffered by many IPP prisoners, the Supreme Court concluded in *Kaiyam* that their approach would 'be more satisfactory in result' than that of the ECtHR in *James, Wells and Lee*. Importantly, it held, inter alia, that this was the case because it would present 'no risk … to public safety'.[40]

[34] ibid.
[35] ibid [30].
[36] ibid [15].
[37] ibid [38].
[38] ibid [39].
[39] ibid [84].
[40] ibid [40].

The issues surveyed here speak more generally to the broader question of the extent to which relevant judges – in England and Wales, at the ECtHR, or indeed elsewhere – are willing to take an 'activist' role in protecting the fundamental rights of citizens.[41] One of us has argued elsewhere that the dominant beliefs of the UK judiciary, the 'senior judicial tradition' (Annison 2014a), resulted in their being 'ill-equipped to contest robustly, *and in their eyes legitimately*, particular instances of the 'pre-emptive turn' in criminal justice (Annison 2014a: 366 original emphasis). Hence the UK courts have, as we have seen, been reluctant to pursue a more strident approach that would strike a more fundamental blow against the IPP sentence (Annison 2014a).

IV. FUNDAMENTAL RIGHTS AND THE POST-TARIFF DISTINCTION

In this section, we interrogate the extent to which the UK courts and the ECtHR have engaged with the normative implications of the pre-tariff and post-tariff elements of the indeterminate IPP sentence. We suggest that the post-tariff *preventive* element should be distinct in terms of practice (notably including the institution and conditions in which the prisoner is held) from the pre-tariff *punitive* element of the sentence. While recognising the difficulties and potential dangers of pursuing more 'benevolent' forms of detention, we nonetheless argue that the case of the IPP demonstrates the limits of the ability of the ECHR – as currently interpreted – to protect the fundamental rights of individuals following criminal conviction.

We develop this argument through two related steps: first, we show that a focus on the proportionality of preventive measures to the *risks* posed by the offender has precluded a focus on the proportionality of *punishment*; second, we demonstrate why and how post-tariff detention should be conceptualised as a distinctive phase in the IPP prisoner's journey toward (and indeed beyond) release.

The potential for preventive detention to impose disproportionate punishment is an issue that has concerned the ECtHR on a number of occasions. The Court has developed an 'anti-subversion doctrine' (Zedner 2016: 12) by giving an 'autonomous meaning' to the term 'sanction' in Article 7.[42] Under this doctrine, the Court will look behind the official designation of a coercive measure as preventive or non-punitive, in order to ensure that the human rights protections applying to criminal proceedings are not circumvented (Zedner 2016: 12). The approach to Article 5 is less stringent, however, as the ECtHR has 'accepted sentences that give officials a discretion that would allow detention far beyond what could be regarded as proportionate to an offence, as long as such

[41] For illuminating discussion of the various meanings of the term 'activist', see Paterson 2013.
[42] See *Engel and others v the Netherlands*; *M v Germany*.

discretionary powers were explicitly part of the original sentence' (Drenkhahn et al 2012: 12).

The 'special measures' doctrine, as conceived of in *James, Wells and Lee*, leaves little space for judging the proportionality of indeterminate sentences, including the IPP, to the seriousness of the offence of which the offender has been convicted. Furthermore, the judgment seemed to imply that post-tariff detention under an IPP sentence handed down for crimes of lesser seriousness is not problematic, provided that the resources are available for prisoners to address their offending behaviour through rehabilitative interventions. This approach may be contrasted with *M v Germany*, a case argued under Article 7 ECHR, in which the Court viewed preventive detention as a form of *punishment* and was concerned by the lack of differentiation in the material conditions under which such detention was served. This raises the prospect that the longer the individual is detained *preventively* under an IPP, the greater the risk that he will be subjected to excessive *punishment* beyond his tariff. The Court of Appeal in *Walker and Wells* hinted at this possibility in recognising that the 'direct and natural consequence' of the Secretary of State's breach of his public law duty to provide adequate resources to the IPP system was

> to make it likely that a proportion of IPP prisoners will, avoidably, be kept in prison for longer than necessary either for punishment or for protection of the public, contrary to the intention of Parliament (and the objective of article 5 [ECHR] to which Parliament must have been mindful).[43]

The distinction drawn by the ECtHR between preventive measures applied after sentence, which may be conceived of as punishments and prohibited under Article 7, and those handed down at the time of sentencing appears artificial. While the ECtHR requires the material conditions of preventive detention to differ from those of punitive detention under Article 7, the potential for the post-tariff 'preventive' period of an IPP sentence to impose punishment in excess of that deserved by the offender appears to escape its scrutiny so long as detention follows a conviction as required by Article 5. This may provide an incentive to states to impose indeterminate sentences with greater frequency, in order to increase the margins of administrative discretion and allow for periods of prevention that far exceed the punishment proportionate to the crime committed.

On the other hand, the ECtHR has shown itself more willing to assess the proportionality of punishment under the rubric of the Article 3 prohibition on inhuman and degrading treatment or punishment. In *Vinter and others v the United Kingdom*,[44] the Fourth Section of the ECtHR held that grossly disproportionate sentences may violate Article 3, but the test was likely to be met only on 'rare and unique occasions'.[45] A whole life sentence would, however,

[43] *R (Wells) v Parole Board; R (Walker) v Secretary of State for the Home Department* (2008) 40.
[44] *Vinter and Others v the United Kingdom* (2012).
[45] ibid [89].

be grossly disproportionate where the prisoner's detention did not serve any legitimate penological purpose, such as punishment, deterrence, rehabilitation and the protection of the public, and where the sentence was irreducible *de facto* and *de iure*.[46]

Subsequently, the Grand Chamber of the ECtHR held that a whole life sentence could, in the absence of a meaningful review of progress in rehabilitation, be inconsistent even with the aim of pure punishment.[47] Thus, Article 3 was to be

> interpreted as requiring reducibility of the sentence, in the sense of a review which allows the domestic authorities to consider whether any changes in the life prisoner are so significant, and such progress towards rehabilitation has been made in the course of the sentence, as to mean that continued detention can no longer be justified on legitimate penological grounds.[48]

Nevertheless, the Grand Chamber made clear that a prisoner could be detained until the end of his life on preventive grounds if, upon review, it was found that he 'continued to pose a danger to society'.[49]

The principle of punishment proportionate to the crime has the potential to curb sentence length in the case of some IPP prisoners, as the seriousness of the offence in many cases would not have justified a life sentence. On the other hand, the principle of public protection seen in both *James* and *Vinter* can justify much lengthier periods of detention on preventive grounds. This is particularly the case where the burden is on the prisoner to satisfy the Parole Board that it 'is no longer necessary for the protection of the public that the prisoner should be confined'.[50]

V. RECONCEPTUALISING REHABILITATION?

Having raised concern at the failure of the ECtHR to sufficiently curb the use of sentences officially justified on the basis of public protection, we now build on the preceding discussion to suggest that a desistance-informed approach might be more appropriate for indeterminate-sentenced prisoners than the conception of rehabilitation as recidivism risk-reduction, seen in *James, Wells and Lee*. Drawing on McNeill's exploration of competing notions of 'rehabilitation' (McNeill 2012), by conceiving of rehabilitation as a set of institutional supports to individual processes of desistance, we can begin to imagine a system that goes beyond a narrow concern with risk of recidivism and may begin to re-address the limits placed on offenders' fundamental rights post-punishment.

[46] ibid [92].
[47] *Vinter and Others v the United Kingdom* (2013), [112].
[48] ibid [199].
[49] ibid [108].
[50] Crime Sentences Act 1997, s 28(6)(b).

It should first be recalled that the distinction between the punitive and preventive elements of an IPP (or indeed the traditional life sentence), while clear in theory, becomes blurred once the offender reaches prison. The whole of the sentence is served in a prison environment, even after the expiry of the punitive tariff. It is possible to move down through security categories to less restrictive prison regimes, but if a post-tariff prisoner is deemed unsuitable, he will remain in high security settings and will have fewer possibilities for reintegration.

The IPP and the system of rehabilitative interventions with which the prisoner is expected to engage tend to be narrowly risk-focused and programme-oriented. While such interventions are widely described as 'treatments', they are largely based on cognitive behavioural therapy and training in social and self-management skills.[51] Such an approach aligns with what McNeill has termed 'psychological rehabilitation', a practice 'concerned with promoting positive individual-level change' (McNeill 2012: 14). Psychologically-informed offending behaviour programmes have also been described as 'remoralizing', as they seek to emphasise the wrongness of offending and to encourage offenders to take individual responsibility for making more 'pro-social' choices in future (Robinson 2008; Rose 2000). In addition to the fact that this form of 'rehabilitation' is primarily expected to be achieved within the artificial nature of the prison environment, it also 'fails to acknowledge the breadth and depth of the inter-related problems that tend to underlie offending' (Jacobson and Hough, 2010: vi).

The ECtHR's reliance on, and increasing promotion of, rehabilitation in pushing back against the dominant public protection ethos (as examined in section III), seems, at first sight, to be a positive and progressive move. The conception of rehabilitation in *James, Wells and Lee* is rather narrow, however, as it is seen mainly as a means of addressing risk factors for offending and demonstrating suitability for release. The primary reason for this appears to be that the ECtHR largely based its decision on the purpose of the IPP as described in judicial and political statements, which focused on the same narrow conception of rehabilitation underpinning the IPP sentence.

We can thus usefully move to reflect on McNeill's notion of 'social rehabilitation'. This is defined as 'the informal social recognition and acceptance of the reformed ex-offender' (McNeill 2012: 14). This alternative conception points to McNeill's broader argument that rehabilitative interventions should be conceived of not as causing ex-offenders to change, but as having 'a supporting role in the wider enterprise of desistance; a process that belongs to the desister' (McNeill 2012: 13). This conception of rehabilitation as a personal journey may be seen in Judge Power-Forde's concurring opinion in *Vinter*, which conceives of rehabilitation more broadly as a process of change and atonement:

> Those who commit the most abhorrent and egregious of acts and who inflict untold suffering upon others, nevertheless retain their fundamental humanity and carry

[51] For a critical discussion of this approach, see Ward and Maruna 2007.

> within themselves the capacity to change. Long and deserved though their prison sentences may be, they retain the right to hope that, someday, they may have atoned for the wrongs which they have committed.[52]

Desistance – prisoners 'making good' and being equipped to lead meaningful lives – is an uncertain and challenging process that requires a great deal of support, understanding and a recognition of its uneven (potentially back and forth) nature (Maruna 2001; McNeill 2006). It is questionable whether such a process can be supported by prisons in England and Wales. Inviting prisoners to 'open up', to seek to engage in deep learning and change, runs directly counter to the requirements to survive in the general prison estate driven by a hyper-masculine culture (Crewe 2009). It is remarkable that so many indeterminate-sentenced prisoners – and particularly those who have found themselves imprisoned up to 10 years beyond their tariff period – have been able to demonstrate their non-dangerousness within an environment that is not only dissimilar to everyday life in England and Wales, but which is also rife with violence. Moreover, the ever-present threat and the experience of recall risks undoing any progress released IPP prisoners have made towards desistance, further undermining the process.

Given the expressly non-punitive nature of the post-tariff period for the indeterminate IPP sentence, we concur with Ashworth and Zedner that any period beyond the punitive element of the sentence 'should be served in non-punitive conditions with restraints no greater than those required by the imperatives of security' (Ashworth and Zedner 2014: 169). Further, where possible, such detention 'should take place in a separate facility, not part of the prison system' (Ashworth and Zedner 2014: 169). The best therapeutic communities and open prisons *may* satisfy the former requirement in practice and the latter in spirit, but this should not be taken for granted and the principled issues in play should not be obscured.

Crucially, the risk-focused and narrow notion of rehabilitation in *James, Wells and Lee* struggles to provide sufficiently robust normative boundaries for the use of indeterminate sentences, and to appropriately guide the specific form that measures such as those identified by Ashworth and Zedner should take. We can here can sketch an alternative approach, based on a 'desistance paradigm'.

McNeill has suggested that desistance as a process occurs 'somewhere in the interfaces between developing personal maturity, forming new or stronger social and individual subjective narrative constructions which offenders build around these key events and changes' (McNeill 2003: 151). This view has proved to be influential, with Ward and Maruna (Ward and Maruna 2007), for example, joining McNeill's call for criminal justice organisations to 'think of themselves less as providers of correctional treatment (that belongs to the expert) and more as supporters of desistance processes (that belong to the desister)' (McNeill 2006: 46).

[52] *Vinter* (2013), [53].

Many leading desistance scholars have further pointed to the tendency for criminal justice interventions 'to impede the processes of going straight by detaching individuals from their families, derailing career paths, and breeding hostility and defiance' (Liebling and Maruna 2005).

Taken together, this perspective would promote changes to the operation of the IPP sentence – and indeed to the English criminal justice system more generally. At a general level, one would look to adjust underlying systems and practices to ensure that there is a 'gravitational pull' tending towards the reintegration of individuals into appropriate conditions in the community, supported by recognition of the uneven nature of the desistance process (Maruna 2001).[53] It would likely lead to over-arching policies that would seek to place all IPP prisoners in the least restrictive, and least harsh, conditions of detention at the earliest opportunity post-tariff.

While there would be compelling reasons to go further and ensure that post-tariff detention is in a non-penal institution, concerns would rightly be raised at the dangers of such 'non punitive' detention (Steiker 1998). Continued deprivation of liberty after the expiry of a punitive prison sentence, even where it is intended primarily to prevent harm to the public, is likely to be experienced by the prisoner as an additional punishment. As Ashworth and Zedner have rightly argued, 'preventive detention is no less in need of justification' than is imprisonment on a punitive basis (Ashworth and Zedner 2014: 168). Drenkhahn and colleagues have argued that a principle of parsimony could be introduced into the ECtHR's interpretation of Article 5, so that deprivation of liberty would only be permitted 'as a last resort and then only for the shortest possible period' (Drenkhahn et al 2012: 12). We would argue that the same caution should be exercised by courts considering imposing any sentence ostensibly justified on the basis of public protection.

VI. CONCLUSION

The indeterminate imprisonment of 'dangerous offenders' continues to have ripple effects within the penal system of England and Wales, notwithstanding the abolition of the particularly contentious IPP sentence in 2012. This specific sentence, further, highlights the severity of the legal consequences of convictions for serious offences and the challenges of reintegration that face those who have been labelled as 'dangerous'. Specifically as regards the IPP sentence, we have suggested that there has been an ongoing failure to distinguish – in theory or practice – the post-tariff period of detention of 'dangerous' individuals from the initial punitive, pre-tariff period. The ECtHR has recognised

[53] And in the context of the IPP, some would challenge the assumption that it is appropriate to view all IPP prisoners as all necessarily embarked on a journey of desistance from a starting position of being genuinely dangerous: an argument that the ECtHR explicitly recognised.

this distinction to a limited extent by requiring rehabilitation to be provided to prisoners detained for preventive purposes under indeterminate, dangerousness-oriented sentences.

While the ECHR provides important protections across many areas, and indeed English common law also provides a means of holding the authorities to account, there is nonetheless force to the argument that Article 5 as currently interpreted by UK courts and the ECtHR fails appropriately to protect the rights of individuals labelled as 'dangerous' serving indeterminate sentences. Indeed, while Article 7 provides important protections against 'penal subversions' (Zedner 2016), Article 5 allows significant incursions into individual liberties where these are permitted at sentencing, through the use of measures such as the IPP modelled on the long-accepted and widely available life sentence.

In this chapter we have argued that the structure of indeterminate sentences such as the IPP may provide a principled response to the predicament of those at risk of disproportionate punishment in the name of public protection. However, we have raised concerns with the ECtHR's reliance on a limited notion of rehabilitation as risk reduction. Thus we have argued that 'desistance' is an important overarching framework, which sensitises us to the complex dynamics involved in prisoners' 'making good'. We argue that within this framework a more nuanced notion of rehabilitation should be utilised, along with an understanding of the role of criminal justice organisations in supporting – but also potentially undermining – desistance.

REFERENCES

Annison, H (2014a) 'Interpreting the Politics of the Judiciary: The British Senior Judicial Tradition and the Pre-emptive Turn in Criminal Justice' *Journal of Law and Society*, 41, 339–66.

—— (2014b) 'Weeding the garden: The Third Way, the Westminster tradition and Imprisonment for Public Protection' *Theoretical Criminology*, 18, 38–55.

—— (2015) *Dangerous Politics* (Oxford, Oxford University Press).

—— (2018) 'Tracing the Gordian Knot: Indeterminate-Sentenced Prisoners and the Pathologies of English Penal Politics' *The Political Quarterly*, Online First.

—— and Condry, R (2019) 'The Pains of Indeterminate Imprisonment for Family Members' *Prison Service Journal*, 241, 11–19.

Ashworth, A and Zedner, L (2014) *Preventive Justice* (Oxford, Oxford University Press).

Brown, M (2011) 'Preventive Detention and the Control of Sex Crime: Receding visions of justice in Australian case law' *Alternative Law Journal*, 36, 10–16.

Carvalho, H (2017) *The Preventive Turn in Criminal Law* (Oxford, Oxford University Press).

Crewe, B (2009) *The Prisoner Society* (Oxford, Oxford University Press).

Drenkhahn, K, Morgenstern, C and van Zyl Smit, D (2012) 'What is in a Name? Preventive Detention in Germany in the Shadow of European Human Rights Law' *Criminal Law Review*, 3, 167–87.

HM Chief Inspector of Prisons (2016a) *Annual Report 2015-6* (London, TSO).

—— (2016b) *Unintended Consequences: Finding a way forward for prisoners serving sentences of imprisonment for public protection* (London, HMIP).
HM Chief Inspectors of Prisons and Probation (2008) *The Indeterminate Sentence for Public Protection: A Thematic Review* (London, Home Office).
Home Office (2006) *Offender Management Caseload Statistics* (London, Home Office).
Jacobson, J and Hough, M (2010) *Unjust Deserts: Imprisonment for public protection* (London, Prison Reform Trust).
Liebling, A and Maruna, S (2005) *The Effects of Imprisonment* (Cullompton, Willan).
Maruna, S (2001) *Making Good: How Ex-Convicts Reform and Rebuild their Lives* (Washington, DC, American Psychological Association).
McNeill, F (2003) 'Desistance-Focussed Probation Practice' in W Chui and M Nellis (eds), *Moving Probation Forward: Evidence, Arguments and Practice.* (Harlow, Pearson Education).
—— (2006) 'A Desistance Paradigm for Offender Management' *Criminology and Criminal Justice*, 6, 39–61.
—— (2012) 'Four forms of "offender" rehabilitation: Towards an interdisciplinary perspective' *Legal and Criminological Psychology*, 17, 18–36.
McSherry, B, Norrie, AW and Bronitt, S, (2009) *Regulating Deviance: The redirection of criminalisation and the futures of criminal law* (Oxford, Hart Publishing).
Ministry of Justice (2018) *Offender Management Statistics Quarterly, England and Wales, January to March 2018* (London, Ministry of Justice).
Padfield, N (2016) 'Justifying Indefinite Detention: On what grounds?' *Criminal Law Review*, 11, 797–822.
Paterson, A (2013) *Final Judgment* (Oxford, Hart Publishing).
Pratt, J (1997) *Governing the Dangerous: Dangerousness, law and social change* (Sydney, Federation Press).
Prison Reform Trust (2007) *Indefinitely Maybe?: How the indeterminate sentence for public protection is unjustified and unsustainable* (London, Prison Reform Trust).
—— (2012) *Bromley Briefings Prison Factfile: June 2012* (London: Prison Reform Trust).
—— (2016) *Bromley Briefing: Summer 2016* (London, Prison Reform Trust).
Robinson, G (2008) 'Late-Modern Rehabilitation: The Evolution of a Penal Strategy' *Punishment & Society*, 10, 429–45.
Rose, N (2000) 'Government and Control' *British Journal of Criminology*, 40, 321–39.
Rutherford, A (2006) 'Dangerous People: Beginnings of a New Labour Proposal' in T Newburn and PE Rock (eds), *The Politics of Crime Control* (Oxford, Oxford University Press).
Sentencing Guidelines Council (2008) *Dangerous Offenders: Guide for Sentencers and Practitioners* (Sentencing Guidelines Council, Crown Copyright).
Steiker, CS (1998) 'The Limits of the Preventive State' *The Journal of Criminal Law and Criminology*, 88, 771–808.
van Zyl Smit, D and Appleton, C (2016) *Life Imprisonment and Human Rights* (Oxford, Hart Publishing).
——, Weatherby, P and Creighton, S (2014) 'Whole Life Sentences and the Tide of European Human Rights Jurisprudence: What Is to Be Done?' *Human Rights Law Review*, 14, 59–84.

Ward, T and Maruna, S (2007) *Rehabilitation: Beyond the Risk Paradigm* (London, Routledge).
Zedner, L (2016) 'Penal subversions: When is a punishment not punishment, who decides and on what grounds?' *Theoretical Criminology*, 20, 3–20.

TABLE OF CASES

Domestic Cases

Associated Provincial Picture Houses Ltd v Wednesbury Corp [1947] 2 All ER 680, [1948] 1 KB 223
Kaiyam [2014] UKSC 66
R (James) v Secretary of State for Justice [2007] EWHC 2027 (Admin)
R (James) v Secretary of State for Justice (Parole Board intervening); R (Lee) v Same (Same intervening); R (Wells) v Same (Same intervening) [2009] UKHL 22, [2009] 2 WLR 1149.
R (Wells) v Parole Board; R (Walker) v Secretary of State for the Home Department [2008] EWCA Civ 30, [2008] H.R.L.R. 22

European Court of Human Rights

Engel and Others v the Netherlands, App nos 5100/71; 5101/71; 5102/71; 5354/72 and 5370/72 (ECHR 8 June 1976)
James, Wells and Lee v the United Kingdom, App nos 25119/09, 57715/09 and 57877/09 (ECHR, 18 September 2012)
M v Germany, App no 19359/04 (ECHR, 17 December 2009)
Vinter and Others v the United Kingdom, App nos 66069/09, 130/10 and 3896/10 (17 January 2012) (Chamber, Fourth Division)
Vinter and Others v the United Kingdom, App nos 66069/09, 130/10 and 3896/10 (9 July 2013) (Grand Chamber)

10

Intensive Supervision of Sexual and Violent Offenders in Germany

AXEL DESSECKER

I. INTRODUCTION

THE LIMITS SET on offenders released from a penal institution after their prison term has been completed – and who might consequently well be called 'ex-offenders' (Atkin and Armstrong 2013; Geiger 2006) – will depend on many factors, such as legal rules, practices of legal cultures or the social capital on which ex-offenders may build. From a criminological point of view, it seems highly improbable that all groups of ex-prisoners will be treated equally as soon as their criminal conviction is known. Public concern about crime will focus on specific risks perceived as especially threatening ways of victimisation. During some periods of time, moral panics will spread.

Although many more or less deviant groups have been identified as catalysts of moral panics since Stanley Cohen's (1972) classical study, sexual offenders have been a somewhat stable reference group, both for the general public and for criminal justice policies in several countries of Western Europe and beyond, since the late 1990s. Public concern about violent offenders might become even more firmly entrenched over a longer period of time. When it comes to the possibilities for reintegration into society and of the legal consequences of sentencing limiting the rights of ex-prisoners, these groups might well face some punitive consequences beyond traditional prison sentences. Intensive supervision might be an increasingly important intervention in this field.

Intensive supervision comprises a set of individualised control efforts directed at probationers or parolees living in the community. It is often seen as one element within a range of rehabilitative interventions, typically for those who are thought to have some specific needs, such as in North American problem-solving courts (Marlowe, Hardin and Fox 2016). The term can be said to have been established in the criminological discourse (Bouchard and

Wong 2018; Gendreau, Cullen and Bonta 1994). It may fit into broader categories, such as that of 'intermediate sanctions', conceived as alternatives to imprisonment (Will 1995). Varieties of intensive supervision exist in the criminal justice systems of many countries, such as the United States (US) (Drake 2018), Canada (Weinrath, Donatelli and Murchison 2016: 293), England and Wales (Homes, Walmsley and Debidin 2005), Australia (Stout, Dalby and Schraner 2017), New Zealand (Bartels 2014: 3), South Africa (Bartels 2014: 43), France (Herzog-Evans, chapter 11 of this volume), Sweden (Nellis and Bungerfeldt 2013: 282) and the Netherlands (Meijer, chapter 5 of this volume).

In the following sections, problems of the intensive supervision approach will be mainly elaborated from a German perspective. The German criminal justice system has developed a specific sanction of intensive supervision (*Führungsaufsicht*), which, since its introduction in 1975, has been revised and expanded on several occasions. Although intensive supervision can be part of the sentence imposed by the court, it will in most cases appear as a collateral consequence of release from prison, a special hospital or even post-sentence preventive detention. Section II will locate the German methods of intensive supervision within the criminal justice system. It will also place this sanction within the broader landscape of collateral consequences of criminal convictions. Section III adds a more criminological perspective on the basis of statistical data and empirical research. It also focuses on the groups of sexual and violent offenders more specifically, to find out if these are more often the target of closer restrictions than those having been sentenced for other types of offences. Before concluding, section IV looks at intensive supervision from a constitutional and human rights perspective.

II. INTENSIVE SUPERVISION AND THE GERMAN CRIMINAL JUSTICE SYSTEM

A. Non-custodial Sanctions and Collateral Consequences of a Criminal Conviction

Intensive supervision is only one of the non-custodial sanctions that exist according to German criminal law, but it is probably the most untypical amongst them. The most common formal sanction in criminal courts will be a fine (Heinz 2016: 208; and Weigend 2016: 100).[1] Should the sentencing decision result in imprisonment, the prison sentence will be suspended in many cases, as this option applies for all sentences of imprisonment up to two years. Both for adult and juvenile offenders, supervision by the probation service is a

[1] Section 40 of the Penal Code – *Strafgesetzbuch* (StGB). For an English translation of the Penal Code, see at www.gesetze-im-internet.de/englisch_stgb/.

legal option in cases of suspended sentences, and in some but not all categories of cases, supervision will be mandatory. The period of supervision is at least one year, but it may amount to up to three years for juveniles and five years for adults. Only a minority of offenders with suspended sentences are supervised by the probation service, but their proportion increased from 31 per cent in 2004 to 37 per cent in 2007 and 39 per cent in 2010 (Heinz 2016: 220; Jehle et al 2016: 74).

It should be noted that the legal variety of non-custodial sanctions is rather limited in Germany compared to other jurisdictions. For instance, community service or unpaid work is an alternative to imprisonment in the case of default in paying a fine, but it is not seen as an option within the sentencing decision of a court for adult offenders. It is a common sanction for juveniles, however (Albrecht 2004: 472; Wilde 2017).

Beyond the traditional scope of criminal sentencing, a considerable number of legal restrictions exist for those convicted of a crime. For some groups of offenders, there will be the cumulative effect of both criminal sanctions and non-criminal legal consequences (Uggen and Stewart 2015). This applies for all those who are not German citizens, for members of some professions, but also for specific groups of offenders. Statistical material, as well as research, being rather limited in this area, it is virtually impossible to determine how many ex-offenders are affected by 'collateral consequences' (Dessecker 2018). Some of these legal consequences will be relevant for many ex-offenders under intensive supervision.

Although Germany does not have a national register for sexual offenders, all federal states – the *Länder* – have introduced specific police programmes based on their own registers for high-risk ex-offenders living in the community since 2010. 'High risk' has been identified with a more or less broadly-defined subgroup of sex offenders everywhere in the country, but some of the programmes have also included some subgroups of violent offenders. The oldest programme, and still the one most widely known, is called HEADS – an acronym for *Haftentlassenen-Auskunftsdatei Sexualstraftäter* (a reference file for sexual offenders released from prison).

B. Intensive Supervision as a Post-sentence Measure

In several aspects, intensive supervision works in a rather similar way to 'regular' supervision by the probation service. In the context of intensive supervision the probation service is even more important, and social work tends to shift its focus towards control of 'high-risk offenders' (Farrall 2016; Klug 2018). Although the probation service has been the best-established social service within the criminal justice system for many years (Grosser 2017; Mutz 2008), in this case it is not the only agency involved, being joined by several other organisations.

i. Post-sentence Execution as a Measure of Correction and Prevention

Intensive supervision is not an ordinary penalty according to German criminal law. It may be pronounced by the court as a part of its sentencing decision, but this is generally not done in practice. Most cases occur in specific situations when the law orders intensive supervision as a binding consequence. This legal construction might suggest classification of intensive supervision as a collateral consequence of criminal conviction, or as a civil disqualification. Collateral consequences may be defined as restrictions 'typically located outside the penal code, implemented by non-criminal justice institutions, and interpreted by the courts as civil regulations rather than criminal penalties' (Uggen and Stewart 2015: 1874). According to a typology of civil disqualifications proposed by Von Hirsch and Wasik (1997), civil measures dealing with risks of certain kinds fall into three main types, such as 'those that take effect automatically on conviction' or 'those that may be imposed by the sentencing judge'. These conceptual frameworks, however, will not provide a perfect classification. The legal foundation of intensive supervision actually is a part of the Penal Code, and it is not simply a legal requirement to desist from certain activities but also to take some action.

The legal foundation of intensive supervision is related to a category of criminal sanctions other than punishment and based on the assumption of dangerousness rather than guilt (Dessecker 2004: 199; Dubber and Hörnle 2014: 32, 61; Meier 2015: 269). Translations of this category have been changing: in an older official translation of the Penal Code, they were called 'measures of reform and prevention', while Bohlander (2008) translates them as 'measures of rehabilitation and incapacitation' and the European Court of Human Rights (ECtHR) uses the term 'measures of correction and prevention' (*M v Germany* 2009). Legal theory implies that the scope of intensive supervision goes beyond the limits of individual guilt for a specific crime, which has been the basis of a conviction.

Although the concept of intensive supervision as a sanction pronounced by the court[2] has existed for many years, this has never been at the core of the measure. Instead, there is a much more influential set of options that use intensive supervision as an additional measure for ex-prisoners and for offenders released from special hospitals and similar institutions. For offenders released from prison, intensive supervision only applies if there has not been a conditional release on parole. Intensive supervision for ex-prisoners requires that they were released only at the end of their full prison terms, or they have 'maxed out' their sentence. There is an additional requirement related to the length of the prison term:

> If a single or aggregate sentence of imprisonment of not less than two years has been imposed for intentional offences, or not less than one year for an offence listed in

[2] Section 68(1) StGB.

> section 181b has been fully served, supervision shall commence upon the release of the convicted person.[3]

This means the threshold of intensive supervision for ex-prisoners depends on the quality of their crimes. Section 181b StGB refers to an almost complete list of sexual offences, including cases of sexual abuse, sexual assault or rape, but excluding exhibitionist acts committed only in the presence of adult victims. For all other crime categories, the sentence may be considerably longer, and intensive supervision will only take place after a two-year minimum. In exceptional cases of post-sentence preventive detention, intensive supervision will not occur. In addition, the court may waive intensive supervision, 'if there is reason to believe that the convicted person will not commit further offences without supervision'.[4]

Another version of intensive supervision comes into play on release from special hospitals, institutions for the treatment of addictions, and preventive detention. In these cases, intensive supervision is a legal obligation for all release situations, no matter how long the period spent in the institution or what the quality of the offence.

The intensity of intensive supervision will depend on many factors. Among them, time will be crucial for many ex-offenders. The period of intensive supervision will be set within a range of between two and five years,[5] but in specific circumstances it may be extended to an indefinite period of time. This option applies to ex-offenders considered to be dangerous because they do not comply with psychological or psychiatric treatment in the community.

During an intensive supervision period, the court may set directions that will intervene in a more or less severe way in the lives of ex-offenders. The Penal Code sets out the following non-exhaustive list of requirements with which an ex-offender is expected to comply:

1. not to leave his place of domicile or his residence or a specified area without the permission of the supervising authority;
2. not to frequent specified places which may induce him to commit further offences;
3. not to make or maintain contact with the victim, or certain persons or persons from a certain group who may induce him to commit further offences, nor to employ, train or harbour them;
4. not to engage in particular activities which in certain circumstances may be exploited for criminal purposes;
5. not to possess, carry or entrust to another for safekeeping particular objects which could induce him to commit further offences;

[3] Section 68f(1) StGB.
[4] Section 68f(2) StGB.
[5] Section 68c(1) StGB.

6. not to possess or drive motor-vehicles or particular types of motor-vehicles or other vehicles, which in certain circumstances may be misused by him for criminal purposes;
7. to report at particular times to the supervising authority, to another public authority or to the probation officer;
8. to report promptly every change of residence or employment to the supervising authority;
9. to report in the case of unemployment to the Public Employment Agency or to another authorised employment agency;
10. not to consume alcohol or other drugs, if based on certain information there is reason to believe that their consumption will contribute to the commission of future offences, and to undergo alcohol and drug tests of a non-invasive nature; or
11. to present himself at certain times or at certain intervals to a doctor, a psychotherapist or the forensic ambulance service, or
12. to carry the equipment for the electronic monitoring of his whereabouts in working order with him at all times and not to tamper with it.[6]

Electronic supervision is not possible in Germany as an independent measure but only as a direction of the sentencing court combined with intensive supervision. This intervention has been designed to prevent more serious sexual and violent crime, and the legal conditions are more restrictive than those for other directions.

ii. Multiple Agencies

Since its introduction in 1975, intensive supervision has been managed by a local supervising authority (*Aufsichtsstelle*), which is to concentrate on control according to the concept of the law as follows:

> The supervising authority shall supervise the conduct of the convicted person and the fulfilment of the directions in cooperation with the court and with the support of the probation officer.[7]

The supervising authority is entitled to exercise some legal competences the probation service does not have, such as the right to request criminal prosecution for violation of the directions of a supervision order (section 145a StGB).

[6] Section 68b(1) StGB. In fact this is only a list of possible rules, which, in the case of non-compliance, may result in punishment for the offence of violating the directions of a supervision order (s 145a StGB). Other aspects of behaviour may also figure in the directions set by the court, but breach will not be a crime. In most cases, courts will give a whole set of directions and will modify them if this seems appropriate.

[7] Section 68a(3) StGB.

As the administration of justice is a matter for the federal States, supervising authorities are organised according to different regional models. In some parts of the country, there is only one central supervising authority for a federal State, but most have established these agencies as annexes of regional courts. This most common model implies that the supervising authority is directed by a judge, who typically has other tasks too. Some have employed specialised social workers within the supervising authority, although this is not the case everywhere.

Since a reform in 2007, the forensic ambulance service has been added to these organisations. Forensic ambulance services had previously been established as parts of special hospitals intended to treat ex-patients during their reintegration into the community. The idea of the reform was to generalise this approach and to expand it to ex-prisoners. This did not mean a complete shift in terms of medicalisation of criminal behaviour. Forensic ambulance services are used for only two kinds of directions aimed at ex-prisoners, both of which imply that psychotherapy or a psychiatric intervention seems appropriate. In the last decade, forensic ambulance services have been established by most federal States, but they still do not exist throughout Germany (Gregório Hertz et al 2017; Sauter, Seewald and Dahle 2017).

The police have traditionally been involved in the supervision of ex-offenders. The most important method in use today is the design of specific management programmes for high-risk sexual and violent offenders released from prison, such as HEADS. There is some evidence that these programmes have been relevant for many more ex-offenders than electronic monitoring (Dessecker 2018; Kasecker 2010: 80), but empirical research is almost non-existent.

III. INTENSIVE SUPERVISION IN PRACTICE

A. Official Statistics and Similar Data Collections

More or less complete official statistics on intensive supervision were collected for several years following the sanction's introduction, but their collection was stopped by an administrative agreement of the *Länder* in the early 1990s. As intensive supervision was introduced as a part of the Penal Code of the Federal Republic of Germany, these data referred to West Germany and the West of Berlin (Table 10.1). Numbers of intensive supervision cases grew quite steadily from the mid-1970s. In 1990, there were over 12,000 cases of intensive supervision, around 9 per cent of the caseload of the probation service. Most of the workload of probation officers consists of probation and parole supervision cases typically less cumbersome and unrelated to intensive supervision.

Table 10.1 Cases of intensive supervision versus probation and parole supervision in West Germany (Probation statistics, 1977–90)*

	Intensive supervision (Führungsaufsicht)	**Probation and parole supervision (Bewährungsaufsicht)**
1977	4,080	71,125
1978	5,083	81,017
1979	6,333	88,971
1980	7,381	93,840
1981	8,416	99,885
1982	9,321	106,126
1983	10,026	114,659
1984	10,698	120,561
1985	10,912	124,868
1986	11,415	127,494
1987	12,176	131,020
1988	12,341	131,572
1989	12,400	130,767
1990	12,462	131,381

Source: Statistisches Bundesamt (1980: Table 1) and following issues.

Later, an unofficial survey was made by *DBH – Fachverband für Soziale Arbeit, Strafrecht und Kriminalpolitik*, a non-governmental organisation in the probation field since 2008, when intensive supervision cases had already doubled in comparison to 1990 (Table 10.2). The most recent survey for 2015 shows some 37,000 cases. For some of the *Länder* more detailed regional statistics are available. On the basis of regional comparison, it may be seen that there is considerable variation (Reckling 2016). Although variation in sentencing is always to be expected in a federal system, there has been some discussion of the possible consequences of regional probation policies (Morgenstern and Hecht 2011: 186; Ruderich 2014: 337).

Table 10.2 Numbers of intensive supervision cases: a *Länder* comparison

	2008	**2009**	**2010**	**2011**	**2012**	**2013**	**2014**	**2015**
Baden-Württemberg	1,665	2,060	2,358	2,499	2,612	2,708	2,758	2,461
Bayern	6,496	6,732	7,100	7,362	7,623	7,847	8,005	8,058
Berlin	2,164	2,306	2,289	2,360	2,561	3,202	2,681	2,687
Brandenburg	513	545	596	611	630	642	679	694
Bremen	245	276	294	310	337	347	386	400

(continued)

Table 10.2 *(Continued)*

	2008	2009	2010	2011	2012	2013	2014	2015
Hamburg	769	807	790	815	829	737	663	645
Hessen	1,177	1,271	1,367	1,592	1,772	1,884	1,987	1,849
Mecklenburg-Vorpommern	520	600	672	758	818	852	866	919
Niedersachsen	1,656	2,001	2,233	2,462	2,588	2,731	2,751	2,887
Nordrhein-Westfalen	4,622	5,132	5,905	6,427	6,830	7,097	8,315	8,594
Rheinland-Pfalz	1,271	1,318	1,474	1,635	1,731	1,781	1,784	1,791
Saarland	369	378	438	469	477	506	502	492
Sachsen	1,184	1,315	1,454	1,580	1,649	1,756	2,251	2,354
Sachsen-Anhalt	1,045	1,134	1,162	1,188	1,249	1,254	1,290	1,223
Schleswig-Holstein	572	576	637	656	706	739	771	808
Thüringen	550	642	726	764	969	1,030	1,035	1,156
	24,818	27,093	29,495	31,488	33,381	35,113	36,724	37,018

Source: Reckling 2016.

Surveys among the *Länder* ministries of justice have been hampered by the fact that there has been inconsistency as regards data sources, counting criteria and control procedures (Kwaschnik 2008: 308; Ruderich 2014: 337). While some regional statistics have been based on intensive supervision cases, others have counted numbers of ex-prisoners involved. Although there are legal rules to avoid multiple supervision procedures for offenders who have been convicted more than once,[8] Morgenstern and Hecht (2011: 185) have shown that these problems still exist. The main difficulty in describing the practice of intensive supervision over time is the lack of statistical data collected and published in a more sophisticated way (Arbeitsgruppe Optimierung des bestehenden kriminalstatistischen Systems 2009: 59).

A new collection of statistical data was launched in 2016, but only preliminary and incomplete results have been published so far. According to these tables, more than 60 per cent of those under intensive supervision are ex-prisoners, the most frequent single direction is to report regularly to the supervising authority or to the probation service, and intensive supervision exceeds the five years threshold for some 22 per cent of cases (Götting 2017).

B. Empirical Research

Intensive supervision has been viewed in a rather critical way by many probation practitioners and criminologists since its introduction in 1975. One early

[8] Sections 68b(4), 68e(1) StGB.

author assumed that the legal rules favoured 'dominance of control over social assistance' and would cause institutional conflicts (Jacobsen 1985: 180). Similar concerns are still to be heard in professional seminars and conferences. When it comes to articles published in probation journals, the pros and cons of specific methods are now being argued in a much more sophisticated way.[9]

More recent research has tried to describe intensive supervision practice and to pinpoint the consequences of several legal reforms in a situation where justice statistics are lacking, sometimes on the basis of more or less consistent regional data collections (Kwaschnik 2008; Rohrbach 2014; Ruderich 2014). The most comprehensive of these recent empirical studies set out to evaluate intensive supervision as conceived by major reform legislation enacted in 2007 and 2011 at the national level. Analysing case files of a sample of supervising authorities all over Germany, Alexander Baur (2015: 49) distinguished three types of intensive supervision he characterised by specific problems. Table 10.3 features a simplified version of this typology, which is a mixture of legal as well as empirical aspects.

Table 10.3 Types of intensive supervision

	Type I	**Type II**	**Type III**
clientele needs	primarily assistance	some control	control
example	suspended hospital order (s 67b StGB)	release at the end of a prison term (s 68f StGB)	release at the end of a prison term (s 68f StGB)
legal prediction	positive	negative	negative
sanction for non-compliance	revocation	offence of violating the directions of a supervision order (s 145a StGB)	offence of violating the directions of a supervision order (s 145a StGB)
dominating agencies	probation service, forensic ambulance service	probation service, supervising authority	probation service, supervising authority, police
offences	all	all	sexual
number of cases in the study	127	377	102

Source: Baur 2015: 51.

Type I intensive supervision is characterised by a clientele who will primarily need social assistance and help to cope with its multiple problems. Its situation is rather similar to that of 'ordinary' probationers, but the legal setting is different. For example, a Type I person might be someone who was convicted

[9] For recent examples, see Cornel et al 2018; and Zobrist 2018.

for a minor robbery by a court that accepted diminished responsibility due to a mental disorder, and which made a suspended hospital order for treatment in the community. According to the law, this is only possible if there is enough reason to expect that special hospital treatment will not be necessary to prevent recidivism.[10] The probation service will mainly have to cooperate with the forensic ambulance service or a psychiatrist. Should the offender commit another crime, the suspension of the hospital order might still be revoked, or hospitalisation for a limited period not exceeding three months and for the purpose of crisis intervention might be ordered.

Clients under Type II intensive supervision will need more control. They will have been convicted for offences for which a suspended prison term combined with 'ordinary' probation would be precluded by the law. The most frequent examples would be offenders who spent several years in prison for certain violent crimes and who were only released at the end of their full prison terms. In these cases, intensive supervision secures some control by agencies of the criminal justice system even beyond the prison sentence, because recidivism is seen as all too common. The supervising authority will pay more attention to these cases, and its powers to intervene will sometimes be used. If an ex-offender from this group commits another crime, he will be prosecuted but no suspended sentence can be revoked. The minor offence of violating the directions of a supervision order (section 145a StGB) will be a more marginal issue in the process, but it may involve other interventions by the criminal justice system.

Type III intensive supervision is even more stringent. In these cases, the intensive supervision is intended to control offenders who are viewed as being in danger of victimising other persons, especially by the commission of more serious sexual offences. This is probably the type of case where intensive supervision's definition as a non-custodial alternative to post-sentence preventive detention (Dessecker 2004: 381) is most convincing. But the tasks of control and of crime prevention in these cases tend to be shifted away from the probation service and even the supervising authority to police agencies (Baur 2015: 230).

C. Sexual and Violent Offenders

Legal accounts of intensive supervision in Germany tend to stress that this measure is largely independent from the specific offences committed (Baur 2015: 37; Groß 2016, section 68 note 6 and section 68f note 6). In his extensive study, Baur (2015) concentrated on differences between the types of intensive supervision. As Table 10.3 shows, only Type III was characterised by sexual offences, while Types I and II refer to any crime. In Baur's expert interviews, several directors of supervising agencies and probation officers said their work with sexual

[10] Section 67b StGB.

offenders was more labour-intensive than supervision of other clients. In particular, intensive supervision of paedosexual clients was seen as problematic (Baur 2015: 75). Unfortunately, more detailed information on the crime characteristics of the cases studied is not available.

Moritz Rohrbach's (2014) study provides further valuable detail. He analysed the files of all intensive supervision cases recorded in the *Land* of Mecklenburg-Vorpommern in 2009. From a total of 192 case files containing sufficient information, he found that 55 per cent related to sexual and violent offenders, the most frequent offence being assault causing bodily harm by dangerous means[11] (17 per cent). This variable simply referred to the offence covered by the original conviction that was the cause of intensive supervision. As previous convictions were not systematically examined, the proportion of sexual and violent offenders might have been underestimated. A typical non-violent offence was theft[12] (6 per cent) (Rohrbach 2014: 204 and 300).

Comparisons can be drawn with the earlier results of Jacobsen (1985), who chose a similar design for his file analysis of a sample of intensive supervision cases from Niedersachsen, recorded in 1981 and 1982. In 557 case files, only 30 per cent could be clearly associated with sexual and violent offences.[13] On the other hand, 33 per cent of the sample were theft cases. Sexual and violent offenders had most often been released from psychiatric institutions, not from prisons (Jacobsen 1985: 84 and 107).

Sex offender registration might affect more persons in Germany, but statistical data have been published only sporadically and no empirical research results have been available. For electronic supervision, an empirical study based on a total of 74 cases that existed in the period from its introduction in 2011 to August 2013 demonstrated that every case involved sexual or violent offenders (Bräuchle 2016: 95). This picture has not changed at all during the last few years. On 31 December 2016, there were 88 offenders under electronic supervision, and 63 of them were sexual offenders (Dessecker 2018).

IV. INTENSIVE SUPERVISION AND HUMAN RIGHTS

A. The Perspective of the Federal Constitutional Court

Intensive supervision is a non-custodial measure that tends to restrict fundamental rights of ex-offenders in a less intensive way than a prison sentence, a hospital order or post-sentence preventive detention. Nonetheless, its legitimacy and its constitutional limits have been questioned on several occasions (Baur 2015: 14).

[11] Section 224 StGB.
[12] Section 242 StGB.
[13] This is almost certainly an underestimation, as some of the offence categories mix up non-violent and violent crimes.

In 1980, an ex-offender complained to the Federal Constitutional Court about intensive supervision's having commenced as he was released at the end of a full prison term of two years for attempted blackmail. In a rather short decision, the Court pointed out that from the position of the Basic Law,[14] there was no objection to a penal sanction constructed to help and control ex-offenders in order to stop them from reoffending (BVerfG, 15 August 1980). References were made to earlier case law on preventive detention (Dessecker 2016: 422). For the Federal Constitutional Court, intensive supervision seemed to be specifically legitimate for those prisoners considered to be dangerous and who were not granted conditional early release. In this situation, intensive supervision was not regarded as another penalty for an act that had been punished before, which would have been contrary to the right to a fair trial as stipulated by Article 103(3) GG. Instead it was one of the legal consequences of a criminal conviction, which was also understood by the person convicted. The Court went on to underline that intensive supervision in these circumstances was not disproportionate, as it was clearly limited to cases where the prerequisites for conditional release were not fulfilled. Moreover, directions as listed in section 68a StGB should secure that the specific arrangement for intensive supervision fit the individual case.

The fundamental acknowledgement that intensive supervision is legitimate from a constitutional law perspective has not precluded the meticulous testing of specific directions in other cases. In 2010, the Federal Constitutional Court (BVerfG 8 December 2010) quashed the following direction made by the Higher Regional Court (*Oberlandesgericht*) of Munich for a period of five years:

> The convicted person is prohibited from publishing ideas of the extreme right or of national socialist ideology, especially by publications of the *Deutsche Stimme* publishing house, in the News of the *Hilfsorganisation für nationale politische Gefangene und deren Angehörige e.V. (HNG)* or by means of the *Freundeskreis UN e.V.*

The complainant had been sentenced to imprisonment for four years and three months for membership of a terrorist organisation, illegal handling of explosives and illegal bearing of a fire-arm. The Higher Regional Court explained that he had tried to spread extremist, anti-Jewish and anti-American slogans even when in prison. Nevertheless, the Federal Constitutional Court's decision did not concentrate on specific issues of intensive supervision but rather on freedom of expression.[15] The direction was deemed vague and as lacking careful consideration of public security versus the complainant's basic right of free speech. Lastly, it was also considered disproportionate, as it hindered the complainant's ability to participate at all in public debate of his political views.

More recently, the Federal Constitutional Court (eg BVerfG, 22 January 2015) dealt with complaints against electronic supervision directions on several occasions.

[14] *Grundgesetz* (GG).
[15] Art 5 GG.

Although these decisions do not elaborate on potential constitutional issues in detail, they leave little doubt that the Court tends to interpret electronic supervision as a legitimate intervention for high-risk offenders.

The Federal Constitutional Court has been considerably more critical about directions not to consume alcohol or other drugs, for a complainant who had a long history of drug addiction and drug offences but no convictions for other offences (BVerfG, 30 March 2016). Abstinence directions might appear disproportionate if there were reasons to suppose that ex-offenders would not be able to comply with them because of their addiction. During the period of intensive supervision, consuming drugs or alcohol would even be deemed a crime. As far as addiction could be diagnosed as a disease from a medical point of view, and given that several trials of therapy had shown it to be unsuccessful, a further abstinence direction would appear to violate the ex-offender's personal freedoms guaranteed by the Constitution.

B. The European Court of Human Rights

On some occasions, German domestic courts have discussed the legal setting of intensive supervision from a European human rights perspective. In a case of indeterminate intensive supervision of a sexual offender released from a special hospital, the Munich Higher Regional Court (OLG München, 14 August 2012) made a remark on the general qualification of intensive supervision. The statement was quite clear, though. The Court said that there was no violation of the *nulla poena sine lege* principle as stated in Article 7(1) of the European Convention on Human Rights (ECHR). Although the ECtHR had held that post-sentence preventive detention, as it used to be implemented in Germany before 2013, was a form of criminal punishment (*M v Germany* 2009), this reasoning was limited to the specific problem of how to separate sentences of imprisonment from preventive detention, and it could not be applied to a non-custodial measure. As Article 5 of the Convention only referred to cases of detention, it was not relevant either.

This decision is in line with the established interpretation of the Convention (Meyer-Ladewig, Harrendorf and König 2017, Article 7 note 8; Schabas 2015: 226), and at least one more case has been decided in the same way by another domestic court (OLG Nürnberg, 10 November 2014). The ECtHR seems never to have dealt with intensive supervision in Germany. The jurisprudence of the Strasbourg institutions, however, has considered a few cases of sex-offender registration from other European countries (*Adamson v United Kingdom* 1999; *Gardel v France* 2009).

As national registers of sexual offenders apply to convicted persons and can be labelled a collateral consequence of conviction, if not a post-sentence measure of prevention, the ECtHR has not seen any major human rights problem in this context. Compared to long periods of imprisonment, these interventions might produce the impression of only minor consequences not beyond the limits of proportionality, and be justified by the protection of possible victims of crime. Moreover, the Convention was not designed to establish a complete or even perfect system of human rights. This might at least partly explain why the question whether a measure such as intensive supervision enters into conflict with the Convention heavily depends on its specific design and on the scope of the directions involved.

V. CONCLUSION

'Intensive supervision' is a comprehensive term for legal interventions that seek to control the behaviour of offenders or ex-offenders in the community. Specific conditions will vary across jurisdictions. As shown by the example of Germany, intensive supervision may function through the cooperation of the courts with the agencies of the police, the probation service and the forensic ambulance service, and it is directed at various groups of offenders.

Although there is a considerable body of empirical research at the national level, specific problems regarding intensive supervision for sexual and violent offenders are under-researched. We are still lacking more precise empirical information on indeterminate intensive supervision and on the practice of management programmes for higher-risk sexual and violent offenders run by the police. Lastly, even the incomplete statistics we have can demonstrate how considerably the numbers of ex-offenders involved have been growing in the long run.

The human rights perspective has shown that intensive supervision is problematic, at least if its circumstances are constructed in a way that blurs the distinction between custody and a non-custodial sanction, such as in cases of compulsory residence, although sex-offender registration is not seen as a major human rights issue in terms of the ECHR. It might be concluded that the non-custodial sanctions of the criminal justice system are much more difficult to confine, as they will always appear as a less serious alternative to imprisonment of high-risk offenders. At this stage we can only speculate about the extent to which country-level differences may be explained by reference to fundamental societal values and the specific characteristics of legal cultures.

REFERENCES

Albrecht, H-J (2004) 'Youth justice in Germany' *Crime and Justice*, 31, 443–93.

Arbeitsgruppe Optimierung des bestehenden kriminalstatistischen Systems (2009) 'Abschlussbericht der Arbeitsgruppe' in Rat für Sozial- und Wirtschaftsdaten (ed), *Optimierung des bestehenden kriminalstatistischen Systems in Deutschland: Empfehlungen der Arbeitsgruppe Optimierung des bestehenden kriminalstatistischen*

Systems unter dem Vorsitz von Prof Dr Wolfgang Heinz, Universität Konstanz (Baden-Baden, Nomos) 33–137.

Atkin, CA and Armstrong, GS (2013) 'Does the concentration of parolees in a community impact employer attitudes toward the hiring of ex-offenders?' *Criminal Justice Policy Review*, 24, 71–93.

Bartels, L (2014) *Literature review on intensive supervision orders: A report prepared for the ACT Justice and Community Safety Directorate* (Canberra, ACT Justice and Community Safety Directorate), available at https://papers.ssrn.com/sol3/papers.cfm?abstract_id=2669069 (last accessed 16 July 2018).

Baur, A (2015) 'Die Führungsaufsicht: eine rechtshistorische, dogmatische und rechtstatsächliche Untersuchung. Zugleich Abschlussbericht zur bundesweiten Evaluation der Führungsaufsicht unter besonderer Berücksichtigung der Reformen 2007 und 2011' in A Baur and J Kinzig (eds), *Die reformierte Führungsaufsicht: Ergebnisse einer bundesweiten Evaluation* (Tübingen, Mohr Siebeck) 1–645.

Bohlander, M (2008) *The German Criminal Code: A modern English translation* (Oxford, Hart Publishing).

Bouchard, J and Wong, JS (2018) 'Examining the effects of intensive supervision and aftercare programs for at-risk youth: A systematic review and meta-analysis' *International Journal of Offender Therapy and Comparative Criminology*, 62, 1509–34.

Bräuchle, A (2016) *Die elektronische Aufenthaltsüberwachung gefährlicher Straftäter im Rahmen der Führungsaufsicht: eine Studie zur Rechtsdogmatik und Rechtswirklichkeit* (Dissertation Universität Tübingen), available at hdl.handle.net/10900/73947 (last accessed 16 July 2018).

Cohen, S (1972) *Folk devils and moral panics: The creation of the Mods and Rockers* (London, MacGibbon & Kee).

Cornel, H et al (2018) 'Wissen, was wir tun: Überlegungen zur Rückbesinnung auf sozialarbeiterisches Handeln in der Arbeit mit straffällig gewordenen Menschen' *Bewährungshilfe*, 65, 77–90.

Dessecker, A (2004) *Gefährlichkeit und Verhältnismäßigkeit: Eine Untersuchung zum Maßregelrecht* (Berlin, Duncker and Humblot).

—— (2016) 'Constitutional limits on life imprisonment and post-sentence preventive detention in Germany' in D Van Zyl Smit and C Appleton (eds), *Life imprisonment and human rights* (Oxford, Hart Publishing) 411–34.

—— (2018) 'Die Kollateralfolgen von Strafen' in K Boers et al (eds), *Kriminologische Welt in Bewegung* (Mönchengladbach, Forum) 476–86.

Drake, EK (2018) 'The monetary benefits and costs of community supervision' *Journal of Contemporary Criminal Justice*, 34, 47–68.

Dubber, MD and Hörnle, T (2014) *Criminal law: A comparative approach* (Oxford, Oxford University Press).

Farrall, S (2016) 'The long-term impacts of probation supervision' in F Dünkel et al (eds), *European treatment, transition management, and re-integration of high-risk offenders: results of the final conference at Rostock-Warnemünde, 3–5 September 2014, and final evaluation report of the Justice Cooperation Network (JCN) project 'European treatment and transition management of high-risk offenders'* (Mönchengladbach, Forum) 45–82.

Geiger, B (2006) 'The case for treating ex-offenders as a suspect class' *California Law Review*, 94, 1191–242.

Gendreau, P, Cullen, FT and Bonta, J (1994) 'Intensive rehabilitation supervision: The next generation in community corrections?' *Federal Probation*, 58, 72–78.

Götting, B (2017) *Statistik der Führungsaufsicht 2015*. Presented at the Fachtagung Führungsaufsicht, Kassel: DBH Fachverband für Soziale Arbeit, Strafrecht und Kriminalpoltik, available at www.dbh-online.de/sites/default/files/doku/vortraege/fa-statistik-stand_nov.17.pdf (last accessed 16 July 2018).

Gregório Hertz et al (2017) *Extramurale Behandlung und Betreuung von Sexualstraftätern: Ergebnisse einer bundesweiten Umfrage zur Nachsorge-Praxis 2016* (Wiesbaden, KrimZ), available at http://www.krimz.de/publikationen/bm-online/bm-online13/ (last accessed 16 July 2018).

Grosser, R (2017) 'Bewährungshilfe' in H Cornel, G Kawamura-Reindl and B-R Sonnen (eds), *Resozialisierung: Handbuch* (4th edn) (Baden-Baden, Nomos) 200–16.

Groß, K-H (2016) 'Kommentierung zu §§ 67e–68g StGB' in W Joecks and K Miebach (eds), *Münchener Kommentar zum Strafgesetzbuch* (3rd edn) (Munich, Beck).

Heinz, W (2016) *Kriminalität und Kriminalitätskontrolle in Deutschland* (Konstanz, Universität Konstanz), available at http://www.uni-konstanz.de/rtf/kis/Kriminalitaet_und_Kriminalitaetskontrolle_in_Deutschland_Stand_2013.pdf (last accessed 16 July 2018).

Von Hirsch, A and Wasik, M (1997) 'Civil disqualifications attending conviction: a suggested conceptual framework' *Cambridge Law Journal*, 56, 599–626.

Homes, A, Walmsley, RK and Debidin, M (2005) *Intensive supervision and monitoring schemes for persistent offenders: Staff and offender perceptions* (London, Home Office).

Jacobsen, H-F (1985) *Führungsaufsicht und ihre Klientel: Intentionen und Realitäten einer Maßregel* (Köln, Heymann).

Jehle, J-M et al (2016) *Legalbewährung nach strafrechtlichen Sanktionen: eine bundesweite Rückfalluntersuchung 2010 bis 2013 und 2004 bis 2013* (Mönchengladbach, Forum), available at http://www.bmjv.de/SharedDocs/Downloads/DE/Service/StudienUntersuchungenFachbuecher/Legalbewaehrung_nach_strafrechtlichen_Sanktionen_2010_2013.pdf?__blob=publicationFile&v=1 (last accessed 16 July 2018).

Kasecker, K (2010) *Die Überwachung rückfallgefährdeter Sexualstraftäter: ein Vergleich der Konzepte und Strategien der Bundesländer unter kriminologischen, rechts- und polizeiwissenschaftlichen Aspekten* (Master Thesis Bochum, Ruhr-Universität).

Klug, W (2018) 'Sozialarbeit mit Sexualstraftätern im Rahmen der Führungsaufsicht: empirische Einblicke in ein schwieriges Handlungsfeld' *Bewährungshilfe*, 65, 138–59.

Kwaschnik, S (2008) *Die Führungsaufsicht im Wandel* (Hamburg, Kovač).

Marlowe, DB, Hardin, CD and Fox, CL (2016) *Painting the current picture: A national report on drug courts and other problem-solving courts in the United States* (Alexandria, National Drug Court Institute), available at www.ndci.org/wp-content/uploads/2016/05/Painting-the-Current-Picture-2016.pdf (last accessed 16 July 2018).

Meier, B-D (2015) *Strafrechtliche Sanktionen* (4th edn) (Berlin, Springer).

Meyer-Ladewig, J, Harrendorf, S and König, S (2017) 'Kommentierung zu Art. 5-7 MRK' in J Meyer-Ladewig, M Nettesheim and S Von Raumer (eds), *Europäische Menschenrechtskonvention: Handkommentar* (4th edn) (Baden-Baden, Nomos).

Morgenstern, C and Hecht, A (2011) 'Rechtstatsachen zur Führungsaufsicht im kriminalpolitischen Kontext' *Bewährungshilfe*, 58, 177–95.

Mutz, J (2008) 'Germany' in AM van Kalmthout and I Durnescu (eds), *Probation in Europe* (Nijmegen, Wolf Legal Publishers) 381–415.
Nellis, M and Bungerfeldt, J (2013) 'Electronic monitoring and probation in Sweden and England and Wales: Comparative policy developments' *Probation Journal*, 60, 278–301.
Reckling, P (2016) 'Der Anstieg der Führungsaufsichtsfälle ist erheblich' in DBH-Fachverband für Soziale Arbeit, Strafrecht und Kriminalpolitik (ed) *40 Jahre Führungsaufsicht: Evaluation, Geschichte und Zahlen* (Köln, DBH) 113–18.
Rohrbach, MP (2014) *Die Entwicklung der Führungsaufsicht unter besonderer Berücksichtigung der Praxis in Mecklenburg-Vorpommern* (Mönchengladbach, Forum).
Ruderich, D (2014) *Führungsaufsicht: die Entwicklung und Ausgestaltung des Instituts der Führungsaufsicht auch im Hinblick auf die einzelnen Bundesländer sowie die Darstellung und Bewertung der Übergangskonzepte zum Umgang mit rückfallgefährdeten Sexualstraftätern* (Frankfurt/M, PL Academic Research).
Sauter, J, Seewald, K and Dahle, K-P (2017) 'Wirksamkeit ambulanter forensischer Nachsorge: was wissen wir wirklich? Übersichtsarbeit über den aktuellen Forschungsstand in der Bundesrepublik Deutschland' *Bewährungshilfe* 64, 146–61.
Schabas, WA (2015) *The European Convention on Human Rights: A commentary* (Oxford, Oxford University Press).
Statistisches Bundesamt (1980) *Bewährungshilfe 1977* (Stuttgart, Kohlhammer).
Stout, B, Dalby, H and Schraner, I (2017) 'Measuring the impact of juvenile justice interventions: What works, what helps and what matters?' *Youth Justice*, 17, 196–212.
Uggen, C and Stewart, R (2015) 'Piling on: Collateral consequences and community supervision' *Minnesota Law Review*, 99, 1871–910.
Weigend, T (2016) 'No news is good news: Criminal sentencing in Germany since 2000' *Crime and Justice*, 45, 83–106.
Weinrath, M, Donatelli, G and Murchison, MJ (2016) 'Mentorship: A missing piece to manage juvenile intensive supervision programs and youth gangs?' *Canadian Journal of Criminology and Criminal Justice*, 58, 291–321.
Wilde, F (2017) 'Wenn Armut zur Strafe wird: die freie, gemeinnützige Arbeit in der aktuellen Sanktionspraxis' *Neue Kriminalpolitik*, 29, 205–19.
Will, R (1995) 'Intensive supervision probation' in M Tonry and K Hamilton (eds), *Intermediate sanctions in overcrowded times* (Boston, MA, Northeastern University Press) 89–90.
Zobrist, P (2018) '"Wissen, was wir tun" heißt: sich für Wissen öffnen. Replik auf den Beitrag von Cornel, Grosser, Lindenberg und Lindenberg' *Bewährungshilfe*, 65, 293–306.

TABLE OF CASES

Domestic Cases

Federal Constitutional Court

BVerfGE 55, 28 (15 August 1980, 2 BvR 495/80)
BVerfG, 1 BvR 1106/08 (8 December 2010, EuGRZ 2011, 88)

BVerfG, 2 BvR 2095/14 (22 January 2015)
BVerfG, 2 BvR 496/12 (30 March 2016, NJW 2016, 2170)

Higher Regional Courts

OLG München, 1 Ws 599/12, 1 Ws 654/12, 1 Ws 655/12, 1 Ws 656/12, 1 Ws 657/12, 1 Ws 658/12 (14 August 2012)
OLG Nürnberg, 2 Ws 509/14 (10 November 2014, R & P 2015, 55)

European Court of Human Rights

Adamson v United Kingdom App no 42293/98 (26 January 1999)
Gardel v France App no 16428/05 (17 December 2009)
M v Germany App no 19359/04 (17 December 2009)

11

Bifurcation and Redemption in France

MARTINE HERZOG-EVANS

I. INTRODUCTION

MODERN LEGAL SYSTEMS are often characterised by 'bifurcation', according to Pratt (2002), who borrowed from Bottoms' earlier predictions (Bottoms 1977, 1980: 6). Bifurcation consists of a legal and practical dichotomy that opposes two main categories of offenders and how they are processed. One finds, on the one hand, 'dangerous' offenders, who are treated more harshly (with more constraints, fewer early prison releases, in some cases the violation of general criminal law principles and so on) but who are also subject to more scrutiny and attention – which may include more support. On the other hand, one finds 'run-of-the-mill' offenders, who are treated managerially, the main focus being on the prevention of prison overcrowding and the processing of cases as quickly as possible, with little attention paid to their psycho-social and criminogenic needs, and where the ideal of rehabilitation is abandoned and replaced by expedient procedures and measures. This prediction seems to have come true in the French (Herzog-Evans 2017a and 2017b) – and the Belgian (Scheirs et al 2015) – contexts. On the one hand, most offenders (the 'run-of-the-mill' ones) are processed via shabby prosecutor-led procedures, devoid of due process, which lead to measures that are purely formal, non-constraining – but also non-protective of victims and unsupportive of rehabilitation (up to 50 per cent of all offences are processed in this way – Danet 2013) – or via 'McJustice' factory-line felony courts processing (Ligue des Droits de l'Homme 2012). On the other hand, a small but increasing number of offenders who have committed serious offences ('the dangerous') have, during the 'Sarkozy era', been the subject of a long series of reforms that have, inter alia, created various legal mechanisms allowing the authorities to subject them to potentially perpetual forms of supervision beyond their sentence.

However, the French penal landscape is in fact more contrasting still: the legal system can be described as the patchwork outcome of opposing political stances and epochs; the dominant orientation being a 'purist' treatment and rehabilitation model, most offenders keeping their citizen's rights and benefitting from a very generous criminal record-expunging system. Even the most dangerous offenders are subject to only rather loose probation. A practical common denominator is also, unfortunately, that the managerial nature of French justice and probation, along with the impact of the merger between prison and probation services in 1999, has led to a purely formal form of supervision and societal re-entry system, where most offenders, whether run-of-the-mill or dangerous, are essentially left to their own devices (see, in 2014, Morgenstern and Robinson's warning).

Before we proceed, it is important to note that the dichotomy between run-of-the-mill and dangerous offenders has little to do with actual dangerousness, whatever this means (Lazerges 2012; Mbanzoulou 2010), and is entirely non-evidence-based (ie does not rely on validated structured risk assessment, whether forensic or criminological). It relies solely on the following criteria and circumstances: purely legal categories (ie the distinction between crimes and felonies); prosecutors' subjective assessments; culture and local particularities, along with prosecutors' personalities (for instance domestic violence cases are typically considered not serious (Herzog-Evans 2017c), whilst insults to the police are (Herzog-Evans ongoing)); whatever makes the headlines versus anonymous yet quantitatively numerous offences.

II. RETENTION OF RIGHTS FOR THE 'RUN-OF-THE-MILL'

The general philosophy that guides French criminal justice and prison norms is very inclusive. It is deemed essential that most offenders be allowed to return to society, both as citizens and as employees. Also, in many cases, the offences at stake are not deemed serious enough to warrant any more constraints than those that were imposed during the execution of the sentence. To illustrate these issues, we shall focus mainly on three important examples: (i) prisoners' right to vote; (ii) criminal records; (iii) and ordinary offender supervision.

A. The Right to Vote

Two opposite visions exist in Europe and beyond. One might first consider that the right to vote should be reserved for law-abiding, and therefore 'deserving', citizens. It follows logically from this that those who have not behaved as good citizens, as illustrated by their committing an offence, should be deprived of this precious right. Those who are of this opinion add that depriving offenders and/or prisoners of their rights will encourage them to get their lives back on track (eg in the United Kingdom (UK): Dhami and Cruise 2013). An opposite view considers that in order to encourage offenders to feel part of the community and thus to act as such, one should encourage them to participate in public life (Easton 2009; Foster 2008). Some even argue that allowing offenders to vote may contribute to the prevention of reoffending (Uggen et al 2004). To this we would like to add that just as other citizens, prisoners and offenders also feel the consequences of political choices and policies, and that they should have a say.

Probably because of its divisive nature, this debate has not been subjected to clear-cut European regulations. The European Convention on Human Rights (ECHR) is silent on the subject matter, and Additional Protocol No 1, Article 3, refers in only very general terms to citizens' right to vote. Only soft law regulations, which can easily be dismissed, and will particularly be ignored in written law jurisdictions, refer to prisoners' right to vote. However, they do so in vague and general terms. In particular, Rule 11 of the European Prison Rules (EPR) 2006 states that '[p]rison authorities shall ensure that prisoners are able to participate in elections, referenda and in other aspects of public life', but it hastens to add that this only applies 'in so far as their right to do so is not restricted by national law'. In other words, the Council of Europe merely allows Member States to do as they please and formulates a rather cynical tautology: prisoners can vote if they are allowed to vote. This constitutes a perfect illustration of what this volume shows: that the ECHR framework offers very little effective protection.

For its part, the European Court of Human Rights (ECtHR) is similarly conciliatory. Three decades ago, it ruled that Member States could limit offenders' rights to vote if this was in pursuit of a legitimate goal and if such limitations were proportionate (*Mathieu-Mohin & Clerfayt v Belgium* 1987). In *Frodl* (2010), it further added that such limitations should be necessary in each individual case. This is a classic case of cold feet: the ECtHR was well aware of the vastly different viewpoints in Member States, and did not want to make a decisive decision one way or another. As a matter of fact, in a later case pertaining to the UK, the Court ruled that Member States could base their own margin of appreciation on the lack of a European consensus (*Hirst v the United Kingdom* 2004: para 40). For this reason, a mere fiscal fraud could, for instance, warrant (in its opinion) the deprivation of the right to vote (*MDU v Italy* 2003). In principle, then, Member States enjoy a considerable amount of discretionary power. However, the UK has been condemned several times, because it deprives most prisoners of the right to vote, and in the *Hirst* case did this both automatically and perpetually. Later, the Grand Chamber also ruled that a prisoner should not be automatically deprived of his right to vote (*Hirst v the United Kingdom* 2005). However, the Grand Chamber, contrary to the section that had ruled in 2004, stated that the hope that depriving offenders of their right to vote would result in their becoming law-abiding citizens did constitute legitimate grounds for such restrictions. In a similar Italian case, the ECtHR ruled that it was essential that the decision to deprive an offender of the right to vote was made by a judge and was explained in writing (*Scoppola v Italy* 2011, para 43).

The UK did not react favourably to the rather undemanding pressure from Europe. It has persisted in opposing European court rulings; it was therefore condemned again in 2015 (*McHugh and others v the United Kingdom* 2015).

In France, since the New Criminal Code (CC) was enacted (1992) and implemented (1994), French offenders have benefitted from very favourable rules. As a principle, felons (who have committed felonies – *délits*) keep their right to vote, even whilst they are detained, but courts can deprive them of their 'civil rights and political liberties' for a maximum duration of five years, 10 if they have committed a serious crime (*crime*);[1] this rises to 15 years in terrorist matters[2] – a rule that has not been amended after the attacks on French soil, even though two law reforms have ensued – Laws of 3 June and of 21 July 2016). At the other extreme of the spectrum, those who have merely committed a misdemeanour (*contravention*)[3] cannot be disenfranchised. Even in crime and felony cases, disenfranchising decisions are very rare (compared with the rest of Europe: Tripkovic 2016), and apply typically only to public figures.

In practice, French judicial authorities seem to be of the opinion that civil and political liberties should not be part of sentences, as they are unrelated to both resocialisation and reoffending; favouring the first and preventing the second are their main goals, according to the law itself.[4] However, the courts analyse this deprivation as being the logical sanction for an undeserving politician or public figure, not as following logically from the simple act of committing an offence.

Importantly, however, offenders who have committed crimes and were sentenced before 1994 remain disenfranchised for the rest of their lives. The European Court of Justice has ruled on this particular issue. It decided that in the case of the applicant, who had been sentenced to 12 years' imprisonment, this was not disproportionate, particularly since he could ask for a legal suspension (*Thierry Delvigne v Commune de Lesparre-Médoc et Préfet de la Gironde* 2015). Interestingly, the French Constitutional Council has ruled that in general, the right to vote is an attribute of citizenship (Decision no 82-146 DC, 1982: para 7), which is roughly defined in the French context as referring to 'belonging to an autonomous political community, which defines rights and duties' (Schnapper 2000: back cover).

In sum, in practice most offenders retain their right to vote, whether they are detained or sentenced to probation, and this whether during or after their sentence. In all cases the right to vote can be reclaimed via a legal rehabilitation procedure.[5]

[1] Art 132-21(1) CC.

[2] Art 422-3(1) CC.

[3] In French criminal law, offences are classified, in a 'tripartite division', as: '*contraventions*' (in US terms misdemeanours) for relatively minor acts (eg parking offences; trespassing), which do not carry custodial sentences and are generally punishable by fines of €38 (in some cases €11) to €1,500; '*délits*' (in US terms 'felonies'), which comprise a large variety of more serious offences (eg theft; violence; domestic violence; apologia of terrorism) and which can carry custodial sentences of up to 10 years and heavy fines; and '*crimes*', ie very serious offences (eg murder; terrorist offences; armed robbery), which can carry a sentence of between 15 to 30 years, or life with or without parole. Each category of offence is handled by different courts: *tribunal de police*; *tribunal correctionnel*; and the *cour d'assises* (with jurors), respectively.

[4] Art 131(19) CC; Art 707 *Code de Procédure Pénale* – Penal Procedure Code (PCC).

[5] Art 131-26 CC.

B. Criminal Records

Legal systems and opinions about criminal records vary greatly, both in Europe and in the rest of the world. A special edition of the *European Journal of Probation*, in 2011, thus uncovered the existence of two different approaches: on the one hand, jurisdictions like England and Wales (Padfield 2011), which consider, similarly to the USA (eg Blumstein and Nakamura 2009) and Australia (Naylor 2011), that once a person has been convicted, it is essential that the public, and particularly potential employers, have access to this information; on the other hand, jurisdictions such as Germany (Morgenstern 2011), Spain (Larrauri 2011) or France (Herzog-Evans 2011), for whom it is imperative that offenders are allowed to re-enter society and find employment, and who therefore block or limit access to this kind of information and/or have a generous criminal record-expunging system; the Netherlands being situated somewhat between these two stances (Boone 2011). Beyond vastly different public opinions, these differences can also be explained by a very different approach to privacy (Jacobs and Larrauri 2012): many Continental jurisdictions consider that a criminal past is a private matter and should not be divulged to all and sundry, whilst other jurisdictions are not particularly concerned by privacy.

In France, by contrast, another concept is also at play: the principle of the 'Right to Be Forgotten' (*Droit à l'Oubli*) (Matsopoulou 2006; Ponseille 2007). According to this principle, people can have a past, but the past does not define an individual. It should not endlessly affect this person's future and, particularly, prevent him or her from being able to study, to obtain employment, and even to have a political career. Thus, it explains, for instance, how former Prime Minister Alain Juppé, who was convicted of a felony, has been able to return to public life. As a matter of fact, he has even been appointed by president Macron as a judge in the highest French court, the Council Constitutional, on February 13, 2019.

Thus, in France, two main principles explain why criminal records are not easily accessible and are easily expunged: the right to be forgotten, and the necessity of supporting the desistance process and of acknowledging achieved desistance (Herzog-Evans 2011). The legal framework of these generous rules is, however, extremely intricate (Herzog-Evans 2017a).

Importantly, not all sentences are mentioned in the criminal record system, and particularly not in Bulletin no 3 ('B3'), which is the part of the criminal record accessible by offenders themselves – and by nobody else. The sentences that are registrable in B3 are only those which are custodial in nature and are in excess of two years unsuspended – unless the suspension has been revoked. However, the court can decide that a sentence shall be registered, even if it is below the two-year threshold.[6] Such decisions are extremely rare. Conversely, the court can grant an exemption from the obligation to mention in B3 a sentence in excess of the two-year threshold. These exemption decisions are more frequent,

[6] Art 777, PPC.

and courts tend to grant them provided the offender or his attorney explains the reason why the exemption is needed. In practice, most employers do not ask for information on a prospective employee's criminal record, unless they are in the security business (Stacey 2014). For this reason, and because of the limited amount of information that is registered in B3, criminal records hardly affect offenders' ability to obtain employment. Moreover, it is illegal to request a copy of B3 from an applicant to university or other forms of training, or to require declarations of people's criminal past when they are seeking to obtain documentation or services. Thus, a criminal past does not affect access to services or education.

Adding to this very protective system, legislators have created a very liberal and intricate expunging system. This very rich body of norms can be roughly divided into three categories: first, rules that expunge the criminal record solely on the basis of the passing of time, and which aim both to declutter the criminal record of very old files and to show mercy to the elderly; second, rules that expunge the criminal record for utilitarian reasons, particularly employment, and which aim at helping with the desistance process, and include minimal merit conditions; and, third, rules that are entirely based on merit, and which acknowledge achieved desistance (Herzog-Evans 2011, 2017a).

However, expunging techniques are less accessible to sex offenders, as legislators have wanted to make sure that administrations – which have direct access to part of the criminal records (called 'B2') and might hire people for positions in charge of children, such as schools and kindergartens – would be in a position to eliminate candidates with a sex-offending past.

Courts also tend to be more demanding in terms of merit when the profession the person wants to pursue warrants higher moral standards. Such is the case for: teachers (Court of Cassation, Criminal Chamber, 25 September 1990, no 89-86.085); university professors (Court of Cassation, Criminal Chamber, 8 February 1995, no 94-81.468); or police officers (Correctional Tribunal of Nantes, 3rd chamber, 26 April 2005, no BL). Courts can also reject the application to expunge if the offence is too serious, or if there are too many of them (eg Court of Cassation, Criminal Chamber, 4 October 2000, no 00-80.181).

Adding to these traditional rules, it is important to note that French re-entry judges (*juges de l'application des peines* – JAP)[7] can also partially expunge criminal records when they decide to release a prisoner early, provided that this is necessary for his or her reinsertion into society, particularly in terms of employment.[8] JAPs are particularly generous in granting this measure, since their professional habitus is mostly focused on desistance (Herzog-Evans 2014).

One category of expunging technique is solely based on merit and is therefore much more demanding (Coltel 2007). Its goal, and the primary interest for

[7] These judges are in charge of releasing prisoners, remission, furlough, of pronouncing sanctions for breach of community sentences and measures (CSM), and for adding or removing obligations attached to CSMs.

[8] Art 712-22 PPC.

former offenders, is to solemnly acknowledge an achieved desistance process, thereby providing it with the full stamp of the judicial ritual advocated by Maruna (2001; 2011). Judicial rehabilitation conversely has a large domain as it applies to all types of offences, including *crimes*.

An application for judicial rehabilitation can only be filed after the passage of sufficient time: one year for a *contravention*; three years for *délits*; and five years for *crimes*. Recidivists have to wait longer: six years for felonies and 10 years for *crimes*. Only heroes who helped the nation at 'the peril of their own lives' are spared these delays, as they have already proved they 'did good' (Maruna 2001).[9] If the court rejects the request, the ex-offender must wait for two more years.

Courts of law have discretion to assess whether the conditions for judicial rehabilitation have been met. Conversely, they cannot, on the one hand, find that the conditions are met, and on the other hand, refer to the seriousness of the crime committed to reject the application (Court of Cassation, 18 March 2015, no 14-82011).

The first condition required for judicial rehabilitation is for the applicant to have paid all the damages due to the victim.[10] A court of law was thus right to reject the application of an ex-offender who had abided by all the other conditions for judicial rehabilitation but had refused to pay damages to the victim (Court of Cassation, 4 November 2015, no 14-85605). On the same basis, and second, the offender must have paid all his or her fines (Court of Cassation, 29 October 2014, no 13-86107).

A third condition is that the person must have had a record of good behaviour whilst incarcerated[11] and demonstrated 'irreproachable behaviour' since his or her release.[12] The latter, rather loose concept concedes great discretion to the courts. In practice, it is required that the person not only has not been sentenced again, but also that he or she has not been on the police radar. A thorough police investigation is thus conducted. Employment, educational achievements, completed treatment, community involvement or charity work (very much in the vein of Maruna's 'Making Good'), type of associates and family life since release are thus additionally subject to scrutiny.

Judicial rehabilitation applications are filed with the Court of Appeal, a second instance court. This is meant to make the procedure even more solemn, with, presumably, an even more convincing judicial stamp on the desistance process.

Since it is easier and swifter to obtain one of the various other forms of partial (mainly automatic) expunging techniques, which will eventually clear most run-of-the-mill offenders' *délits* criminal records, judicial rehabilitation is essentially for those convicted of serious crimes who cannot access other simpler and swifter techniques. In practice, this concerns fewer than 20 offenders per year.

[9] Art 789 PPC.
[10] Art 788(1) PPC.
[11] Art 792(2) PPC.
[12] Art 787(4) PPC.

C. Ordinary Offender Supervision

Unless they have also been sentenced to a suspended sentence with probation, run-of-the-mill prisoners typically benefit from very short release measures. Indeed, such supervision measures can only last for the duration of what is left on their sentence, that is, typically only a few weeks or months (Herzog-Evans 2017b).

The vast majority of offenders under supervision have a maximum of two to three obligations imposed upon them (to pay damages, seek treatment and employment). Only violent or sex offenders will find themselves subject to non-contact obligations, and compliance with such obligations is not verified. Moreover, addicts are not subject to drug tests, because the state cannot afford to perform them.

Run-of-the-mill offenders on parole or probation will also have very few appointments to attend. The norm is one appointment about every two months; once a month if it is an 'intensive' supervision: every fortnight is exceptional and may only apply to the most dangerous sex offenders. In the majority of instances, the nature of the supervision itself mostly consists in the verification of obligations (Dindo 2011), lightyears away from dosage standards according to the risk principle in the risk-need-responsivity (RNR) model (eg Carter and Sarkowitz 2014) and in spite of such an approach clearly being inefficient (Lowenkamp et al 2010).

Beneath this apparently lenient supervision also lies a lack of support and care for run-of-the-mill offenders, as predicted by Bottoms. As Morgenstern and Robinson (2014) pointed out, European legal systems are increasingly abandoning active and concrete support for prisoner re-entry and offender rehabilitation. Many reasons can explain this: lesser eligibility policies; punitive policies; and, in the case of France, essentially managerial penal (Danet 2013) and probation processing (Dubourg 2015), where moving dockets or processing files and prisoners (Herzog-Evans 2017b) has become the sole goal of run-down and overburdened agencies and staff. To sum up a depressing context, offenders are expected to prepare their own release plans single-handedly, to obtain employment and housing without support, and to engage with community agencies and the health system essentially on their own, except for the help of their families and holistic attorneys (Herzog-Evans 2016a).

At the opposite end of the spectrum, we shall now see that dangerous offenders may appear to be treated more harshly; yet they also tend to be more supported.

III. MANDATORY AND PROLONGED SUPERVISION FOR THE 'DANGEROUS'

A. Determining the Identity of Dangerous Offenders

What constitutes a 'dangerous' offender has changed over the decades. In the 1970s, this concept used to refer to organised crime related to drug trafficking.

During the same decade, it also applied to the small number of French left-wing extremist terrorists (*Action Directe*). During the 1990s, the French public 'discovered' sex offending, after the Belgian Dutroux case and shortly after France created 'true life' (Law of 1 February 1994), a form of life sentence without parole (but in reality, parole is exceptionally possible after serving 30 years). Following this, sex offenders also 'became' dangerous in the eyes of the legal system – at least to a certain extent (the Law of 17 June 1998 was to be followed by several other reforms focusing on sex offences). During Nicolas Sarkozy's reign, first as Minister of the Interior then as President, three laws were passed against recidivists (12 December 2005; 10 August 2007; 10 March 2010), another category of 'dangerous' offenders, thereby going full circle back to the Third Republic at the end of the nineteenth century (Badinter 1992). Following 9/11, and even though France was spared any attacks at the time, a new law profoundly reformed the fate of organised crime offenders (Law of 9 March 2004). After the 2015 and 2016 terrorist attacks on French soil, two further laws were thus passed in 2016 focusing on terrorists (Laws of 3 June and 21 July 2016).

Clearly, then, dangerous offenders are defined by legislators, who essentially react to high-profile '*faits divers*'. If, in the past, the left has strongly criticised such reforms, when in power it has never modified the legal framework implemented by its more conservative predecessors. Clearly, the classic dichotomy between the left and the right has become blurred, with both political camps agreeing on the dichotomy between run-of-the-mill and dangerous offenders (Herzog-Evans 2015a).

Most of the reforms of the 1998–2016 era consisted of making sentences more punitive – although they have mostly failed in view of the courts' discretion – and in creating various schemes destined to give legal grounds for mandatory supervision beyond the sentence. While in 1998 the law created a new sentence called 'socio-judicial supervision' (SSJ: *suivi socio-judiciaire*), which consisted of the courts' attaching a long period of mandatory supervision either as a stand-alone sentence or as a measure applied after release, the new schemes ('safety measures') now consist of imposing supervision even beyond the limits of what the courts had imposed.

In practice, SSJ is used more frequently than safety measures, as courts favour measures that are compatible with essential criminal law principles. Whereas 'sentences' must abide by these principles, safety measures do not. The main explanation for this dichotomy is indeed that whereas sentences punish an offence, safety measures aim to protect society.

The concept of such safety measures is, however, rather blurry, and frankly unconvincing. For indeed, most sentences also aim to protect society, and both sentences and safety measures aim to rehabilitate offenders. After all, the nature of the supervision imposed is in both cases identical, and is found in Articles 132-44 and 132-45 of the Penal Code. Lastly, most safety measures, and all of those that will be presented in the rest of this chapter, necessitate the commission of an offence for which the offender has previously been sentenced.

The 'safety measure' concept originally derived from the School of Social Defence, as modernised by Marc Ancel (1966). Before the arrival of Nicolas Sarkozy in government it had all but disappeared from the legal system (Danet 2008), for it seemed out-dated and, as mentioned, it was virtually impossible to clearly distinguish sentences from safety measures (Patin 1948; Schmelck 1966). Therefore, 'safety measures' is just a legal tag that allows the violation of fundamental legal principles, such as the prohibition of harsher retrospective penal laws (Court of Cassation, Criminal Chamber, 16 December 2009, no 09-85.153, and 14 April 2010, no 09-82.291; 12 October 2011, no 10-88.126; Constitutional Council, 21 February 2008, no 2008-562 DC), even though this principle is mentioned both in the French Constitution and in the ECHR.[13]

The decision to reinstate safety measures in order to impose mandatory supervision upon released sexual and very violent offenders was made in 2005 (Law of 12 December 2005) and 2008 (Law of 25 February 2008). The decision was made because the vast majority of these offenders serve rather short sentences, with, for instance, an average of eight years for those convicted of rape (Tournier 2013) and many fathers convicted of incest being sentenced to community sentences or short custodial sentences. As Razac has fittingly put it, safety measures may be perceived as 'the ambulatory treatment of a behavioural anomaly, which is a source of danger for the community' (Razac 2008: 397).

B. Supervision of Dangerous Offenders

There are currently five safety measures available to the courts, the first four of which apply to sexual and seriously violent offenders. The first two, Judicial Supervision of Dangerous Persons (*Surveillance Judiciaire des Personnes Dangereuses* (SJPD)) and GPS-electronic monitoring (*Placement sous Surveillance Electronique Mobile* (PSEM)), created in 2005, did not truly exceed the length of the sentence as they were in fact based on remissions granted during the person's incarceration. If, for instance, the offender has benefitted from a two-year remission, he or she can then be supervised for exactly two years upon release. The third measure (Safety Surveillance, SS), which was created in 2008, aims to extend these limited durations, potentially ad infinitum. If the offender fails to comply with his or her – perpetual – obligations, he or she can then be placed in a custodial setting (Safety Detention), also created in 2008.

One last safety measure was created in 2014 (Law of 15 August 2014) in order to place offenders who had been declared partially irresponsible by reason

[13] Art 8 of the French Declaration of Human Rights (*Déclaration des Droits de l'Homme et du Citoyen* 1789); and Art 7 ECHR.

of insanity[14] under psychiatric watch. This does not require the offender to be dangerous, and will therefore not be discussed here.

The imposition of safety measures cannot be based solely on the nature of the offence. Given their rather extreme legal consequences, they can only be pronounced by way of reference to a criterion of 'dangerousness' or 'risk of recidivism' – or both. Depending on the type of safety measure, the criterion used and the consequences and duration of it vary (see Herzog-Evans 2016b).

This rather complex legal framework is further complicated by the fact that those offenders who have committed the most serious offences of all[15] can see more lenient safety measures (SJPD and PSEM) prolonged via the imposition of the most stringent one (SS).

The conditions of dangerousness or risk of reoffending that are imposed in most cases, albeit in confusingly different terms (Van der Wolf and Herzog-Evans 2015), are not established by an evidence-based assessment. Quite the contrary, they are subject to so-called 'expert evaluation' by psychiatrists who, in most cases, have not been trained in evidence-based techniques (Baratta et al 2012) and tend to refer to mental disorders that are not recognised anywhere else in the world and date back to Freudian psychoanalysis (eg Pirlot and Pedinielli 2013). Not only do most psychiatrists use non-evidence-based techniques, but currently the majority of re-entry judges also seem to be opposed to structured risk assessment tools (Herzog-Evans 2015b).

The dangerousness criterion has also been criticised in principle by the quasi-unanimous French legal doctrine (eg Lazerges 2012; Delage 2008; Mbanzoulou et al 2008; Mbanzoulou 2010), including by conservative lawyers (Conte et al 2010). This is on the grounds that it could not be and has never been defined in legal terms, in violation of the general principle of penal legality, according to which criminal law rules must be absolutely clear and understandable.

In principle, then, safety measures pose a serious risk in terms of human rights and civil liberties, and violate numerous fundamental principles of criminal law, notably, on the one hand, the prohibition of punitive retrospective penal rules and, on the other hand, the rule prohibiting obligations and restrictions being imposed beyond the term of a sentence. Yet in practice, the content of the mandatory supervision to which offenders are subjected is strictly identical to the ordinary forms of probation imposed on run-of-the-mill offenders. They are governed by exactly the same legal rules, that is Articles 132-44 and 132-45 of the Criminal Code. Judges may be slightly more strict with these offenders and impose, on top of the three main ones described above, non-contact obligations (which are also imposed on domestic violence offenders) (Herzog-Evans 2017c). It is only in the rare instances when a GPS form of electronic monitoring is imposed that the order becomes more difficult to bear in the long run, since the

[14] Art 706-131(1) PPC.
[15] As listed in Art 706-53(13) PCC.

technology frequently malfunctions, which impacts on the offender's life much more than the device should in itself.

Sex offenders benefit from the very same loose form of supervision, devoid of drug or alcohol testing or control over their movements, and devoid of any control of their computers – unless new charges are brought against them. Added to this, in practice, safety measures are rarely imposed, most judges being wary of their extreme legal, if not practical, consequences, and because the procedural constraints imposed on the courts are very cumbersome. Statistics are unfortunately not regularly available. Thankfully, a 2012 parliamentary report showed that there were only 53 people placed under GPS-EM at the time, and a total of 132 individuals have been thus controlled since 2007 (Blanc 2012). No statistics are available for other measures. We do know, however, thanks to a parliamentary question, that in 2012 there had been 22 people subjected to Safety Surveillance since the 2008 Act, and that 19 were still under supervision at the time (Ministry of Justice, France 2012). As to the custodial form of safety measure, Safety Detention, in 2015 the Deprivation of Liberty General Controller (Contrôleur général des lieux de privation de liberté 2015) revealed that only five people had been subjected to it since 2008, and only for very short periods of time. The courts' extreme caution actually generated difficulties, as the Safety Detention Centre had initially planned on delivering group work, which was never made possible; the most people that the centre ever boarded never exceeded two. Therefore, most of the time these offenders have de facto been placed in conditions of solitary confinement.

Importantly, whether they benefit from an ordinary early release measure or are placed under mandatory supervision in the shape of a safety measure, dangerous offenders are significantly more supported in developing their release plans than run-of-the-mill offenders. A first factor is sheer time: their sentences are long enough for this to be doable. A second factor is that public agencies are more concerned with their possible risk of reoffending, and they are therefore more proactive. Whatever the reasons, this results in dangerous offenders' re-entry preparations being better supported, which confirms, several decades later, Bottoms' prediction.

Most sex and violent offenders are in practice sentenced to ordinary custodial and community sentences, devoid of all the conditions required of specialised sentences or measures. However, these offenders can be made to notify any new address at which they might live.

C. Sex Offender Register

France's 'Right to Be Forgotten' principle (see section II.B) does not benefit sex offenders to the same degree as the rest of the offending population. Like many Western jurisdictions and, in Europe, the UK (eg Lueb 2000), France has created a Sex Offender Register (*Fichier National Judiciaire des Auteurs d'Infractions Sexuelles ou Violentes*: FJNAIS). The FJNAIS was established in 2004 and has been operational since 2005. Originally created to register sex offenders, it has gradually been extended to various forms of serious violent offence. Its main goal is to help the police geo-localise sex offenders. However, the only obligation the FJNAIS entails is for offenders to notify the police of their address.[16]

Other than being listed in Article 706-47 of the PPC, the offence must have been punished by at least five years' imprisonment. When these conditions are met, the registration of the offender is mandatory and automatic. For sentences of exactly five years, the principle is registration and the exception, by special court decision, is non-registration. Conversely, for sentences of less than five years, the principle is non-registration and registration is the exception.[17] The prosecutor is in charge of both the registration and its deletion.

Once on the register, a person must notify the police, by giving proof of his or her address, in principle, once a year. If he or she has been sentenced for commission of a *crime* or a *délit* that carries a 10-year sentence, this obligation is biannual. For those whose 'dangerousness justifies it', the court or the JAP can make notification a monthly obligation.[18]

Registration in the FJNAIS and the obligation attached to it cannot be perpetual; they can, however, be required for a very long period. This cannot exceed 30 years if the person has committed a crime or a felony punishable by at least 10 years; it cannot exceed 20 years for shorter *délit* sentences.

The 'Right to Be Forgotten' rule nonetheless partly protects sex offenders and other serious offenders. For, as with criminal records, access to the register is limited to public officials. In this respect, France has not followed in the footsteps of the US *Megan* or the UK *Sarah* laws, which have allowed the police, in certain circumstances, to inform the parent of a child that his or her partner has a sex-offending past (Kemshall and Weaver 2012). In France, only judicial authorities[19] and police forces,[20] and then only on a need-to-know basis and for the purpose of specific missions, designated public services, notably Prefectures, which are in charge of local public safety,[21] or prison services' sentence register services[22] can consult the FJNAIS. Every consultation leaves a trace for three years,[23] which allows those controlling the register to ensure that is used appropriately.

IV. CONCLUSION

We saw that Bottoms' observation in the 1970s, pertaining to a binary dichotomy between run-of-the-mill and dangerous offenders, has, overall, been confirmed in the French twenty-first-century criminal justice system. On the one

[16] Art 706-53-1 PPC.
[17] Art 706-53-2 PPC.
[18] Art 706-53-5 PPC.
[19] Art 706-53-1 PPC.
[20] Arts 706-53-7 and R. 53-8-24 PPC.
[21] Art R. 53-8-24 PPC.
[22] Art 706-53-7(4) PPC.
[23] Art R. 53-8-34 PPC.

hand, run-of-the-mill offenders go mostly unsupported upon their re-entry into society, and are hardly supervised at all; on the other hand, at least in principle, dangerous offenders are better prepared for their release, and are supposedly supervised more intensively.

Bottoms did not focus on offenders' rights, and therefore could not have foreseen how this particular aspect would play out. What Bottoms could also not have predicted in the French context was that most offenders would retain most of their rights, including dangerous offenders. For in spite of their being subject to registration and less favourable criminal records norms, they remain invisible to the public, who, for the most part, have no way of accessing either one of these filing systems.

France does offer a rather contrasting picture, which limits the consequences and scope of Bottoms' dichotomy. Indeed, we saw that a series of specificities limit the consequences of the dichotomy.

First, the criminal justice and probation systems are run down and burned out, and have extremely limited financial, material and human resources, demonstrating a serious weakness in terms of efficacy. This reduces how strict supervision can be and to what extent rights can be limited for both run-of-the-mill and dangerous offenders. Similarly, and second, French practitioners and agencies have a professional culture and ethics of very loose control and restrictions, which results in a general lack of awareness of danger and little attention being paid to victims.

Third, and more positively, France has a solid culture of abiding by general criminal law principles along with human rights, such as the right to privacy and its traditional appendix, the 'Right to Be Forgotten'. If safety measures do carry serious limitations to dangerous offenders' rights, they are in practice used parsimoniously by French courts, and the forms of supervision to which these offenders are submitted remain loose.

Fourth, the sheer complexity and intricacy of France's legal system further limits the use of safety measures: in many cases, courts and practitioners simply do not want to put themselves to the trouble. Fifth, the legal definition of dangerousness being very vague violates the cardinal principle of legality, which deters the courts from using it as a reliable criterion.[24]

In brief, then, it is the combination of both positive and negative internal factors that contributes to limiting how many restrictions are imposed on offenders. Importantly, the Human Rights Convention framework has played a very limited part in France's development of this intricate combination. France has decided to create this generous system on its own, without any outside influence. Other factors, such as the very unfavourable economic situation and managerialism in both public services and the criminal justice system, are at work. In combination with repeated political knee-jerk reactions to high-profile

[24] Although, as various contributions to this volume show, responses of national courts may differ significantly in relation to dangerous offenders.

crime, and particularly terrorist attacks, Bottoms' traditional dichotomy might be increasingly validated, even if the very definition of what constitutes 'dangerous offenders' might shift from sex offenders to terrorists.

REFERENCES

Ancel, M (1966) *La défense sociale nouvelle* (Paris, Persée).

Badinter, M (1992) *La prison républicaine* (Paris, Fayard).

Baratta, A, Morali, A and Halleguen, O (2012) 'La vérité sur l'expertise post-sentencielle' *Annales Médico-Psychologiques*, 170, 96–98.

Blanc, E (2012) *Rapport d'information sur le suivi des auteurs d'infractions à caractère sexuel, en conclusion des travaux d'une mission d'information relative à l'exécution des décisions de justice*, Commission presided over by MJ-L Warsmann, 29 February, National Assembly, no 4421.

Blumstein, A, and Nakamura, K (2009) 'Redemption in the presence of widespread criminal background checks' *American Society of Criminology*, 47(2), 327–59.

Boone, M (2011) 'Judicial rehabilitation in the Netherlands: Balancing between safety and privacy' *European Journal of Probation*, 3(1), 63–78.

Bottoms, AE (1977) 'Reflections on the renaissance of dangerousness' *Howard Journal of Criminal Justice*, 16, 70–96.

—— (1980) 'An introduction to "the coming crisis"' in AE Bottoms and RD Preston (eds), *The coming penal crisis: A criminological and theological exploration* (Edinburgh, Scottish Academic Press) 1–24.

Carter, MM and Sarkowitz, RJ (2014) *Dosage probation. Rethinking the structure of probation sentences* (National Institute of Corrections, Center for Effective Public Policy, January).

Coltel, A (2007) 'Le pardon ou l'oubli? La réhabilitation judiciaire en France sous la IIIe République: le cas d'Angers' *Crimes, Histoire & Société*, 11(2), 89–106.

Conte, P, Tzitzis, S and Bernard, G (2010) *Peine, dangerosité. Quelles certitudes?* (Paris, LGDJ.).

Contrôleur général des lieux de privation de liberté (2015) Avis du 5 octobre 2015 relatif à la rétention de sûreté, *Official Journal* (5 November).

Danet, J (2008) 'La dangerosité, une notion criminologique séculaire et mutante' *Champ Pénal* (2008), available at champpenal.revues.org/6013 (last accessed 19 March 2017).

Danet, J (coordinator) (2013) *La réponse pénale. Dix ans de traitement des délits* (Rennes, Presses Universitaires de Rennes).

Delage, PJ (2008) 'La dangerosité comme éclipse de l'imputabilité et de la dignité' *Reue Générale de Droit Médical*, 26, 39–66.

Dhami, MK, and Cruise, PA (2013) 'Prisoners' disenfranchisement. Prisoners and public views of an invisible punishment' *Analyses of Social Issues and Public Policy*, 13(1), 211–27.

Dindo, S (2011) *Sursis avec mise à l'épreuve: la peine méconnue. Une analyse des pratiques de probation en France* (Study for the French Direction of the Prison Services, Bureau PMJ1, May).

Dubourg, E (2015) *Les services pénitentiaires d'insertion et de probation. Fondements juridiques. Evolution. Evaluation et avenir*, PhD in criminal law and criminal sciences, University of Nantes.

Easton, S (2009) 'The prisoner's right to vote and civic responsibility: Reaffirming the social contract?' *Probation Journal*, 56(3), 224–37.

Foster, S (2008) *Human rights and civil liberties* (Harlow, Pearson).

Herzog-Evans, M (2007) 'Récidive' in *Encyclopaedia Droit Pénal et Procédure Pénale*, 3rd edn (Paris, Dalloz).

—— (2011) 'Judicial rehabilitation in France: Helping with the desisting process and acknowledging achieved desistance' *European Journal of Probation*, 3(1), 4–19.

—— (2014) *French re-entry courts and rehabilitation: Mister Jourdain of desistance* (Paris, L'Harmattan).

—— (2015a) 'France: Legal architecture, political posturing, "prisonbation" and adieu social work' in G Robinson and F McNeill (eds), *Community punishment. European perspective* (Abingdon, Routledge and COST UE) 51–71.

—— (2015b) 'What on earth can this possibly mean? French re-entry courts and experts risk assessment' *International Journal of Law and Psychiatry*, 44, 98–108.

—— (2016a) 'Release and supervision: Relationships and support from classic and holistic attorneys' *International Journal of Therapeutic Jurisprudence*, 1(1), 23–58.

—— (2016b) 'Legal Constraints on the Indeterminate Control of "Dangerous" Sex Offenders in the Community: The French Perspective' *Erasmus Law Journal*, 2, 67–82.

—— (2017a) *Droit de l'exécution des peines*, 5th edn (Paris, Dalloz).

—— (2017b) *La mise en oeuvre de la libération sous contrainte dans le Nord Est de la France* (Report to the Mission Droit et Justice, GIP).

—— (2017c) 'Violence against women programmes in a north east French city. Issues of safety, collaboration, gender, 'McJustice', and evidence-based practices' in D Halder, T Nadu and K Jaishankar (eds), *Therapeutic jurisprudence and overcoming violence against women* (Hershey, PA, IGI Global) 85–105.

—— (Ongoing) *One year of felony trials at the tribunal of X. Issues of legitimacy, procedural justice, and therapeutic jurisprudence* (Research study, University of Reims, Law Faculty).

Jacobs, JB, and Larrauri, E (2012) 'Are criminal convictions a public matter? The USA and Spain' *Punishment and Society*, 14(1), 3–28.

Kemshall, H, and Weaver, B (2012) 'The sex offender public disclosure pilots in England and Scotland. Lessons for "marketing strategies" and risk communication with the public' *Criminology & Criminal Justice*, 12(5), 549–65.

Larrauri, H (2011) 'Conviction records in Spain: Obstacles to reintegration of offenders?' *European Journal of Probation*, 3(1), 50–62.

Lazerges, C (2012) 'Le choix de la fuite en avant au nom de la dangerosité, Les lois 1, 2, 3, 4, 5, etc. sur la prévention et la répression de la récidive' *Revue de Science Criminelle et de Droit Pénal Comparé*, 1, 274–79.

Ligue des droits de l'homme de Toulouse (2012) *Comparutions immédiates: quelle justice* (Toulouse, Erès).

Lowenkamp, CT et al (2010) 'Intensive supervision programs: Does program philosophy and the principles of effective intervention matter?' *Journal of Criminal Justice*, 38, 368–75.

Lueb, R (2000) 'Social policy and sexual offenders: Contrasting United States' and European policies' *European Journal on Criminal Policy and Research*, 8, 423–40.

Maruna, S (2001) *Making Good. How ex-convicts reform and rebuild their lives* (Washington, DC, American Psychological Association).

—— (2011) 'Re-entry as a rite of passage' *Punishment and Society*, 13(1), 1–27.

Matsopoulou, H (2006) 'L'oubli en droit pénal' in *Les droits et le Droit*, Mélanges dédiés à Bernard Boulot (Paris: Dalloz) 771–806.
Mbanzoulou, P (2010) 'La dangerosité' in M Herzog-Evans (ed), *Transnational criminology manual* (Nijmegen, Wolf Legal Publishers) 109–26.
——, Bazex, H, Razac, O and Alvarez, J (2008) *Les nouvelles figures de la dangerosité* (Paris, L'Harmattan).
Ministry of Interior, France Parliamentary Question. National Assembly no 100922. Question raised by MP Mr Michel Vergnier, available at www2.assemblee-nationale.fr/questions/detail/14/QE/100922.
Ministry of Justice, France (2012) Answer to the Parliamentary question no 00845, *JO Sénat* 20 December 2007, Written Question by Mr Jacques Mézard, Senator, *JO Sénat* 19 July.
Ministry of Justice, France (2017) Press Statement of 14 March, available at www.presse.justice.gouv.fr/archives-communiques-10095/communiques-de-2017-12858/droit-de-vote-des-personnes-detenues-29787.html.
Morgenstern, C (2011) 'Judicial rehabilitation in Germany – the use of criminal records and the removal of recorded convictions' *European Journal of Probation*, 3(1), 20–35.
—— and Robinson, G (2014) 'Consent and cooperation of the unfree: Introduction to the special issue' *European Journal of Probation*, 6(3), 203–08.
Naylor, B (2011) 'Criminal records and rehabilitation in Australia' *European Journal of Probation*, 3(1), 79–96.
Padfield, N (2011) 'Judicial rehabilitation? A view from England' *European Journal of Probation*, 3(1), 36–49.
Patin, M (1948) 'La place des mesures de sûreté dans le droit positif moderne' *Revue de Sciences Criminelles et de Droit Pénal Comparé*, 3, 415–30.
Pirlot, G and Pedinielli, HL (2013) *Les perversions sexuelles et narcissiques*, 3rd edn (Paris, Armand Colin).
Ponseille, A (2007) 'La peine et le temps' *Archives de Politique Criminelle*, 29(1), 69–93.
Pratt, J (2002) *Punishment and civilisation. Penal tolerance and intolerance in modern society* (London, Sage).
Razac, O (2008) 'Les ambiguïtés de l'évolution de l'application des peines à l'aune des nouvelles mesures de sûreté' *Actualité Juridique Pénal*, 397–414.
Sands, C (2016) *Growing up, moving on. The international treatment of childhood criminal records* (Report to The Standing Committee for Youth Justice, March).
Scheirs, V, Beyens, K and Snacken, S (2015) 'Mixed system: Belgium. Who's in charge? Conditional release in Belgium as a complex bifurcation practice' in M Herzog-Evans (ed), *Offender release and supervision: The role of courts and the use of discretion* (Nijmegen, Wolf Legal Publishers) 149–64.
Schnapper, D (2000) *Qu'est-ce que la citoyenneté?* (Paris, Folio Actuel).
Schmelck, VR (1966) 'La distinction entre la peine et la mesure de sûreté' in Collective, *Recueil d'études à la mémoire de Maurice Patin* (Paris, Cujas) 179–98.
Stacey, C (2014) *Rehabilitation and desistance vs disclosure. Criminal records: learning from Europe* (Report for Winston Churchill Memorial Trust and Unlock for people with convictions, March).
Tournier, PV (2013) *Observatoire des prisons et autres lieux d'enfermement. Tableau de bord du 1er mai 2013*, available at www.assemblee-nationale.fr/14/controle/lois/pdf/observatoire-0712.pdf (last accessed 31 December 2018).

Tripkovic, M (2016) 'The Modern Cives Sine Suffraggio: Dimensions of Criminal Disenfranchisement in Europe' *The Howard Journal* 55(1–2), 4–23.
Uggen, C, Manza, J and Berhens, A (2004) '"Less than the average citizen": stigma, role transition and the civic reintegration of convicted felons' in S Maruna and R Immarigeon (eds), *After crime and punishment: Pathways to offender reintegration* (Cullompton, Willan Publishing) 261–93.
Van der Wolf, MJF and Herzog-Evans, M (2015) 'Mandatory measures: "safety measure". Supervision and detention of dangerous offenders in France and the Netherlands: A comparative and human rights perspective' in M Herzog-Evans (ed), *Offender release and supervision: The role of courts and the use of discretion* (Nijmegen, Wolf Legal Publishers) 193–234.

TABLE OF CASES

Domestic Cases

French Constitutional Council Decision no 82-146 DC (18 November 1982)
French Court of Cassation, Criminal Chamber, no 10-86832 (14 February 2012)
French Court of Cassation, Criminal Chamber, no 14-82011 (18 March 2015)
French Court of Cassation, Criminal Chamber, no 14-85605 (4 November 2015)
French Court of Cassation, Criminal Chamber, no 13-86107 (29 October 2014)
French Court of Cassation, Criminal Chamber, no 09-85.153 (16 December 2009)
French Court of Cassation, no 09-82.291 (14 April 2010)
Paris Court of Appeal, DP 1919, 2,9 (11 February 1914)

European Court of Human Rights

Frodl v Austria App no 20201/04 (8 April 2010)
Hirst v the United Kingdom App no 74025/0 (30 March 2004)
Hirst v the United Kingdom App no 74025/01 (6 October 2005, Great Chamber)
Mathieu-Mohin & Clerfayt v Belgium App no 9267/81 (2 March 1987)
McHugh and others v the United Kingdom App no 51987/08 (10 February 2015)
MDU v Italy App no 58540/00 (28 January 2003)
Scoppola v Italy App no 126/05 (18 January 2011)

European Court of Justice

Thierry Delvigne v Commune de Lesparre-Médoc et Préfet de la Gironde Case C-650/13, ECLI:EU:C:2015:648.

12

Australia's Expanding Jurisprudence of Risk

A Critical Analysis of Australian Preventive Detention and Post-Sentence Supervision Systems

PATRICK KEYZER AND DARREN O'DONOVAN

I. INTRODUCTION: DATA-CENTRED POLICING AND AUSTRALIA'S EXPANDING 'JURISPRUDENCE OF RISK'

IN THIS CHAPTER, we focus upon the post-sentence consequences that have flowed from the growth of preventive and data-driven policing in Australia. The existence of a past conviction can result in entry into a complex web of supervisory mechanisms, including the deprivation of liberty and incarceration, according to opaque procedures of risk assessment. As discussed throughout, Australia's 'jurisprudence of risk' extends from predictive policing of those with an existing criminal record to extensive schemes of preventive detention and supervision. The 'risk-based' consequences of conviction also extend to the immigration system, where upon completion of their sentence, offenders also face possible preventive deportation. We argue that the use of opaque risk-centred criteria threatens to displace the principle of proportionality, resulting in a diminution of fundamental rights. The chapter offers an analytical framework for understanding how these systems have taken root and expanded, and how they might be reformed.

In countries that do not have the death penalty, indefinite detention is clearly the most serious consequence that can accompany conviction for a crime.[1]

[1] See the extensive discussion of this by the Australian High Court in *Veen v The Queen (No 2)* (1988) 164 CLR 465, 472–75.

Notwithstanding this, preventive detention on *civil* grounds following the completion of sentence is now an established part of the Australian legal system at the federal and state level.[2] It is now possible to be incarcerated indefinitely on the basis of risk assessments, in circumstances where no fresh crime has been committed. In its decisions in *Fardon v Australia* (2007) and *Tillman v Australia* (2007), the United Nations Human Rights Committee (HRC) condemned both Queensland and New South Wales (NSW) respectively as having arbitrarily deprived past offenders of liberty and freedoms without the application of traditional criminal standards of proof or adequate safeguards.[3] Under some of these regimes, serious questions have been raised whether these risk assessment reviews are sufficiently regular or 'periodic' to satisfy international human rights standards.[4] Nevertheless, the Australian Government has recently elected to expand preventive detention to the Commonwealth level with the creation of the *Criminal Code Amendment (High Risk Terrorist Offenders) Act 2016*, which permits post-sentence detention for a range of non-violent terrorist offences.

While this detention system deals with a defined (but expanding) population of serious offences, there is also increasing evidence that risk assessment frameworks applied to previously convicted offenders are being integrated into everyday policing. In 2017, empirical research into the use of data profiling by NSW police found extensive reliance upon risk-based algorithms as part of day-to-day police investigations and operations (Sentas and Pandolfini 2017). Past contact with police, often not rising to the level of conviction, was found to result in juveniles being made subject to a suite of monitoring measures, including home visits and 'stop and search'.

This chapter analyses this trend that, upon conviction or contact with police, prisoners become vulnerable to a growing regulatory framework of punitive, 'risk-based powers' that condition their reintegration and future in society.

[2] Preventive detention in Australia commenced with the State jurisdictions, which are the primary but not exclusive creators of criminal law standards. Constitutionally the Commonwealth Parliament enjoys general power to legislate in relation to crime. State and Territory governments are mandated by their Constitutions to legislate for the peace, order and good government of their jurisdictions. Historically, the federal criminal jurisdiction has been quite limited, with the offences created by the *Crimes Act 1914 (Cth)*, being modest in scope and largely confined to the protection of Commonwealth interests. Since the 1980s, however, Australia's federal criminal law expanded to address criminal activity with international or national networks. Commonwealth criminal law is created under the external affairs power (s 51(xxix) of the Constitution of Australia) or incidental to other heads of power specifically vested in the federal Government under s 51 of the Constitution (or, in the case of the Territories, s 122 of the Constitution). As discussed in this chapter, preventive detention powers now attach to a range of federal terrorism offences under Commonwealth law.

[3] See further Keyzer 2010.

[4] In *KA, KB, KC and KD* (2014), the President of the Australian Human Rights Commission, Professor Gillian Triggs AO, criticised the incarceration of four indigenous men who had been found not guilty by reason of mental impairment, and yet had been incarcerated for long periods of time (one, for over two decades). It is arguable that the monitoring of cases falls a long way short of the requirement of regular review required by the United Nations HRC in *Rameka v New Zealand* (2002).

We argue that three overarching trends have marked and shaped the operation of current risk-centred statutory schemes:

(a) *The arbitrary application of risk logic*. Australian preventive detention and supervision regimes are often centred upon overly broad, unstructured discretionary powers, which fail to comply with the proportionality principle. These extensive powers are frequently not accompanied by genuine, detailed measures designed to advance the treatment or rehabilitation of prisoners in preventive detention, which are essential to avoiding arbitrary and punitive systems (*Fardon v Australia* (2007): para 7.4; *Tillman v Australia* (2007): para 7.4(4)).

(b) *The political management of fear*. Preventive detention and supervision regimes rely upon and reinforce images of the 'just in time' state, whereby visible, punitive interventions obscure the state's broader duty to build an infrastructure to respond to complex social problems. At a time when the welfare state in Australia faces challenges, and where justice reinvestment advocacy is to the fore, we critically analyse the political distancing and administrative closures that underpin the continuing emphasis upon post-sentence preventive regimes. Australia, which has been subjected to direct condemnation and successful individual complaints before the United Nations human rights bodies, provides key insights into how preventive detention and data-driven policing are constructed and maintained politically.

(c) *The obscured realities of administering risk regimes*. Australia now possesses a defined landscape of preventive detention and supervision *administration* that is not foregrounded in public debates. Recent research has begun to construct the empirical reality of preventive systems, through interviews with professional experts and staff in the system (Keyzer and McSherry 2013, 2015). Studying the operation of these regimes at the coalface reveals evidence of practical deficiencies, such as unclear functional divisions of labour and the vague drafting of supervision requirements.

The contributions to this book chart and analyse the worrying global trend in the negative consequences that now flow from past conviction. This chapter underlines that in experiencing these consequences, offenders are often confronted with a specific *form* of state authority and decision-making: one centred on 'risk logic'. The Australian experience of this type of administrative decision-making is that it is often not transparent in its operation and is difficult to challenge through traditional judicial mechanisms. Overall, we argue that discretionary powers centred on 'risk' assessment can have corrosive effects upon the rule of law and prompt a normative drift towards rights deprivation. Australia's treatment of convicted offenders has seen the emergence of the worrying dynamic identified by Amoore, namely that 'risk is uncertainty made certain … it acts on the uncertain future in a way that undercuts law's conventional reliance on precedent, evidence and judgment in the present' (Amoore 2006).

II. LEGISLATING RISK: THE REQUIREMENT OF PROPORTIONALITY

As is discussed by other contributors to this volume, the European Court of Human Rights ruling in *Bergmann v Germany* (2016), underlines that measures of post-sentence supervision or detention should be subjected to a traditional three-step proportionality analysis prior to their employment. First, the *principle of legality* requires that the parameters of any detention or rights-limiting supervision be set out in law, and be adopted for clear purposes and according to foreseeable terms in pursuit of a genuine public interest. Second, administrative decision-makers face a higher burden of justification where *less restrictive measures* are available to prevent the feared conduct. Lastly, despite the uncertainty associated with determining the risk assessment, limitations placed upon rights must represent a *fair balance* when weighed against purported benefits to community safety. Australia's current preventive detention regimes, however, have been consistently found to feature elements of arbitrariness and disproportionality that are contrary to international human rights law.[5]

Australia's presence at the forefront in adopting the preventive management of past offenders is at least partly attributable to the limited domestic legal hurdles such frameworks have to clear. The Australian constitutional context, lacking a bill of rights, means that any challenge to a state preventive detention or post-sentence supervision regime can only be framed on narrow grounds.[6] The prevailing approaches to constitutional law frame any inquiry through an institutionalist lens, asking whether the relevant state provision impugns the 'institutional integrity' of State Supreme Courts. The federal High Court is thus limited to evaluating the relevant state legislation by considering whether the tasks envisioned by the legislation depart in serious respects from the usual judicial process. Notwithstanding the difficulties associated with mounting a constitutional challenge in the absence of a bill of rights, litigation has challenged the appropriateness of post-sentence supervision orders issued on a civil standard of proof.

In the first challenge, *Kable v DPP (NSW)* (1996), the High Court held that a predecessor of the current NSW legislation did impair the institutional integrity of the NSW Supreme Court, in violation of the Federal Constitution:

> [W]hilst imprisonment pursuant to Supreme Court order is punitive in nature, it [was] not [made] consequent upon any adjudgment by the Court of criminal guilt.

[5] It is important to note that an alternative to preventive detention – the indefinite sentence – has been the subject of superior court decisions, and is, in practice, used only in rare circumstances. In *R v Moffatt* (1998), the Victorian Court of Appeal confirmed the legality of the Victorian indefinite sentence provisions, emphasising that the deprivation of liberty under the provisions was to be rooted in the finding of guilt for the offence and used sparingly. In *Buckley v R* (2006), Australia's federal highest court, the High Court, held that Queensland provisions authorising the imposition of indefinite sentences were constitutionally valid, while also stressing that care was to be exercised when such a sentence is ordered.

[6] Statutory bills of rights exist only in two provincial jurisdictions in Australia: the State of Victoria and the Australian Capital Territory.

> Plainly ... such an authority could not be conferred by a law of the Commonwealth upon this Court, any other federal court, or a State court exercising federal jurisdiction ... [N]ot only is such an authority non-judicial in nature, it is repugnant to the judicial process in a fundamental degree.[7]

Unfortunately, the decision in *Kable*, while centred firmly on the general rule-of-law principle, was fragmented in its treatment of the offending aspects of the state legislation, with four distinctive judgments forming the majority. In addition, the legislation at issue in *Kable* was expressed to apply only to Mr Kable himself: it was *ad hominem* in nature. Thus, in a subsequent challenge to Queensland's sex-offender legislation in *Fardon v Attorney-General (Queensland)* (2004), which applied to a *class* of offenders, 'serious sex offenders', the majority of the High Court distinguished *Kable* on the facts. The majority also dismissed the argument that the legislation was unconstitutional as it permitted double punishment, holding that detention in prison should not be characterised as punishment if it is for a non-punitive purpose (Keyzer 2008).

The latter finding was underpinned by a certain conception of the judicial role. The High Court stressed its focus was upon a narrow constitutional point – a first principles characterisation of the nature of the function the Court was being tasked to perform – not an evaluation of the policy underpinnings of the scheme. The findings of the High Court majority diverged from pre-existing judicial pronouncements regarding the punitive character of imprisonment.[8] Furthermore, the actual substantive content of the legislation provided little evidence of, or commitment to, the broader rehabilitative purpose asserted to exist by the Queensland government in proceedings. Justice Kirby, in his dissent in *Fardon v Attorney-General (Queensland)* (2004), strongly underlined this failure:

> If the real objective of the Act were to facilitate rehabilitation of certain prisoners retained in prison under a 'continuing detention order', significant, genuine and detailed provisions would have appeared in the Act for care, treatment and rehabilitation. There are none. Instead, the detainee remains effectively a prisoner. He or she is retained in a penal custodial institution, even as here the very prison in which the sentences of judicial punishment have been served. After the judicial sentence has concluded, the normal incidents of punishment continue. They are precisely the same.[9]

The grounded nature of Kirby J's critique underscores the abstract quality of the reasoning of the majority – which held effectively that extraordinary forms of civil commitment sat comfortably within the traditional modes of criminal

[7] *Kable v DPP (NSW)* (1996), 116–117.

[8] In *Power v The Queen* (1974) 131 CLR 623, 627, a unanimous High Court had said that we 'cannot understand how ... imprisonment, either with or without hard labour, can, however enlightened the prison system is, be regarded as otherwise than a severe punishment'.

[9] *Fardon v Attorney-General (Queensland)* (2004) 223 CLR 575, 643.

process and sentencing that had hitherto operated in Australia.[10] The Queensland law differs from the well-known regimes for the detention of sexually violent predators in the United States (US), which require a finding of mental abnormality and only authorise detention in a secure treatment facility (not a prison) (*Fardon v Australia* (2007); *Tillman v Australia* (2007)). It requires no finding of mental abnormality and authorises civil commitment to prison (Keyzer, Pereira and Southwood 2004).

The disproportionality of the Australian system was confirmed by the United Nations HRC, which made multiple findings of violation of the International Covenant on Civil and Political Rights in the decisions of *Fardon v Australia* and *Tillman v Australia*.[11] In its existing jurisprudence, the HRC had stressed that the concept of 'arbitrariness' proscribed detention 'that is inappropriate, unjust and unpredictable' (*Van Alphen v the Netherlands* (1988): para 5.8). This does not prohibit State Parties to the Covenant from authorising their courts to order indefinite sentences that contain a preventive component (*Rameka v New Zealand* (2002): para 7.3). If, however, a State Party is able to achieve its legitimate ends by means less invasive than that of detention then detention will be considered to be arbitrary. In *Fardon* and *Tillman* it was accepted by the HRC that the rehabilitation and treatment of sex offenders was a legitimate objective, but the unmodulated use of re-imprisonment was not proportionate to this goal. A more balanced approach would require the use of purpose-designed non-punitive facilities directed towards the objectives of offender treatments, together with long-term strategies contemplating monitored release into community settings.[12]

In its submission to the Committee, the Australian Government had argued that the mere fact that the detention takes place in a prison did not give it a punitive character. In the Government's five-page response to the Committee's finding that there had been violations of the Covenant, the Australian Government sought to outsource its response to State governments (even though it has constitutional power to override any State legislation to obviate the impediment to any federal reservation) and failed to address the underlying issue of a lack of rehabilitation in community settings (O'Donovan and Keyzer 2015: 151). It reiterated that in detaining Mr Tillman, the NSW government was satisfied that at the relevant time, there was no treatment available in the community suitable to address his offending behaviour. In relation to Mr Fardon, it repeated that the Queensland government had 'advised that the intensive counselling and rehabilitation programs Mr Fardon was required to undergo during his

[10] The claim that the scheme reflected the traditional values and aims of criminal sentencing shaped the judgments of Callinan and Heydon JJ in particular.

[11] On 18 March 2010 the HRC, in an 11:2 ruling, upheld Fardon and Tillman's complaints under Art 9. The Committee also concluded that the Queensland legislation breached the Art 14 guarantee of a fair trial and the Art 15 guarantee against the retroactive infliction of punishment.

[12] See Carroll, Lyall and Forrester 2004, which was referred to with approval by the HRC in the *Tillman* decision.

preventive detention were not available in psychiatric facilities outside of the prison environment'. The non-existence of sufficient facilities and alternatives being the source of its violation, the Government was effectively instancing its own shortcomings as a defence (O'Donovan and Keyzer 2015). The Australian Government has persisted with this approach: in response to a successful claim in the Australian Human Rights Commission (AHRC) by four indigenous men that their detention in prison was arbitrary (*KA, KB, KC and KD* (2014)), the Attorney-General, George Brandis, observed:

> The issue of detention raised by this report is primarily a matter for state and territory governments given their responsibilities for the criminal justice system, including police, courts and corrections …
>
> … [T]he Commonwealth disagrees with the [AHRC's] interpretation of Australia's international human rights obligations. Australia, comprised of the Commonwealth and the states and territories, is a party to a range of United Nations international human rights treaties. The Commonwealth and the states and territories are responsible for compliance with Australia's human rights obligations within their constitutional responsibilities.
>
> In this report, the [AHRC] appears to have conflated Australia, as a State Party to relevant treaties, with the Commonwealth Government. The [AHRC] has relied upon this rationale to make adverse findings against the Commonwealth, holding it responsible for the actions of state and territory governments, without due regard for the allocation of responsibilities under the Constitution between the Commonwealth and the states and territories. The Commonwealth does not accept this analysis.[13]

Given that Australia has clear constitutional power to implement human rights principles in its States and Territories, this can only be characterised as a direct repudiation by Australia of its international legal obligations.

The Australian submissions in *Fardon* and *Tillman* also argued that the availability of judicial review of decisions to detain meant that the system was not arbitrary in its operation. Domestic judicial review proceedings do not, however represent an application of the proportionality principle as contemplated by international human rights law. As is discussed throughout this chapter, the mechanism is heavily conditioned by the traditional reluctance of Australian courts to get involved in issues of distributive justice and the specific terms of the domestic legislation.

The Australian litigation on preventive detention ultimately illustrates how governments will invoke institutionalist arguments in an effort to 'close the calculus' and foreclose a proper proportionality analysis. First, while politicians often link preventive detention powers to the existence of adequate rehabilitation facilities and managed transition procedures to community supervision, such a link is not present in primary legislation. The asserted 'rehabilitative' goal is also displaced by the nature of court processes. Judicial review is, by its nature, temporally-bounded, and tied to discrete administrative events and

[13] *KA, KB, KC and KD* (2014) AusHRC 80, 53.

actors. Systems of preventive detention are usually segmented into a range of individual administrative actions, thereby limiting a court's ability to adopt or enforce a 'whole of life course' perspective on the individual's treatment. As will be discussed later on this chapter, courts have often proved reluctant to engage in the active balancing of rights and risk. This is particularly the case where legislation centres upon an evaluative judgement about the individual at the time of the court action, abstracted from his or her broader engagement with services, the possibilities of supervision and other supports. The rest of this chapter will explore how proportionality has been 'crowded' out through selective political debates, before moving to examine how an under-resourced administrative state can fail to treat the management and rehabilitation of offenders holistically.

III. THE 'JUST IN TIME' STATE: FROM PREVENTIVE DETENTION TO PREVENTIVE EXILE

The growing actuarial discourse in Australian law enforcement is no longer limited to high-end or particularly dangerous offenders but is gradually beginning to redefine policing, and in turn the consequences that flow from conviction. While the 'risk society' (Beck 1992) may be nominated as the unifying element, it may equally be said that these risk frameworks have proved politically powerful by feeding the idea of the 'just in time' state, which acts to remove risk through highly visible legal acts of incapacitation or surveillance. This image and political discourse of 'just in time' state power often operates to obscure failings in relation to rehabilitation, social inclusion and community policing, which policies and programmes are equally vital to addressing issues of public safety.

Despite the controversy and international condemnation surrounding the State legislation in *Fardon* and *Tillman*, the federal Government recently extended the Commonwealth scheme of preventive detention for high-risk offenders. This supplements the existing system of control order supervision and detention by allowing the detention of those previously convicted of terrorist offences under the Commonwealth Criminal Code.[14] The political case for this legislation was tied to claims of a rising terrorist threat – yet control orders in Australia have been rarely used, and Australia has already expanded its range of preparatory terrorism offences to enable police to intervene, arrest and obtain criminal convictions for a wide range of conduct prior to any planned attack.[15]

[14] For a description of both systems and their interoperability, see Commonwealth of Australia, Independent National Security Legislation Monitor, *Review of Divisions 104 and 105 of the Criminal Code: Control Orders and Preventative Detention Orders* (Commonwealth of Australia 2017).

[15] The control order regime is outlined in Division 104 of the *Commonwealth Criminal Code 1995*. The first Commonwealth system of Preventative Detention (Division 105 of the *Commonwealth Criminal Code 1995*), which was supplemented by the recent 2016 Act, permits preventive detention for a short period of time in order to prevent a likely terrorist attack.

The extension of such detention powers at the federal level does attract greater judicial scrutiny than that applied by the High Court in the *Kable* and *Fardon* cases, where it was reviewing whether State-level legislation was compatible with the institutional integrity of State courts. The debate around the 2016 Act underlined that core procedural fairness protections and preserving judicial ability to consider alternatives represented key flashpoints for the constitutionality of this new scheme. The 2016 Act, reflecting the higher standard of justification required for a federal scheme, features some limited modifications from State regimes. First, it requires that a court may only make a continuing detention order if satisfied that there is 'no other less restrictive measure that would be effective in preventing the unacceptable risk'. This requirement of satisfaction is undermined, however, by the fact that the legislation does not empower the court to make an order other than a continuing detention order. Currently control orders are issued by federal courts, while applications for a continuing detention order under the 2016 Act are made to the Supreme Court of a State or Territory. The Act therefore does not offer a forum for holistic consideration but remains mired in institutional division.

The legislation also limits the consideration of whether the continuing detention order is the least rights-restrictive option only to the particular time at which the order is before the court, or towards the end of the sentence. In our view, consideration of the availability of effective de-radicalisation, rehabilitation or supervision programmes, both prior to and *after* the making of an order, is required for the system to be assessed as proportionate. The limited time horizon for the court's supervision and analysis represents a lack of commitment to the idea that post-sentence detention is a measure of last resort and is actually aimed at the detainee's rehabilitation and reintegration into society. The failure to create a Risk Management Monitor to develop best practices for risk assessments, expert accreditation and the creation of risk management plans, also places the federal regime out of step with comparator jurisdictions.[16] The lack of professional support and infrastructure necessary to achieve proportionality in practice will be analysed in the final section of this chapter.

The requirement of confirming, in substance, the preventive rather than punitive nature of the proposed detention is also occluded in the federal scheme. Section 105A8(e) of the legislation contemplates that the court is to have regard to any treatment or rehabilitation programmes in which the offender has had an opportunity to participate, and to the level of the offender's participation in any such programmes. Crucially, the proposed legislation does not require the court to consider whether such interventions were made available and whether

[16] In Scotland, The Risk Management Authority is an independent statutory body, established under the Criminal Justice (Scotland) Act 2003 (see further McSherry and Keyzer 2009). The State of Victoria has recently created a Post-Sentence Authority to address this problem, but this is in only one of the five Australian jurisdictions where post-sentence preventive detention regimes operate (at the State level). There is no such agency at the federal level.

they were adequate. In its response to the Joint Parliamentary Committee on Human Rights, the Attorney General's Department expressly argued for the passage of the preventive detention legislation before there was consideration of how it will interact with control orders (Australia, Commonwealth Parliament, Joint Committee on Human Rights, 2017: paras 2–64). This again illustrates the recurring dynamics of goal displacement – whereby a legislative scheme framed as a risk management intervention becomes detached from broader commitment to risk management infrastructure. Ultimately, the Australian Parliament's Joint Committee on Human Rights, in a rare determination given the Government's majority in Parliament, held that the Act was not compatible with the right to liberty.

The eventual passage of the Act attracted a range of public comment and media coverage. The reader should not, however, attribute the rapid growth of 'risk'-centred post-conviction powers simply to the age of global terrorism or concern regarding sex offenders. The consequences of an earlier conviction, or simply the bare fact of contact with police, are rapidly triggering daily surveillance and supervision. Actuarial, data-driven policing is now increasingly shaping everyday, community-based police operations in a manner that recalls the Phillip K Dick literary concept of 'pre-crime' (Dick 1956). On 19 July 2018, the Australian Government announced that it will introduce post-sentence preventive detention of people convicted of planning or preparing for terror attacks.

The prevalence of actuarial and data-driven policing is also supported by a recent landmark empirical study into the application of NSW Police Force's 'Suspect Targeting Management Plan' (STMP) to NSW residents under the age of 25 (Sentas and Pandolfini 2017). The STMP is a police intelligence tool that uses risk assessment to identify potential offenders and guide police interaction with individuals subject to the programme. It uses quantitative risk assessment tools to assess the risk of reoffending. Criteria for placement on the STMP are not publicly available and individuals cannot access their STMP plan. The report found that young people subjected to a STMP had:

- only minor non-violent convictions;
- no prior convictions but extensive contact with the police;
- prior convictions for violence offences;
- cognitive impairments and/or mental health issues;
- been subjected to cautions or warning, or had availed themselves of diversion services.

The report found that those individuals placed upon an STMP had experienced a pattern of continual intervention by police, including the use of stop-and-search powers, move-on powers and presentations by police at the individuals' homes. It identified three instances where the courts had found that the mere existence of a STMP did not ground a 'reasonable suspicion' as is required under legislation (Sentas and Pandolfini 2017). No therapeutic interventions or services accompanied the placement of an individual on the STMP, despite the youth of the individuals involved. The lack of transparency regarding the use of past conviction within police datasets recalls the recent US Supreme Court matter of *Loomis v State of Wisconsin* (2017), where a secret algorithm, COMPAS, was used to calculate the risk of recidivism of an offender in the US in the context of a sentence calculation.[17] The STMP is thus just one example of how the process of actuarial risk assessment, drawing from the bare fact of past conviction, has permeated throughout the criminal justice system.

In the field of migration, Australia has also pursued a system of 'preventive exile', whereby individuals who have served their sentences are deemed to fail a character test and are deported on the basis of their potential risk to the public. A person is presumed to fail the character test if he or she has a 'substantial criminal record', which the relevant policy, *Ministerial Direction 65*, defines as a criminal conviction attracting a sentence of 12 months or more.[18] The removal of individuals occurs without notice, with individuals being taken to immigration detention pending the hearing of their case. Suspended sentences or criminality expressly described as lying at the low end of the relevant offence range have triggered findings that the safety of the Australian community requires the cancellation of the individual's visa and his or her removal from the country. The relevant policy only requires that 'there is more than a minimal or remote chance' that a person remaining in Australia would engage in criminal conduct or 'other disruptive conduct'. The instability of this threshold requirement is increased by the fact that no existing risk assessment tools use the term 'minimal' or 'remote' (Coyle and Keyzer 2016). The policy does not expressly require that any *expert* evaluation actually take place, with decision-makers only being required to have regard to 'information and evidence on the risk of the non-citizen re-offending' (Coyle and Keyzer 2016). The system seems liable to expand in the short term, with a Cabinet briefing note, leaked in 2016, proposing the introduction of 'a visa risk assessment tool that establishes an intelligence-led threat identification and risk profiling capability incorporating immigration as well as national security and criminality risk for visa applicants' (Lipson 2016). The scheme underlines that Australia has seen the migration of preventive logic from areas of high risk (which have attracted the bulk of professional research and reflection) towards lower-end offences.

Significantly, attempts to judicially review cancellations have frequently foundered on separation of powers concerns. The relevant sections of the *Migration Act* permitting visa cancellation are framed as 'public interest' powers, and discretions shaped by risk, based on community expectations. The full Federal Court, in the leading case of *Minister for Immigration and Border Protection v Stretton* (2016), has stressed the limited role of the courts in challenging

[17] See further Keyzer 2017.

[18] This can include cumulative convictions and sentences, adding up to a year.

ministerial evaluation of risk and community expectations. Chief Justice Allsop observed:

> The decision to be made under s 501 called for an evaluative balancing of *unquantifiable* (though low) risk, possibly serious harm to a person or persons unknown if re-offending occurred, and known immediate human hardship if removal takes place. The decision to be made *did not admit of a ready answer by some calculus*. The decision as made was one that can be seen to have been reached by reasoning which was intelligible and directed towards, and related intelligibly to, the purposes of the power. It was one that, though having harsh consequences for Mr Stretton and his family, can be seen to be reasonably within the purview of the provision. (emphasis added)

The contradictory, halting nature of the phrase 'unquantifiable (though low) risk' arguably reflects the court's reluctance to hinge the cancellation power upon professional standards of risk identification. The deportation regime is not, therefore, defined by a principled commitment to forensic psychological analysis, but rather upon facilitating a political judgment on the balance of risk, public safety and consequences of deportation for the individual. This is also underlined by the passive approach to professional resourcing taken within the Ministerial Direction, which merely requires that the Minister should consider any evidence from independent and authoritative sources on the risk of reoffending, not that it should be secured (Minister for Immigration and Border Protection 2014: para 11.1.2.3). The ruling also underlined that the Minister enjoyed the power, once a risk had been found to exist, of determining its acceptability to the public:

> The low risk of re-offending was, having regard to what happened, of behaviour that was uncontrolled and contributed to by alcohol. In circumstances where the risk of such re-offending could not be eliminated it is difficult to conclude that such risk (though low) was necessarily acceptable because of the hardship that removal would cause to him and his family. (*Minister for Immigration and Border Protection v Stretton* (2016))

It is thus only an exceptional case where the quality of the Minister's risk assessment has led to the decision's being struck down as unreasonable. This occurred, for instance, in the case *Cotterill v Minister for Immigration and Border Protection* (2016), where the Minister concluded that Mr Cotterill presented a low risk of reoffending – and therefore was liable to deportation – despite the fact that he had no convictions for 51 years, had not been required to attend a sex-offenders' programme while in jail and was well integrated into the community. Section 501 of the *Migration Act* is thus a powerful example of how 'risk' logic can become unmoored from professional judgement and become a tool for the expression of political viewpoints on threats to public safety. This scheme of preventive exile illustrates how a legislative concept of 'risk' is often combined with, and interacts with, under-expressed ideas of community values or public safety. The task of commensurating a risk with these other values is opaque, and for Australian judges is one more suited to political institutions. This deference to evaluative or political judgement, when combined with an overall lack of transparency as to how a risk is quantified, underlines the manner in which traditional rule-of-law protections are effectively recalibrated to reflect a new form of preventive governmental decision-making.[19]

IV. THE PRACTICAL CHALLENGES OF ADMINISTRATING RISK-DRIVEN SCHEMES

This chapter has shown that the rights of individuals are increasingly being rendered dependent upon risk-assessment frameworks and professional judgement. Opening up the 'black box' of professional resourcing and culture is a key future lever in the effective functioning and supervision of these systems. Grounded studies of professional standards and the underlying predictive validity of forensic risk assessment tools underline that a selective or reductive approach to risk management can often shape the individual's experience of post-sentence supervision. The emerging use of computer algorithms in preventive detention and post-sentence supervision regimes also suggests that ensuring greater transparency and interdisciplinary exchange are going to be key future challenges.

A number of continuing detention order reviews have featured judicial discussion of the lack of predictive validity of some actuarial tools used by the relevant clinicians (*McLean* (2006): para 26; *Mangolamara* (2007): paras 165–66 (overturned on appeal); *George* (2009): para 33). In one of these decisions, *DPP(WA) v Samson* (2014), McKechnie J of the Western Australian Supreme Court refused to issue a continuing detention order despite the high-risk classification given by the Static-99, a sex-offender risk assessment tool. His Honour stressed that this tool had not been validated on the indigenous Australian population, and therefore could not be relied upon for assessment of the indigenous prisoner. These decisions may yet become significant in light of the international trend, which sees default risk-assessment tools struggle to adjust for individuals of different social and cultural backgrounds, especially in light of federal and State policies that emphasise the need for distinctive recognition of distinctive populations.

The gradual expansion of detention into a more diverse range of offences raises serious questions about the underlying accuracy of the risk assessments. For instance, the development of actuarial or structured professional judgement clinical assessment tools, available for use to assess the recidivism risk for terrorists, is in its relative infancy compared with these tools as used in the sex-offender and violent-offender regimes in Australia. As Nolan (2016: 8) has argued, there

[19] To like effect, in a different context, see Annison 2014.

> is a danger that the decisions made in relation to terrorist offenders will default to often secret risk assessments made of groups and classes of offenders rather than on the psychological orientations towards offending and the criminogenic thinking of a particular individual prison incarcerated for a relevant terrorism offence.

This echoes our earlier discussion of deportation under the *Migration Act*, in underlining that the Government's recourse to preventive powers is episodic and reactive, and is often shaped by political trends rather than the established efficacy of the professional intervention that will occur under the proposed legislation. It also echoes earlier warnings about the weakness of risk-assessment methodologies that rely on historical or static variables, applying group data to the individual, ignore difference in particular groups and morph tools designed to assist prescriptions for treatment into devices for the control of risks that cannot be predicted (McSherry and Keyzer 2009).

Nevertheless, Australian court decisions upholding the operation of systems of preventive detention, such as *Fardon* and the Victorian Court of Appeal ruling in *Nigro & Ors v Secretary to the Department of Justice* (2013), have often stressed that such systems are to be shaped by expert knowledge and professional standards. In justifying the Victorian system of preventive detention in the latter case, the Victorian Court of Appeal stressed that the prediction of future offending

> requires expertise which judges do not have. It calls for observation and assessment of those who commit the particular type of offence and a detailed knowledge of the types of factors, both personal and environmental, which increase or reduce the risk of further offending. The necessary expertise combines the ability to make a qualitative assessment of the individual and the ability to utilise the available quantitative risk assessment instruments ... A risk assessment report would ordinarily be at the centre of any court evaluation of the level of risk.[20]

Despite this principle's being invoked, a recent empirical study involving those working within the system found a lack of resources and expertise in key areas. The study, conducted by one of the authors and Professor Bernadette McSherry, consisted of qualitative interviews with a significant sample of lawyers and psychologists from three State jurisdictions. The first key dynamic agreed to mark Australian systems was the failure to match the regulatory intervention to the level of risk. In-prison interventions were marred by a tendency to provide one size fits all, with a reported practice of placing offenders who engaged in sexual offences against adults in the same programme as people who offend against children being cited by participants as one of the major failings of in-prison treatment programmes. A majority of the participants in this research stressed that if preventive detention regimes must be deployed, they should include programmes that are designed to address past

[20] *Nigro & Ors v Secretary to the Department of Justice* (2013) 41 VR 359, 392–3.

offending behaviours. This is not always or even often the case (Keyzer and McSherry 2015).

The study also found that while there was strong support for offender participation in sex-offender treatment programmes, there were mixed opinions about the *effectiveness* of such programmes as currently offered. Participants agreed that there was simply not enough research on the effectiveness of interventions. It was noted that there were 'no measurement tools being used [and] there are no outcome studies' (Keyzer and McSherry 2015: 809). They highlighted the fundamental need to tailor treatment and medication to individual requirements and characteristics, and emphasised the importance of 'whole of lifestyle' concerns, such as community connections, post-imprisonment relationships and employment opportunities. Despite these criticisms, custody-based treatment programmes have become unofficial prerequisites for discharge from prison according to lawyers in each of the three States.

Participants also registered concern about the heavy burden of justification attaching to exiting risk management schemes (Keyzer and McSherry 2015: 812). It is often the detainees themselves, as opposed to another more appropriate authority, who must identify accommodation and social contacts in their release plan and outline any of their 'triggers' for possible reoffending. Offenders may be unable to formulate these plans because they lack the intellectual capacity to do so. The recent Queensland case of *Attorney-General for the State of Queensland v Guy* (2017) illustrates the persisting lack of infrastructure to support the exit of past offenders into supported accommodation in the community. The applicant in this case had, in 1998, been sentenced to 10 years' imprisonment for 34 sexual offences against children. Upon completion of his sentence, he was preventively detained as posing a risk to the public. Having been assessed as low intelligence earlier in life, he had been diagnosed with Parkinson's Disease while in custody, necessitating the provision of a carer. In assessing the need to renew his continuing detention order in 2017, Chief Justice Holmes noted that the respondent's disabilities and lack of support or contacts outside prison meant that independent accommodation was not suitable. Her Honour also found that placing him in a mainstream nursing home would pose a risk of future offending. Queensland Corrective Services had admitted there was no other facility in which to place the applicant. Chief Justice Holmes warned:

> It seems to me that a time will come when there are enough offenders in the respondent's category of age and debility falling within the compass of the *Dangerous Prisoners (Sexual Offenders) Act* to require the setting up of supported accommodation for them. It is deeply troubling to think that people who could be managed and rendered relatively risk-free with appropriate support and accommodation, must instead, be imprisoned as the only option.[21]

[21] *Attorney-General v Guy* (2017) QSC 105, 108.

Despite this systemic failure however, the individualised, constricted nature of the court's role meant that Her Honour ruled:

> It is not feasible to expect the Department to devise supported accommodation designed around the respondent. It may be that in the future some private organisation will take him, but the chances are very limited, given the risk he poses.[22]

Even where it does occur, an individual's exit from a preventive detention programme is often not accompanied by appropriate support, creating a clear risk of his or her being repeatedly subject to detention orders. This can grow out of people simply not understanding the content of their supervision order, through a lack either of capacity or of English language skills. One Queensland lawyer noted that some of the supervision orders are between four and six pages long, and 'they're written in language that even lawyers have great difficulty in understanding'. The standard order is 'vague and terribly drafted', ultimately resulting in an unintentional breach, 'resigned despondency' or even 'a desire to challenge' out of frustration (Keyzer and McSherry 2015: 820). Since there is no clear body responsible for organising accommodation and other post-release services for prisoners, the task often falls to legal aid solicitors. While government legal aid departments employ social workers, the reintegration of sexual offenders into the community is not the responsibility of those organisations. This issue of drafting orders represents just one visible example of the need for greater attentiveness to, and supervision of, the day-to-day practice of proportionate risk-centred rights limitation.

The lack of prominence given to this 'coalface' activity is often indicative of expertise and resource 'cliffs' in post-sentence supervision systems. While the extensive litigation and debate that has accompanied the creation of preventive detention has slowly generated a greater (if partial) level of access to forensic psychology services, there is an abiding lack of expert knowledge and training in the design and oversight of supervision orders in the community. Beyond detention services, there is an overreliance on what is termed 'distance administrative management' (eg use of Global Positioning System tracking devices), reflected in a lack of resourcing and clinical training. There are also insufficient oversight and appeal avenues available to those who wish to challenge the actions of parole and probation officers managing released offenders.

V. CONCLUSION: IS THE RIGHT TO LIBERTY BEING 'BALANCED TO BLANDNESS' IN AUSTRALIA?

As we have seen throughout this collection, the proportionality principle represents the primary response of national and international legal systems to balancing the competing interests of community safety and the rights

[22] ibid para 8.

of offenders. Australian experiences, however, show how the proportionality principle can be effectively crowded out by the legislative design of risk-based legislation. Where primary legislation does not adopt a 'whole of life course' perspective, by linking detention or supervision powers to the existence of adequate rehabilitation and support facilities, the rights of the offender are often permanently deferred by the application of risk-based logic. The individual, point in time nature of judicial review offers a highly constricted frame for the oversight of governmental actions.

Australia's experience of preventive detention and supervision thus raises a familiar challenge for public lawyers. While proportionality is central, its practical operation is heavily circumscribed by institutionalist arguments and judicial deference to political or administrative actors. As Chief Justice of New Zealand Dame Sian Elias has stressed (2009: 61), there is a continual danger that rights can become mere markers for a process, rather than protections to affirm in everyday decision-making:

> [I]f the emphasis upon rationality in decision-making leads to a 'tick the box' scrutiny of process, if rights are 'balanced' to blandness, if justifications for incursions on rights are used to manage them down, then there will be setbacks for human rights.

While international jurisprudence has the ability to address the Government as a single entity, Australia has failed to act to remedy these violations of its international legal obligations. In expanding its risk-centred detention and supervision of offenders, the Australian Government pursued the political imagery of the 'just in time' state, which prioritises limited, visible acts of intervention over a coherent, professional approach to human rights, rehabilitation and risk management.

REFERENCES

Amoore, L (2006) 'Biometric borders: Governing mobilities in the war on terror' *Political Geography*, 25, 336–51.

Annison, H (2014) 'Interpreting the Politics of the Judiciary: the British Senior Judicial Tradition and the Pre-emptive Turn in Criminal Justice' *Journal of Law and Society*, 41(3), 339–66.

Australia, Commonwealth Parliament, Independent National Security Legislation Monitor (2017) *Review of Divisions 104 and 105 of the Criminal Code: Control Orders and Preventative Detention Orders*.

——, Joint Parliamentary Committee on Human Rights (2017) *Report 2 of 2017* (Canberra, Parliament of Australia).

——, (2012) *Response of the Australian Government to the Views of the Committee in Communication No 1635/2007 Tillman v Australia and Communication No 1629/2007 Fardon v Australia* (Canberra, Attorney General's Department).

Beck, U (1992) *Risk Society: Towards a New Modernity* (Sage Publications).

Carroll, A, Lyall, M and Forrester, A (2004) 'Clinical Hopes and Public Fears in Forensic Mental Health' *The Journal of Forensic Psychiatry and Psychology*, 15(3), 407–25.

Coyle, I and Keyzer, P (2016) 'The removal of convicted noncitizens from Australia: is there only a "minimal and remote" chance of getting it right?' 41, 2, *Alternative Law Journal* 86–88.

Dick, PK (1956) 'The Minority Report', 4,5, *Fantastic Universe* 4–36.

Elias, S (2009) 'Administrative Law for Living People', *Cambridge Law Review*, 68(1), 47–66.

Keyzer, P (2008) 'Preserving Due Process or Warehousing the Undesirables? To What End the Separation of Judicial Power of the Commonwealth?' *Sydney Law Review*, 30, 101–14.

—— (2010) 'The United Nations Human Rights Committee's views about the legitimate parameters of the preventive detention of serious sex offenders' *Criminal Law Journal*, 34, 283–91.

—— (2017) 'Open Rights or Secret Risk Assessments? New Challenges for Public Law in an Age of Artificial Intelligence and the Law' in M Poblet, P Casanovas and E Plaza (eds), *Linked Democracy: Artificial Intelligence for Democratic Innovation*, CEUR Workshop Proceedings, vol 1897, 6–14, Melbourne, Australia, 19 August 2017.

——, Pereira, C and Southwood, S (2004) 'Pre-emptive Imprisonment for Dangerousness' *Psychiatry, Psychology and Law*, 11, 244–53.

—— and McSherry, B (2013) 'The Preventive Detention of "Dangerous" Sex Offenders in Australia: Perspectives at the Coalface' *International Journal of Criminology and Sociology*, 2, 296–305.

—— and McSherry, B (2015) 'The Preventive Detention of Sex Offenders: Law and Practice' *University of New South Wales Law Journal*, 38, 792–822.

La Fond, J (2011) 'Sexual Offender Commitment Laws in the USA: The Inevitable Failure of Misusing Civil Commitment to Prevent Future Sex Crimes' in B McSherry and P Keyzer (eds), *Dangerous People* (London, Routledge) 51–70.

Lipson, D (2016) 'Leaked Government document outlines tougher migration program, increased monitoring of refugees', *ABC News*, 4 February 2016.

McSherry, B and Keyzer, P (2009) *Sex Offenders and Preventive Detention: Politics, Policy and Practice* (Annandale, Federation Press).

Minister for Immigration and Border Protection (2014) *Ministerial Direction No 65 – Visa Refusal and Cancellation under S 501 and Revocation of Mandatory Cancellation under S 501CA* (Canberra, Department of Home Affairs).

Nolan, M (2016) Submission to Parliamentary Joint Committee on Intelligence and Security, *Inquiry into the Criminal Code Amendment (High Risk Terrorist Offender) Bill 2016*, 12 October 2016.

O'Donovan, D and Keyzer, P (2015) '"Visions of a distant millennium?" The effectiveness of the UN Human Rights Petition System' in P Keyzer, V Popovski and C Sampford (eds), *Access to International Justice* (London, Routledge) 148–77.

Sentas, V and Pandolfini, C (2017) *Policing Young People in NSW: A Study of the Suspect Targeting Management Plan, A Report of the Youth Justice Coalition NSW* (Sydney, Youth Justice Coalition NSW).

Slobogin, C (2013) 'Preventive Detention in Europe, the United States, and Australia' in P Keyzer (ed), *Preventive Detention: Asking The Fundamental Questions* (Cambridge, Intersentia) 31–54.

TABLE OF CASES

Australian Case Law

Attorney-General for the State of Queensland v Guy [2017] QSC 105
Buckley v R [2006] HCA 7, (2006) 224 ALR 416
Cotterill v Minister for Immigration and Border Protection [2016] FCAFC 61
DPP(WA) v Samson [2014] WASC 199
Fardon v Attorney-General (Queensland) [2004] 223 CLR 575
George [2009] QSC 2
KA, KB, KC and KD [2014] AusHRC 80
Kable v DPP (NSW) (1996) 189 CLR 51
Mangolamara [2007] WASC 71
McLean [2006] QSC 137
Minister for Immigration and Border Protection v Stretton [2016] FCAFC 11, 237 FCR 1
Nigro & Ors v Secretary to the Department of Justice [2013] VSCA 213, [124]; 41 VR 359
Power v The Queen (1974) 131 CLR 623
R v Moffatt [1998] 2 VR 229
Veen v The Queen (No 2) (1988) 164 CLR 465

European Court of Human Rights

Bergmann v Germany App no 23279/14 (7 January 2016)

UN Human Rights Committee

Fardon v Australia (2007), UN Doc CCPR/C/98/D/1629/2007 (10 May 2010)
Rameka v New Zealand (2002), UN Doc CCPR/C/79/D/1090/2002 (6 November 2003)
Tillman v Australia (2007), UN Doc CCPR/C/98/D/1635/2007 (12 April 2010)
Van Alphen v the Netherlands (1988), UN Doc CCPR/C/39/D/305/1988 (23 July 1990)

US Cases

Loomis v State of Wisconsin 137 S Ct 2290 (2017)

Part IV

Juvenile Offenders and Legal Consequences of Criminal Conviction

13

The Albatross of Juvenile Criminal Records

NICOLA CARR*

> [The present cases] … addressed a regime which condemned people to suffer, like an albatross which they could never shake off, permanent adverse consequences of ancient wrong-doing notwithstanding completion of the ostensible punishment (if any) and irrespective of its continuing significance.[1]

> Ah/ well a-day! what evil looks
> Had I from old and young!
> Instead of the cross, the Albatross
> About my neck was hung.
> (*The Rime of the Ancient Mariner*, Samuel Taylor Coleridge)

I. INTRODUCTION

WITHIN THE UNITED Kingdom (UK), an increasing emphasis on public protection, evident in criminal justice and wider social policy, has formed the background for the expansion of a criminal record regime that allows for the disclosure of old criminal records and even non-conviction information. Examples of disclosures on criminal record certificates include information on investigations that did not proceed to prosecution, circumstances where a person has been acquitted of an offence (ie where he or she is found to be legally innocent) and other background information considered to be relevant. The justification for such an intrusion into a person's private life is that it serves a wider public interest, on the basis that disclosure of such information may prevent future harm.

The criminal record schemes in the various jurisdictions of the UK (England and Wales, Scotland and Northern Ireland) are notable for their breadth, and stand in contrast to those in other European countries where access to criminal records is much more restricted and where greater emphasis

* I would like to thank Andy Henley for his helpful comments on a draft of this chapter.

[1] *R (on the application of T and another) v Secretary of State for the Home Department and another*, [48] per Lord Wilson.

is placed on their private nature (Jacobs and Larrauri 2012; Larrauri 2014b; Kurtovic and Rovira 2017). In most European countries, a criminal record is considered to be a private matter and therefore not subject to public disclosure (Jacobs and Larrauri 2012). This principle even extends to the sharing of criminal record information amongst agencies within the criminal justice system. Furthermore, where criminal records are disclosed, they typically only contain information on convictions. They do not provide information on so-called 'administrative sanctions' such as cautions, nor do they contain information on acquittals or police intelligence indicating that a person was previously investigated for an offence (Larrauri 2014a, 2014b).

A further notable feature of criminal record regimes within the UK is the failure to adequately differentiate between criminal records acquired as a juvenile and those acquired as an adult. This is despite the fact that part of the rationale for the establishment of separate systems for dealing with juvenile offending is the view that children should be treated in a manner that limits the potentially harmful impacts of contact with the criminal justice system. Thus, from their earliest foundations, youth courts have underscored the importance of confidentiality and sought to limit the identification of children involved in criminal proceedings (Jacobs 2014). That a child's welfare should be the paramount consideration in all proceedings is a fundamental tenet of the United Nations Convention on the Rights of the Child (UNCRC). Rights instruments specifically addressing juvenile justice emphasise the importance of privacy, and therefore the limiting of the disclosure of criminal records acquired as a juvenile.

Looking specifically at the criminal record regime in England and Wales, this chapter will highlight how records acquired as a juvenile for minor offending have been subject to disclosure many years after the event, even in circumstances where the penalty issued at the time was considered to be 'diversionary' and, as such, on the understanding that fewer consequences would accrue as a result.[2] Given the low age of criminal responsibility in England and Wales – age 10 – in comparison to a European average of 14 years (Goldson 2013) and the scope for a wide range of criminal information, including so-called 'diversionary' measures, to be included in a criminal record check, the disclosure of criminal records acquired as a child is particularly problematic. A series of legal challenges in domestic and European courts have highlighted the difficulties with the current regime and the negative impact it has had on areas of life including education, employment, travel and family. In this chapter, the implications of this regime will be considered in relation to children's rights standards. Furthermore, it will highlight the paradoxical situation whereby greater access to criminal records has in many instances been justified by a stated aim to 'protect the public', and in particular to protect children.

[2] This chapter focuses on the regime in England and Wales, although there are similar issues with criminal record regimes in Northern Ireland (Mason 2011) and Scotland (Weaver 2018), where different legal regimes apply.

II. CHILDREN'S RIGHTS AND CRIMINAL RECORDS

Various children's rights standards recognise the differential status of children in criminal proceedings (Kilkelly 2008; Goldson and Muncie 2012). In these standards, specific emphasis is placed on the need to safeguard a child's right to a private and family life, and to avoid the negative impacts of stigmatisation resulting from contact with the criminal justice system. To this end, in many countries throughout the world criminal justice proceedings involving children are held in private and only participants with direct involvement in a case are allowed to attend (Council of Europe 2010). This emphasis on privacy also extends to prohibitions on the publication of information that would identify a child involved in criminal proceedings. Specifically in relation to criminal records, the *United Nations Standard Minimum Rules for the Administration of Juvenile Justice* (The Beijing Rules) (1985), state that:

> Records of juvenile offenders shall be kept strictly confidential and closed to third parties. Access to such records shall be limited to persons directly concerned with the disposition of the case at hand or other duly authorized persons. (Rule 21.1)
>
> Furthermore, these rules state that records acquired as a juvenile offender should not be used in any subsequent proceedings when a child reaches adulthood. (Rule 21.2)

The Committee on the Rights of the Child (CRC), the forum through which State Parties' compliance with the UNCRC is periodically reviewed, specify in 'Comment No 10, Children's Rights in Juvenile Justice' (2007) that records of diversionary measures within the juvenile justice system should not be viewed as 'criminal records', and that states should introduce rules that allow for the automatic removal of juvenile criminal records when a child becomes an adult, or which allow for the removal of certain limited serious offences when specific conditions are met (eg not having committed further offences within two years of the last conviction).

In their submission for the last periodic inspection of the UK's compliance with the UNCRC, the Children's Commissioners of England, Wales, Scotland and Northern Ireland recommended the introduction of a mechanism to allow for juvenile criminal records to be cleared (allowing for exceptions when it is deemed necessary for public protection) when a child reaches the age of 18 (UK Children's Commissioners 2015).[3] In their concluding observations the CRC recommended that within the UK jurisdictions, the minimum age of criminal responsibility should be raised in accordance with acceptable international standards and that diversionary measures should not appear in criminal records (CRC 2016).

[3] Children's Commissioners are appointed in each of the countries comprising the UK: England, Wales, Northern Ireland and Scotland. Their roles are established in legislation and their primary purpose is to promote and protect the rights of children with particular reference to the UNCRC. There are some differences in the remit and level of independence from government of the Children Commissioners across the UK jurisdictions, for instance some are involved directly in case work with individual children, while others are not. Equivalent roles are carried out by Children's Ombudsmen in European countries (see Thomas 2011 for a comparative analysis).

The main thrust of children's rights standards therefore is to privilege diversionary measures as the most appropriate response to dealing with children in the criminal justice system, to emphasise the importance of privacy for children involved in criminal proceedings and to limit the longer-term impacts of contact with the system by restricting the disclosure of criminal records acquired as a juvenile. The rationale for such approaches is grounded in the view that the labelling and stigmatisation inherent in the mark of a criminal record impacts negatively on rehabilitation and reintegration.

III. DIFFERENCES IN CRIMINAL RECORD REGIMES

The merits or otherwise of criminal record disclosure tend to be demarcated by two competing imperatives – risk and rehabilitation. Those who argue that criminal records are relevant information that should be subject to disclosure do so on the basis that an information-holder (whether an employer or otherwise) can make an informed decision about whether a person is a suitable candidate in whom to place trust. Through this reasoning, a criminal record can tell us something about the character of a person (ie his or her behaviour in the past), but it also invites an assessment about that person's behaviour in the future – that is to say, an assessment of future risk. Such a view is contrary to the fact that we know that most offending escapes the attention of the criminal justice system and that people frequently commit serious offences without a prior record of offending. Furthermore, even where a record does exist, its predictive validity decreases over time (Kurlychek et al 2007; Weaver 2018).

Some of the reasons for varying approaches to criminal records internationally can be explained by different socio-cultural contexts and the distinctions between common law and civil law systems (Jacobs and Larrauri 2012). They are also reflective of different approaches and attitudes towards privacy and rehabilitation (Kurtovic and Rovira 2017), and towards children and young people. Comparative analysis of the treatment of juvenile criminal records shows that many European countries treat records acquired as a child as confidential, meaning that they cannot be disclosed to third parties or in subsequent criminal proceedings when the child attains adulthood (Jehle et al 2008; Carr et al 2015). In Spain, for instance, the records of juveniles are held on a separate database, and information provided on a criminal records certificate will not contain any information on records acquired as a juvenile (Carr et al 2015). Similarly, in France and Belgium, juvenile criminal records are not subject to disclosure for the purpose of certificates issued to employers (Herzog-Evans 2011; Baert and Verhofstadt 2013).[4] In some countries provisions also exist allowing for the

[4] It is worth noting, however, that while these general principles regarding the confidentiality of juvenile criminal records apply, juvenile criminal records can be disclosed in the context of immigration, asylum and residence applications (Carr et al 2015).

expungement of juvenile criminal records. The following section will outline how the approach to criminal record retention and disclosure in England and Wales falls well short of international rights standards. It begins with an overview of the evolution of the criminal record regime, the various changes made over time, and the specific impacts on individuals of the treatment of records acquired as a juvenile.

IV. CRIMINAL RECORD REGIME IN ENGLAND AND WALES

In 1972, the organisation JUSTICE (the British Section of the International Commission of Jurists), NACRO (previously the National Association for the Care and Resettlement of Offenders) and the Howard League for Penal Reform jointly established an independent committee (The Gardiner Committee) to consider a procedure for limiting the disclosure of criminal records. At the time, the UK was the only member of the Council of Europe that did not have a mechanism in place for limiting disclosure requirements. The ensuing report of the Committee – *Living it Down – The Problem of Old Convictions* (Gardiner Committee 1972) proposed a system through which criminal convictions would be considered 'spent' after a period of time, and this proposal ultimately led to the enactment of the Rehabilitation of Offenders Act (ROA) 1974. As the title of this legislation suggests, the intention was to support the rehabilitation of persons who had been convicted of offences by limiting the circumstances in which they would be required to disclose their criminal records (Henley 2018). Under the ROA 1974, a criminal conviction may become 'spent' after a certain period of time.[5] A caution is considered spent immediately, unless it was imposed with conditions attached. Within the legislation, a distinction is made between records of juvenile and adult offending, in that shorter time periods apply for a juvenile criminal record to be considered 'spent' than for offences committed as an adult. However, ever since its original enactment this legislation has been limited in the type of rehabilitation it affords (eg certain convictions can never be considered spent). Subsequent amendments to the ROA 1974 provided exemptions for certain professions,[6] and changes to the law over the years have shifted the balance further from the rehabilitation of the individual towards the protection of the public (Thomas 2007; Padfield 2011).[7]

[5] This legislation was originally enacted in England and Wales and Scotland. The Rehabilitation of Offenders (NI) Order 1978 is the equivalent legislation for Northern Ireland.

[6] For example the Rehabilitation of Offenders Act 1974 (Exceptions) Order 1975 (SI 1975/1023) listed specific professions to which the legislation did not apply, and the range of exceptions detailed in the Exceptions Order has expanded significantly over time (Mason 2010).

[7] The lengthy time periods before a conviction can be considered spent and the threshold at which this is set have been criticised (Padfield 2011). Provisions in the Legal Aid, Sentencing and Punishment of Offenders Act 2012 reduced the rehabilitation periods of the ROA 1974 and extended the provisions of the legislation to include prison sentences up to and including four years (see Henley 2018).

The most significant of these changes was the introduction of a system for different levels of criminal record disclosures. The Police Act 1997 introduced a new regime of standard and enhanced disclosure for those wanting to work (or to volunteer to work) with children and vulnerable adults. The legislation provides for three types of certificates to be issued: (i) Criminal Conviction Certificates; (ii) Criminal Record Certificates; and (iii) Enhanced Criminal Record Certificates (ECRCs). The difference between the three types of certificates concerns the amount of information that is disclosed in each. In the first category, Criminal Conviction Certificates (more commonly referred to as 'Basic Certificates') include information on current convictions and cautions (ie those that are not considered spent). In the second category, Criminal Record Certificates (more commonly referred to as 'Standard Certificates') contain all convictions and cautions, whether spent or otherwise, unless they have been subject to 'filtering'.

A system of 'filtering' was introduced by the Government in 2013, which allows for certain old and minor convictions and cautions to be filtered (meaning that they do not appear on a person's criminal record certificate). A caution is filtered if it was given at least six years previously in the case of an adult, and at least two years previously in the case of a person who was under 18 at the time of the conviction. A conviction can be filtered if it is a person's only conviction; it did not result in a custodial sentence; it occurred at least 11 years previously in the case of an adult, and at least five years previously in the case of a person who was under 18 at the time of conviction; and it was not for a 'listed offence'. Listed offences include a range of offending encompassing the most serious offences (eg murder, sexual assault and rape).

In the last category, ECRCs contain all conviction and caution information spent or otherwise, and also any additional information deemed relevant by the police. As Grace (2014: 121) outlines, such information encompasses the following:

> allegations, records of arrest and/or charge and/or prosecution, statements by witnesses and (alleged) offenders themselves, cautions, convictions, records of penalty notices for disorder, sentencing reports, tax and/or benefit investigations, the placement of individuals on barring lists, and covert or overt police surveillance intelligences – as well as more peripheral 'intelligence' such as anti-social behaviour orders and reports of anti-social behaviour itself (despite the seemingly non-criminal nature of this behaviour by its very definition).

The Disclosure and Barring Service (DBS) conducts criminal record checks in England and Wales, and issues a criminal record certificate that lists all 'relevant matters' recorded against the individual who is the subject of the application (Law Commission 2017). Equivalent bodies carry out these functions in Scotland (Disclosure Scotland) and in Northern Ireland (Access NI). On request for a criminal record check, the certificate is issued to the subject of the check, who then provides it to any prospective employer or other relevant party (eg a professional body or a licensing authority). Criminal record checks are becoming increasingly routine and disclosures are made for a number of other purposes, including in criminal trials (where a person's previous criminal history is considered relevant); in civil court proceedings; in university admissions; in insurance applications; and for travel or resident visas (House of Commons Justice Committee 2017).

The system governing disclosure is complex, and in some instances information is required on 'spent' convictions (eg in criminal proceedings for the purposes of sentencing or for adducing 'bad character'), while in other instances information must only be disclosed on 'unspent' convictions (eg insurance applications). The picture is further complicated in the case of travel and residence visas, where the requirement to disclose spent and/or unspent convictions varies by country. The wide use of criminal records is illustrated by the fact that in 2015 the DBS processed 4.2 million applications in England and Wales alone (Law Commission 2017).[8] The charity Unlock, which campaigns on behalf of people with convictions, estimates that over the past five years over 850,000 people have been affected by the disclosure of a youth criminal record (Stacey 2018).

V. DIVERSION AND THE ILLUSION OF LESS CONSEQUENCE

In England and Wales, a separate youth justice system, distinct from the adult criminal justice system, operates for juvenile offenders. Children from age 10 (the minimum age of criminal responsibility) up to age 17 are dealt within this system. Traditionally, the purpose of separating the treatment of children from that of adult offenders has been in recognition of the fact that most young people grow out of crime, and that involvement with the criminal justice system may lead to negative consequences. Debates around different approaches to youth justice have tended to oscillate between welfare and justice perspectives (Muncie and Goldson 2013). In the case of the former, promoting the welfare of the child is seen as the primary consideration, but this has sometimes been used as justification for extensive intervention. A justice perspective is more typically associated with strategies of responsibilisation – that is, holding young people to account for their actions and ensuring that they are adequately punished for wrongdoing (Muncie 2008). In reality, however, youth justice systems tend to embody a range of contradictory rationales (McAlister and Carr 2014), and this becomes manifest in the different approaches adopted towards young people who transgress the law and in the nature of interventions undertaken.

The question of how interventionist the youth justice system should be is one that has been extensively debated. Many commentators, including

[8] The DBS describes its role as follows: 'The DBS helps employers make safer recruitment decisions and prevent unsuitable people from working with vulnerable groups, including children.' Disclosure and Barring Service, 'About Us', available at www.gov.uk/government/organisations/disclosure-and-barring-service/about (last accessed 29 March 2018).

children's rights advocates, favour less intervention through practices such as diversion from formal processing through the criminal justice system (Smith 2018). Insights from labelling theory (Lemert 1951; Becker 1963; Schur 1973) and empirical research exploring the effects of contact with the criminal justice system on children (McAra and McVie 2007; Petrosino et al 2010) have informed the view that diverting children away from the criminal justice system avoids potential negative effects, such as association with offending peers and self-identification as an offender. However, the point at which children and young people are diverted is clearly important, as is the question of what they are diverted to. In England and Wales, community resolutions, cautions and conditional cautions (see Table 13.1) are characterised as diversionary or 'out-of-court' measures, in that young persons are diverted from formal processing through the courts. However, this does not mean that they are diverted from contact with the youth justice system. In certain circumstances, young people subject to diversionary disposals still encounter a good deal of contact with the system, for example through requirements to engage with Youth Offending Services, aimed at reducing their risk of reoffending (Kelly and Armitage 2014; Smith 2014; Taylor 2016). Most importantly, such 'diversions' also lead to the acquisition of a criminal record.

Table 13.1 provides an overview of diversionary or 'out-of-court' disposals currently available within the youth justice system in England and Wales, the intervention involved, criminal record implications and the police entitlement to gather bio-information (eg fingerprints and DNA). As will be evident, 'diversionary' disposals also result in the child's acquiring a criminal record. If they do not meet the criteria for filtering, such disposals may remain on a person's criminal record *ad infinitum*, regardless of the age at which he or she acquired the record. Therefore, one of the main justifications for the use of diversionary disposals – to reduce the negative effects of system contact, including the labelling of young people as offenders – is fundamentally undermined by the criminal record regime that currently operates in England and Wales. A further difficulty arises from treating such 'administrative' or 'regulatory' measures in the same manner as court convictions, in that the evidence is not tested to the same degree as it would be in court, and the person makes an admission of guilt without recourse to an independent and impartial tribunal (Larrauri 2014a). Further still, research with young people shows that there is an inherent incentive to accede to diversionary measures precisely because they are perceived as being less consequential (Carr et al 2015).

The fact that a person may admit guilt does not mean that that person fully understands the implications of doing so, particularly in relation to the longer-term consequences of criminal record disclosure. As outlined, the system relating to criminal record regimes in England and Wales is particularly complex and unwieldy, and by virtue of their maturity and level of understanding, children and young people are placed in a particularly invidious situation. Research conducted with children and young people to ascertain their understanding of

Table 13.1 Diversionary 'out-of-court' disposals for juveniles in England and Wales

	Community Resolution	Youth Caution	Youth Conditional Caution
Description	Community resolution is the term for the resolution of a minor offence or anti-social behaviour incident through informal agreement between the parties involved.	May be given for an offence when the young person admits the offence and there is sufficient evidence for a realistic prospect of conviction, but it is not in the public interest to prosecute.	As per youth caution, but **there is a compulsory assessment and intervention attached. The conditions must have one or more of the following objectives: rehabilitation, reparation and/or punishment.**
Consent required	The young person's agreement is required in order to participate in and accept a community resolution.	Children are required to make an admission of offending in order to receive a caution, but they are not required to consent to a caution, unlike in the case of adults.	The Youth Offending Team (YOT) must assess the young person and advise on appropriate conditions. The young person must also agree to accept the Youth Conditional Caution and the conditions attached, and as such a child must consent to receiving a conditional caution. If the young person does not comply with the conditions set, he or she can be prosecuted for the original offence.
Criminal record implications	Community resolutions are an informal out-of-court disposal and do not form part of a criminal record. **However, their use is recorded and this record may be disclosed as part of an enhanced criminal record certificate.**	A caution is an admission of guilt, and as such a record of the caution will be kept by the police and **will appear on standard and enhanced criminal record checks (unless subject to filtering).**	

(continued)

Table 13.1 *(Continued)*

	Community Resolution	Youth Caution	Youth Conditional Caution
Fingerprints and DNA		Supporting fingerprints are required. Where fingerprints are not taken at the time, the young person can be required to provide fingerprints within two years of receiving the caution or conditional caution. DNA samples can be taken for certain offences and can be retained for specified time periods.	

Sources: Youth Justice Board for England and Wales (2013) *Youth Out-of-Court Disposals. Guide for Police and Youth Offending Services* (London, YJB); Ministry of Justice (2013) *Code of Practice for Youth Conditional Cautions* (London, Home Office); Home Office (2017) *CODE D Revised. Code of Practice for the identification of persons by Police Officers* (London, Home Office).

the criminal record regime shows that many are under the misapprehension that when they reach adulthood their childhood record of offending is 'wiped clean' (Carr et al 2015).[9] Furthermore, many children may admit guilt in the absence of sufficient legal advice (Kemp et al 2011). And even if children do receive legal advice, the changes to the system over time mean that the future consequences of diversionary disposals may be unforeseeable.

VI. LEGAL CHALLENGES TO THE CRIMINAL RECORD REGIME

The wide scope of the criminal record regime in England and Wales has been challenged in a number of court appeals in recent years. Some of the concerns articulated in these cases include practices in relation to the retention of criminal record data and other information on the Police National Computer (PNC), and the disclosure of this data in criminal record checks. Significantly, a number of the appeal cases relate to adults who had acquired records as juveniles and who were subsequently required to disclose these records many years later. In some cases, evidence was given that the individuals concerned erroneously believed that their records were considered 'spent' or deleted. However, policy in respect of the retention of data and the requirements for the police to disclose this had changed in the intervening years, meaning that for some individuals, childhood transgressions would be subject to disclosure for the rest their lives. In one legal case, the judge likened this to an albatross around one's neck, which could never be shaken off.[10]

[9] This research was commissioned by NIACRO and conducted in Northern Ireland, where the criminal record regime is broadly similar to that of England and Wales (Mason 2011).

[10] Lord Wilson in *R (on the application of T and another) v Secretary of State for the Home Department and another*, [48]. The albatross in Coleridge's *Rime of the Ancient Mariner* is fastened

In one of the most significant legal cases – *R (T and others) v Chief Constable of Greater Manchester* – the applicants argued that the blanket disclosure of all convictions and cautions was contrary to Article 8 of the European Convention on Human Rights (respect for family and private life). In this case one of the appellants, 'T', who was aged 21 at the time of the legal action, challenged the disclosure of warnings[11] he had received as an 11-year-old for the theft of two bicycles, when he applied for a place on a sports studies course at university. These warnings were disclosed in an Enhanced Criminal Record Check, required because the course involved work with children.[12] The Court ultimately held that blanket disclosures of all convictions and cautions were disproportionate to the legitimate aim of public protection, and that the relevant legislation (the Rehabilitation of Offenders Act Exceptions Order and the Police Act 1997) was incompatible with Article 8 and therefore ultra vires.

The Government appealed this decision, and in the subsequent Supreme Court judgment – *R (on the application of T and another) v Secretary of State for the Home Department and another* – the Court held that as cautions take place in private, they are part of a person's private life from the outset. Drawing on the line of reasoning set out in *R (L) v Commissioner of Police of the Metropolis*, which concerned the disclosure of a conviction, the Court further confirmed the view that with the passage of time, criminal records should become part of a person's private life. On the question of the disclosure of information in ECRCs, the Court agreed that such disclosure significantly jeopardised the respondents' entry into education or employment:

> In the present appeals it is true that, in the end, T was allowed to enroll on the sports studies courts and it is possible, albeit unlikely, that, not withstanding the refusal of the provider of the training course to put her forward for work in the care sector, JB could have secured it by direct application. But the point is that, in both cases, the disclosure in the ECRCs of the cautions issued to them significantly jeopardised entry into their chosen field of endeavour.[13]

The Supreme Court noted that the respondents' criminal records, once disclosed, interfered with their Article 8 rights. Drawing on a European Court

around the neck of the sailor after he has killed it. He prays and the albatross falls from his neck, and he is eventually rescued from the sea, but he is forced to retell the story for the rest of his life.

[11] For offenders under the age of 18, reprimands and warnings were formerly available instead of cautions (Crime and Disorder Act 1998, s 65), and the provisions of the ROA 1974 relating to cautions apply equally to warnings and reprimands. The provisions of the Crime and Disorder Act 1998 have since been amended, and 'cautions' and 'conditional cautions' replace reprimands and warnings.

[12] The other two appellants in this case were JB, who received a caution for the theft of false nails from a store over a decade earlier, and AW, who aged 16 was charged with offences of manslaughter and robbery. AW was 26 at the time of the application and wished to join the army. Both T and JB were granted leave to appeal, but AW's application was rejected.

[13] *R (on the application of T and another) v Secretary of State for the Home Department and another*, [20] per Lord Wilson.

of Human Rights judgment in relation to the retention of DNA samples and fingerprints of persons suspected but never convicted of offences (*S v United Kingdom* 2009), which held that such blanket retention was in contravention of Article 8 rights, the Court considered that compared to the 'highly personal and sensitive nature' of DNA material, criminal record information was 'not in that league' but that retention of the information could nevertheless be open to further challenge. The Supreme Court allowed the appeal in parts and found that despite the introduction of a 'filtering system', the current system still failed to adequately determine the relevance of data for the purpose disclosed, the time elapsed since the commission of the offence, the nature of the offence and the disposal (Law Commission 2017). In other words, the wide breadth of criminal record disclosure does not adequately account for *relevance*, that is, whether the matter being disclosed is pertinent to the situation in question. So for instance, one can appreciate that a record of a driving offence would be relevant to a position where a person was required to drive as part of a job, but it would not be relevant if that person was working in an administrative role. Further still, the current system does not adequately account for the passage of time and it does not reflect relevant contextual information, such as the circumstances surrounding the offence.

While the filtering system was introduced following the initial legal challenge in *T and Others* and was intended to limit disclosures of 'old and minor' offences, its scope has been limited by the number of preconditions that apply. The list of 'non-filterable' offences is unwieldy and complex. Problematically, the range of non-filterable offences draws on various pieces of legislation, so that it is unclear what exactly is included in the 'listed' offences, rendering it unintelligible to those without relevant expertise or resources. Further still, there is a lack of clarity about jurisdictional equivalence, meaning that offences that may be filterable or non-filterable in one UK jurisdiction (ie England and Wales, or Scotland and Northern Ireland) may not be in another. The restriction that only one conviction or caution meeting the criteria outlined above can ever be filtered is also problematic, and particularly so when multiple offences are committed in the course of one incident.

In a recent review, the Law Commission noted the complexity of a criminal records disclosure system that has been overlaid with different reforms:

> [It] makes it hard to understand and inaccessible to users … These difficulties arises both from the fact that a number of different pieces of legislation must be referred to in order to identify offences that are non-filterable, and that an up to date copy of the relevant legislation is currently only accessible from legal databases available on subscription. (Law Commission 2017: 9)

Aside from general concerns regarding intelligibility, it also noted that 'the system might be regarded as disproportionately harsh in its effect on young offenders', in that a sufficient distinction is not made between criminal records acquired as a juvenile and those acquired in adulthood (Law Commission 2017:14). The concerns regarding the disproportionate effects of the regime on children and young people have been echoed in a review of the youth justice system (Taylor 2016) and a report from the House of Commons Justice Committee (2017). All of these bodies have called for rationalisation and reform.

VII. CONCLUSION

The criminal record regime in England and Wales does not adequately recognise the possibility for rehabilitation. Legislation introduced over 40 years ago, which aimed at the 'Rehabilitation of Offenders' and provided for certain convictions to be considered 'spent' after a specific time period, has been eroded by further laws and regulations geared towards public protection. The emphasis on public protection is predicated on a belief that knowing about a person's past record of offending can lead to informed decisions about what risks he or she may pose. This is in spite of evidence that shows the limited predictive validity of a criminal record over time.

Although there is separate justice system for children, the regime for criminal record disclosure does not adequately differentiate between children and adults. The range of circumstances in which people are required to disclose criminal records has broadened, and in some situations old records of juvenile offending are routinely disclosed. This has meant that a criminal record hangs like an albatross around a person's neck, requiring a constant retelling of past misdeeds. The situation in England and Wales is in clear contravention of children's rights standards, and it stands in contrast to the situation in other countries where records of juvenile offending are sealed. Reforming the current system to limit criminal record disclosure would be a positive step in reducing the impacts of system contact, long after that contact has ceased.

REFERENCES

Baert, S and Verhofstadt, E (2013) 'Labour market discrimination against juvenile delinquents: Evidence from a field experiment' *Working Paper 2013/852*, available at wps-feb.ugent.be/Papers/wp_13_852.pdf.

Becker, HS (1963) *Outsiders* (New York, Free Press).

Carr, N, Dwyer, C and Larrauri, E (2015) *Young People, Criminal Records and Employment Barriers* (Belfast, NIACRO).

Committee on the Rights of the Child (2016) *Concluding Observations on the Fifth Periodic Report of the United Kingdom of Great Britain and Northern Ireland.*

Council of Europe (2010) *Guidelines of the Committee of Ministers of the Council of Europe on Child Friendly Justice* (Adopted by the Committee of Minister on 17 November 2010 at the 1098th meeting of the Ministers' Deputies), Strasbourg, Council of Europe.

House of Commons Justice Committee (2017) *Disclosure of Youth Criminal Records. First Report of Session 2017–19* (London, House of Commons).

Gardiner Committee (1972) *Living it Down – The Problem of Old Convictions. A Report of the Gardiner Committee* (London, Stevens & Sons).

Goldson, B and Muncie, J (2012) 'Towards a global "child friendly" juvenile justice' *International Journal of Law, Crime and Justice*, 40, 47–64.

Grace, J (2014) 'Old Convictions Never Die, They Just Fade Away: The Permanency of Convictions and Cautions for Criminal Offences in the UK' *The Journal of Criminal Law*, 78, 121–35.

Henley, A (2018) 'Mind the Gap: Sentencing, Rehabilitation and Civic Purgatory' *Probation Journal*, DOI: 10.1177/0264550518776773.

Herzog-Evans, M (2011) 'Judicial Rehabilitation in France: Helping with the Desisting Process and Acknowledging Achieved Desistance' *European Journal of Probation*, 3(1), 4–19.

Jacobs, JB and Larrauri, E (2012) 'Are criminal convictions a public matter? The USA and Spain' *Punishment & Society*, 14(1), 3–28.

Jacobs, JB (2014) 'Juvenile Criminal Record Confidentiality' in FE Zimring and DS Tanenhaus (eds), *Choosing the Future for American Juvenile Justice* (New York, New York University Press) 149–68.

Jehle, J, Lewis, C and Sobota, P (2008) 'Dealing with Juvenile Offenders in the Criminal Justice System' *European Journal of Criminal Policy Research*, 14(2–3), 237–47.

Kelly, L and Armitage, V (2014) 'Diverse Diversions: Youth Justice Reform, Localized Practices, and a "New Interventionist Diversion"?' *Youth Justice*, 15(2), 117–33.

Kemp, V, Pleasance, P and Palmer, NJ (2011) 'Children, young people and requests for police station legal advice: 25 years on from PACE' *Youth Justice*, 11(1), 28–46.

Kilkelly, U (2008) 'Youth Justice and Children's Rights: Measuring Compliance with International Standards' *Youth Justice*, 8(3), 187–92.

Kurlychek, MC, Brame, R and Bushway, SD (2007) 'Enduring Risk? Old Criminal Records and Predictions of Future Criminal Involvement' *Crime and Delinquency*, 53(1), 64–83.

Kurtovic, E and Rovira, M (2017) 'Contrast between Spain and Netherlands in the hidden obstacles to re-entry in the labour market due to a criminal record' *European Journal of Criminology*, 14(5), 505–21.

Larrauri, E (2014a) 'Are Police Records Criminal Records? Disclosure of Criminal Information and the Presumption of Innocence' *European Journal of Crime, Criminal Law and Criminal Justice*, 22(4), 377–95.

—— (2014b) 'Legal protections against criminal background checks in Europe.' *Punishment and Society*, 16(1), 50–73.

Law Commission (2017) *Criminal Records Disclosure: Non-Filterable Offences* (Law Com 371) (London, Stationery Office).

Lemert, E (1951) *Social Pathology* (New York, McGraw-Hill).

McAlister, S and Carr, N (2014) 'Experiences of youth justice: Youth justice discourses and their multiple effects' *Youth Justice*, 14(3), 241–54.

McAra, L and McVie, S (2007) 'Youth Justice? The Impact of System Contact on Patterns of Desistance from Offending' *European Journal of Criminology*, 4(3), 315–34.

Mason, S (2010) *A Balanced Approach. Independent Review by Sunita Mason. Safeguarding the Public Through the Fair and Proportionate Use of Accurate Criminal Record Information*, available at webarchive.nationalarchives.gov.uk/20100418065544/http:/police.homeoffice.gov.uk/publications/about-us/ind-review-crim/a-balanced-approach-12835.pdf?view=Binary (last accessed 4 May 2018).

—— (2011) *A Managed Approach. A Review of the Criminal Records Regime in Northern Ireland. Part 1* (Belfast, Department of Justice).

Muncie, J (2008) 'The "Punitive Turn" in Juvenile Justice: Cultures of Control and Rights Compliance in Western Europe and the USA' *Youth Justice*, 8, 2, 107–21.

—— and Goldson, B (2013) 'Youth Justice: In a Child's Best Interests?' in R Sparks and J Simon (eds), *The Sage Handbook of Punishment and Society* (London, Sage) 341–55.

Naylor, B (2011) 'Criminal Records and Rehabilitation in Australia' *European Journal of Probation*, 3(1), 79–96.

Padfield, N (2011) 'Judicial Rehabilitation? A View from England' *European Journal of Probation*, 3(1), 36–49.

Petrosino, A, Turpin-Petrosino, C and Guckenburg, S (2010) 'Formal System Processing of Juveniles: Effects on Delinquency' *Campbell Systematic Review*, (1).

Schur, E (1973) *Radical Nonintervention: Rethinking the Delinquency Problem.* (Englewood Cliffs, NJ, Prentice-Hall).

Smith, R (2014) 'Re-inventing Diversion' *Youth Justice*, 14(2), 109–21.

—— (2018) *Diversion in Youth Justice. What Can we Learn from Historical and Contemporary Practices* (London, Routledge).

Stacey, C (2018) *A Life Sentence for Young People. A Report into the Impact of Criminal Records Acquired in Childhood and Early Adulthood* (Kent, Unlock).

Taylor, C (2016) *Review of the Youth Justice System in England and Wales* (London, Ministry of Justice).

Thomas, N (2011) 'The role and impact of independent children's rights institutions in the UK and Europe' *Journal of Social Welfare and Family Law*, 33(3), 279–88.

Thomas, T (2007) *Criminal Records: A Database for the Criminal Justice System and Beyond* (Basingstoke, Palgrave Macmillan).

United Kingdom Children's Commissioners (2015) *Report of the UK Children's Commissioners. UN Committee on the Rights of the Child Examination of the Fifth Periodic Report of the United Kingdom of Great Britain and Northern Ireland*, available at www.childcomwales.org.uk/wp-content/uploads/2016/04/Report-of-the-UK-CCs-UNCRC-Examination-of-the-Fifth-Periodic-Report.pdf.

United Nations Committee on the Rights of the Child (2007) *General Comment No 10: Children's Rights in Juvenile Justice*, Forty-fourth session, 15 January–2 February (Geneva, Office of the High Commissioner for Human Rights).

Weaver, B (2018) 'Time for Policy Redemption? A Review of the Evidence on Disclosure of Criminal Records' (Glasgow, SCCJR).

Youth Justice Board for England and Wales (2013) *Youth Out-of-Court Disposals. Guide for Police and Youth Offending Services* (London, YJB).

TABLE OF CASES

European Court of Human Rights

S v United Kingdom (2009) 48 EHRR 1169

Domestic Cases

R (L) v Commissioner of Police of the Metropolis [2009] UKSC 3
R (on the application of T and another) v Secretary of State for the Home Department and another [2014] UKSC 35
R (T and others) v Chief Constable of Greater Manchester [2013] EWCA Civ 25

14

Dutch Criminal Record Screening in Light of International Children's Rights Standards

ELINA VAN 'T ZAND-KURTOVIC

I. INTRODUCTION

CHILDREN IN CONFLICT with the law are considered to be in need of particular care. Children's rights standards, therefore, explicitly encourage consideration of the child's best interests and respect for the child's privacy. More specifically, they encourage the promotion of the child's dignity, worth, reintegration and social participation, and the avoidance of processes of stigmatisation. Accordingly, these principles should be taken into account when applying measures that limit young offenders in their fundamental rights beyond their sentence.

This chapter explores how a childhood criminal record can result in collateral consequences after conviction in the Dutch labour market. In particular, it examines the Dutch system of storing criminal record information and using this information for pre-employment screening. The relevant law, policy guidelines and case law will then be evaluated using international children's rights standards. Alongside this, findings from qualitative, empirical research are discussed that depict the impact of having a criminal record on juveniles' and young adults' processes of re-entry, particularly into the Dutch labour market.[1] The question this chapter thus aims to answer is to what extent the special position of juveniles, according to international children's rights standards, is respected when restricting access both to employment and to education based on a juvenile criminal record. Lastly, this chapter suggests how children's rights standards could be better upheld in applying collateral consequences, ensuring that due consideration is given to the child's best interests.

[1] This chapter draws on parts of the findings of the author's PhD research: Zand-Kurtovic 2017.

II. COLLATERAL CONSEQUENCES

> When Benjamin[2] was 17 years old, he was experimenting with web cam sex with an 11-year old girl. The girl's parents found out and reported him to the police. He was charged with sexual abuse of a minor. The public prosecutor offered him an out-of-court settlement of 40 hours of community service. Benjamin and his parents wanted the case to be over with as quickly as possible. Still, before they agreed to the settlement offered, they asked whether the offence would raise any problems for becoming a physician, as Benjamin intended to study medicine after high school. They were told it would not raise any obstacles, so they agreed to the sentence. Seven years later, Benjamin had finished his studies and wanted to work as a general practitioner. He had to submit to a criminal record screening during which the offence popped up. With the help of a lawyer, he passed the screening eventually, yet it took several months to be 'cleared' for the job. He is afraid employers will not hire him because of the considerable delay, which might also signal to them that he has a criminal history.[3]

This case gives an insight into several issues concerning criminal records and collateral consequences that restrict ex-offenders on the labour market. It raises questions as to what types of sentences are stored in criminal record databases and for what period; whether there is a separate database for storing childhood criminal records; and what the rules are for access and disclosure for the purpose of pre-employment screening. Acceptance of an out-of-court settlement as a child may have, as the case above illustrates, negative consequences for access to employment several years later.

In this regard, scholars have argued that so-called collateral consequences of convictions are often not foreseeable as they operate largely beyond public knowledge and public view. They are not a part of the criminal sanction, but are often imposed as additional, administrative measures (Pinard 2010). Thus, 'despite their impact on individuals who cycle through the criminal justice system, they are not considered part of this system. … [They] for the most part are ignored throughout the criminal process' (Pinard 2010: 1215). Consequently, they can be considered as 'invisible punishment[s]' (Travis 2002; Thomas and Hebenton 2013; Corda 2016), or at least as 'low-visibility restrictions' (Garland 2017). As a result, the 'powerfully effective stigma' of 'ex-convict' can follow convicted persons beyond the realm of the criminal justice system, 'in the guise of collateral, or non-penal, sanctions' (Roberts 2008). In other words, these formal collateral consequences, 'although not formally part of the offender's punishment', are 'burdens imposed' as a result of having received official punishment (Duff 2013: 186). However, special provisions laid down in international children's rights instruments suggest that children in contact with the criminal justice system are considered to be in need of particular care and should, in principle, be protected against the damaging effects of both processes of

[2] Not his real name.
[3] District Court of Utrecht, 8 May 2018, UTR 17 / 2426 WET V60.

stigmatisation and actual restrictions affecting their economic and social activities. These standards are explained in section III.

III. CHILDREN'S RIGHTS STANDARDS

The United Nations Convention on the Rights of the Child of 1989 (CRC) explicitly refers to the need to extend particular care to the child. Children, by reason of their physical and mental immaturity, are considered to need special safeguards and care, including appropriate legal protection. Therefore, the CRC prescribes that the best interests of the child shall be a primary consideration:

- In all actions concerning children, the best interests of the child shall be a primary consideration. (Article 3(1) CRC)

This 'best interests' principle is explained in more detail in the UN's General Comment No 5 (2003), which provides general measures for the implementation of the CRC. A concrete application of this principle is, for example, that decision-makers should *systematically* consider how their decisions affect children's rights and interests. Later in this chapter, it is examined *whether* and *how* the best interests of the child are systematically taken into account in criminal record screening for employment purposes:

- Every legislative, administrative and judicial body or institution is required to apply the best interests principle by systematically considering how children's rights and interests are or will be affected by their decisions and actions. (General Comment No 5, para 12)

The CRC moreover provides special provisions for children in contact with the criminal justice system, such as provisions promoting dignity, worth and reintegration, and the right to privacy:

- Every child should be treated in a manner consistent with the promotion of the child's sense of dignity and worth, and which takes into account the desirability of promoting the child's reintegration and the child's assuming a constructive role in society. (Article 40(1) CRC)
- Every child alleged as or accused of having infringed the penal law has at least the following guarantees: To have his or her privacy fully respected at all stages of the proceedings. (Article 40(2)(b)(vii) CRC)
- The establishment of laws, procedures, authorities and institutions should be promoted specifically applicable to children alleged as, accused of, or recognized as having infringed the penal law. (Article 40(3) CRC)

Full respect for the privacy of the child is one, concrete way to promote his or her reintegration into society. In addition to these general rules of the Convention, concerning the position of children in general, there are specific recommendations for storing, using and disseminating children's criminal record information.

The United Nations Standard Minimum Rules for the Administration of Juvenile Justice 1985 (The Beijing Rules) lay down the principle of strict confidentiality and limited access to juvenile criminal records in adult proceedings:

- Records of juvenile offenders shall be kept strictly confidential and closed to third parties. (Rule 21(1) Beijing Rules)
- Records of juvenile offenders shall not be used in adult proceedings in subsequent cases involving the same offender. (Rule 21(2) Beijing Rules)

According to the UN's commentary on these rules, these principles are aimed at striking a balance between the conflicting interests underlying the use of criminal record information. On the one hand, there are the general interests of the police, the public prosecutor and other authorities in improving public protection. On the other, there are the interests of the juvenile (ex-)offender. Rule 8(1) aims to balance these interests by prescribing that the juvenile's right to privacy shall be respected at all stages of the case in order to avoid harm being caused to him or her by undue publicity and by the process of labelling. The commentary on this rule explains that young persons are considered particularly susceptible to stigmatisation, as criminological research on labelling processes has provided evidence of the detrimental effects resulting from the permanent identification of young persons as 'delinquent' or 'criminal'.

Based on criminological theories, labelling a young offender as a 'criminal' may indeed impair his or her opportunities for full social acceptance, whether informally by family or friends, or formally by employers or schools. It could, moreover, lead to secondary deviance if the offender internalises the label and adjusts his or her self-image and social roles to this label (Becker 1963), thereby preventing successful desistance and rehabilitation. Therefore, it should be considered to what extent a childhood criminal record should follow a juvenile into adulthood, and how the tension between the rehabilitative approach of juvenile justice and the interests of public protection should be managed (Stone 2016).

In this regard, the UN General Comments, which elaborate on the right of a child to have his or her privacy respected (as laid down in Article 40 CRC), state that access to the criminal record information of minors should be seriously restricted in order to prevent a negative impact on access to education, work or housing. General Comment No 10 specifies that full respect should be given to the juvenile's privacy rights, and stresses the importance of preventing harm caused by processes of stigmatisation:

- No information shall be published that may lead to the identification of a child offender because of its effect of stigmatization, and possible impact on his/her ability to have access to education, work, housing or to be safe. (General Comment No 10, para 64)
- With a view to avoiding stigmatization and/or prejudgements, records of child offenders should not be used in adult proceedings in subsequent cases involving the same offender. (Rules 21 Beijing Rules)

- The States parties [are recommended to] introduce rules which would allow for an automatic removal from the criminal records of the name of the child who committed an offence upon reaching the age of 18, or for certain limited, serious offences where removal is possible at the request of the child, if necessary under certain conditions (eg not having committed an offence within two years after the last conviction). (General Comment No 10, para 67)

In addition to the recommendation to restrict access to childhood criminal records in adult proceedings, General Comment No 10 explicitly recommends the expungement of the criminal records of juveniles upon reaching the age of majority. The same recommendation is made in the Child-friendly Justice Guidelines of the Council of Europe, which aim to facilitate juveniles' reintegration and therefore prescribe restricted access to criminal record information by third parties upon the individual's reaching the age of majority:

- In order to promote the reintegration within society, and in accordance with the national law, criminal records of children should be non-disclosable outside the justice system on reaching the age of majority. Exceptions for the disclosure of such information can be permitted in cases of serious offences. (Child-friendly Justice Guidelines, para 83)

It can be concluded that the recommendations mentioned above make a clear distinction between the age of minority and the age of majority, and aim to restrict the disclosure of childhood criminal record information insofar as possible. This, in order to avoid a negative impact on a child's ability to be accepted for either education or employment. Reintegration and avoidance of the label of 'criminal' are thus promoted. If, however, disclosure of criminal record information would be necessary for reasons of public protection, this should be balanced with the child's best interests. For example, by disclosing only information on serious offences, or allowing for convictions to become spent after a period of two years without criminal justice contacts. In the next section, the Dutch framework for storing and disseminating criminal record information will be evaluated in light of these children's rights standards. Subsequently, the way in which this information is used in criminal record screening for employment purposes will be examined.

IV. THE CRIMINAL RECORD SYSTEM

In the Netherlands, basic information on criminal cases that has been registered in an official database has become known as the 'criminal record' – although this is not an official, legal term and is only used colloquially. This record consists of information that is registered in the Dutch *Judicial Documentation System* (JDS). This central system registers information on criminal cases as soon as the police submit a case to the public prosecutor's office. Then the public prosecutor registers the case under the alleged offender's name in the judicial documentation system, and that person will then have a 'criminal record'.[4] This means that a person receives a criminal record when he or she is *only suspected* of an offence, without being prosecuted or convicted. In other European countries, the criminal record database does not register suspects of a crime but only convicted persons. Also, contrary to other European countries (Jacobs and Larrauri 2015), the Dutch 'criminal record' registers all sorts of different types of outcomes of criminal cases, such as dismissals (decisions not to prosecute) and out-of-court settlements – both decided upon by the public prosecutor.[5] Dutch criminal records thus consist of criminal cases that are being processed (ie alleged offences), or which have been processed by the public prosecution service or the criminal court.

Alongside the *type of information* that is registered, *storage periods* determine the impact a criminal record can have on young ex-offenders' reintegration into society. After criminal cases have been dealt with, information remains stored in the Dutch JDS. Before 2004, the legal provisions on storage periods explicitly aimed to promote the rehabilitation of ex-offenders by applying short periods.[6] They contained three special provisions that explicitly promoted the reintegration of juveniles. First, if a juvenile had not reached the age of 16 when he or she committed the offence, it would not be registered on his or her criminal record. Second, an explicit distinction was made between the age of minority and the age of majority. Minors who had been punished by a juvenile court would have the registration of this conviction removed from their criminal records after two years, or four years if a prison sentence had been imposed.[7] Third, relatively minor convictions (ie suspended sentences, fines below €113, or community service of less than 40 hours) would not be registered on the juvenile's criminal record.[8]

In 2004, a radical shift regarding storage periods took place in the Netherlands, as these periods were largely extended for both juveniles and adults.[9] Information on criminal cases are now, regardless of age, stored for 20 years, or 30 years for more severe offences (ie those that are punishable by a prison sentence of six years or more).[10] In addition, information on sexual offences is kept for 80 years (eg distributing child pornography, indecent assault, sexual abuse or rape). The current law prescribes that instances of contact between juveniles and the criminal justice system are registered in the JDS from 12 years of age onwards, rather than from 16 years of age, regardless of the type or severity of the punishment that may be imposed or whether the case might

[4] Art 2 *Besluit justitiële en strafvorderlijke gegevens (Bjsg).*
[5] Arts 6, 7 *Besluit justitiële en strafvorderlijke gegevens (Bjsg).*
[6] *Wet op de justitiële documentatie en op de verklaringen omtrent het gedrag (Wjd) 1959.*
[7] Art 7a *Wjd.*
[8] Art 4(3)(4) *Wjd.*
[9] *Wet justitiële en strafvorderlijke gegevens (Wjsg) 2002.*
[10] Art 4 *Wjsg.*

be dismissed.[11] This may have serious consequences for young ex-offenders' process of rehabilitation, for example if they apply for a job a few years after conviction and are rejected following a criminal record screening. For juvenile sex offenders, these extended storage periods may have an even greater hindering effect on their reintegration opportunities.

This development, following which more young offenders may possibly encounter obstacles to their reintegration due to their having a criminal record for longer periods of time, does not seem to be in line with the international standards outlined in section III. These explicitly aim to support juveniles' reintegration and their assuming a constructive role in society. In most continental European countries, childhood criminal records are distinguished from adult criminal records by having entirely separate databases in place (Sands 2016). The Dutch legal framework, however, makes no distinction between minors and adults with regard to the type of information that is stored and the storage periods. Moreover, unlike other countries (Carr, Dwyer, and Larrauri 2015), the Netherlands does not provide the possibility for criminal records to become spent or expunged once a juvenile reaches the age of majority.

It can be concluded that storage periods in the Netherlands are relatively lengthy compared to other countries, both for minor and adult (alleged) offenders. The Dutch system is, therefore, far removed from the recommendation of the automatic removal of a minor's criminal record upon reaching the age of majority (General Comment No 10, para 67). The distinction made between severe and minor offences is unlikely to promote juveniles' reintegration into society, as this still allows the retention of records for 20 years (rather than 30). The only difference made between childhood and adult criminal records is the so-called 'expiry period': the period during which criminal record information can be used for pre-employment screening. Such periods are shorter for young ex-offenders than for adults. Although this 'expiry period' does not mean that the juvenile criminal record is wiped or sealed, the person can no longer be refused access to jobs or education based on his or her juvenile criminal record. The legal framework for pre-employment screening is explored in section V.

V. CRIMINAL RECORD SCREENING

Unlike the United States and other European countries (such as Germany, France, Belgium and Spain), the Netherlands does not allow individuals to obtain an extract of their criminal record (Kurtovic and Rovira 2017). This prevents 'enforced subject access' (Loucks, Lyner, and Sullivan 1998), which means that third parties, such as employers, may require a potential employee to hand in a copy of their criminal record before being hired. Employers do not have access

[11] Arts 6, 7 *Bjsg*.

to the criminal record database themselves, yet they can still require inspection of a criminal record before making a hiring decision. In the Netherlands, however, criminal record disclosure is highly restricted due to the weight given to the protection of privacy (Boone 2011; 2012). This significant emphasis on privacy protection, combined with a strong desire on behalf of employers to obtain criminal background knowledge of potential employees, led to the creation of new legal provisions in 2004. The new legal framework aims to respect ex-offenders' privacy rights as well as to meet the concerns of employers who want to know whether a potential employee has a (relevant) criminal history. Therefore, the only way for most employers to acquire information on criminal backgrounds is by means of an official request for a *certificate of conduct*.[12]

The certificate of conduct is a document in which the State Secretary for Justice and Security declares that the applicant for the certificate has not committed any criminal offences that are relevant to the performance of his or her duties. Consequently, with regard to its use of criminal record information for employment restrictions, the Dutch system is very different from those in neighbouring western European countries. It neither allows employers direct access to the criminal record database, nor can individuals obtain an extract from their criminal record to provide to a prospective employer. Instead, the certificate of conduct is issued by a central administrative screening authority of the Ministry of Justice and Security, called *Justis*. Once issued, the certificate does not reveal any criminal record information. When the applicant for the certificate has convictions that are considered relevant to the performance of his or her duties, the application will be refused and the certificate of conduct denied. Given the privacy of criminal records, the refusal is always sent to the applicant himself or herself – never directly to the employer. When a potential employee cannot hand over the certificate because it has been refused, this is a clear signal to the employer that the administrative agency has judged that the applicant has a criminal conviction relevant to the occupation proposed; if no risk had been observed, the applicant would have received the certificate. This particular instrument for disseminating criminal record information ensures that the actual criminal history of convicted persons remains concealed and, therefore, a private matter. Only the state can assess the applicant's fitness for performing the job desired based on his or her criminal records. This seems to be in line with the children's rights standards discussed in section III, which promote full respect for privacy. However, privacy protection is not an aim in itself; it should enhance the avoidance of labelling juveniles as 'ex-convicts' and prevent the obstruction of their successful reintegration into society.

Since the introduction of new laws and policy rules for issuing certificates of conduct in 2004, the use of criminal record information for employment screenings has sharply increased. One policy change, intended to make the certificate

[12] Beleidsregels VOG-NP-RP 2018 ('Policy Rules on the Certificate of Conduct 2018').

of conduct a strong risk-prevention instrument that would be popular with employers, is that they are now allowed to request a certificate for any occupation, both paid and unpaid. This means Justis also assesses requests connected with voluntary work, internships and education.[13] The number of requests for a certificate of conduct has since skyrocketed. Between 2004 and 2017 the number of requests increased almost eightfold: from 135,000 to 1,063,632.[14] Regarding juveniles and young adults under the age of 23 an even greater increase can be observed: from 23,780 requests in 2004 to 221,147 in 2017.[15] The number of refusals, however, does not show a similar increase over the same period. On average, the refusal is about 3,000 for applicants in general and about 600 for applicants under the age of 23 per year. The number of refused certificates may thus be considered extremely low, therefore it is often argued that the certificate is not a great stumbling block to ex-offenders' re-entry into the labour market.[16]

Based on the number of applications, however, it can be concluded that certificates have become a fairly cheap, easily accessible instrument that enables all employers – regardless of whether there is a substantial societal interest at stake – to request the state to perform background screening and subsequently decide whether a potential employee is fit for the job. Because of the ever-increasing number of requests for a certificate of conduct, the stigma of having a criminal record may become more weighty and long-lasting, and thus obstruct juveniles' process of re-entry into the labour market. The more often background screening is carried out, the more it limits their (legal) possibilities to secure employment. This is particularly the case if employers adhere strictly to the screening outcome, so that a negative decision directly leads to a young person's being dismissed from his or her job. If an employer will not put the official refusal aside – for reasons of official policy requiring a certificate of all employees, or of avoiding professional liability if anything goes wrong – there is no room for the ex-offender to discuss his or her criminal past and be granted a second chance.

Recent research has indicated that there is a strong stigmatising effect attached to this preventive screening instrument, in the sense that juveniles exclude themselves from applying for a certificate of conduct, or for a job in general, due to fear of being rejected because of their criminal past (Gosliga 2015; Kruize and Gruter 2016; van 't Zand-Kurtovic 2017). This stigmatising effect, as well as the self-exclusion resulting from it, can be expected to keep expanding as numbers of requests for certificates of conduct keep rising sharply each year. Although it

[13] This is often the case for vocational training courses, particularly those that require internships in the field of care (for children or the elderly), social work, youth work and education. See at www.rijksoverheid.nl/binaries/rijksoverheid/documenten/rapporten/2017/02/01/analyse-438-vog-weigeringen-jongeren/VOG+onderzoek+Justis+438.pdf (last accessed 12 July 2018).

[14] See at www.justis.nl/binaries/Kwartaalcijfers%20Verklaring%20Omtrent%20het%20Gedrag%20(VOG)%202017_tcm34-304771.pdf (last accessed 12 July 2018).

[15] See at www.justis.nl (last accessed 12 July 2018).

[16] Kamerstukken II 2016/17, 34550 VI, 98 (Parliamentary Documents).

is argued that the excluding effect of criminal record screening is negligible due to the very low number of refusals, there are no data on the 'dark number' of persons who avoid applying for a certificate. Therefore, it is difficult to estimate the actual effects of pre-employment screening on ex-offenders' labour market position.

VI. SCREENING AND CHILDREN'S RIGHTS

When a certificate of conduct is refused, the applicant for the certificate can appeal to an administrative court. Some applicants have invoked children's rights in appeal proceedings because the offences that have led to the refusal were committed *as a minor*. A district court ruled that, as a principle, the CRC is not applicable beyond the age of minority.[17] It held that the CRC does not apply if a childhood criminal record leads to exclusion from employment when the person has since reached the age of 18, as Article 1 CRC determines that a 'child' means every human being below the age of 18 years. Nevertheless, in cases concerning minors who have been refused a certificate of conduct, the highest administrative court in the Netherlands (the Council of State) has decided that the CRC is not applicable for several reasons.

First, the Council of State has ruled on the question of whether the preventive purposes of criminal record screening could lead to violation of privacy rights (Articles 16 and 40 CRC). It held that, after criminal proceedings have ended, Article 40(2) CRC (full respect for the child's privacy at all stages of the proceedings) does not render criminal record information inadmissible in subsequent administrative proceedings, as it has a merely preventive purpose.[18] Although the applicant for the certificate in that case argued that the use of criminal records can hinder the specific aim of juvenile justice, to promote reintegration of the minor into society, the Council of State ruled nonetheless that the right to privacy as laid down in Article 40(2) is not applicable, since the certificate of conduct is neither part of nor connected to criminal procedure, but rather is a preventive instrument embedded in administrative law. In addition, it held that the right to privacy according to Article 16 was not violated by criminal record screening. Privacy rights can be restricted in order to protect rights and freedoms of others, and the certificate of conduct does this by preventing risks to public safety.

Second, the Council of State ruled that the best interest principle (Article 3 CRC) was not violated by criminal background screening, since although this article prescribes that the best interests of the child should be involved in decision-making, they do not necessarily have to be the determining factor.[19]

[17] District Court of Zwolle-Lelystad, 28 August 2012, ECLI:NL:RBZLY:2012:BX6023.
[18] Council of State, 24 June 2009, ECLI:NL:RVS:2009:BI9706.
[19] Council of State, 19 October 2011, ECLI:NL:RVS:2011:BT8577.

The Council of State stated that it follows from Article 3 that the Government should create provisions that safeguard children's interests, and gave the example of barring a young ex-offender who was convicted for public assault from working as a trainee in a childcare centre in close contact with children. The Council considered that such a refusal would be in accordance with the best interests of the children placed in day-care.[20]

Lastly, the Council of State has ruled on the recommendations regarding the removal of criminal records of minors. It held that applicants for a certificate cannot invoke General Comment No 10, in particular the recommendation that a child's criminal record be removed upon reaching the age of 18, because it is merely a recommendation and therefore non-binding.[21]

It can be concluded that, in the Netherlands, applicants who have been refused a certificate of conduct based on offences committed when they were minors cannot successfully invoke children's rights standards before the highest administrative court as laid down in the CRC and concurring rules and comments. Yet since 2011 three important developments have taken place in favour of the position of juveniles in certificate of conduct cases. In 2011, the policy rules for deciding on certificate of conduct requests were adjusted, so that it now should explicitly be taken into account whether the offender was a *minor* at the time of committing the offence. This was already taken into account in practice, but only implicitly, whereas now due consideration should be given to whether the age of the offender at the time of the offence does or does not weigh in his or her favour. This policy change was the result of politicians and probation officers advocating for children to be given a so-called 'second chance' (Hilhorst 2011). Explicit consideration of the young age of the offender should make decision-makers aware that some behaviours result from youthful rashness, therefore such misbehaviours should be seen as youthful sins and should not be held against ex-offenders.

A second adjustment is the 'expiry' period of offences. In 2013, this period was reduced for minors and young adults below the age of 23. Now the expiry period is two years for juveniles who are not yet 23 years old when applying for a certificate of conduct – whereas it is four years in general. This two-year expiry period does not apply for violent offences punishable by a prison sentence of six years or more; in such cases the expiry period is four years. Sexual offences never expire, and will always be taken into account when deciding whether someone is fit for the job at hand. This age threshold was created in order to bring the policy into line with the new criminal law provisions applicable to young adults from 16 to 23 years old ('*adolescentenstrafrecht*' (Van der Laan et al. 2016)).[22]

[20] Council of State, 24 June 2009, ECLI:NL:RVS:2009:BI9706.
[21] Council of State, 2 June 2011, ECLI:NL:RVS:2011:BQ8830.
[22] Stcrt 2013, 5409 (Commentary to the Policy Rules on the Certificate of Conduct 2013).

A third adjustment follows from a verdict of the Council of State in which it was held that minor sex offenders cannot be treated in the same manner as adult sex offenders.[23] It was ruled that applying the same strict regime for minor sex offenders as for adult ones is disproportionate. Decision-making should differentiate with regard to the age of sex offenders, so that their opportunities for completing education or obtaining relevant employment would not be seriously restrained. When a sexual offence committed as a minor leads to a refusal of a certificate of conduct, the decision-makers should explicitly consider whether this refusal is not 'manifestly disproportionate' given the minor age of the offender. To do so, four aspects should be considered, according to the Council of State: (i) the circumstances in which the offences had been committed; (ii) whether the minor offender was less blameworthy than an adult offender would have been; (iii) whether the risk of reoffending – given the fact that the offence was committed as a minor – should be considered as equal to the risk posed by an adult offender; and (iv) whether it is justified that the applicant is deprived of education, or employment based on his qualifications. These aspects are only determined in case law, however, and have not led to a change in official policy. This means that although decision-makers consider these criteria in practice, the official guidelines for decision-making do not reflect this more lenient approach, so applicants may not be aware of it and cannot invoke it.

Since several legal developments have taken place that seem to have brought criminal record screening more in line with the best interests principle, let us now turn to practice in order to observe to what extent they help to protect children who have been in conflict with the law, by promoting their reintegration and social participation and avoiding processes of stigmatisation.

VII. PRACTICAL OBSTACLES

The empirical research reported here consisted of a qualitative, longitudinal design, and aimed to provide a subjective perspective on how having a criminal record impacts upon the process of re-entry into society, particularly into the labour market. The outcomes discussed below are based on the lived experiences of 31 young adults who have a criminal record, aged between 16 and 30 (with an average age of 23.6), who were followed during their process of reintegration into the labour market for average periods of between six and 18 months. While most of these respondents are young adults and have also committed offences while they were adults, their stories are nonetheless important to consider here, as they clearly demonstrate the underlying mechanisms of how young persons deal with the stigma of a criminal record in the labour market. To date, no

[23] Council of State, 5 September 2012, ECLI:NL:RVS:2012:BX6537.

empirical research has been carried out on the collateral consequences of convictions for children in particular.

Most respondents appeared to be unaware that they were 'labelled' from the moment they became a suspect, that is, that when the public prosecution service registers an alleged offence in the JDS, they have a so-called criminal record; a status upon which employment restrictions can be based. However, many suspects only become aware of this if they applied for jobs and then had their requests for certificates of conduct refused. Patrick,[24] for example, said, when asked how he had reacted after receiving the message that he did not qualify for a certificate of conduct, 'First I tried to figure out why, because I thought I didn't have a criminal record anymore.' Patrick had committed a sexual offence 14 years ago (at the age of 12) and had never been confronted with his having a criminal record, until he requested a certificate to become a taxi driver (at the age of 26). During criminal proceedings, most young suspects are not explicitly informed about what it means to have a criminal record. Due partly to the complexity of the Dutch legal regime regarding criminal records, suspects remain uninformed and, thus, unaware of the consequences of a conviction in the years ahead. It can therefore be argued that employment restrictions based on having a criminal record create 'invisible' barriers to the labour market.

As well as not knowing precisely what information would be disclosed on their criminal record, many respondents were unaware of how much time had to elapse before they would be issued with a certificate of conduct. After his certificate was refused, Ajouad (22 years old) texted me the following question: 'Can you look up for me how long before I've served my time?' At age 18, the only thing Ajouad wanted to do, in order to make a living, was to become a taxi driver. At age 20 he applied for a certificate for the first time. Both his first and second requests were refused. At age 23 he applied for a third time and – due to the lapse of time – the certificate was issued to him. The offences committed as a minor had thus been following him for almost five years into adulthood. This was due to the fact that the 'expiry' period is calculated from the date of the last conviction – not from the date the offence was committed – which in his case was almost two years later. Consequently, although a young offender – even a one-off offender – may already have demonstrated that he or she did not fall back into crime throughout the entire pre-trial period, employment restrictions can still be imposed for several years post-sentence.

Young ex-offenders' general unawareness is partly due to the policy rules on issuing certificates providing for different expiry periods (ranging from two years to indefinite). For taxi drivers, for example – a seemingly highly desired occupation amongst ex-offenders – a special period of five years applies. Respondents generally expected that they would be offered a new chance earlier in their reintegration process – sometimes much earlier. The discovery that employment

[24] All respondents' names are fictitious.

restrictions still applied was accompanied by a sense of resignation that the restrictions were likely to last a long time and that the expiry date was not fixed. The discovery thereof is often accompanied by feelings of being demotivated and distraught, as is illustrated by this statement by Milad (21):

> The toughest part is how other people look at you and how other people judge you. When you're trying to get your life back on track, have a normal place in society, in some way you feel judged, no matter what. ... Somehow I want to do something about it, but there's nothing you can do, you cannot change it. ... I don't know what else I could do. I don't see another solution. ... I live my life one day at a time now. Not knowing what I want to do. Confused and everything ...

VIII. ANTICIPATED STIGMA

For young adults trying to create a 'normal' life after conviction, deep insecurities can be experienced by their not knowing what information is registered on a criminal record, how long it will apply, what its expiry date will be and how offences (including alleged offences) are weighed in the decision of whether to issue a certificate of conduct. Two-thirds of the respondents who participated in the research explicitly stated that, at some point, their criminal record had led to restrictions on obtaining employment or education. This was the case not only for young adults with a serious criminal record (ie those with at least one prison sentence), but also for those who had a relatively minor record.

About one out of four respondents said they had been refused education. For example, Riccardo (16) was refused entry into a training programme for the armed forces. The certificate had not been issued to him because he was suspected of theft. The school did not want to take the risk of awaiting the outcome of the complaint proceedings against the refusal of his certificate, and therefore did not let him start his training. Riccardo did not understand this: after all, he argued, he had explained to the school that he had a good chance of success during the proceedings. So he presumed that the school had another reason: it did not want to take the risk of accepting him in order to avoid responsibility, since then the school would be held responsible for providing alternative education:

> They didn't want to accept me and then await the decision. If they accepted me onto the programme, they'd be obliged to keep me. Cause I'm still a minor. And if I start there, they cannot easily shift me to another programme or school. It'd be their responsibility to give me education. That'd be the problem, because they cannot kick me out of the school. ... They'd have to arrange a new programme for me. They'd rather say: let's reject him now, so we don't run into trouble later. (Riccardo, 16)

As a consequence, in their search for both education and employment, young ex-offenders generally try to avoid jobs for which a certificate is required.

However, this requirement is not always apparent in a job vacancy. In many cases, it is mentioned during the hiring process, or even when an ex-offender has already been hired, as people are usually hired first and the certificate requested later. The certificate is then treated as a formality that has to be completed before an employment contract is drafted. This leaves many young ex-offenders very afraid of being labelled as ex-criminals and of being dismissed when an employer discovers that they cannot provide the certificate required. One of the respondents, who had been caught for embezzling money six years ago, expressed these fears clearly:

> I don't dare to apply for all sorts of jobs. First you check whether they want a certificate. Even once you're in the job application process, you're afraid they'll bring it up and ask for one after all. It remains a very big obstacle in the way of job applications. (Sabia, 26)

These insecurities thus remain after ex-offenders have been hired, and sometimes after they have already started the job. Almost all of the respondents recalled the shame they felt during the job-search process. Such shame often goes hand-in-hand with the fear of rejection, which is based less on official refusal of their certificate than on having to face an employer and announce that they did not qualify for a certificate of conduct. Moreover, even if they were allowed to retain their job, they would still have to deal with the stigma of being an 'ex-convict', as the employer and possibly some co-workers would be aware of their past.

Precious (24), who had been detained from age 20 to 21, had been rebuilding her life over the last three years. She had started a training course in care for the elderly, but was refused a certificate, so she could not do her internships. She had to discuss this with several school teachers, as she had to plead with them to make special arrangements for her – which they eventually did. She said that she would be relieved when the four years since her release from prison were over and she would qualify for a certificate:

> Next year my criminal past will finally be over and done with. I'll then be able to get a certificate of conduct again, so my background will no longer give me all kinds of trouble. At last I'll no longer have to tell anyone about it, so I can start my next training programme and find a job without people knowing anything about it!

IX. SELF-EXCLUSION

By following these young respondents during the course of their reintegration process, it became clear that many of them adopt self-exclusion as a strategy for avoiding rejection on the basis of the stigma of a criminal record. A consequence of this strategy is that it impacts on ex-offenders' positions in the labour market in a way that relegates them to second-rate jobs, that is hard, physical work, irregular hours and temporary contracts with no job security. Due to their criminal records, all the young adult offenders and ex-offenders in this study had experienced difficulties in the labour market. Hence, they found it difficult to stay motivated about finding employment. For example, Bryan (27) believed that – without official qualifications – he hardly had a chance on the labour market:

> Basically, without the certificate, without a contract, you have almost nothing. I've found a temporary solution now. And I'm a person who lives one day at a time, I don't think days ahead. But actually I do want to make long-term plans.

The primary concern of most was to find a stable job that would allow them to think confidently about their future and make long-term plans. The temporary nature of their jobs ensured that they continued to worry not only about obtaining employment, but also about repeatedly encountering problems due to their criminal background. Abdel (20), who was expelled from a training programme during his imprisonment, tried to apply for a new training programme after he was released, but was refused because of his background. He says he did not try to start a training programme again: 'You become discouraged and think: I'll never be accepted.' Some respondents rather opt to 'take the honourable way out' than to face rejection by their employer or colleagues and being sent away from the job. This was expressed by Sabia (26), who had been required by her employer to submit a certificate but had delayed requesting it for almost six months:

> This fear of not getting the certificate is all-pervading. But I'd rather leave the job myself than tell them honestly what has happened and then be forced to leave. … I think they will label you as a sort of criminal.

In sum, a significant reason why many ex-offenders exclude themselves from employment seems to be their uncertainties about the invisible barriers to the labour market, that is, not knowing when they will run into one. What adds to their insecurities is that employers can oblige a prospective employee to undergo criminal record screening. These striking instances of self-exclusion are fuelled by the fact that ex-offenders cannot know beforehand whether they will qualify for a certificate. A difficulty for many of them is that the current certificate policy provides no opportunities to know in advance – before accepting a job, for example – whether a certificate will be issued for that specific job. They first need an employer to fill in and sign the application for a certificate connected with a specific job. Applicants with a criminal record thus have no choice but to await the decision after they have already been hired – and possibly to withdraw from the job to avoid the personal rejection that will follow if their certificate is refused.

X. TOWARDS CHILD-FRIENDLY CRIMINAL RECORD SCREENING

The lived experiences of juveniles and young adults described in section IX illustrate that the Dutch legal system seems insufficient to promote the avoidance of processes of stigmatisation in the labour market based on their having a criminal record. These empirical findings show that mechanisms of both exclusion and self-exclusion relegate young ex-offenders to an unfavourable position in the labour market. It can therefore be concluded that children's rights standards have very little effect in Dutch practice regarding criminal record screening for employment purposes, in particular the issuing of certificates of conduct. The UN CRC prescribes that in all decisions concerning minors, the best interests of the child should be a primary consideration (Article 3(1) CRC). The current policy rules, however, consider the minor age of the offender as only one of several aspects to be taken into account, along with aspects such as the number and severity of the offences and the time that has elapsed. Although a policy change in 2011 made explicit consideration of the applicant's minor age mandatory, this does not necessarily mean that the best interests of the child are now a *primary* consideration in cases concerning minors. It only means that the minor age of the offender should be taken into account, regardless of whether it is weighed in his or her favour given the other merits of the case (Kurtovic 2012). Since 2013, the policy has changed in a way that has more of an impact on balancing young ex-offenders' interest in successful reintegration with the interests of public safety. By reducing the expiry period for offences to two – instead of four – years for applicants for the certificate below the age of 23, their chances have increased of successfully qualifying for a certificate of conduct after two years have elapsed without contact with the criminal justice system.

Still, in light of the CRC and other international or European standards, more improvements can be made to provide special safeguards and care for children who have been in conflict with the law. With regard to the right of the child to have his or her privacy respected in full, at all stages of the proceedings (Article 40(2) and Article 16 CRC), it can be argued that the Dutch criminal record database should make a distinction between childhood and adult criminal records. Juveniles seem to experience many stigmatising responses due to their having a criminal record, without knowing *what information* is registered, *how long* it will apply, what its *expiry date* will be and whether they are likely to *qualify* for a certificate of conduct due to their record. The Beijing Rules (Rule 21), as well as the Child-Friendly Justice Guidelines (paragraph 83), prescribe that records of juvenile offenders shall be kept strictly confidential, closed to third parties outside the criminal justice system, and should not be used in adult proceedings involving the same offender. General Comment No 10 (paragraph 67) takes this one step further by recommending that the law should allow for the automatic removal of the criminal record of the child upon his or her reaching the age of 18, except for certain limited, serious offences. Yet the Dutch criminal record database stores the same information regarding offences of both adult and minor offenders for the same period of time (generally 20 or 30 years, and 80 years for sexual offences).

A better balance could be struck between the seemingly conflicting interests of storing and using criminal record information for crime prevention and control, on the one hand, and the avoidance of detrimental effects on juveniles' reintegration process, resulting from the stigma of having a criminal record, on the other. There are, however, no special legal provisions that explicitly aim to avoid the detrimental effects of the process of labelling young persons as 'delinquent' or 'criminal'. The Dutch regime should therefore offer a possibility for youngsters to 'wipe the slate clean', in order to avoid harm being caused to them by labelling. This could be done by creating provisions that allow criminal records to become spent, either after a certain period or at the discretion of decision-makers after young ex-offenders have demonstrated their desistance from crime. A discretionary procedure should, according to General Comment No 10, be used only for certain limited, serious offences, for which removal will not take place automatically but at the request of the child and under certain conditions.

Currently, however, the criminal record will be kept for at least 20 years, and it is left to the Ministry of Justice and Security to determine in its policy guidelines on the certificate of conduct for how long an offence is taken into account in pre-employment screening. Consequently, different political regimes can lead to different policy rules. In addition, the certificate policy appears to be easily changed based on public opinion or populist politicians' call to toughen preventive measures. For example, following a security incident concerning a young convicted Jihadist who was able to work at an airport,[25] the shorter expiry period for juveniles and young adults no longer applies in case of (alleged) crimes of terrorism.[26] Parliament also accepted a motion by politicians, requiring that convictions concerning child abuse should never expire.[27] It can thus be argued that the policy rules on the certificate of conduct are vulnerable to current events and incidents, public opinion and political pressure.[28] To balance this vulnerability, however, there are neither legal provisions that allow juveniles' records to be spent after a fixed period, nor possibilities for juveniles to 'earn' judicial rehabilitation after having demonstrated serious efforts in their process of desisting from crime, for example by completing a treatment or training programme, or volunteering.

This is all the more important since empirical research has demonstrated that there are indeed serious adverse effects of increasingly widespread criminal record screening in the Netherlands. Both juveniles and young adults appear to adopt a strategy of self-exclusion to avoid rejection and exclusion from the labour market. Combined with the long periods of retention of criminal record information, those convicted as juveniles can be confronted with the effect of stigmatisation due to their having a criminal record well into their

[25] Kamerstukken II, 2017/18, 2017-2018, 34775-X, 6 (Parliamentary Documents).

[26] Stcrt. 2017, 68620 (Commentary to the Policy Rules on the Certificate of Conduct 2018).

[27] Kamerstukken II, 2017/18, 31322, 359 (Parliamentary Documents).

[28] Ministry of Security and Justice (2013) *Beleidsdoorlichting Preventiemaatregelen* ('Policy Audit on Preventive Measures'), annex to Kamerstukken II, 2012/13, 33199, 2.

adult life. This can have a negative impact on their ability to have access to both education and work. Children's rights standards should thus be upheld more rigorously to protect children in conflict with the law, and to ensure that in criminal record-screening procedures, due consideration is given to the child's best interests.

REFERENCES

Becker, HS (1963) *Outsiders: Studies in the sociology of deviance* (New York, The Free Press).

Boone, MM (2011) 'Judicial rehabilitation in The Netherlands: Balancing between safety and privacy' *European Journal of Probation*, 3(1), 63–78.

— (2012) 'Criminal records as an instrument of incapacitation' in M Malsch and M Duker (eds), *Incapacitation. Trends and new perspectives* (Surrey: Ashgate) 203–20.

Carr, N, Dwyer, C and Larrauri, E (2015) 'Young people, criminal records and employment barriers', in NIACRO and The Bytes Project, *New Directions: Understanding and Improving Employment Pathways in Youth Justice in Northern Ireland* (Belfast, Department of Employment and Learning) 7–62.

Corda, A (2016) 'More justice and less harm: Reinventing access to criminal history records' *Howard Law Journal*, 60(1), 1–60.

Duff, RA (2013) 'Who must presume whom to be innocent of what?' *Netherlands Journal of Legal Philosophy*, (42)3, 170–192.

Garland, D (2017) 'Penal power in America: Forms, functions and foundations' *Journal of the British Academy*, 5, 1–35.

Gosliga, FP (2015). *De stem van de uitvoering in perspectief. Een experimentele verkenning van de beleving van risicojongeren en jeugdprofessionals rond de aanvraag van de VOG* (Almere, SenseGuide).

Hilhorst, P (2011) *Iedereen verdient een tweede kans. Getuigenissen van jeugdreclasseerders over de nadelige effect van het VOG-systeem* (VARA, De Ombudsman).

Jacobs J and Larrauri E (2015) 'European Criminal Records & Ex-Offender Employment' *NYU School of Law, Public Law Research Paper No 15-41*.

Kruize, P and Gruter, P (2016) *Eens een dief, altijd een dief? Een verkenning rond het meten van de effectiviteit van de Verklaring Omtrent het Gedrag* (Amsterdam, WODC).

Kurtovic, EG (2012) 'Jeugdzonde, eeuwig zonde? Een onderzoek naar de beoordelingswijze van Verklaring Omtrent het Gedrag-aanvragen van jongeren', *PROCES: Tijdschrift voor Strafrechtspleging*, 91(2), 115–27.

— and Rovira, M (2017) 'Contrast between Spain and the Netherlands in the hidden obstacles to re-entry into the labour market due to a criminal record' *European Journal of Criminology*, 14(5), 1–17.

Laan, AM van der et al (2016) *Adolescentenstrafrecht. Beleidstheorie en eerste empirische bevindingen (WODC)* (The Hague, Boom).

Loucks, N, Lyner, O and Sullivan, T (1998) 'The employment of people with criminal records in the European Union' *European Journal on Criminal Policy and Research*, 6(2), 195–210.

Pinard, M (2010) 'Reflections and Perspectives on Reentry and Collateral Consequences' *Journal of Criminal Law and Criminology*, 100, 1213–24.

Roberts, J (2008) 'Mythical divide between collateral and direct consequences of criminal convictions: Involuntary commitment of sexually violent predators' *Minnesota Law Review*, 93, 670–740.

Sands, C (2016) *Growing up, Moving on. The International Treatment of Childhood Criminal Records* (Standing Committee for Youth Justice, United Kingdom).

Stone, N (2016) 'Expunging Juvenile Criminal Histories: Towards a "Clean Break"?' *Youth Justice*, 16(1), 71–81.

Thomas, T and Hebenton, B (2013) 'Dilemmas and consequences of prior criminal record: a criminological perspective from England and Wales' *Criminal Justice Studies*, 26(2), 228–42.

Travis, J (2002), *Invisible punishment: An instrument of social exclusion* (New York, The New Press).

Zand-Kurtovic, EG van 't (2017) *Invisible bars. The impact of having a criminal record on young adults' position in the labour market* (Doctoral Dissertation, Utrecht University) (The Hague, Eleven International Publishing).

TABLE OF CASES

Domestic Cases

Council of State, 24 June 2009, ECLI:NL:RVS:2009:BI9706.
Council of State, 2 June 2011, ECLI:NL:RVS:2011:BQ8830.
Council of State, 19 October 2011, ECLI:NL:RVS:2011:BT8577.
Council of State, 5 September 2012, ECLI:NL:RVS:2012:BX6537.
District Court of Zwolle-Lelystad, 28 August 2012, ECLI:NL:RBZLY:2012:BX6023.
District Court of Utrecht, 8 May 2018, UTR 17 / 2426 WET V60.

Index

NB – Page locators in **bold** refer to information in table

www.ingramcontent.com/pod-product-compliance
Ingram Content Group UK Ltd.
Pitfield, Milton Keynes, MK11 3LW, UK
UKHW020905190926
475560UK00010B/278

9 781509 920976